Social Engineering

Social Engineering

The Art of Human Hacking

Christopher Hadnagy

WILEY

Wiley Publishing, Inc.

Social Engineering: The Art of Human Hacking

Published by
Wiley Publishing, Inc.
10475 Crosspoint Boulevard
Indianapolis, IN 46256
www.wiley.com

Copyright © 2011 by Christopher Hadnagy

Published by Wiley Publishing, Inc., Indianapolis, Indiana

Published simultaneously in Canada

ISBN: 978-0-470-63953-5
ISBN: 978-1-118-02801-8 (ebk)
ISBN: 978-1-118-02971-8 (ebk)
ISBN: 978-1-118-02974-9 (ebk)

Manufactured in the United States of America

10 9 8

For general information on our other products and services please contact our Customer Care Department
within the United States at (877) 762-2974, outside the United States at (317) 572-3993 or fax (317) 572-4002.

Wiley also publishes its books in a variety of electronic formats. Some content that appears in print may
not be available in electronic books.

Library of Congress Control Number: 2010937817

To my beautiful wife and my wonderful family; without you this would not have been possible. Mati, there are no words to describe the gratitude I feel for what you have done.

ABOUT THE AUTHOR

CHRISTOPHER HADNAGY is the lead developer of www.social-engineer.org, the world's first social engineering framework. In more than 14 years of security and IT activity, he has partnered with the team at www.backtrack-linux.org and worked on a wide variety of security projects. He also serves as trainer and lead social engineer for Offensive Security's penetration testing team.

ABOUT THE TECHNICAL EDITOR

JIM O'GORMAN is a professional penetration tester and social engineering auditor with more than 14 years of experience working for companies ranging from small ISPs to Fortune 100 corporations. Jim is co-trainer of the Offensive Security Advanced Windows Exploitation class, one of the most difficult exploit development classes available. A founding member of www.social-engineer.org, Jim is an authority on educating the public about social engineering threats.

CREDITS

EXECUTIVE EDITOR
Carol Long

PROJECT EDITOR
Brian Herrmann

TECHNICAL EDITOR
Jim O'Gorman

PRODUCTION EDITOR
Kathleen Wisor

COPY EDITOR
Paula Lowell

EDITORIAL DIRECTOR
Robyn B. Siesky

EDITORIAL MANAGER
Mary Beth Wakefield

FREELANCER EDITORIAL MANAGER
Rosemarie Graham

MARKETING MANAGER
Ashley Zurcher

PRODUCTION MANAGER
Tim Tate

VICE PRESIDENT AND EXECUTIVE
GROUP PUBLISHER
Richard Swadley

VICE PRESIDENT AND
EXECUTIVE PUBLISHER
Barry Pruett

ASSOCIATE PUBLISHER
Jim Minatel

PROJECT COORDINATOR, COVER
Lynsey Stanford

COMPOSITOR
Maureen Forys,
Happenstance Type-O-Rama

PROOFREADER
Jen Larsen, Word One New York

INDEXER
Johnna VanHoose Dinse

COVER IMAGE
© Digital Vision/Getty Images

COVER DESIGNER
Ryan Sneed

CONTENTS

FOREWORD

Security is a puzzle with two sides. From the inside, we look for a sense of comfort and assurance. From the outside, thieves, hackers, and vandals are looking for gaps. Most of us believe our homes are safe until one day, we find ourselves locked out. Suddenly, our perspective shifts and weaknesses are easily found.

To completely understand any kind of security it is essential to step outside of the fence, in essence locking ourselves out, and start looking for other ways in. The problem is that most of us are blinded to potential problems by our own confidence or our belief that strong locks, thick doors, a high-end security system, and a guard dog are more than enough to keep most people at bay.

I'm not most people. In the last ten years I have pulled more cons and scams than anyone in history. I've beaten casinos, faked sports events, fixed auctions, talked people out of their dearest possessions, and walked right past seemingly unbeatable levels of security.

I have made a living exposing the methods of thieves, liars, crooks, and con men on a hit TV show called *The Real Hustle*. If I'd been a real criminal I would probably be rich, famous, or dead—probably all three. I have used a lifetime of research into all forms of deception to teach the public just how vulnerable they really are.

Each week, along with Alexis Conran, I pull real scams on real people who have no idea they are being ripped off. Using hidden cameras, we show the audience at home what is possible so they can recognize the same scam.

This unusual career has resulted in a unique understanding of how criminals think. I've become a sheep in wolves' clothing. I've learned that, no matter how impossible something might seem, there's almost always a clever, unexpected way to solve the problem.

An example of this is when I offered to show how easy it would be to not only steal a woman's purse, but also to get her to tell me the PIN to her ATM or credit cards. The BBC didn't think it was possible to accomplish this. When we presented this as an item for *The Real Hustle*, the BBC commissioner wrote "will never happen" beside it and sent it back. We knew it was entirely possible because different versions of the same scam had been reported, where victims of theft were talked into revealing their PINs in several clever scams around the UK. We took elements from different scams to illustrate exactly how someone might be duped into giving someone else complete access to their bank account.

To prove our point we set up the scam at a local cafe. The cafe was on the top floor of a mall on Oxford Street in London. It was relatively quiet as I sat at an empty table wearing a business suit. I placed my briefcase on the table and waited for a suitable victim. In a few moments, just such a victim arrived with a friend and sat at the table next to mine, placing her bag on the seat beside her. As was probably her habit, she pulled the seat close and kept her hand on the bag at all times.

I needed to steal the entire bag, but, with her hand resting on it and her friend sitting opposite, she was beginning to look like bad news. But, after a few minutes, her friend left to find a restroom. The mark was alone so I gave Alex and Jess the signal.

Playing the part of a couple, Alex and Jess asked the mark if she would take a picture of them both. She was happy to do so. She removed her hand from her bag to take the camera and snap a picture of the "happy couple" and, while distracted, I casually reached over, took her bag, and calmly locked it inside my briefcase. My victim was yet to notice the empty chair as Alex and Jess left the cafe. Once out of sight, Alex headed quickly for the parking garage.

It didn't take long for her to realize her bag was gone. Instantly, she began to panic. She stood up and looked around, frantically. This was exactly what we were hoping for so, I asked her if she needed help.

She started to ask me if I had seen anything. I told her I hadn't but convinced her to sit down and think about what was in the bag. A phone. Make-up. A little cash. And her credit cards. Bingo!

I asked who she banked with and then told her that I worked for that bank. What a stroke of luck! I reassured her that everything would be fine but she would need to cancel her credit card right away. I called the "help-desk" number, which was actually Alex, and handed my phone to her. She was hooked and it was now up to Alex to reel her in.

Alex was downstairs in the van. On the dashboard, a CD player was playing office noises we had downloaded from the Internet. He kept the mark calm, strung her along, and then assured her that her card could easily be canceled but, to verify her identity, she needed to enter her PIN on the keypad of the phone she was using.

My phone and my keypad.

You can guess the rest. Once we had her PIN, I left her with her friend and headed for the door. If we were real thieves, we would have had access to her account via ATM withdrawals and chip and PIN purchases. Fortunately for her, it was just a TV show and she was so happy when I came back to return her bag and tell her it was all a fake scam. She even thanked me for giving her bag back to which I replied, "Don't thank me. I'm the one who stole it."

No matter how secure a system is, there's always a way to break through. Often, the human elements of the system are the easiest to manipulate and deceive. Creating a state of panic, using influence, manipulation tactics, or causing feelings of trust are all methods used to put a victim at ease.

The scenario outlined here is an extreme example, but it shows that, with a little creativity, seemingly impossible scams can be pulled off.

The first step in becoming more secure is simply conceding that a system is vulnerable and can be compromised. On the contrary, by believing a breach is impossible, a blindfold is placed over your eyes as you run full speed ahead. *Social Engineering* is designed to provide you with invaluable insight into the methods used to break seemingly secure systems and expose the threats that exist in the largest vulnerability, the people. This book is not a guide for hackers—they already know how to break in and are finding new ways every day. Instead, Chris Hadnagy offers those inside the fence an opportunity to take a look from the other side, the dark side, as he exposes the thinking and methods of the world's most malicious hackers, con men, and social engineers.

Remember: those who build walls think differently than those who seek to go over, under, around, or through them. As I often tell my audiences, if you think you can't be conned, you're just the person I'd like to meet.

Paul Wilson
October 2010

PREFACE AND ACKNOWLEDGMENTS

It was just a few years ago that I was sitting with my friend and mentor, Mati Aharoni, deciding to launch www.social-engineer.org. The idea grew and grew until it became an amazing website supported by some truly brilliant people. It didn't take long to come up with the idea to put those years of research and experience down into the pages of a book. When I had the idea, I was met with overwhelming support. That said, some specific acknowledgements are very important to how this book became what it is today.

From a very young age I was always interested in manipulating people. Not in a bad way, but I found it interesting how many times I was able to obtain things or be in situations that would be unreal. One time I was with a good friend and business associate at a tech conference at the Javits Center in New York City. A large corporation had rented FAO Schwarz for a private party. Of course, the party was by invitation only, and my friend and I were two small fish in a large pond: the party was for the CEOs and upper management of companies like HP, Microsoft, and the like. My friend said to me, "It would be really cool to get into that party."

I simply responded, "Why can't we?" At that point I thought to myself, "I know we can get in there if we just ask the right way." So I approached the women in charge of the ticket booth and the guest list and I spoke to them for a few minutes. As I was speaking to them, Linus Torvalds, the creator of the Linux kernel, walked by. I had picked up a Microsoft plush toy at one of the booths and as I joke I turned to Linus and said, "Hey, you want to autograph my Microsoft toy?"

He got a good laugh out of it and as he grabbed his tickets he said, "Nice job, young man. I will see you at the party."

I turned back to the women in charge of the ticket booth and was handed two tickets to an exclusive party inside FAO Schwartz.

It wasn't until later in life that I began to analyze stories like this, after some started calling it "the Hadnagy Effect." As funny as that sounds, I began to see that much of what occurred to me wasn't luck or fate, but rather knowing how to be where I needed to be at the right time.

That doesn't mean it didn't take hard work and a lot of help along the way. My muse in life is my wonderful wife. For almost two decades you have supported me in all my ideas and efforts and you are my best friend, my confidant, and my support pillar. Without you I would not be where I am today. In addition, you have produced two of the most beautiful children on this planet. My son and my daughter are the motivation to keep doing all of this. If anything I do can make this place just a little more secure for them, or teach them how to keep themselves safe, it is all worthwhile.

To my son and daughter, I cannot express enough gratitude for your support, love, and motivation. My hope is that my son and my little princess will not have to deal with the malicious, bad people out in this world, but I know just how unlikely that is. May this information keep you both just a little more secure.

Paul, aka rAWjAW, thanks for all your support on the website. The thousands of hours you spent as the "wiki-master" paid off and now we have a beautiful resource for the world to use. I know I don't say it enough, but "you're fired!" Combined with the beautiful creation of Tom, aka DigIp, the website is a work of art.

Carol, my editor at Wiley, worked her butt off to get this organized and following some semblance of a timeline. She did an amazing job putting together a great team of people and making this idea a reality. Thank you.

Brian, I meant what I said. I am going to miss you when this is over. As I worked with you over the last few months I began to look forward to my editing sessions and the knowledge you would lay on me. Your honest and frank counsel and advice made this book better than it was.

My gratitude goes out to Jim, aka Elwood, as well. Without you a lot of what has happened on `social-engineer.org` as well as inside this book, heck in my life in the last couple years, would not be a reality.   Thank you for keeping me humble and in check.   Your constant reality checks helped me stay focused and balance the many different roles I had to play.   Thank you.

Liz, about twelve years ago you told me I should write a book. I am sure you had something different in mind, but here it is. You have helped me through some pretty dark times. Thank you and I love you.

Mati, my mentor, and my *achoti*, where would I be without you? Mati, you truly are my mentor and my brother. Thank you from the bottom of my heart for having the faith in me that I could write this book and launch `www.social-engineer.org` and that both would be good. More than that, your constant counsel and direction have been translated on the pages of this book to make me more than I thought I could be.

Your support with the BackTrack team along with the support of the team at `www.offensive-security.com` have transcended all I could have expected. Thank you for helping me balance and prioritize. My *achoti*, a special thanks to you for being the voice of reason and the light at the end of some frustrating days. With all my love I thank you.

Each person I mentioned here contributed to this book in some fashion. With their help, support and love this book has become a work that I am proud to have my name on. For the rest of you who have supported the site, the channel, and our research, thank you.

As you read this book, I hope it affects you the way writing it has affected me.

Albert Einstein once said, "Information is not knowledge." That is a powerful thought. Just reading this book will not somehow implant this knowledge into your being. Apply the principles, practice what is taught in these pages, and make the information a part of your daily life. When you do, you will then see this knowledge take effect.

Christopher Hadnagy
October 2010

Social Engineering

1

A Look into the World of Social Engineering

*If you know the enemy and know yourself you need
not fear the results of a hundred battles.*

—SUN TZU

Social engineering (SE) has been largely misunderstood, leading to many differing opinions on what social engineering is and how it works. This has led to a situation where some may view SE as simply lying to scam trivial free items such as pizza or obtaining sexual gratification; others think SE just refers to the tools used by criminals or con men, or perhaps that it is a science whose theories can be broken down into parts or equations and studied. Or perhaps it's a long-lost mystical art giving practitioners the ability to use powerful mind tricks like a magician or illusionist.

In whatever camp your flag flies, this book is for you. Social engineering is used every day by everyday people in everyday situations. A child trying to get her way in the candy aisle or an employee looking for a raise is using social engineering. Social engineering happens in government or small business marketing. Unfortunately, it is also present when criminals, con men, and the like trick people into giving away information that makes them vulnerable to crimes. Like any tool, social engineering is not good or evil, but simply a tool that has many different uses.

Consider some of these questions to drive that point home:

» Have you been tasked to make sure your company is as secure as possible?

» Are you a security enthusiast who reads every bit of the latest information out there?

» Are you a professional penetration tester who is hired to test the security of your clients?

» Are you a college student taking some form of IT specialization as your major?

> »   Are you presently a social engineer looking for new and improved ideas to utilize in your practice?

> »   Are you a consumer who fears the dangers of fraud and identity theft?

Regardless of which one of those situations fits you, the information contained within this book will open your eyes to how you can use social engineering skills. You will also peer into the dark world of social engineering and learn how the "bad guys" use these skills to gain an upper hand. From there, you learn how to become less vulnerable to social engineering attacks.

One warning up front: This book is not for the weak. It takes you into those dark corners of society where the "black hats," the malicious hackers, live. It uncovers and delves into areas of social engineering that are employed by spies and con men. It reviews tactics and tools that seem like they are stolen from a James Bond movie. In addition, it covers common, everyday situations and then shows how they are complex social engineering scenarios. In the end, the book uncovers the "insider" tips and tricks of professional social engineers and yes, even professional criminals.

Some have asked why I would be willing to reveal this information. The answer is simple: The "bad guys" don't stop because of a contractual limitation or their own morals. They don't cease after one failed attempt. Malicious hackers don't go away because companies don't like their servers to be infiltrated. Instead, social engineering, employee deception, and Internet fraud are used more and more each day. While software companies are learning how to strengthen their programs, hackers and malicious social engineers are turning to the weakest part of the infrastructure—the people. Their motivation is all about return on investment (ROI); no self-respecting hacker is going to spend 100 hours to get the same results from a simple attack that takes one hour, or less.

The sad result in the end is that no way exists to be 100% secure—unless you unplug all electronic devices and move to the mountains. Because that isn't too practical, nor is it a lot of fun, this book discusses ways to become more aware and educated about the attacks out there and then outlines methods that you can use to protect against them. My motto is "security through education." Being educated is one of the only surefire ways to remain secure against the increasing threats of social engineering and identity theft. Kaspersky Lab, a leading provider of antivirus and protection software, estimated that more than 100,000 malware samples were spread through social networks in 2009. In a recent report, Kaspersky estimated that "attacks against social networks are 10 times more successful" than other types of attacks.

The old hacker adage, "knowledge is power" does apply here. The more knowledge and understanding one has of the dangers and threats of social engineering each consumer and business can have and the more each attack scenario is dissected, the easier it will be to protect from, mitigate, and stop these attacks. That is where the power of all this knowledge will come in.

Why This Book Is So Valuable

Many books are available on the market on security, hacking, penetration testing, and even social engineering. Many of these books have very valuable information and tips to help their readers. Even with all the information available, a book was needed that takes social engineering information to the next level and describes these attacks in detail, explaining them from the malicious side of the fence. This book is not merely a collection of cool stories, neat hacks, or wild ideas. This book covers the world's first framework for social engineering. It analyzes and dissects the very foundation of what makes a good social engineer and gives practical advice on how to use these skills to enhance the readers' abilities to test the biggest weakness— the *human infrastructure*.

The Layout

This book offers a unique approach to social engineering. It is structured closely to the in-depth social engineering framework found at www.social-engineer.org/ framework. This framework outlines the skills and the tools (physical, mental, and personality) a person should strive to possess to be an excellent social engineer.

This book takes a "tell and show approach" by first presenting a principle behind a topic then defining, explaining, and dissecting, then showing its application using collections of real stories or case studies. This is not merely a book about stories or neat tricks, but a handbook, a guide through the dark world of social engineering.

Throughout the book you can find many Internet links to stories or accounts as well as links to tools and other aspects of the topics discussed. Practical exercises appear throughout the book that are designed to help you master not only the social engineering framework but also the skills to enhance your daily communications.

These statements are especially true if you are a security specialist. As you read this book, I hope to impress upon you that security is not a "part-time" job and is not something to take lightly. As criminals and malicious social engineers seem to go from bad to worse in this world, attacks on businesses and personal lives seem to get more intense. Naturally, everyone wants to be protected, as evidenced by the increase in sales for personal protection software and devices. Although these items are important, the best protection is knowledge: security through education. The only true way to reduce the effect of these attacks is to know that they exist, to know how they are done, and to understand the thinking process and mentality of the people who would do such things.

When you possess this knowledge and you understand how malicious hackers think, a light bulb goes off. That proverbial light will shine upon the once-darkened corners and enable you to clearly see the "bad guys" lurking there. When you can see the way these attacks are used ahead of time, you can prepare your company's and your personal affairs to ward them off.

Of course, I am not contradicting what I said earlier; I believe there is no way to truly be 100% secure. Even top-secret, highly guarded secrets can be and have been hacked in the simplest of manners.

Look at the archived story at `www.social-engineer.org/resources/book/TopSecretStolen.htm`, from a newspaper in Ottawa, Canada. This story is very interesting, because some documents ended up in the wrong hands. These weren't just any documents, but top-secret *defense* documents that outlined things such as locations of security fences at the Canadian Forces Base (CFB) in Trenton, the floor plan of the Canadian Joint Incident Response Unit, and more. How did the breach occur? The plans were thrown away, in the trashcan, and someone found them in the dumpster. A simple dumpster dive could have led to one of that country's largest security breaches.

Simple-yet-deadly attacks are launched every day and point to the fact that people need education; need to change the way they adhere to password policies and the way they handle remote access to servers; and need to change the way they handle interviews, deliveries, and employees who are hired or fired. Yet without education the motivation for change just isn't there.

In 2003 the Computer Security Institute did a survey along with the FBI and found that 77% of the companies interviewed stated a disgruntled employee as the source of a major security breach. Vontu, the data loss prevention section of Symantec (`http://go.symantec.com/vontu/`), says that 1 out of every 500 emails contains confidential data. Some of the highlights of that report, quoted from `http://financialservices.house.gov/media/pdf/062403ja.pdf`, are as follows:

- » 62% reported incidents at work that could put customer data at risk for identity theft.
- » 66% say their co-workers, not hackers, pose the greatest risk to consumer privacy. Only 10% said hackers were the greatest threat.

» 46% say it would be "easy" to "extremely easy" for workers to remove sensitive data from the corporate database.

» 32%, about one in three, are unaware of internal company policies to protect customer data.

These are staggering and stomach-wrenching statistics.

Later chapters discuss these numbers in more detail. The numbers show a serious flaw in the way security itself is handled. When there is education, hopefully *before* a breach, then people can make changes that can prevent unwanted loss, pain, and monetary damage.

Sun Tzu said, "If you know the enemy and know yourself you need not fear the results of a hundred battles." How true those words are, but knowing is just half the battle. Action on knowledge is what defines wisdom, not just knowledge alone.

This book is most effective used as a handbook or guide through the world of social attacks, social manipulation, and social engineering.

What's Coming Up

This book is designed to cover all aspects, tools, and skills used by professional and malicious social engineers. Each chapter delves deep into the science and art of a specific social engineering skill to show you how it can be used, enhanced, and perfected.

The next section of this chapter, "Overview of Social Engineering," defines social engineering and what roles it plays in society today, as well as the different types of social engineering attacks, including other areas of life where social engineering is used in a non-malicious way. I will also discuss how a social engineer can use the social engineering framework in planning an audit or enhancing his own skills.

Chapter 2 is where the real meat of the lessons begins. Information gathering is the foundation of every social engineering audit. The social engineer's mantra is, "I am only as good as the information I gather." A social engineer can possess all the skills in the world, but if he or she doesn't know about the target, if the social engineer hasn't outlined every intimate detail, then the chance of failure is more likely to occur. Information gathering is the crux of every social engineering engagement, although people skills and the ability to think on your feet can help you get out of a sticky situation. More often than not, the more information you gather, the better your chances of success.

The questions that I will answer in that chapter include the following:

» What sources can a social engineer use?

» What information is useful?

» How can a social engineer collect, gather, and organize this information?

» How technical should a social engineer get?

» How much information is enough?

After the analyzation of information gathering, the next topic addressed in Chapter 2 is communication modeling. This topic closely ties in with information gathering. First I will discuss what communication modeling is and how it began as a practice. Then the chapter walks through the steps needed to develop and then use a proper communication model. It outlines how a social engineer uses this model against a target and the benefits in outlining it for every engagement.

Chapter 3 covers elicitation, the next logical step in the framework. It offers a very in-depth look into how questions are used to gain information, passwords, in-depth knowledge of the target, and his or her company. You will learn what is good and proper elicitation and learn how important it is to have your elicitations planned out.

Chapter 3 also covers the important topic of preloading the target's mind with information to make your questions more readily accepted. As you unravel this section you will clearly see how important it is to become an excellent elicitor. You will also clearly see how you can use that skill not just in your security practices but in daily life.

Chapter 4, which covers pretexting, is powerful. This heavy topic is one of the critical points for many social engineers. Pretexting involves developing the role the social engineer will play for the attack on the company. Will the social engineer be a customer, vendor, tech support, new hire, or something equally realistic and believable? Pretexting involves not just coming up with the storyline but also developing the way your persona would look, act, talk, walk; deciding what tools and knowledge they would have; and then mastering the entire package so when you approach the target, you *are* that person, and not simply playing a character. The questions covered include the following:

» What is pretexting?

» How do you develop a pretext?

» What are the principles of a successful pretext?

» How can a social engineer plan and then execute a perfect pretext?

The next step in the framework is one that can fill volumes. Yet it must be discussed from the viewpoint of a social engineer. Chapter 5 is a no-holds-barred discussion on some very confrontational topics, including that of *eye cues*. For example, what are the varying opinions of some professionals about eye cues, and how can a social engineer use them? The chapter also delves into the fascinating science of microexpressions and its implications on social engineering.

Chapter 5 goes on analyzing the research, yielding answers to these questions:

» Is it possible to use microexpressions in the field of security?

» How would you do so?

» What benefit are microexpressions?

» Can people train themselves to learn how to pick up on microexpressions automatically?

» After we do the training, what information is obtained through microexpressions?

Probably one of the most debated-on topics in Chapter 5 is *neurolinguistic programming* (NLP). The debate has many people undecided on what it is and how it can be used. Chapter 5 presents a brief history of NLP as well as what makes NLP such a controversy. You can decide for yourself whether NLP is usable in social engineering.

Chapter 5 also discusses one of the most important aspects of social engineering in person or on the phone: knowing how to ask good questions, listen to responses, and then ask more questions. Interrogation and interviewing are two methods that law enforcement have used for years to manipulate criminals to confess as well as to solve the hardest cases. This part of Chapter 5 puts to practical use the knowledge you gained in Chapter 3.

In addition, Chapter 5 discusses how to build instant rapport—a skill you can use in everyday life. The chapter ends by covering my own personal research into "the human buffer overflow": the notion that the human mind is much like the software that hackers exploit every day. By applying certain principles, a skilled social engineer can overflow the human mind and inject any command they want.

Just like hackers write overflows to manipulate software to execute code, the human mind can be given certain instructions to, in essence, "overflow" the target and insert custom instructions. Chapter 5 is a mind-blowing lesson in how to use some simple techniques to master how people think.

Many people have spent their lives researching and proving what can and does influence people. Influence is a powerful tool with many facets to it. To this end, Chapter 6 discusses the fundamentals of persuasion. The principles engaged in Chapter 6 will start you on the road toward becoming a master of persuasion.

The chapter presents a brief discussion of the different types of persuasion that exist and provides examples to help solidify how you can use these facets in social engineering.

The discussion doesn't stop there—framing is also a hot topic nowadays. Many different opinions exist on how one can use framing, and this book shows some real-life examples of it. Then dissecting each, I take you through the lessons learned and things you can do to practice reframing yourself as well as use framing in everyday life as a social engineer.

Another overwhelming theme in social engineering is *manipulation*:

» What is its purpose?

» What kinds of incentives drive manipulators?

» How can a person use it in social engineering?

Chapter 6 presents all a social engineer needs to know on the topic of manipulation, and how to successfully apply such skills.

Chapter 7 covers the tools that can make a social engineering audit more successful. From physical tools such as hidden cameras to software-driven information gathering tools, each section covers tested-and-tried tools for social engineers.

Once you understand the social engineering framework, Chapter 8 discusses some real-life case studies. I have chosen two excellent accounts from world-renowned social engineer Kevin Mitnick. I analyze, dissect, and then propose what you can learn from these examples and identify the methods he used from the social engineering framework. Moreover, I discuss what can be learned from his attack vectors as well as how they can be used today. I discuss some personal accounts and dissect them, as well.

What social engineering guide would be complete without discussing some of the ways you can mitigate these attacks? The appendix provides this information. I answer some common questions on mitigation and give some excellent tips to help secure you and your organization against these malicious attacks.

The preceding overview is just a taste of what is to come. I truly hope you enjoy reading this book as much as I have enjoyed writing it. Social engineering is a passion for me. I do believe there are certain traits, whether learned or inherent, that can make someone a great social engineer. I also subscribe to the belief that with enough time and energy anyone can learn the different aspects of social engineering and then practice these skills to become a proficient social engineer.

The principles in this book are not new; there is no mind-blowing technology that you will see that will change the face of security forever. There are no magic pills. As a matter of fact, the principles have been around for as long as people have. What this book *does* do is combine all of these skills in one location. It does give you clear direction on how to practice these skills as well as examples of real-life situations where they are used. All of this information can help you gain a true sense of understanding the topics discussed.

The best place to start is with the basics, by answering one fundamental question: "What is social engineering?"

Overview of Social Engineering

What is social engineering?

I once asked this question to a group of security enthusiasts and I was shocked at the answers I received:

"Social engineering is lying to people to get information."

"Social engineering is being a good actor."

"Social engineering is knowing how to get stuff for free."

Wikipedia defines it as "the act of manipulating people into performing actions or divulging confidential information. While similar to a confidence trick or simple fraud, the term typically applies to trickery or deception for the purpose of information gathering, fraud, or computer system access; in most cases the attacker never comes face-to-face with the victim."

Although it has been given a bad name by the plethora of "free pizza," "free coffee," and "how to pick up chicks" sites, aspects of social engineering actually touch many parts of daily life.

Webster's Dictionary defines *social* as "of or pertaining to the life, welfare, and relations of human beings in a community." It also defines *engineering* as "the art or science of making practical application of the knowledge of pure sciences, as physics or chemistry, as in the construction of engines, bridges, buildings, mines, ships, and chemical plants or skillful or artful contrivance; maneuvering."

Combining those two definitions you can easily see that social engineering is the art or better yet, science, of skillfully maneuvering human beings to take action in some aspect of their lives.

This definition broadens the horizons of social engineers everywhere. Social engineering is used in everyday life in the way children get their parents to give in to their demands. It is used in the way teachers interact with their students, in the way doctors, lawyers, or psychologists obtain information from their patients or clients. It is definitely used in law enforcement, and in dating—it is truly used in every human interaction from babies to politicians and everyone in between.

I like to take that definition a step further and say that a true definition of social engineering is the act of manipulating a person to take an action that *may* or *may not* be in the "target's" best interest. This may include obtaining information, gaining access, or getting the target to take certain action.

For example, doctors, psychologists, and therapists often use elements I consider social engineering to "manipulate" their patients to take actions that are good for them, whereas a con man uses elements of social engineering to convince his target to take actions that lead to loss for them. Even though the end game is much different, the approach may be very much the same. A psychologist may use a series of well-conceived questions to help a patient come to a conclusion that change is needed. Similarly, a con man will use well-crafted questions to move his target into a vulnerable position.

Both of these examples are social engineering at its truest form, but have very different goals and results. Social engineering is not just about deceiving people or lying or acting a part. In a conversation I had with Chris Nickerson, a well-known social engineer from the TV series *Tiger Team,* he said, "True social engineering is not just believing you are playing a part, but for that moment you *are* that person, you are that role, it is what your life is."

Social engineering is not just any one action but a collection of the skills mentioned in the framework that when put together make up the action, the skill, and the science I call social engineering. In the same way, a wonderful meal is not just one ingredient, but is made up by the careful combining, mixing, and adding of many ingredients. This is how I imagine social engineering to be, and a good social engineer is like a master chef. Put in a little dab of elicitation, add a shake of manipulation, and a few heaping handfuls of pretexting, and *bam!*—out comes a great meal of the perfect social engineer.

Of course, this book discusses some of these facets, but the main focus is what you can learn from law enforcement, the politicians, the psychologists, and even children to better your abilities to audit and then secure yourself. Analyzing how a child can manipulate a parent so easily gives the social engineer insight into how the human mind works. Noticing how a psychologist phrases questions can help to see what puts people at ease. Noticing how a law enforcement agent performs a successful interrogation gives a clear path on how to obtain information from a target. Seeing how governments and politicians frame their messages for the greatest impact can show what works and what doesn't. Analyzing how an actor gets into a role can open your eyes to the amazing world of pretexting. By dissecting the research and work of some of the leading minds in microexpressions and persuasion you can see how to use these techniques in social engineering. By reviewing some of the motivators of some of the world's greatest salespeople and persuasion experts you can learn how to build rapport, put people at ease, and close deals.

Then by researching and analyzing the flip side of this coin—the con men, scam artists, and thieves—you can learn how all of these skills come together to influence people and move people in directions they thought they would never go.

Mix this knowledge with the skills of lock picks, spies who use hidden cameras, and professional information gatherers and you have a talented social engineer.

You do not use every one of these skills in each engagement, nor can you master every one of these skills. Instead, by understanding *how* these skills work and *when* to use them, anyone can master the science of social engineering. It is true that some people have a natural talent, like Kevin Mitnick, who could talk anyone into anything, it seemed. Frank Abagnale, Jr., seemed to have the natural talents to con people into believing he was who he wanted them to believe he was. Victor Lustig did the unbelievable, actually convincing some people that he had the rights to sell the Eiffel Tower, topped only by his scam on Al Capone.

These social engineers and many more like them seem to have natural talent or a lack of fear that enables them to try things that most of us would never consider attempting. Unfortunately in the world today, malicious hackers are continually improving their skills at manipulating people and malicious social engineering attacks are increasing. DarkReading posted an article (`www.darkreading.com/database_security/security/attacks/showArticle.jhtml?articleID=226200272`) that cites that data breaches have reached between $1 and $53 million per breach. Citing research by the Ponemon Institute DarkReading states, "Ponemon found that Web-borne attacks, malicious code, and malicious insiders are the most costly types of attacks, making up more than 90 percent of all cybercrime costs per organization per year: A Web-based attack costs $143,209; malicious code, $124,083; and malicious insiders, $100,300." Malicious insiders being listed on the top three suggests that businesses need to be more aware of the threats posed by malicious social engineering, even from employees.

Many of these attacks could have been avoided if people were educated, because they could act on that education. Sometimes just finding out how malicious people think and act can be an eye opener.

As example on a much smaller and more personal scale, I was recently discussing with a close friend her financial accounts and how she was worried about being hacked or scammed. In the course of the conversation we started to discuss how easy it is to "guess" people's passwords. I told her that many people use the same passwords for every account; I saw her face go white as she realized this is her. I told her that most people use simplistic passwords that combine things like their spouse's name, his or her birthday, or anniversary date. I saw her go an ever-brighter shade of pale. I continued by saying that most of the time people chose the simplest "security question" such as "your (or your mother's) maiden name" and how easy finding that information is via the Internet or a few fake phone calls.

Many people will list this information in Blippy, Twitter, or Facebook accounts. This particular friend didn't use social media sites too much, so I asked her that if she thought with a few phone calls she could picture herself giving over this information. Of course she said no. To illustrate how easily people hand over personal information, I told her that I once saw a placemat in a restaurant that had a $50-off coupon for a local golf course—a very attractive offer. To take advantage of this offer, you only had to provide your name, date of birth, and street address, and provide a password for an account that would be set up and sent to your e-mail address. (I only noticed this in the first place because someone had started filling out the coupon and left it on the table.) Every day websites are created to collect such sensitive information.

A phone call with a survey or some quick research on the Internet can yield a birth date or anniversary date, and armed with this information I have enough to build a password attack list. Plus, a dozen sites offer detailed records of all sorts of personal information on an individual for a mere $9–$30 USD.

Realizing how malicious social engineers think, how scammers react to information, and how con men will try anything, can help people to be more aware of what is going on around them.

A team of security enthusiasts and I have scoured the Internet collecting stories that show many different aspects of social engineering. These stories can help answer a vital question—"how is social engineering used in society over time?"—and see where social engineering's place is and how it is used maliciously.

Social Engineering and Its Place in Society

As already discussed social engineering can be used in many areas of life, but not all of these uses are malicious or bad. Many times social engineering can be used to motivate a person to take an action that is good for them. How?

Think about this: John needs to lose weight. He knows he is unhealthy and needs to do something about it. All of John's friends are overweight, too. They even make jokes about the joys of being overweight and say things like, "I love not worrying about my figure." On one hand, this is an aspect of social engineering. It is social proof or consensus, where what you find or deem acceptable is determined by those around you. Because John's close associations view being overweight as acceptable, it is easier for John to accept it. However, if one of those friends lost weight and did not become judgmental but was motivated to help, the possibility exists that John's mental frame about his weight might change and he might start to feel that losing weight is possible and good.

This is, in essence, social engineering. So you can clearly see how social engineering fits into society and everyday life, the following sections present a few examples of social engineering, scams, and manipulation and a review of how they worked.

The 419 Scam

The 419 scam, better known as the Nigerian Scam, has grown into an epidemic. You can find an archived story and article about this scam at `www.social-engineer` `.org/wiki/archives/ConMen/ConMen-Scam-NigerianFee.html`.

Basically an email (or as of late, a letter) comes to the target telling him he has been singled out for a very lucrative deal and all he needs to do is offer a little bit of help. If the victim will help the letter sender extract a large sum of money from foreign banks he can have a percentage. After the target is confident and "signs on," a problem arises that causes the target to pay a fee. After the fee is paid another problem comes up, along with another fee. Each problem is "the last" with "one final fee" and this can be stretched out over many months. The victim never sees any money and loses from $10,000–$50,000 USD in the process. What makes this scam so amazing is that in the past, official documents, papers, letterhead, and even face-to-face meetings have been reported.

Recently a variation of this scam has popped up where victims are literally sent a real check. The scammers promise a huge sum of money and want in return only a small portion for their efforts. If the target will wire transfer a small sum (in comparison) of $10,000, when they receive the promised check they can deposit the check and keep the difference. The problem is that the check that comes is a fraud and when the victim goes to cash it she is slapped with check fraud charges and fines, in some cases *after* the victim has already wired money to the scammer.

This scam is successful because it plays on the victim's greed. Who wouldn't give $10,000 to make $1,000,000 or even $100,000? Most smart people would. When these people are presented with official documents, passports, receipts, and even official offices with "government personnel" then their belief is set and they will go to great lengths to complete the deal. Commitment and consistency play a part in this scam as well as obligation. I discuss these attributes in greater detail in later chapters, and when I do, you will see why this scam is so powerful.

The Power of Scarcity

The article archived at www.social-engineer.org/wiki/archives/Governments/Governments-FoodElectionWeapon.html talks about a principle called *scarcity*.

Scarcity is when people are told something they need or want has limited availability and to get it they must comply with a certain attitude or action. Many times the desired behavior is not even spoken, but the way it is conveyed is by showing people who are acting "properly" getting rewards.

The article talks about the use of food to win elections in South Africa. When a group or person does not support the "right" leader, foodstuffs become scarce and jobs people once had are given to others who are more supportive. When people see this in action, it doesn't take long to get them in line. This is a very malicious and hurtful form of social engineering, but nonetheless, one to learn from. It is often the case that people want what is scarce and they will do anything if they are lead to believe that certain actions will cause them to lose out on those items. What makes certain cases even worse, as in the earlier example, is that a government took something necessary to life and made it "scarce" and available only to supporters—a malicious, but very effective, manipulation tactic.

The Dalai Lama and Social Engineering

The interesting article archived at www.social-engineer.org/wiki/archives/Spies/Spies-DalaiLama.html details an attack made on the Dalai Lama in 2009.

A Chinese hacker group wanted to access the servers and files on the network owned by the Dalai Lama. What methods were used in this successful attack?

The attackers convinced the office staff at the Dalai Lama's office to download and open malicious software on their servers. This attack is interesting because it blends both technology hacking and social engineering.

The article states, "The software was attached to e-mails that purported to come from colleagues or contacts in the Tibetan movement, according to researcher Ross Anderson, professor of security engineering at the University of Cambridge Computer Laboratory, cited by the *Washington Times* Monday. The software stole passwords and other information, which in turn gave the hackers access to the office's e-mail system and documents stored on computers there."

Manipulation was used as well as common attack vectors such as phishing (the practice of sending out emails with enticing messages and links or files that must be opened to receive more information; often those links or files lead to malicious payloads) and exploitation. This attack can work and has worked against major corporations as well as governments. This example is just one in a large pool of examples where these vectors cause massive damage.

Employee Theft

The topic of employee theft could fill volumes, especially in light of the staggering statistic found at www.social-engineer.org/wiki/archives/DisgruntledEmployees/DisgruntledEmployees-EmployeeTheft.html that more than 60 percent of employees interviewed admitted to taking data of one sort or another from their employers.

Many times this data is sold to competitors (as happened in this story from a Morgan Stanley employee: www.social-engineer.org/wiki/archives/DisgruntledEmployees/DisgruntledEmployees-MorganStanley.html). Other times employee theft is in time or other resources; in some cases a disgruntled employee can cause major damage.

I once talked to a client about employee discharge policies, things like disabling key cards, disconnecting network accounts, and escorting discharged employees out of the building. The company felt that everyone was part of the "family" and that those policies wouldn't apply.

Unfortunately, the time came to let go of "Jim," one of the higher-ranking people in the company. The "firing" went well; it was amicable and Jim said he understood. The one thing the company did right was to handle the firing around closing time to avoid embarrassment and distraction. Hands were shook and then Jim asked the fateful question, "Can I take an hour to clean out my desk and take some personal pictures off my computer? I will turn my key card into the security guard before I leave."

Feeling good about the meeting, they all quickly agreed and left with smiles and a few laughs. Then Jim went to his office, packed a box of all his personal items, took the pictures and other data off his computer, connected to the network, and wiped clean 11 servers' worth of data—accounting records, payroll, invoices, orders, history, graphics, and much more just deleted in a matter of minutes. Jim turned in his key card as he promised and calmly left the building with no proof that he was the one to initiate these attacks.

The next morning a call came in to me from the owner describing the carnage in the ex-employee's wake. Hoping for a silver bullet, the client had no choice but try to recover what could be recovered forensically and start over from the backups, which were more than two months old.

A disgruntled employee who is left unchecked can be more devastating than a team of determined and skilled hackers. To the tune of $15 billion USD, that is what the loss is estimated at being to businesses in the U.S. alone due to employee theft.

These stories may leave a question about what different categories of social engineers are out there and whether they can be classified.

DarkMarket and Master Splynter

In 2009 a story broke about an underground group called DarkMarket—the so-called eBay for criminals, a very tight group that traded stolen credit card numbers and identity theft tools, as well as the items needed to make fake credentials and more.

An FBI agent by the name of J. Keith Mularski went under deep cover and infiltrated the DarkMarket site. After a while, Agent Mularski was made an administrator of the site. Despite many trying to discredit him he hung in for more than three years as the admin of the site.

During this time, Mularski had to live as a malicious hacker, speak and act as one, and think as one. His pretext was one of a malicious spammer and he was knowledgeable enough to pull it off. His pretext and his social engineering skills paid off because Agent Mularski infiltrated DarkMarket as the infamous Master Splynter, and after three years was essential in shutting down a massive identity theft ring.

The three-year social engineering sting operation netted 59 arrests and prevented over $70 million in bank fraud. This is just one example of how social engineering skills can be used for good.

The Different Types of Social Engineers

As previously discussed, social engineering can take on many forms. It can be malicious and it can be friendly, it can build up and it can tear down. Before moving on to the core of this book, take a brief look at the different forms of social engineers and a very short description of each:

» **Hackers:** Software vendors are becoming more skilled at creating software that is *hardened*, or more difficult to break into. As hackers are hitting more hardened software and as software and network attack vectors, such as remote hacking, are becoming more difficult, hackers are turning to social engineering skills. Often using a blend of hardware and personal skills, hackers are using social engineering in major attacks as well as in minor breaches throughout the world.

» **Penetration testers:** Since a real-world penetration tester (also known as a pentester) is very offensive in nature, this category must follow after hackers. True penetration testers learn and use the skills that the malicious hackers use to truly help ensure a client's security. Penetration testers are people who might have the skills of a malicious black hat but who never use the information for personal gain or harm to the target.

» **Spies:** Spies use social engineering as a way of life. Often employing every aspect of the social engineering framework (discussed later in this chapter), spies are experts in this science. Spies from all around the world are taught different methods of "fooling" victims into believing they are someone or something they are not. In addition to being taught the art of social engineering, many times spies also build on credibility by knowing a little or even a lot about the business or government they are trying to social engineer.

» **Identity thieves:** Identity theft is the use of information such as a person's name, bank account numbers, address, birth date, and social security number without the owner's knowledge. This crime can range from putting on a uniform to impersonating someone to much more elaborate scams. Identity thieves employ many aspects of social engineering and as time passes they seem more emboldened and indifferent to the suffering they cause.

» **Disgruntled employees:** After an employee has become disgruntled, they often enter into an adversarial relationship with their employer. This can often be a one-sided situation, because the employee will typically try to hide their level of displeasure to not put their employment at risk. Yet the more disgruntled they become, the easier it becomes to justify acts of theft, vandalism, or other crimes.

» **Scam artist:** Scams or cons appeal to greed or other principles that attract people's beliefs and desires to "make a buck." Scam artists or con men master the ability to read people and pick out little cues that make a person a good "mark." They also are skillful at creating situations that present as unbeatable opportunities to a mark.

» **Executive recruiters:** Recruiters also must master many aspects of social engineering. Having to master elicitation as well as many of the psychological principles of social engineering, they become very adept at not only reading people but also understanding what motivates people. Many times a recruiter must take into consideration and please not only the job seeker but also the job poster.

» **Salespeople:** Similar to recruiters, salespeople must master many people skills. Many sales gurus say that a good salesperson does not manipulate people but uses their skills to find out what people's needs are and then sees whether they can fill it. The art of sales takes many skills such as information gathering, elicitation, influence, psychological principles, as well as many other people skills.

» **Governments:** Not often looked at as social engineers, governments utilize social engineering to control the messages they release as well as the people they govern. Many governments utilize social proof, authority, and scarcity to make sure their subjects are in control. This type of social engineering is not always negative, because some of the messages governments relay are for the good of the people and using certain elements of social engineering can make the message more appealing and more widely accepted.

» **Doctors, psychologists, and lawyers:** Although the people in these careers might not seem like they fit into the same category as many of these other social engineers, this group employs the same methods used by the other groups in this list. They must use elicitation and proper interview and interrogation tactics as well as many if not all of the psychological principles of social engineering to manipulate their "targets" (clients) into the direction they want them to take.

Regardless of the field, it seems that you can find social engineering or an aspect of it. This is why I hold firmly to the belief that social engineering is a science. Set equations exist that enable a person to "add up" elements of social engineering to lead to the goal. In the example of a con man, think of the equation like this: pretext + manipulation + attachment to greed = target being social engineered.

In every situation, knowing what elements will work is the hard part, but then learning how to utilize those elements is where the skill comes in. This was the basis for thought behind developing the social engineering framework. This framework has revolutionized the way social engineering is dissected, as discussed in the next section.

The Social Engineering Framework and How to Use It

Through experience and research I have tried to outline the elements that make up a social engineer. Each of these elements defines a part of the equation that equals a whole social engineer. These aspects are not set in stone; as a matter of fact, from its original state until now the framework has grown.

The purpose of the framework is to give enough information for anyone to build on these skills. The framework is not designed to be an all-inclusive resource for all information in each chapter. For example, the portion of Chapter 5 that covers microexpressions is based on the research of some of the greatest minds in this field and my experience in using that information. By no means is it meant to replace the 50 years of research by such great minds as Dr. Paul Ekman.

As you read through the framework you will see that by utilizing the many skills within it, you can not only enhance your security practice, but also your mindset about how to remain secure, how to communicate more fully, and how to understand how people think.

Refer to the table of contents for a clear picture of the framework or view it online at www.social-engineer.org/framework. At first glance the framework may appear daunting, but inside this book you will find an analysis of each topic that will enable you to apply, enhance, and build these skills.

Knowledge is power—it is true. In this sense, education is the best defense against most social engineering attacks. Even the ones that knowledge can't protect 100 percent against, having details of these attacks keeps you alert. Education can help you enhance your own skills, as well as be alert.

Along with education, though, you need practice. This book was not designed to be a once-read manual; instead it was designed to be a study guide. You can practice and customize each section for your needs. The framework is progressive in the sense that it is the way a social engineering attack is laid out. Each section of the framework discusses the next topic in the order that a social engineer might utilize that skill in their engagement or planning phases.

The framework shows how an attack might be outlined. After the attack is planned out, the skills that are needed can be studied, enhanced, and practiced before delivery.

Suppose, for example, that you are planning a social engineering audit against a company that wanted to see whether you could gain access to its server room and steal data.

Maybe your plan of attack would be to pretend to be a tech support person who needs access to the server room. You would want to gather information, maybe even perform a dumpster dive.

Then under the pretext of being the tech guy, you could utilize some covert camera tools as well as practice the proper language and facial/vocal cues for how to act, sound, and look like a tech guy.

If you locate what company your client uses for tech support you may need to do info gathering on it. Who does your client normally get to service them? What are the names of the employees with whom they interact? The attack needs to be planned out properly.

This book is not just for those who perform audits, though. Many readers are curious about what the attacks are, not because they are protecting a company, but because they need to protect themselves. Not being aware of the way a malicious social engineer thinks can lead someone down the path toward being hacked.

College students in the field of security have also used the framework. The information in the framework outlines a realistic path for these vectors, or methods of attack, and enables the reader to study them in depth.

Generally, this information can also help enhance your ability to communicate in everyday life. Knowing how to read facial expressions or how to use questions to put people at ease and elicit positive responses can enhance your ability to communicate with your family and friends. It can assist you in becoming a good listener and more aware of people's feelings.

Being able to read people's body language, facial expressions, and vocal tones can also enhance your ability to be an effective communicator. Understanding how to protect yourself and your loved ones will only make you more valuable and more aware of the world around you.

Summary

Like any book, the knowledge contained herein is only useful if you put it into practice. The more you practice the more you will succeed at mastering these skills.

Previously, I discussed how social engineering is like mastering the art of cooking. By mixing the right ingredients in the right quantity you can have a meal that is full of flavor and excitement. The first time you try to cook a meal it might have too much salt or it might lack flavor altogether, but you don't immediately throw in the towel—you keep trying until you get it right. The same goes for social engineering. Some of the necessary skills may come more naturally to you and others may be more difficult.

If a particular topic is hard to understand or difficult for you to grasp, do not give up, and do not assume you cannot learn it. Anyone can learn and use these skills with the right amount of effort and work.

Also keep in mind that, just like a real recipe, many "ingredients" go into a good social engineering gig. The first ingredient might make more sense after you get down the line a little more. Certain skills—such as "the human buffer overflow" covered in Chapter 5—will only make sense after you master some of the other skills discussed in this book.

Regardless, keep practicing and make sure to do extra research on topics for which you need clarity. Now let's start cooking. Your "recipe" starts in the next chapter with the first ingredient, information gathering.

2 Information Gathering

War is ninety percent information.

—Napoleon Bonaparte

It has been said that no information is irrelevant. Those words ring true when it comes to this chapter on information gathering. Even the slightest detail can lead to a successful social engineering breach.

My good friend and mentor, Mati Aharoni, who has been a professional pentester for more than a decade, tells a story that really drives this point home. He was tasked with gaining access to a company that had an almost nonexistent footprint on the Web. Because the company offered very few avenues to hack into, gaining this access would prove to be very challenging.

Mati began scouring the Internet for any details that could lead to a path in. In one of his searches he found a high-ranking company official who used his corporate email on a forum about stamp collecting and who expressed an interest in stamps from the 1950s. Mati quickly registered a URL, something like `www.stampcollection.com`, and then found a bunch of old-looking 1950 stamp pictures on Google. Creating a quick website to show his "stamp collection," he then crafted an email to the company official:

> *Dear Sir,*
>
> *I saw on* `www.forum.com` *you are interested in stamps from the 1950s. Recently my grandfather passed away and left me with a stamp collection that I would like to sell. I have a website set up; if you would like to see it please visit* `www.stampcollection.com`.
>
> *Thanks,*
> *Mati*

Before he sent the email to the target, he wanted to ensure there would be maximum impact. He took the office number from the forum post and placed a phone call to the man. "Good morning, sir, this is Bob. I saw your posting on www.forum.com. My grandfather recently passed and he left me a bunch of stamps from the 1950s and 60s. I took pictures and made a website. If you are interested I can send you the link and you can take a look."

The target was very eager to see this collection and readily accepted the email. Mati sent the man the email and waited for him to click the link. What Mati did was embed a malicious frame on the website. This frame had code in it that would exploit a vulnerability then known in the popular Internet Explorer browser and give control over the target's computer to Mati.

The wait was not long: as soon as the man received the email he clicked the link and the company's perimeter was compromised.

A tiny piece of information—the corporate email this man used to look for stamps—is what led to this compromise. No piece of information is irrelevant. With that knowledge in mind, here are questions that come up with regard to information gathering:

>> How can you gather information?

>> What sources exist for social engineers to gather information?

>> What can you glean from this information to profile your targets?

>> How can you locate, store, and catalog all this information for the easiest level of use?

These are just a few of the questions that you will need to find answers for in order to accomplish proper and effective information gathering. With the plethora of social networking sites out there, people can easily share every aspect of their lives with anyone they choose, making potentially damaging information more readily available than ever before. This chapter focuses on the principles of information gathering by presenting examples of how it can be used in social engineering and the devastating effects some of the information people release on the Web can have on their personal and business security.

Many of the skills or methods that a social engineer may use come from other fields. One field that is superb at gathering information is sales. Salespeople tend to be very talkative, easygoing, and very good at collecting data about those with whom they interact.

I once read a book on sales in which the author encouraged salespeople to gather referrals from the buyer—something along these lines: "Can you tell me one person who you think could benefit from this product as much as you will?"

Using simple wording can get a person to open up and refer family, friends, and maybe even coworkers. *Harvesting*, or gathering this information and then storing it, allows the sales people to have what they call "warm leads" to call on. A warm lead is where they have a person with an "in," a way to get in the door without having to cold call.

The salesperson can now call on those referrals and say something like, "I was just at Jane's house two doors down, and she bought our premium policy. After reviewing the benefits and paying for the year upfront she said you might benefit from the same coverage. Do you have a minute for me to show you what Jane purchased?"

These skills used by salespeople are often mirrored by social engineers. Of course a social engineer is not asking for referrals, but think about the flow of information in and out of this conversation. The salesperson gathers information from his present client, then he relays that information in a way that will make the new "target" more susceptible to listen and let him in. In addition, by dropping hints on what the first customer bought and using words like "premium" and "in advance" the salesperson is preloading the new target with the keywords he wants to use on him in just a little while. This technique is effective in that it builds trust, uses familiarity, and allows the target to feel comfortable with the salesperson, or the social engineer, giving their mind a bridge over the gap that normally would exist there. This chapter, as well as the following chapter, will delve deep into these topics.

As a social engineer, both angles are of vital importance to understand and then to use effectively. To return to the illustration used in Chapter 1 of being a chef, a good chef knows all about how to spot good quality products, fresh vegetables, and quality meats. They are knowledgeable about what goes into the recipe, but unless the right quantities are used the food may be too bland or too strong or not good enough to eat at all. Simply knowing that a recipe calls for salt doesn't make you a chef, but knowing how to mix the right amount and types of ingredients can help you master the art of cooking. A social engineer needs to master the type and quantity of skills to be used (the "recipe"). When that is done they can become a master social engineer.

This chapter helps identify this balance. The first ingredient in any recipe for a social engineer is information (detailed in the next section). The higher the quality of the information the more likely you are to achieve success. This chapter begins by discussing how to gather information. Then it moves on to discuss what sources can be used to harvest information. This chapter would not be complete without discussing how to tie it all together and utilize these resources as a social engineer.

Gathering Information

Gathering information is like building a house. If you try to start with the roof your house will surely be a failure. A good house will be built using a solid foundation and from there it will be built literally from the ground up. As you gather information you may be overwhelmed with how to organize and then use this data, so starting a file or an information gathering service to gather this data in is a good idea.

Many tools exist to assist in collecting and then using this data. For penetration tests and social engineering audits I use a Linux distribution called BackTrack that is specifically designed for this purpose. BackTrack is like most Linux distributions in that it is free and open source. Perhaps its greatest asset is that it contains more than 300 tools designed to assist in security auditing.

All of the tools within BackTrack are also open source and free. Especially attractive is the high quality of BackTrack's tools, many of which rival and even surpass tools you would pay an arm and a leg for. Two BackTrack tools that are particularly useful for information gathering and storing are called Dradis and BasKet. The following sections take a quick look at each.

Using BasKet

BasKet is similar in functionality to Notepad, but more like Notepad on steroids. It is presently maintained by Kelvie Wong and can be found for free either in BackTrack or at http://basket.kde.org/. The website has full instructions for how to install BasKet. Once installed BasKet is easy to use and the interface is not difficult to understand.

As seen in Figure 2-1, the interface is easy to figure out. Adding a new "Basket" to hold data is as simple as right clicking on the left side of the screen and selecting New Basket.

Once new Baskets are added the sky is the limit. You can copy and paste data, place screen shots in the Basket, or even tie in OpenOffice or other types of charts, graphs, and other utilities.

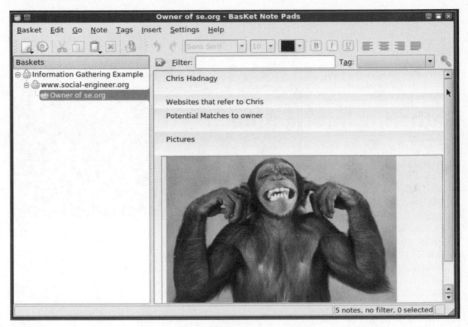

Figure 2-1 BasKet allows for easy organization of the data found during information gathering.

Adding a screenshot can be done in a few ways. The easiest is to copy the image then right mouse click on the new Basket and click Paste. As shown in Figure 2-1, adding images is simple but also shows the image right away. Notes can be typed or pasted around the images by simply clicking in the Basket and starting to type.

In a normal security audit, what makes BasKet attractive is the way it catalogs data and shows it on the screen. I usually add a different Basket for each type of data such as Whois, social media, and so on. After that, I will do some recon using Google Maps or Google Earth to capture some images of the client's building or facility, which I can store in BasKet as well. When the audit is complete, being able to pull up and utilize this information quickly is very easy. Figure 2-2 illustrates a nearly complete BasKet that contains a lot of useful information and tabs.

As shown in Figure 2-2, BasKet is easy to store the information in an easy-to-read format. I try to include as much information as possible because no information is too small to store. The information I include is items from the client's website, WhoIs information, social media sites, images, employee contact info, resumes found, forums, hobbies, and anything else I find linked to the company.

Figure 2-2 A nearly completed BasKet with lots of useful information.

When I am done, I simply click on the menu called Basket then Export and export the whole BasKet as an HTML page. This is great for reporting or sharing this data.

For a social engineer, collecting data, as will be discussed in detail later, is the crux of every gig, but if you cannot recall and utilize the data quickly, it becomes useless. A tool like BasKet makes retaining and utilizing data easy. If you give BasKet a try and use it once, you will be hooked.

Using Dradis

Although BasKet is a great tool, if you do a lot of information gathering, or if you work on team that needs to collect, store, and utilize data, then a tool that allows for multi-user sharing of this data is important. Enter Dradis. According to the creators of the open-source Dradis, the program is a "self-contained web application that provides a centralized repository of information" you have gathered, and a means by which to plan for what's to come.

Like BasKet, Dradis is a free, open-source tool that can be found at http:// dradisframework.org/. Whether you are using Linux, Windows, or a Mac, Dradis has easy-to-use set up and installation instructions found at http://dradisframework .org/install.html.

Once Dradis is installed and set up, you simply browse to the localhost and port you assigned, or use the standard 3004. You can do this by opening a browser and typing `https://localhost:3004/`.

Once logged in, you're greeted with the screen shown in Figure 2-3. Notice the Add Branch button at the top left. Adding a branch allows you to add similar details as you can in BasKet: notes, images, and more, and you can even import notes.

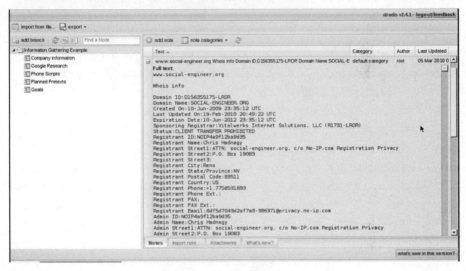

Figure 2-3 Dradis has a nice, easy-to-use interface.

Dradis and BasKet are just two tools that I have used to collect and store data. The websites for both Dradis and BasKet have very nice tutorials on setting up and using these powerful tools.

Whatever operating system you use—Mac, Windows, or Linux—there are choices out there for you. What is important is to use a tool that you are comfortable with and that can handle large amounts of data.

For that reason I suggest staying away from things like Notepad in Windows or Smultron or TextEdit in Mac. You want to be able to format and highlight certain areas to make them stand out. In my Dradis server, pictured in Figure 2-3, I have a section for phone scripts. This functionality is handy for transcribing ideas that might work based on the information I gathered.

These tools suggest how a social engineer begins to utilize the information he collects. The first stage in utilizing the information you gather is thinking like a social engineer.

Thinking Like a Social Engineer

Having a few hundred megabytes of data and pictures is great, but when you start reviewing it, how do you train yourself to review and then think of the data in a way that has maximum impact?

Of course you could just open a browser and type in long-winded random searches that may lead to some form of information, some of which may even be useful. If you are hungry you probably don't just run to the kitchen and start to throw whatever ingredients you see into a bowl and start digging in. Planning, preparation, and thought all cause the meal to be good. Similar to a real meal, a social engineer needs to plan, prepare, and think about what information he will try to obtain and how he will obtain it.

When it comes to this vital step of information gathering many people will have to change the way they think. You have to approach the world of information in front of you with a different opinion and mindset than what you normally may have. You have to learn to question everything, and, when you see a piece of information, learn to think of it as a social engineer would. The way you ask questions of the web or other sources must change. The way you view the answers that come back must also change. Overhearing a conversation, reading what seems like a meaningless forum post, seeing a bag of trash—you should assimilate this information in a different way than you did before. My mentor Mati gets excited when he sees a program crash. Why? Because he is a penetration tester and exploit writer. A crash is the first step to finding a vulnerability in software, so instead of being irritated at losing data he gets excited at the crash. A social engineer must approach information in much the same way. When finding a target that utilizes many different social media sites, look for the links between them and the information that can create a whole profile.

As an example, one time I rented a car to drive a few states away for business. My companion and I loaded all of our luggage in the trunk; as we were entering the car we noticed a small bag of trash in the back seat. The other person said something like, "Service today just stinks. You figure for what you pay they would at least clean out the car."

True, you would expect that, but I stopped that bag from just being chucked into the nearest can, and I said, "Let me just look at that really quick." As I opened the bag and pushed aside the Taco Bell wrappers, what was lying in plain sight was a shock to me—half of a ripped-up check. I quickly dumped out the bag and found a bank receipt and the other half of the check. The check was written out for a couple thousand dollars, then just ripped up—not into tiny little pieces, but just into four large chunks, then thrown into a small bag with a Taco Bell wrapper. Taping it back together revealed this person's name, company name, address, phone number, bank account number, and bank routing number. Together with the bank receipt I now had the balance of his account. Thankfully for him I am not a malicious person because only a couple more steps are needed to commit identity theft.

This story personifies how people view their valuable information. This guy rented the car before me and then because he threw the check away he felt it was gone, disposed of safely. Or so he thought; but this is not an isolated case. At this URL you can find a recent story about very valuable things people just threw away or sold for next to nothing at a garage sale: www.social-engineer.org/wiki/archives/BlogPosts/LookWhatIFound.html.

Things like:

» A painting that a museum bought for $1.2 million

» 1937 Bugatti Type 57S Atalante with a mere 24,000 miles sold for $3 million

» A copy of the Declaration of Independence

If people throw away a painting with a hidden copy of the Declaration of Independence in it, then throwing away bills, medical records, old invoices, or credit card statements probably isn't such a huge deal.

How you interact with people in public can have devastating effects. In the following scenario I was asked to audit a company and before I could proceed I needed to gather some data. Take a look at how simple, seemingly meaningless information can lead to a breach.

Simply following one of the higher ups of the target company for a day or two showed me that he stopped for coffee every morning at the same time. Since I was aware of his 7:30 a.m. coffee stop at the local coffee shop I could plan a "meeting." He would sit for 30–35 minutes, read the paper, and drink a medium cafe latte. I enter the shop about 3–5 minutes after he sits down. I order the same drink as him and sit down next to him in the shop. I look over as he places one section of the paper down and ask whether I can read the paper he is done with. Having already picked up a paper on the way I knew that page three contained an article about a recent murder in the area. After acting as if I just read it, I say out loud, "Even in these small towns things are scary nowadays. You live around here?"

Now at this point the target can blow me off, or if I played my cards right, my body language, vocal tone, and appearance will put him at ease. He says, "Yeah, I moved in a few years back for a job. I like small towns, but you hear this more and more."

I continue, "I am just traveling through the area. I sell high-end business consulting services to large companies and always enjoy traveling through the smaller towns but I seem to hear more and more of these stories even in the rural areas." Then in a very joking tone I say, "You don't happen to be a bigwig in a large company that needs some consulting do you?"

He laughs it off and then as if I just challenged him to prove his worth says, "Well I am a VP of finance at XYZ Corp. here locally, but I don't handle that department."

"Hey, look, I am not trying to sell you something, just enjoy coffee, but if you think I can stop by and leave you some information tomorrow or Wednesday?"

This is where the story gets interesting, as he says, "Well I would but I am heading out for a much-needed vacation on Wednesday. But why don't you mail it to me and I will call you." He then hands me a card.

"Going somewhere warm and sunny, I hope?" I ask this knowing that I am probably getting close to my point where I need to cut it off.

"Taking the wife on a cruise south." I can tell he doesn't want to tell me where, which is fine, so we shake hands and part ways.

Now could he have been blowing me off? Probably, but I have some valuable information:

» His direct number

» When he is leaving for vacation

» What type of vacation

» That he is local

» The name of his company

» His title in his company

» That he recently relocated

Of course, some of this information I already had from previous information gathering, but I was able to add a substantial amount to it after this meeting. Now to launch the next part of the attack, I call his direct line the day after he is supposed to be gone and ask for him, only to be told by his receptionist, "Sorry, Mr. Smith is on vacation—can I take a message?"

Excellent. The information is verified and now all I need to do is launch the final phase, which means dressing up in a suit and taking my $9 business cards to his office. I enter, sign in, and tell the receptionist I have an appointment with Mr. Smith at 10:00 a.m. To which she replies, "He is on vacation, are you sure it is today?"

Using my practice sessions on microexpressions, a topic addressed in Chapter 5, I show true surprise: "Wait, his cruise was this week? I thought he left next week."

Now this statement is vital—why?

I want the appointment to be believable and I want the receptionist to trust me by proxy. By stating I know about his cruise this must mean Mr. Smith and I have had intimate conversation—enough so that I know his itinerary. But my helplessness elicits pity and right away the secretary comes to my aid. "Oh, honey, I am sorry, do you want me to call his assistant?"

"Ah, no." I reply. "I really wanted to leave some information with him. How about this—I will just leave it with you and you can give it to him when he gets back? I am terribly embarrassed; maybe you can avoid even telling him I did this?"

"My lips are sealed."

"Thank you. Look I am going to crawl out of here, but before I do can I just use your bathroom?" I know that I normally would not be buzzed in, but I hope the combination of my rapport, my helplessness, and their pity will lead to success—and it does.

While in the bathroom, I place an envelope in one stall. On the cover of the envelope I put a sticker that says PRIVATE. Inside the "private" envelope is a USB key with a malicious payload on it. I do this in one stall and also in the hallway by a break room to increase my chances and hope that the person that finds one of them is curious enough to insert it into their computer.

Sure enough, this method seems to always work. The scary thing is that this attack probably wouldn't work if it weren't for a useless little conversation in a coffee shop.

The point is not only about how small data can still lead to a breach, but also how you collect this data. The sources that you can use to collect data are important to understand and test until you are proficient with each method and each source of collection. There are many different types of sources for collecting data. A good social engineer must be prepared to spend some time learning the strengths and weaknesses of each as well as the best way to utilize each source. Thus the topic of the next section.

Sources for Information Gathering

Many different sources exist for information gathering. The following list cannot possibly cover every source out there, but it does outline the major choices you have.

Gathering Information from Websites

Corporate and/or personal websites can provide a bounty of information. The first thing a good social engineer will often do is gather as much data as he can from the company's or person's website. Spending some quality time with the site can lead to clearly understanding:

- » What they do
- » The products and services they provide
- » Physical locations
- » Job openings
- » Contact numbers
- » Biographies on the executives or board of directors
- » Support forum
- » Email naming conventions
- » Special words or phrases that can help in password profiling

Seeing people's personal websites is also amazing because they will link to almost every intimate detail about their lives—kids, houses, jobs, and more. This information should be cataloged into sections because it will often be something from this list that is used in the attack.

Many times company employees will be part of the same forums, hobby lists, or social media sites. If you find one employee on LinkedIn or Facebook, chances are that many more are there as well. Trying to gather all that data can really help a social engineer profile the company as well as the employees. Many employees will talk about their job title in their social media outlets. This can help a social engineer to profile how many people may be in a department and how the departments are structured.

Search Engines

Johnny Long wrote a famous book called *Google Hacking for Penetration Testers* and really opened up many people's eyes to the amazing amount of information that Google holds.

Google forgives but it never forgets, and it has been compared to the Oracle. As long as you know how to ask, it can tell you most anything you want to know.

Johnny developed a list of what he calls "Google Dorks," or a string that can be used to search in Google to find out information about a company. For example if you were to type in: **site:microsoft.com filetype:pdf** you would be given a list of every file with the extension of PDF that is on the microsoft.com domain.

Being familiar with search terms that can help you locate files on your target is a very important part of information gathering. I make a habit of searching for **filetype:pdf**, **filetype:doc**, **filetype:xls**, and **filetype:txt**. It is also a good idea to see if employees actually leave files like DAT, CFG, or other database or configuration files open on their servers to be harvested.

Entire books are dedicated to the topic of using Google to find data, but the main thing to remember is learning about Google's operands will help you develop your own.

A website like www.googleguide.com/advanced_operators.html has a very nice list of both the operands and how to use them.

Google is not the only search engine that reveals amazing information. A researcher named John Matherly created a search engine he called Shodan (www.shodanhq.com).

Shodan is unique in that it searches the net for servers, routers, specific software, and so much more. For example, a search of **microsoft-iis os:"windows 2003"** reveals the following number of servers running Windows 2003 with Microsoft IIS:

» United States 59,140

» China 5,361

» Canada 4,424

» United Kingdom 3,406

» Taiwan 3,027

This search is not target-specific, but it does demonstrate one vital lesson: the web contains an amazing wealth of information that needs to be tapped by a social engineer seeking to become proficient at information gathering.

Whois Reconnaissance

Whois is a name for a service and a database. Whois databases contain a wealth of information that in some cases can even contain full contact information of the website administrators.

Using a Linux command prompt or using a website like www.whois.net can lead you to surprisingly specific results like such as a person's email address, telephone number, or even DNS server IP address.

Whois information can be very helpful in profiling a company and finding out details about their servers. All of this information can be used for further information gathering or to launch social engineering attacks.

Public Servers

A company's publicly reachable servers are also great sources for what its websites don't say. Fingerprinting a server for its OS, installed applications, and IP information can say a great deal about a company's infrastructure. After you determine the platform and applications in use, you could combine this data with a search on the corporate domain name to find entries on public support forums.

IP addresses may tell you whether the servers are hosted locally or with a provider; with DNS records you can determine server names and functions, as well as IPs.

In one audit after searching the web using the tool called Maltego (discussed in Chapter 7), I was able to uncover a publicly facing server that housed literally hundreds of documents with key pieces of information about projects, clients, and the creators of those documents. This information was devastating to the company.

An important note to keep in mind is that performing a *port scan*—using a tool like NMAP or another scanner to locate open ports, software, and operating systems used on a public server—can lead to problems with the law in some areas.

For example, in June 2003, an Israeli, Avi Mizrahi, was accused by the Israeli police of the offense of attempting the unauthorized access of computer material. He had port scanned the Mossad website. About eight months later, he was acquitted of all charges. The judge even ruled that these kinds of actions should not be discouraged when they are performed in a positive way (www.law.co.il/media/computer-law/mizrachi_en.pdf).

In December 1999, Scott Moulton was arrested by the FBI and accused of attempted computer trespassing under Georgia's Computer Systems Protection Act and Computer Fraud and Abuse Act of America. At the time, his IT service company had an ongoing contract with the Cherokee County of Georgia to maintain and upgrade the 911 center security (www.securityfocus.com/news/126).

As part of his work, Moulton performed several port scans on Cherokee County servers to check their security and eventually port scanned a web server monitored by another IT company. This provoked a lawsuit, although he was acquitted in 2000. The judge ruled that no damage occurred that would impair the integrity and availability of the network.

In 2007 and 2008, England, France, and Germany passed laws that make unlawful the creation, distribution, and possession of materials that allow someone to break any computer law. Port scanners fall under this description.

Of course, if you are involved in a paid audit of a company most of this will be in the contract, but it is important to state that it is up to the social engineer auditor to be aware of the local laws and make sure you are not breaking them.

Social Media

Many companies have recently embraced social media. It's cheap marketing that touches a large number of potential customers. It's also another stream of information from a company that can provide breadcrumbs of viable information. Companies publish news on events, new products, press releases, and stories that may relate them to current events.

Lately, social networks have taken on a mind of their own. When one becomes successful it seems that a few more pop up that utilize similar technology. With sites like Twitter, Blippy, PleaseRobMe, ICanStalkU, Facebook, LinkedIn, MySpace, and others, you can find information about people's lives and whereabouts in the wide open. Later, this book will discuss this topic in much more depth and you will see that social networks are amazing sources of information.

User Sites, Blogs, and So On

User sites such as blogs, wikis, and online videos may provide not only information about the target company, but also offer a more personal connection through the user(s) posting the content. A disgruntled employee who's blogging about his company's problems may be susceptible to a sympathetic ear from someone with similar opinions or problems. Either way, users are always posting amazing amounts of data on the web for anyone to see and read.

Case in point: Take a look at a new site that has popped up—www.icanstalku .com (see Figure 2-4). Contrary to its name, it does not encourage people to actually stalk others. This site points to the complete thoughtlessness of many Twitter users. It scrapes the Twitter site and looks for users who are silly enough to post pictures using their smart phones. Many people do not realize that most smart phones embed GPS location data in their photos. When a user posts a picture to the web with this data embedded it can lead a person right to their location.

Displaying location-based information is a scary aspect of social media websites. Not only do they allow you to post pictures of yourself, they also implicitly reveal your location—possibly without your knowledge.

Sites like ICanStalkU underscore the danger of this information. Check out a story (one of many) that shows how this data is used for home break-ins, robberies, and sometimes more at www.social-engineer.org/wiki/archives/BlogPosts/ TwitterHomeRobbery.html.

This type of information can give you a very detailed profile of your target. People love to tweet about where they are, what they are doing, and who they are with. Blippy allows a person to connect their bank accounts and in essence it will "tweet" with each purchase, where it was from, and how much it costs. With pictures including embedded location data and then sites like Facebook, which many use to put personal pictures, stories, and other related info, it is a social engineer's dream. In a short while a whole profile can be developed with a person's address, job, pictures, hobbies, and more.

Another aspect of social media sites that makes them excellent sources of information gathering is the ability to be anonymous. If the target is a recently divorced middle-aged man who loves his Facebook page, you can be a young woman who is looking for a new friend. Many times, while flirting, people divulge valuable pieces of information. Combine the ability to be anyone or anything you want on the web with the fact that most people believe everything they read as gospel fact and what you have is one of the greatest risks to security.

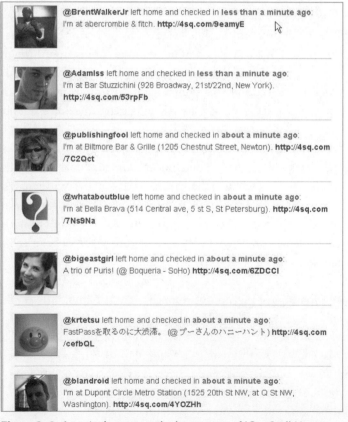

Figure 2-4 A typical scene on the homepage of ICanStalkU.com.

Public Reports

Public data may be generated by entities inside and outside the target company. This data can consist of quarterly reports, government reports, analyst reports, earnings posted for publicly traded companies, and so on. An example of these are Dunn and Bradstreet reports or other sales reports that are sold for very little money and contain a lot of details on the target company.

Another avenue discussed in more detail later is using background checkers such as those found at www.USSearch.com and www.intelius.com. These sites, along with many others, can offer background check services for as little as $1 for one limited report to a $49 per month fee that lets you run as many checks as you want. You can get much of this information for free using search engines, but some of the detailed financial data and personal information can only be obtained easily and legally through a paid-for service. Perhaps most shocking is that many of these companies may even provide data like a person's Social Security Number to some customers.

Using the Power of Observation

Though not used enough as a social engineering tool, simple observation can tell you much about your target. Does the target's employees use keys, RFID cards, or other methods to enter the building? Is there a designated area for smoking? Are dumpsters locked, and does the building have external cameras? External devices such as power supplies or air conditioning units usually reveal who the service company is, and that can allow the social engineer another vector to gain access.

These are just a few of the questions that you can get answers for through observation. Taking some time to watch the target, film using a covert camera, and then studying and analyzing the information later can teach you a lot and give your information file a major boost.

Going through the Garbage

Yes, as hard as it is to imagine enjoying jumping through the trash, it can yield one of the most lucrative payoffs for information gathering. People often throw away invoices, notices, letters, CDs, computers, USB keys, and a plethora of other devices and reports that can truly give amazing amounts of information. As mentioned previously, if people are willing to throw away art that is worth millions, then things they view as trash will often go without a second thought, right into the garbage.

Sometimes companies shred documents they deem as too important to just throw out, but they use an inefficient shredder that leaves paper too easy to put back together, as shown in Figure 2-5.

Figure 2-5 Large one-way shreds leave some words still readable.

This image shows a few documents after shredding, but some whole words are still discernable. This type of shredding can be thwarted with a little time and patience and some tape, as seen in Figure 2-6. Documents that can be even partially taped back together can reveal some very devastating information.

Figure 2-6 Putting documents back together only takes time and patience.

However, using a shredder that shreds both directions into a fine minced mess makes taping documents back together nearly impossible, as shown in Figure 2-7.

Figure 2-7. You can hardly tell this was once money.

Many companies use commercial services that take their shredded documents away for incineration. Some companies even leave the shredding to a third party, which, as you probably guessed, leaves them open to another attack vector. A social engineer who finds out the name of their vendor for this can easily mimic the pickup person and be handed all their documents. Nevertheless, dumpster diving can offer a quick way to find all the information you want. Remember some key pointers when performing a dumpster dive:

» **Wear good shoes or boots:** Nothing will ruin your day faster than jumping in a dumpster and having a nail go through your foot. Make sure your shoes tie on nice and tight as well as offer protection from sharp objects.

» **Wear dark clothing:** This doesn't need much explanation. You probably want to wear clothes you don't mind having to get rid of, and dark clothes to avoid being detected.

» **Bring a flashlight**

» **Grab and run:** Unless you are in such a secluded area that you have no chance of being caught, grabbing some bags and going elsewhere to rummage through them might be best.

Dumpster diving almost always leads to some very useful information. Sometimes a social engineer doesn't even have to dive into a dumpster to find the goods. Already mentioned in Chapter 1 is the article found at `www.social-engineer.org/resources/book/TopSecretStolen.htm`, but it solidifies this thought. The Canadian CTU (Counter-Terrorism Unit) had plans for a new building that outlined its security cameras, fences, and other top-secret items. These blueprints were just thrown away—yes, just tossed in the trash, not even shredded, and fortunately found by a friendly person.

This story is just one of many that show "the height of stupidity," as the article stated, but from a social engineer's point of view, trash diving is one of the best information gathering tools out there.

Using Profiling Software

Chapter 7 discusses the tools that make up some of the professional toolsets of social engineers, but this section offers a quick overview.

Password profilers such as Common User Passwords Profiler (CUPP) and Who's Your Daddy (WYD) can help a social engineer profile the potential passwords a company or person may use.

How to use these tools is discussed in Chapter 7, but a tool like WYD will scrape a person or company's website and create a password list from the words mentioned on that site. It is not uncommon for people to use words, names, or dates as passwords. These types of software make it easy to create lists to try.

Amazing tools such as Maltego (see Chapter 7 for more details), made by Paterva, are an information gatherer's dream. Maltego allows a social engineer to perform many web-based and passive information gathering searches without having to use any utilities but Maltego itself.

Then it will store and graph this data on the screen to be used in reporting, exporting or other purposes. This can really help in developing a profile on a company.

Remember, your goal as you collect data is to learn about the target company and the people within the company. Once a social engineer collects enough data, a clear picture will form in their minds as to the best way to manipulate the data from the targets. You want to profile the company as a whole and find out roughly how many employees are part of some club, a hobby, or group. Do they donate to a certain charity or do their kids go to the same school? All of this information is very helpful in developing a profile.

A clear profile can help the social engineer not only in developing a good pretext, but can also outline what questions to use, what are good or bad days to call or come onsite as well as many other clues that can make the job so much easier.

All of the methods discussed so far are mostly physical, very personal methods of information gathering. I didn't touch on the very technical side of information gathering like services such as SMTP, DNS, Netbios, and the almighty SNMP. I do cover some of the more technical aspects that Maltego can help with in Chapter 7 in more detail. These methods are worth looking into but are very much technical in nature as opposed to more "human" in nature.

Whatever the method you utilize to gather information logically, the question that may come up is now that you know where to gather, how to gather, and even how to catalog, store, and display this info, what do you do with it?

As a social engineer, after you have information you must start planning your attacks. To do that you need to start modeling an outline that will use this information. One of the best ways to start utilizing this data is to develop what is called a communication model.

Communication Modeling

> *The more elaborate our means of communication,*
> *the less we communicate.*
>
> —Joseph Priestley

Communication is a process of transferring information from one entity to another. Communication entails interactions between at least two agents, and can be perceived as a two-way process in which there is an exchange of information and a progression of thoughts, feelings, or ideas toward a mutually accepted goal or direction.

This concept is very similar to the definition of social engineering, except the assumption is that those involved in the communication already have a common goal, whereas the goal of the social engineer is to use communication to create a common goal. Communication is a process whereby information is enclosed in a package and is channeled and imparted by a sender to a receiver via some medium. The receiver then decodes the message and gives the sender feedback. All forms of communication require a sender, a message, and a receiver. Understanding how communication works is essential to developing a proper communication model as a social engineer. Modeling your communication as a social engineer will help us to decide the best method of delivery, the best method for feedback, and the best message to include.

Communication can take many different forms. There are auditory means, such as speech, song, and tone of voice, and there are nonverbal means, such as body language, sign language, paralanguage, touch, and eye contact.

Regardless of the type of communication used, the message and how it is delivered will have a definite effect on the receiver.

Understanding the basic ground rules is essential to building a model for a target. Some rules cannot be broken, such as communication always has a sender and a receiver. Also everyone has different personal realities that are built and affected by their past experiences and their perceptions.

Everyone perceives, experiences, and interprets things differently based on these personal realities. Any given event will always be perceived differently by different people because of this fact. If you have siblings, a neat exercise to prove this is to ask them their interpretation or memory of an event, especially if it is an emotional event. You will see that their interpretation of this event is very different from what you remember.

Each person has both a physical and a mental personal space. You allow or disallow people to enter that space or get close to you depending on many factors. When communicating with a person in any fashion, you are trying to enter their personal space. As a social engineer communicates they are trying to bring someone else into their space and share that personal reality. Effective communication attempts to bring all participants into each other's mental location. This happens with all interactions, but because it is so common people do it without thinking about it.

In interpersonal communications two layers of messages are being sent: verbal and nonverbal.

Communication usually contains a verbal or language portion, whether it is in spoken, written, or expressed word. It also usually has a nonverbal portion—facial expressions, body language, or some non-language message like emoticons or fonts.

Regardless of the amount of each type of cue (verbal or nonverbal), this communication packet is sent to the receiver and then filtered through her personal reality. She will form a concept based on her reality, then based on that will start to interpret this packet. As the receiver deciphers this message she begins to unscramble its meaning, even if that meaning is not what the sender intended. The sender will know whether his packet is received the way he intended if the receiver gives a communication packet in return to indicate her acceptance or denial of the original packet.

Here the packet is the form of communication: the words or letters or emails sent. When the receiver gets the message she has to decipher it. Many factors depend on how it is interpreted. Is she in a good mood, bad mood, happy, sad, angry, compassionate—all of these things as well as the other cues that alter her perception will help her to decipher that message.

The social engineer's goal has to be to give both the verbal and nonverbal cues the advantage to alter the target's perception so as to have the impact the social engineer desires.

Some more basic rules for communication include the following:

» Never take for granted that the receiver has the same reality as you.

» Never take for granted that the receiver will interpret the message the way it was intended.

» Communication is not an absolute, finite thing.

» Always assume as many different realities exist as there are different people involved in the communication.

Knowing these rules can greatly enhance the ability for good and useful communications. This is all good and great but what does communication have to do with developing a model? Even more, what does it have to do with social engineering?

The Communication Model and Its Roots

As already established, communication basically means sending a packet of information to an intended receiver. The message may come from many sources like sight, sound, touch, smell, and words. This packet is then processed by the target and used to paint an overall picture of "What's being said." This method of assessment is called the *communication process.* This process was originally outlined by social scientists Claude Shannon and Warren Weaver in 1947, when they developed the Shannon-Weaver model, also known as "the mother of all models."

The Shannon-Weaver model, according to Wikipedia, "embodies the concepts of information source, message, transmitter, signal, channel, noise, receiver, information destination, probability of error, coding, decoding, information rate, [and] channel capacity," among other things.

Shannon and Weaver defined this model with a graphic, as shown in Figure 2-8.

In a simple model, also known as the transmission model, information or content is sent in some form from a sender to a destination or receiver. This common concept of communication simply views communication as a means of sending and receiving information. The strengths of this model are its simplicity, generality, and quantifiability.

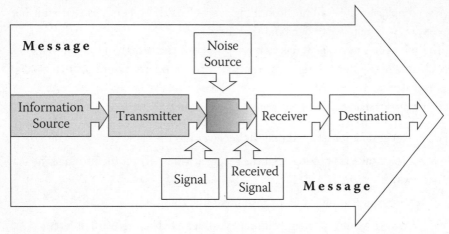

Figure 2-8 The Shannon-Weaver "mother of all models."

Shannon and Weaver structured this model based on:

» An information source, which produces a message

» A transmitter, which encodes the message into signals

» A channel, to which signals are adapted for transmission

» A receiver, which "decodes" (reconstructs) the message from the signal

» A destination, where the message arrives

They argued that three levels of problems for communication existed within this theory:

» The technical problem—How accurately can the message be transmitted?

» The semantic problem—How precisely is the meaning conveyed?

» The effectiveness problem—How effectively does the received meaning affect behavior? (This last point is important to remember for social engineering. The whole goal of the social engineer is to create a behavior that the social engineer wants.)

Almost 15 years later, David Berlo expanded on Shannon and Weaver's linear model of communication and created the Sender-Message-Channel-Receiver (SMCR) model of communication. SMCR separated the model into clear parts, as shown in Figure 2-9.

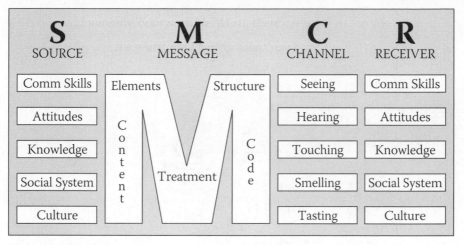

Figure 2-9 The Berlo model.

You can think of communication as processes of information transmission governed by three levels of rules:

» Formal properties of signs and symbols

» The relations between signs/expressions and their users

» The relationships between signs and symbols and what they represent

Therefore, you can further refine the definition of communication as social interaction where at least two interacting agents share a common set of signs and a common set of rules.

In 2008 another researcher, D. C. Balmund, combined the research of many of his previous cohorts with his own and developed the transactional model of communication, as shown in Figure 2-10.

In this model you can see that the channel and message can take on many forms, not just spoken, as represented by the picture. The message can be in written, video, or audio form and the receiver can be one person or many people. The feedback also can take on many forms.

Combining and analyzing this research can help a social engineer develop a solid communication model. Not only social engineers can benefit from doing this—everyone can. Learning how to develop a plan of communication can enhance the way you deal with your spouse, your kids, your employer or employees—anyone you communicate with.

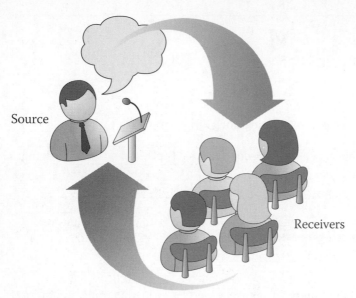

Figure 2-10 The new and improved communication model.

Because the focus of this book is social engineers, you need to analyze what a social engineer can take away from all of this. After reading all this theory you may begin to wonder how this can be used. Remember, a social engineer must be a master at communication. They must be able to effectively enter into and remain in a person's personal and mental space and not offend or turn off the target. Developing, implementing, and practicing effective communication models is the key to accomplishing this goal. The next step then is developing a communication model.

Developing a Communication Model

Now that you know about the key elements of a communication model, take a look at them from the eyes of a social engineer:

» **The Source:** The social engineer is the source of the information or communication that is going to be relayed.

» **The Channel:** This is the method of delivery.

» **The Message:** Probably the biggest part of the message is knowing what you are going to say to the receiver(s).

» **The Receiver(s):** This is the target.

» **The Feedback:** What do you want them to do after you effectively give them the communication?

How can you use these elements effectively? The first step into the world of communication modeling is starting with your goal. Try working with a couple of the scenarios that might be part of a typical social engineering gig:

» Develop a phishing email targeted against 25–50 employees and attempt to have them go during work hours to a non-business website that will be embedded with malicious code to hack into their networks.

» Make an onsite visit to portray a potential interviewee who has just ruined his resume by spilling coffee on it and needs to convince the front-desk person to allow a USB key to be inserted into a computer to print a copy of the resume.

When developing a communication strategy you may find working on the model in reverse order to be beneficial.

» **Feedback:** What is your desired response? The desired response is to have the majority of the employees you send this email to click on it. That is ideal; of course, you might be happy with just a handful or even one, but the goal, the desired feedback, is to have the majority of targets click on the phishing link.

» **Receivers:** This is where your information gathering skills come in handy. You need to know all about the targets. Do they like sports? Are they predominantly male or female? Are they members of local clubs? What do they do in their off time? Do they have families? Are they older or younger? The answers to these questions can help the social engineer decide what type of message to send.

» **Message:** If the target is predominantly 25–40-year-old males, with a few being part of a fantasy football or basketball league, your targets may click on a link about sports, women, or a sporting event. Developing the email's content is essential, but also grammar, spelling, and punctuation are very important to consider. One of the biggest tip-offs to phishing emails in the past has been the bad spelling.

Getting an email that reads like this: "Click here and enter ur pasword to verify ur account settings," is a dead giveaway to its being a non-legitimate email. Your email must be legit with good spelling and an appealing offer that fits the target. Even with the same goal the message will change depending on gender, age, and many other factors. The same email would probably fail if the targets were predominately female.

» **Channel:** This answer to this element is easy, because you already know it is going to be an email.

» **Source:** Again, this element is a no-brainer, because you, the social engineer, are the source. How believable you are depends on your skill level as a social engineer.

Scenario One: Phishing Email

The targets are 45 males ranging from the age of 25 to 45. Out of the 45 targets, 24 are in the same fantasy basketball league. They all go daily to a site (www.myfantasybasketballleague.com) to register their picks. This is verified by posts on the forums.

The goal is to drive them to a site that is available and that you now own, www.myfantasybasketballeague.com, which is a slight misspelling. This site is a clone of the site they visit with one change—it has an embedded iframe. There will be a Login button in the center of the page that when clicked, brings them back to the real site. The delay in loading and clicking will give the code the time it needs to hack their systems.

How would you write the email? Here is a sample that I wrote:

Hello,

We have some exciting news at My Fantasy Basket Ball League. We have added some additional features that will allow you more control over your picks as well as some special features. We are working hard on offering this to all of our members but some additional service fees may apply.

We are excited to say that the first 100 people to log in will get this new service for free. Click this link to be taken to the special page, click the gray LOGIN button on the page, and log in to have these features added to your account. www.myfantasybasketballeague.com

Thanks,
The MFBB Team

This email would mostly likely get at least the 24 who are already in the league interested enough to click the link and check out the site and try these new features for free.

Analyze that email. First, it contains an offer that would attract the present members of that fantasy league. Many of them realize the offer is limited to only the first 100, so they would click on it soon as they get the email, which more than likely is at work. The site that the email drives them to has the malicious code and although the majority will fall victim, all the malicious social engineer needs is one victim.

Also notice that the email contains good grammar and spelling, an enticing hook, and enough motivation to click quickly. It is a perfect email based off a solid communication model.

Scenario Two: USB Key

The onsite scenario is a little more difficult to do because it is in person. You can only do so much to "spoof" your identity in person. In this scenario remember that you must have all these details in memory because you can't be pulling out and using cue cards. It is also important to remember that oftentimes we have only one chance to make an impression. If we do a bad job at it, it can ruin the rest of the gig.

» **Feedback:** The goal with this scenario is to get the front desk receptionist to accept your USB drive that has a malicious program on it. The program will auto load and scrape her system for all information, such as usernames, passwords, email accounts, SAM files that contain all the passwords on the system, and more, copying it all to a directory on the USB drive. It also creates a reverse connection from the receptionist's machine to your servers, giving you access to her machine and hopefully the network. I am fond of using the Metasploit framework or the Social Engineering Toolkit (see Chapter 7) that ties in with Metasploit. Metasploit executes exploit code on its victims and it has a built-in handler called Meterpreter. The user can script many things like keylogging, screenshots, and recon from the victim's machines.

» **Receivers:** Having one true target can be tricky because if your target is unreceptive to the idea, your plan is shot. You must be warm, friendly, and convincing. This must be done fast, too, because too much time will allow doubt to set in. But if you move too fast you can cause doubt and fear, killing your chances. A perfect balance must be accomplished.

» **Message:** Because you're delivering the message in person, it must be clear and concise. The basic story is that you saw the ad in the paper for a database administrator and you called in and spoke to Debbie, the HR person. She said she was booked today but you should stop in and drop off a resume for her review and then meet her at the end of the week. While you were driving over, a squirrel ran out, causing you to slam on the brakes and causing your coffee to come out of the holder and spill in your bag, ruining your resumes and other stuff. Anyhow, you have another appointment but really need this job and wonder whether she would print you a fresh copy from your USB drive.

» **Channel:** You are going in person using verbal, facial, and body language communication.

» **Source:** Again, this is you as the social engineer, unless you have a good reason to have a stand in.

Holding a coffee-stained folder with some wet papers in it can help sell the story. Looking dejected and not alpha-male-ish can also help sell it. Politely speaking to her and not using foul language will help her feel a liking to you and maybe even some pity. The USB key should contain a file called myresume.doc or myresume.pdf and be printable. PDFs are the most commonly used formats since most companies are running an older version of Adobe Reader that is vulnerable to many different exploits. Make sure the resume is in a format that allows for the most people to be able to open it—not some odd format.

> *Most of the time people want to help. They want to be able to assist a person in distress if the story is believable as well as heart wrenching. For a special twist if you really lack a heart as a social engineer, you can put a spin on the story: On my way over, it was my turn today to drop my daughter off at school. When she climbed over the seat to give me a kiss goodbye she knocked over my coffee into my bag. I was already running late and closer to here than home; could you print me a fresh copy?*

Either way, this story usually works and will lead to the USB key being inserted into the computer and most likely a complete compromise of the receptionist's computer, which can lead to a total compromise of the company.

The Power of Communication Models

Communication modeling is a powerful tool that is a must-have skill for every social engineer. The hardest part about communication modeling is to ensure your information-gathering sessions are solid.

In both of the earlier scenarios, not having a good plan and model will lead to failure. A good way to practice communication modeling is to write out a model for manipulating people you know well—a husband, wife, parent, child, boss, or friend—to do something you want, to take some action you desire.

Set a goal, nothing malicious, such as getting someone to agree to a different vacation spot or a to go to a restaurant you love and your partner hates, or to allow you to spend some money on something you normally wouldn't ask for. Whatever it is you come up with, write out the five communication components and then see how well the communication goes when you have a written plan. You will find that with your goals clearly defined, you can better test your social engineering communication methods, and be able to achieve your goals more easily. List the following five points and fill them out one by one, connecting the dots as you go along.

» Source

» Message

» Channel

» Receivers

» Feedback

Communication modeling yields very valuable information and without it, most communication will not be successful for a social engineer. As previously mentioned, information gathering is the crux of every social engineering gig, but if you become proficient at information gathering and you are able to gather amazing amounts of data but don't know how to use it, it is a waste.

Learn to become a master at information gathering and then practice putting that into action with communication modeling. This is just the start, but it can literally change the way you deal with people both as a social engineer and in everyday contexts. Yet so much more goes into developing a solid message in the communication model.

One key aspect of learning how to communicate, how to manipulate, and how to be a social engineer is learning how to use questions, as discussed in the next chapter.

3

Elicitation

The supreme art of war is to subdue the enemy without fighting.

—SUN TZU

Being able to effectively draw people out is a skill that can make or break a social engineer. When people see you and talk to you they should feel at ease and want to open up.

Have you ever met someone and instantly felt, "Wow I like that person"? Why? What was it about him that made you feel that way? Was it his smile? The way he looked? The way he treated you? His body language?

Maybe he even seemed to be "in tune" with your thoughts and desires. The way he looked at you was non-judgmental and right away you felt at ease with him.

Now imagine you can tap into that and master that ability. Don't shrug off this chapter as a simple "how to build rapport" lesson. This chapter is about *elicitation*, a powerful technique used by spies, con men, and social engineers, as well as doctors, therapists, and law enforcement, and if you want to be protected or be a great social engineer auditor then you need to master this skill. Used effectively, elicitation can produce astounding results.

What is elicitation? Very few aspects of social engineering are as powerful as elicitation. This is one of the reasons it is near the top of the framework. This skill alone can change the way people view you. From a social engineering standpoint, it can change the way you practice security. This chapter dissects examples of expert elicitation and delves deep into how to utilize this powerful skill in a social engineering context.

Before getting in too deep, you must begin with the basics.

What Is Elicitation?

Elicitation means to bring or draw out, or to arrive at a conclusion (truth, for instance) by logic. Alternatively, it is defined as a stimulation that calls up (or draws forth) a particular class of behaviors, as in "the elicitation of his testimony was not easy."

Read that definition again and if it doesn't give you goose bumps you may have a problem. Think about what this means. Being able to effectively use elicitation means you can fashion questions that draw people out and stimulate them to take a path of a behavior you want. As a social engineer, what does this mean? Being effective at elicitation means you can fashion your words and your questions in such a way that it will enhance your skill level to a whole new level. In terms of information gathering, expert elicitation can translate into you target *wanting* to answer your every request.

I want to take this discussion one step further because many governments educate and warn their employees against elicitation because it is used by spies all over the earth.

In training materials, the National Security Agency of the United States government defines elicitation as "the subtle extraction of information during an apparently normal and innocent conversation."

These conversations can occur anywhere that the target is—a restaurant, the gym, a daycare—anywhere. Elicitation works well because it is low risk and often very hard to detect. Most of the time, the targets don't ever know where the information leak came from. Even if a suspicion exists that there is some wrong intent, one can easily pass it off as an angry stranger being accused of wrong doing for just asking a question.

Elicitation works so well for several reasons:

> »   Most people have the desire to be polite, especially to strangers.

> »   Professionals want to appear well informed and intelligent.

> »   If you are praised, you will often talk more and divulge more.

> »   Most people would not lie for the sake of lying.

> »   Most people respond kindly to people who appear concerned about them.

These key factors about most humans are why elicitation works so well. Getting people to talk about their accomplishments is too easy.

In one scenario in which I was tasked to gather intel on a company, I met my target at a local chamber of commerce function. Because it was a mixer I hung back until I saw the target approaching the bar. We got there at the same time and because the purpose of these functions is to meet and greet people and exchange business cards, my first move wasn't extreme.

I said, "Escaping from the vultures?"

He replied with a chuckle, "Yeah, this is what makes these things worth the time—open bar."

I listened to him order, and I ordered a similar drink. I lean over with my hand out, and said, "Paul Williams."

"Larry Smith."

I pulled out a business card I had ordered online. "I work with a little import company as the head of purchasing."

He said as he handed me his card, "I am the CFO for XYZ."

With a chuckle I responded, "You're the guy with the bucks—that's why everyone is after you out there. What exactly do you guys do?"

He bagan to relate a few details of his company's products, and when he listed one that is well known, I said, "Oh right, you guys make that *widget*; I love that thing. I read in *XYZ Magazine* it hit a new sales record for you guys." From my previous information gathering I knew he had personal interest in that device so my praise was well received.

He began to puff his chest out a bit. "Did you know that device sold more in the first month that our previous and next five products combined?"

"Yikes, well I can see why, because I bought five myself." I chuckled through the mild praise.

After another drink and some more time I was able to discover that they recently purchased accounting software, the name of the CSO (and the fact he was on vacation for a few days), and that my friend here was also going on vacation soon to the Bahamas with his wife.

This seemingly useless info is not useless at all. I have a list of details about software, people, and vacations that can help me plan an attack. But I didn't want to stop there; I went in for the kill with a question like this:

"I know this is a weird question, but we are a small company and my boss told me I am to research and buy a security system for the doors. We just use keys now, but he was thinking RFID or something like that. Do you know what you guys use?"

This question I thought would send up red flares and smoke signals. Instead, he said "I have no clue; I just signed the checks for it. What I do know is I have this fancy little card…" as he pulls out his wallet to show me his card. "I think it is RFID, but all I know is that I wave my wallet in front of the little box and the door opens."

We exchanged laughs and I walked away with knowledge that led to some very successful attack vectors. As you may have noticed, elicitation is similar to and linked to information gathering. This particular information-gathering session was made so much easier by a solid pretext (discussed in Chapter 4) as well good elicitation skills. Elicitation skills are what made the questions flow smoothly and what made the target feel comfortable answering my questions.

Knowing that he was on vacation and what kinds of accounting software they used as well as the door locking security I was able to plan an onsite visit to repair a "faulty" RFID box and time clock. Simply telling the front desk receptionist, "Larry called me before he left for the Bahamas and said there was a time clock by the manufacturing department that is not registering properly. It will take me a few minutes to test and analyze it." I was given access in a matter of seconds without ever being questioned.

Elicitation led me to that success because with the knowledge I was given there was no reason for the receptionist to doubt my pretext.

Simple, light, airy conversation is all it takes to get some of the best information out of many people. As discussed so far, clearly defining your goals to achieve maximum results is vital. Elicitation is not used merely for information gathering, but it can also be used to solidify your pretext and gain access to information. All of this depends on a clearly defined and thought-out elicitation model.

The Goals of Elicitation

Reviewing the definition for elicitation can give you a clear path of what your goals are. Really, though, you can boil it down to one thing. A social engineer wants the target to take an action, whether that action be as simple as answering a question or as big as allowing access to a certain restricted area. To get the target to comply, the social engineer will ask a series of questions or hold a conversation that will motivate the target to that path.

Information is the key. The more information that you gather, the more successful the attack will be. Because elicitation is non-threatening it is very successful. Count how many times in a week you have meaningless little conversations with someone at a store, coffee shop, or elsewhere. The whole methodology of holding conversations is steeped in elicitation and it is used in a non-malicious way daily. That is why it is so effective.

In one episode of the popular British television show *The Real Hustle*, the hosts demonstrated the ease of many social engineering attacks. In this episode the goal was to draw a target into a game of luck that was rigged. To do so someone had a partner who acted as a complete stranger play a role in being interested and conversational with the attacker. This conversation draws in the surrounding people, which made eliciting proper responses from the target very easy. This is one method that works well.

Whichever method is used, the goal is to obtain information then utilize that information to motivate a target to the path the social engineer wants him to take. Understanding this fact is important. Later chapters cover pretexting and other manipulation tactics, but you don't want to confuse elicitation with those. Realizing that elicitation is conversation is important. Sure, it may be closely linked to your pretext, body language, and eye cues, but all of those pale in comparison to your ability to engage people in conversation.

Some experts agree that mastering the art of conversation has three main steps:

1. **Be natural.** Nothing can kill a conversation quicker than seeming to be uncomfortable or unnatural in the conversation. To see this for yourself try this exercise. Have a conversation with someone about something you know a lot about. If you can record it somehow or have someone else take notice, see how you stand, your posture, and the way you assert your knowledge. All of these things will scream confidence and naturalness. Then inject yourself in a conversation you know nothing about and have the same recording or friend observing. See how all those nonverbal aspects change for you when you try to inject an intelligent thought into a conversation you know nothing about.

   This exercise shows you the difference in being natural and not being natural. The person(s) you are conversing with will be able to see it easily, which will kill all chances of successful elicitation. How do you seem natural in conversations? Thus we arrive at step 2.

2. **Educate yourself.** You must have knowledge of what it is you will be talking to your targets about. This section should come with a big fat red neon light warning, but because every book can't include one let me emphasize this part:

   It is *imperative* that you not pretend you are more than you can reasonably be believed you are.

   Confused? Here's an example to break it down. If you wanted to obtain the chemical composition for a top-secret product and your elicitation target is one of the chemists involved in making the product, and you decide to start talking chemistry, do not play yourself off as a world-class chemist (unless you are). He may throw something at you that will show you know nothing and then your cover is blown and so is the elicitation.

A more realistic approach may be that you are a research student studying XYZ, and was told he had amazing knowledge in this area. Due to his expertise, you just wanted to ask him a question on a chemical formula you are working on and why it doesn't seem to be working out.

The point is that whatever you chose to converse about and whomever with, do research, practice, and be prepared. Have enough knowledge to speak intelligently about a topic that will interest the target.

3. **Don't be greedy.** Of course, the goal is to *get* information, *get* answers, and be *given* the key to the kingdom. Yet, do not let that be the focus. That you are only there for yourself will quickly become evident and the target will lose interest. Often, giving someone something will elicit the feeling of reciprocation (discussed in Chapter 6), where he or she now feels obligated to give you something in return. Being this way in conversation is important. Make the conversation a give and take, unless you are conversing with a person who wants to dominate the conversation. If he wants to dominate, let him. But if you get a few answers, feel the conversation out and don't get greedy trying to go deeper and deeper, which can raise a red flag.

Sometimes the people who are labeled as the "best conversationalists" in the world are those who do more listening than talking.

These three steps to successful elicitation can literally change the way you converse with people daily, and not just as a social engineer or a security auditor, but as an everyday person. I personally like to add one or two steps to the "top three."

For example, an important aspect to elicitation is facial expressions during a conversation. Having your gaze be too intense or too relaxed can affect the way people react to your questions. If your words are calm and you have engaged the target in a conversation but your body language or facial expressions show disinterest, it can affect the mood of the person, even if she doesn't realize it.

This may seem odd to bring up here, but I am a fan of Cesar Milan, aka, The Dog Whisperer. I think that guy is a genius. He takes dogs that seem unruly and in a matter of minutes has both the dogs and their owners produce high-quality personality traits that will merit a very successful relationship for both. He basically teaches people how to communicate with a dog—how to ask and tell it to do things in a language it understands. One of the things he preaches that I fully believe in is that the "spirit" or energy of the person affects the "spirit" or energy of the dog. In other words, if the person approaches the dog all tense and anxious, even if the words are calm, the dog will act tense, bark more, and be more on edge.

Obviously, people are not the same as dogs but I truly believe that this philosophy applies. As a social engineer approaches a target her "spirit" or energy will affect the person's perception. The energy is portrayed through body language, facial expressions, dress, and grooming, and then the words spoken to back that up. Without even knowing it, people pick up on these things. Have you ever thought or heard someone say, "That guy gave me the creeps" or "She looked like such a nice person"?

How does that work? The person's spirit or energy is relayed to your "sensors," that data is correlated with past experiences, and then a judgment is formed. People do it instantaneously, many times without even knowing it. So your energy when you are going to elicit must match the role you are going to play. If your personality or mental makeup doesn't enable you to easily play a manager then don't try. Work with what you have. Personally, I have always been a people person and my strong suit is *not* topics like chemistry or advanced math. If I were in the situation mentioned earlier I would not try to play the role of a person who knows about those things. Instead my elicitation might be as simple as a stranger interested in starting a conversation about the weather.

Whatever methods you chose to use, you can take certain steps to have the upper edge. One of these steps is called *preloading*.

Preloading

You stand in line to buy your $10 movie ticket and are barraged with sensory overload of posters of upcoming movies. You stand in line to buy your $40 worth of popcorn and drinks, see more posters, and then you push your way through to get a seat. Finally, when the movie starts you are presented with a series of clips about upcoming movies. Sometimes these movies aren't even in production yet, but the announcer comes on and says, "The funniest movie since..." or the music starts with an ominous tone, a dense fog fills the screen, and the voiceover intones, "You thought it was over in *Teenage Killer Part 45*...."

Whatever the movie is, the marketers are telling you how to feel—in other words, preloading what you should be thinking about this movie—before the preview starts. Then the short 1–3 minutes they have to show you what the movie is about is spent showing you clips to entice your desire to see the movie and to appeal to the crowd that wants the comedy, horror, or love story.

Not much has been written about preloading, but it is a very serious topic. Preloading denotes that you can do just what it says—preload targets with information or ideas on how you want them to react to certain information. Preloading is often used in marketing messages; for example, in the national restaurant chain ads that show beautiful people laughing and enjoying the meal that looks so beautiful and perfect. As they say "yummm!" and "ohhh!" you can almost taste the food.

Of course as a social engineer you can't run a commercial for your targets so how can you use preloading?

As with much in the social engineering world, you have to start from the end results and work backward. What is your goal? You might have the standard goal of elicitation to gain information from a target on a project she is working on or dates she will be in the office or on vacation. Whatever it is, you must set the goal first. Next you decide the type of questions that you want to ask, and then decide what type of information can preload a person to want to answer those questions.

For example, if you know that later tonight you want to go to a steak place that your coupon-loving wife doesn't really enjoy, but you are in the mood for a rib eye, you can preload to get a response that may be in your favor. Maybe earlier in the day you can say something like, "Honey, you know what I am in the mood for? A big, juicy, grilled steak. The other day I was driving to the post office and Fred down the road had his grill out. He had just started cooking the steaks on charcoal and the smell came in the car window and it has been haunting me ever since." Whether this elicits a response at this exact moment is not important; what you did is plant a seed that touched every sense. You made her imagine the steaks sizzling on the grill, talked about seeing them go on, talked about smelling the smoke, and about how much you wanted one.

Suppose then you bring home the paper and as you're going through it you see an ad with a coupon for the restaurant you want to go to. You simply leave that page folded on the table. Again, maybe your wife sees it or maybe she doesn't, but chances are that because you left it with the mail, because you mentioned steak, *and* because she loves coupons she will see the coupon left on the table.

Now later on she comes to you and says, "What do you want for dinner tonight?" Here is where all your preloading comes in—you mentioned the smell, sight, and desire for steak. You left an easy-to-find coupon on the table for the steak restaurant of choice and now it is dinner discussion time. You answer her with, "Instead of making you cook and having a mess to clean up tonight, we haven't been to XYZ Steaks in a while. What if we just hit that place tonight?"

Knowing she doesn't like that place all you can hope is the preloading is working. She responds, "I saw a coupon for that place in the newspaper. It had a buy one meal get a second half off. But you know I don't like...."

As she is speaking you can jump in and offer praise: "Ha! Coupon queen strikes again. Heck, I know you don't like steak too much but I hear from Sally that they have awesome chicken meals there, too."

A few minutes later you are on the way to steak heaven. Whereas a frontal assault stating your desire to go to XYZ would have most likely met with a resounding "No!" preloading helped set her mind up to accept your input and it worked.

One other really simplistic example before moving on: A friend walks up and says, "I have to tell you a really funny story." What happens to you? You might even start smiling before the story starts and your anticipation is to hear something funny, so you look and wait for opportunities to laugh. He preloaded you and you anticipated the humor.

How do these principles work within the social engineering world?

Preloading is a skill in itself. Being able to plant ideas or thoughts in a way that is not obvious or overbearing sometimes takes more skill than the elicitation itself. Other times, depending on the goal, preloading can be quite complex. The earlier steak scenario is a complex problem. The preload took some time and energy, where a simplistic preload might be something as simple as finding out what kind of car they drive or some other innocuous piece of information. In a very casual conversation where you "happen" to be in the same deli at the same time as your target you start a casual conversation with something like, "Man, I love my Toyota. This guy in a Chevy just backed into me in the parking lot, not even a scratch." With any luck as you engage the target in conversation, your exclamation about your car might warm him up to the questions that you can then place about types of cars or other topics you want to gather intel on.

The topic of preloading makes more sense as you start to analyze how you can utilize elicitation. Social engineers have been mastering this skill for as long as social engineering has been around. Many times the social engineer realizes he has this skill way before he turns to a life of social engineering. As a youth or a young adult he finds interacting with people easy, and later finds that he gravitates toward employment that uses these skills. Maybe he is the center of his group of friends and people seem to tell him all their problems and have no problem talking to him about everything. He realizes later that these skills are what gets him through doors that might be closed otherwise.

When I was young I always had this talent. My parents would tell me stories of how I at five or six years old would strike up conversations with complete strangers, sometimes even walking into the kitchen of busy restaurants to ask questions about our order or inquire how things were being done. Somehow I got away with it—why? Probably because I didn't know this behavior wasn't acceptable and because I did it with confidence. As I got older, that skill (or a lack of fear) came into full effect.

It also seemed that people, sometimes even complete strangers, loved to tell me their problems and talk to me about things. One story that I think helps to see how I was able to utilize not only preloading but also good elicitation skills was when I was around 17 or 18 years old.

I was an avid surfer and would do odd jobs to support my hobby—basically anything from pizza delivery to fiberglass cutter to lifeguard. One time I ran errands for my father who owned an accounting/financial consulting company. I would deliver papers to his clients, get signatures, and bring them back. Often, many of the clients would open up and tell me all about their lives, their divorces, and their business successes and failures. Usually this started with a small session with them telling me how great my Dad was to them. At the time I never understood why people, especially adults, would open up to a 17–18 year old with the reasons their universe is breaking apart.

One particular client I would visit often owned an apartment complex. It was nothing huge and fancy; he just had a few properties that he owned and managed. This poor guy had real problems—family problems, health problems, and personal problems—all of which he routinely would tell me about for as long as I would sit and listen. This is when it began to hit me that I could get away with saying or doing amazing things if I just spent time listening to people. It made them feel important and like I was a good person. It didn't matter if I sat there thinking about my next great wave; what mattered was that I listened.

Normally I would listen for as long as I could stand the amazing amount of tobacco smoke he put out (he smoked more than any person I ever have seen in my life). But I would sit and listen and because I was young and had no experience I would offer no advice, no solution, just an ear. The thing was that I was truly concerned; I didn't fake it. I wished I had a solution. One day he told me about how he wanted to move back out West where his daughter was and be closer to family.

I wanted to move on in life and get a job I thought would be cool, fun, and give me some more cash for surfboards and other things I "needed." During one of my listening sessions, a crazy idea popped in my head, and he viewed me as a responsible, compassionate young man with a "good head" on my shoulders. The preloading took place over the months I spent sitting with him and listening. Now it was time to cash in on that. I said, "Why don't you go back and let me run your apartment complex for you?" The idea was so absurd, so ridiculous that looking back now I would have laughed in my face. But for weeks, months even, I had listened to his problems. I knew the man and his woes. On top of that, I never laughed at or rejected him. Now he had shared a problem with me, and here was a perfect solution, one that took care of all of his problems as well as mine. My income needs were low, and he wanted to be close to his family. We had built a relationship over the last few months and thus he "knew" me and trusted me.

After some discussion we came to an agreement and he up and moved back out West and I was a 17-year-old running a 30-unit apartment complex as the vice-landlord. I could go on and tell you much more on this story but the point is already made. (I will tell you the job went great until he asked me to try to sell his complex for him, which I did in record time, at the same time selling myself out of a job.)

The point is that I developed a rapport, a trust, with someone and without trying and without malicious intent, I had a chance to preload him over months with the ideas that I was kind and compassionate and intelligent. Then when the time arose I was able to present an absurd idea, and because of the months of preloading, it was accepted.

It wasn't until later in life that it hit me what was going on here. There were so many factors at play that I didn't realize at the time. Preloading from a social engineering standpoint involves knowing your goal before you start. In this case, I didn't know I was going to try and land a crazy job with this guy. But preloading still worked.

In most social engineering cases it would much quicker, but I think the principles apply. Being as genuine as you can is essential. Because preloading involves the person's emotions and senses, give them no reason to doubt. The question you ask should match your pretext. For preloading to work you have to ask for something that matches the belief you built into them. For example, if my offer was to have me go visit my client's family and take pictures rather than manage his apartment complex, it wouldn't have matched the belief system he had of me, namely that I was a smart, business-minded, caring young man. Finally, the offer, when made, must be of benefit to the target, or at least perceived as benefit. In my case, there was lots of benefit to my client. But in social engineering the benefit can be as little as "bragging rights": giving the person a platform to brag a bit. Or the benefit can be much more and involve physical, monetary, or psychological benefits.

Practicing elicitation and becoming proficient at it will make you a master social engineer. Logically, the next section is how to become a successful elicitor.

Becoming a Successful Elicitor

Analyzing just my own experiences I can identify some key components that led to my success from five-years-old to now:

» A lack of fear to talk to people and be in situations that are not considered "normal."

» I truly do care for people, even if I don't know them. I want to and enjoy listening to people.

» I offer advice or help only when I have a real solution.

» I offer a non-judgmental ear for people to talk about their problems.

These are key elements to successful elicitation. The United States Department of Homeland Security (DHS) has an internal pamphlet on elicitation it hands out to its agents that I was able to obtain and archive at www.social-engineer.org/wiki/archives/BlogPosts/ocso-elicitation-brochure.pdf.

This brochure contains some excellent pointers. Basically, as stated in it and in this chapter, elicitation is used because it works, is very hard to detect, and is non-threatening. The DHS pamphlet approaches elicitation from a "how to avoid" point of view, but the following sections take some of the scenarios and show you what can be learned.

Appealing to Someone's Ego

The scenario painted in the DHS brochure goes like this:

Attacker: "You must have an important job; so and so seems to think very highly of you."

Target: "Thank you, that is nice of you to say, but my job isn't that important. All I do here is..."

The method of appealing to someone's ego is simplistic but effective. One caution, though: Stroking someone's ego is a powerful tool but if you overdo it or do it without sincerity it just turns people off. You don't want to come off as a crazy stalker: "Wow, you are the most important person in the universe and you are so amazing-looking, too." Saying something like that might get security called on you.

Using ego appeals needs to be done subtly, and if you are talking to a true narcissist avoid eye rolls, sighs, or argumentativeness when she brags of her accomplishments. Subtle ego appeals are things like, "That research you did really changed a lot of people's viewpoints on…" or "I overheard Mr. Smith telling that group over there that you are one of the most keen data analysts he has." Don't make the approach so over the top that it is obvious.

Subtle flattery can coax a person into a conversation that might have never taken place, as stated in the DHS brochure, and that is exactly what you want as a social engineer.

Expressing a Mutual Interest

Consider this mock scenario:

Attacker: "Wow, you have a background in ISO 9001 compliance databases? You should see the model we built for a reporting engine to assist with that certification. I can get you a copy."

Target: "I would love to see that. We have been toying with the idea of adding a reporting engine to our system."

Expressing mutual interest is an important aspect of elicitation. This particular scenario is even more powerful than appealing to someone's ego because it extends the relationship beyond the initial conversation. The target agreed to further contact, to accept software from the attacker, and expressed interest in discussing plans for the company's software in the future. All of this can lead to a massive breach in security.

The danger in this situation is that now the attacker has full control. He controls the next steps, what information is sent, how much, and when it is released. This is a very powerful move for the social engineer. Of course, if the engagement were long-term, then having a literal piece of software that can be shared would prove even more advantageous. Sharing usable and non-malicious software would build trust, build rapport, and make the target have a sense of obligation.

Making a Deliberate False Statement

Delivering a false statement seems like it would backfire off the top, but it can prove to be a powerful force to be reckoned with.

Attacker: "Everybody knows that XYZ Company produced the highest-selling software for this widget on earth."

Target: "Actually, that isn't true. Our company started selling a similar product in 1998 and our sales records have beaten them routinely by more than 23%."

These statements, if used effectively, can elicit a response from the target with real facts. Most people must correct wrong statements when they hear them. It's almost as if they are challenged to prove they are correct. The desire to inform others, appear knowledgeable, and be intolerant of misstatements seems to be built into human nature. Understanding this trait can make this scenario a powerful one. You can use this method to pull out full details from the target about real facts and also to discern who in a group might have the most knowledge about a topic.

Volunteering Information

The DHS brochure makes a good point about a personality trait many of us have. A few mentions of it have appeared in the book already and it's covered in much more detail later on, but *obligation* is a strong force. As a social engineer, offering up information in a conversation almost compels the target to reply with equally useful information.

Want to try this one out? Next time you are with your friends say something like, "Did you hear about Ruth? I heard she just got laid off from work and is having serious problems finding more work."

Most of the time you will get, "Wow, I didn't hear that. That is terrible news. I heard that Joe is getting divorced and they are going to lose the house, too."

A sad aspect of humanity is that we tend to live the saying "misery loves company"—how true it is in this case. People tend to want to share similar news. Social engineers can utilize this proclivity to set the tone or mood of a conversation and build a sense of obligation.

Assuming Knowledge

Another powerful manipulation tool is that of *assumed knowledge*. It is commonplace to assume that if someone has knowledge of a particular situation, it's acceptable to discuss it with them. An attacker can deliberately exploit this trait by presenting information as if he is in the know and then using elicitation to build a conversation around it. He then can regurgitate the information as if it were his own and continue to build the illusion that he has intimate knowledge of this topic. This scenario might be better illustrated with an example.

One time I was going to China to negotiate a large deal on some materials. I needed to have some intimate knowledge about my target company in the negotiations and had to find a way to get it before I met with them. We had never met face to face but I was heading to a conference in China before my negotiations started. While at the conference I happened to overhear a conversation starting about how to place yourself in a higher position when dealing with the Chinese on negotiations.

I knew this was my opportunity, and to make the situation even sweeter one of the people in the small group was from the company I was going to be meeting with. I quickly injected myself into the conversation and knew that if I didn't say something quick I would lose face. My knowledge was limited but they didn't need to know that. When a small pause arose I began to talk about the Guanxi theory. Guanxi is basically how two people who may not have the same social status can become connected, and then one is pressed upon to perform a favor for the other. I talked about how this connection can be used, and then concluded by tying it in with how important it is as an American to not simply take a business card and stick it in my back pocket but to review it, comment on it, then place it somewhere respectful.

This conversation was enough to set me up as someone who had some knowledge and deserved to stay in the circle of trust there. Now that I had established my knowledge base I sat back and listened to each person express his or her experience and personal knowledge on how to negotiate properly with large Chinese companies. I paid very close and particular attention when the gentlemen who worked for my target company spoke. As he talked I could tell the "tips" he was giving were closely linked to the business philosophies of his company. This knowledge was more valuable than anything I could have paid for and it led to a very successful trip.

There are a couple more scenarios I feel are often used in elicitations.

Using the Effects of Alcohol

Nothing loosens lips more than the juice. This is an unfortunate but true fact. Mix any one of the preceding five scenarios with alcohol and you can magnify its effects by 10.

Probably the best way to describe this scenario is with a true story.

In 1980 a senior scientist from Los Alamos National Laboratory traveled to a research institute in the People's Republic of China (PRC) to talk about his specialty, nuclear fusion. He had extensive knowledge of U.S. nuclear weapons information but knew the situation he was entering was dangerous and he needed to be determined to stick to his topic.

Yet he was constantly barraged with increasingly detailed inquiries directly related to nuclear weapons. The attackers' tactics would change and they would ask many benign questions about fusion and astrophysics, his specialty.

Once they even threw a cocktail party in his honor. They gathered around and applauded his knowledge and research—each time with a toast and a drink. They began to inquire about classified matters such as the ignition conditions of deuterium and tritium, the two components in the then-new neutron bomb. He did well at fending off the constant questions, but after many toasts and a party in *his* honor, he decided to give an analogy. He mused to the group that if you rolled those two components into a ball and then rolled them off the table they would most likely ignite because they had such low temperature threshold levels.

This seemingly useless story and information most likely caused the researchers in China to discern a clear path of research on nuclear weapons. They would take this information to yet another scientist and now armed with a little more knowledge, use that knowledge to get to the next stage with him or her. After many attempts, it is very likely the Chinese scientist would possess a clear picture of what path to take.

This is a serious example of how using elicitation can lead to gaining a clear picture of the whole answer. In social engineering it may be the same for you. All the answers might not come from one source. You may elicit some information from one person about their whereabouts on a particular date, and then use that information to elicit more information from the next stage, and so on and so forth. Putting those nuggets of information together is often the hard part of perfecting elicitation skills. That is discussed next.

Using Intelligent Questions

As a social engineer you must realize that the goal with elicitation is not to walk up and say, "What is the password to your servers?"

The goal is getting small and seemingly useless bits of information that help build a clear picture of the answers you are seeking or the path to gaining those answers. Either way, this type of information gathering can help give the social engineer a very clear path to the target goal.

How do you know what type of questions to use?

The following sections analyze the types of questions that exist and how a social engineer can use them.

Open-Ended Questions

Open-ended questions cannot be answered with yes or no. Asking, "Pretty cold out today, huh?" will lead to a "Yes," "Uh-uh," "Yep," or some other similar affirmative guttural utterance, whereas asking, "What do you think of the weather today?" will elicit a real response: the person must answer with more than a yes or no.

One way a social engineer can learn about how to use open-ended questions is to analyze and study good reporters. A good reporter must use open-ended questions to continue eliciting responses from his or her interviewee.

Suppose I had plans to meet a friend and he canceled, and I wanted to know why. I can ask a question like, "I was curious about what happened to our plans the other night."

"I wasn't feeling too well."

"Oh, I hope you are better now. What was wrong?"

This line of questioning usually gets more results than doing an all-out assault on the person and saying something like, "What the heck, man? You ditched me the other night!"

Another aspect of open-ended questions that adds power is the use of *why* and *how*. Following up a question with *how* or *why* can lead to a much more in-depth explanation of what you were originally asking.

This question again is not "yes" or "no" answerable, and the person will reveal other details you may find interesting.

Sometimes open-ended questions can meet with some resistance, so using the *pyramid approach* might be good. The pyramid approach is where you start with narrow questions and then ask broader questions at the end of the line of questioning. If you really want to get great at this technique learn to use it with teenagers.

For example, many times open-ended questions such as, "How was school today?" will be met with an "OK" and nothing more, so asking a narrow question might open up the flow of information better.

"What are you doing in math this year?" This question is very narrow and can be answered only with a very specific answer: "Algebra II."

"Ah, I always hated that. How do you like it?"

From there you can always branch out into broader questions, and after you get the target talking, getting more info generally becomes easier.

Closed-Ended Questions

Obviously, closed-ended questions are the opposite of open-ended questions but are a very effective way to lead a target where you want. Closed-ended questions often cannot be answered with more than one or two possibilities.

In an open-ended question one might ask, "What is your relationship with your manager?" but a closed-ended question might be worded, "Is your relationship with your manager good?"

Detailed information is usually not the goal with closed-ended questions; rather, leading the target is the goal.

Law enforcement and attorneys use this type of reasoning often. If they want to lead their target down a particular path they ask very closed questions that do not allow for freedom of answers. Something like this:

"Do you know the defendant, Mr. Smith?"

"Yes I do."

"On the night of June 14th, did you see Mr. Smith at the ABC Tavern?"

"I did."

"And at what time was that?"

"11:45pm."

All of these questions are very closed ended and only allow for one or two types of responses.

Leading Questions

Combining aspects from both open- and closed-ended questions, leading questions are open ended with a hint leading toward the answer. Something like, "You were at the ABC Tavern with Mr. Smith on June 14th at around 11:45pm, weren't you?" This type of question leads the target where you want but also offers him the opportunity to express his views, but very narrowly. It also preloads the target with the idea that you have knowledge of the events being asked about.

Leading questions often can be answered with a yes or no but are different from closed-ended questions because more information is planted in the question that when answered gives the social engineer more information to work with. Leading questions state some facts and then ask the target to agree or disagree with them.

In 1932 the British psychologist Frederic C. Bartlett concluded a study on reconstructive memory. He told subjects a story and then asked them to recall the facts immediately, two weeks later, and then four weeks later. Bartlett found that subjects modified the story based on their culture and beliefs as well as personality. None were able to recall the story accurately and in its entirety. It was determined that memories are not accurate records of our past. It seems that humans try to make the memory fit into our existing representations of the world. When asked questions, many times we respond from memory based on our perceptions and what is important to us.

Because of this, asking people a leading question and manipulating their memory is possible. Elizabeth Loftus, a leading figure in the field of eyewitness testimony research, has demonstrated through the use of leading questions how distorting a person's memory of an event is easily possible. For example, if you showed a person a picture of a child's room that contained no teddy bear, and then asked her, "Did you see *a* teddy bear?" you are not implying that one was in the room, and the person is free to answer yes or no as they wish. However, asking, "Did you see *the* teddy bear?" implies that one was in the room and the person is more likely to answer "yes," because the presence of a teddy bear is consistent with that person's schema of a child's room.

Because of this research the use of leading questions can be a powerful tool in the hands of a skilled social engineer. Learning how to lead the target can also enhance a social engineer's ability to gather information.

Assumptive Questions

Assumptive questions are just what they sound like—where you assume that certain knowledge is already in the possession of the target. The way a social engineer can determine whether or not a target possesses the information he is after is by asking an assumptive question.

For example, one skill employed by law enforcement is to assume the target already has knowledge—for example, of a person—and ask something like, "Where does Mr. Smith live?" Depending on the answer given, the officer can determine whether the target knows the person and how much she knows about him.

A good point to note is that when a social engineer uses assumptive questions the whole picture should never be given to the target. Doing so gives all the power to the target and removes much of the social engineer's ability to control the environment. The social engineer never wants to use assumptive questions to accuse the target of a wrong. Doing so alienates the target and again costs the social engineer power.

A social engineer should use assumptive questions when he has some idea of the real facts he can use in the question. Using an assumptive question with bogus information may turn the target off and will only confirm that the target doesn't know about something that didn't happen. Back to an earlier example, if I wanted to gain information from a leading chemist and I did some research and knew enough to formulate one intelligent sentence I could make an assumptive question but it would ruin future follow up if I was not able to back up the assumption the target would make of my knowledge.

For example, if I were to ask, "Because deuterium and tritium have such low temperature thresholds, how does one handle these materials to avoid ignition?" The follow-up information might be hard to follow if I am not a nuclear physicist. This is counterproductive and not too useful. Plan your assumptive questions to have the maximum effect.

One adjunct that is taught to law enforcement officials that comes in very handy when using assumptive questions is to say, "Now think carefully before you answer the next question…" This kind of a statement preloads the target's mind with the idea that he must be truthful with his next statement.

It can take months or years to master these skills. Don't get disheartened if the first few attempts are not successful, and keep trying. Don't fear, though, there are some tips to mastering this skill. I will review these in closing.

Mastering Elicitation

This chapter has a lot of information for you to absorb, and if you are not a people person, employing the techniques covered might seem like a daunting task. Like most aspects of social engineering, elicitation has a set of principles that when applied will enhance your skill level. To help you master these principles, remember these pointers:

» Too many questions can shut down the target. Peppering the target with a barrage of questions will do nothing but turn off the target. Remember, conversation is a give and take. You want to ask, but you have to give to make the target feel at ease.

» Too few questions will make the target feel uncomfortable. Have you ever been in a conversation that is filled with "awkward silences"? It isn't good is it? Don't assume that your target is a skilled and willing conversationalist. You must work at making a conversation an enjoyable experience.

» Ask only one question at a time. Chapter 5 covers buffer overflows on the human mind, but at this time your goal is *not* to overflow the target. It is to merely gather information and build a profile. To do this you can't seem too eager or non-interested.

As you have probably gathered, making elicitation work right is a delicate balance. Too much, too little, too much at once, not enough—any one of them will kill your chances at success.

However, these principles can help you master this amazing talent. Whether you use this method for social engineering or just learning how to interact with people, try this: Think of conversation as a funnel, where on the top is the largest, most "neutral" part and at the bottom is the very narrow, direct ending.

Start by asking the target very neutral questions, and gather some intel using these questions. Give and take in your conversation, and then move to a few open-ended questions. If needed, use a few closed-ended questions to direct the target to where you want to go and then if the situation fits, move to highly directed questions as you reach the end of funnel. What will pour out of the "spout" of that funnel is a river of information.

Think about it in the situation discussed in this chapter of my target at the chamber of commerce gathering. My goal was to gather intel on anything that might lead to a security breach.

I started off the conversation with a very neutral question. "Escaping the vultures?" This question broke the ice on the conversation as well as used a little humor to create a bridge that allowed us to exist on the same plane of thought. I asked a few more neutral questions and handed him my card while inquiring what he does. This segues smoothly into the open-ended questions.

A brief information-gathering session that occurred earlier, using carefully placed closed-ended or assumptive questions was key. After hearing about the company's recent purchase for new accounting software and network upgrades I wanted to go in for the kill. Having scoped out the building I knew it used RFID, but I wasn't sure if the target would go so far as to describe the card and show it to me.

This is where the use of direct questions played a role: coming right out and asking what security the company used. By the time I used that type of question our rapport and trust factor was so high he probably would have answered any questions I asked.

Understanding how to communicate with people is an essential skill for an elicitor. The social engineer must be adaptive and able to match the conversation to his or her environment and situation. Quickly building even the smallest amount of trust with the target is crucial. Without that rapport, the conversation will most likely fail.

Other key factors include making sure that your communication style, the questions used, and the manner in which you speak all match your pretext. Knowing how to ask questions that force a response is a key to successful elicitation, but if all that skill and all those questions do not match your pretext then the elicitation attempt will most surely fail.

Summary

This chapter covered some of the most powerful points in this whole book—powerful in the sense that applying them can change not only your social engineering abilities but also your abilities as a communicator. Knowing how to ask the right questions in the right tense and the right manner can open so many opportunities. As a social engineer, this is what separates success from failure. First impressions are based initially on sight, but what comes out of your mouth first can make or break the deal. Mastering elicitation can almost guarantee success as a social engineer and can add serious weight to any pretext you decide to use.

Throughout this chapter I mentioned the power of pretexting. This is another topic that every social engineer, both malicious and professional, must master. But how can you ensure you accomplish this goal? To answer this you must learn about pretexting and understand exactly what it is, as discussed in Chapter 4.

4

Pretexting: How to Become Anyone

Honesty is the key to a relationship. If you can fake that, you're in.

—RICHARD JENI

At times we probably all wish we could be someone else. Heck, I would love to be a little skinnier and better looking. Even though medical science hasn't come up with a pill that can make that possible, a solution to this dilemma does exist—it's called *pretexting*.

What is pretexting? Some people say it is just a story or lie that you will act out during a social engineering engagement, but that definition is very limiting. Pretexting is better defined as the background story, dress, grooming, personality, and attitude that make up the character you will be for the social engineering audit. Pretexting encompasses everything you would imagine that person to be. The more solid the pretext, the more believable you will be as a social engineer. Often, the simpler your pretext, the better off you are.

Pretexting, especially since the advent of the Internet, has seen an increase in malicious uses. I once saw a t-shirt that read, "The Internet: Where men are men, women are men, and children are FBI agents waiting to get you." As slightly humorous as that saying is, it has a lot of truth in it. On the Internet you can be anyone you want to be. Malicious hackers have been using this ability to their advantage for years and not just with the Internet.

In social engineering playing a role or being a different person to successfully accomplish the goal is often imperative. Chris Hadnagy might not have as much pull as the tech support guy or the CEO of a major importing organization. When a social engineering situation arises, having the skills needed to become the pretext is important. In a discussion I was having with world-renowned social engineer Chris Nickerson, on this topic, he said something I think really hits home.

Nickerson stated that pretexting is not about acting out a role or playing a part. He said it is not about living a lie, but actually becoming that person. You are, in every fiber of your being, the person you are portraying. The way he walks, the way he talks, body language—you become that person. I agree with this philosophy on pretexting. Often when people watch a movie the ones we feel are the "best we have ever seen" are where the actors get us so enthralled with their parts we can't separate them from their portrayed characters.

This was proven true to me when many years ago my wife and I watched a great movie with Brad Pitt, *Legends of the Fall.* He was a selfish jerk in this movie, a tormented soul who made a lot of bad decisions. He was so good at playing this part my wife literally hated him as an actor for a few years. That is a good pretexter.

The problem with using pretexting for many social engineers is that they feel it is just dressing up as a part and that's it. True, the dress can help, but pretexting is a science. In a way, your whole persona is going to portray you in a light that is different than who you are. To do this, you, as a social engineer, must have a clear picture of what pretexting really is. Then you can plan out and perform the pretext perfectly. Finally, you can apply the finishing touches. This chapter will cover those aspects of pretexting. First is a discussion of what pretexting really is. Following that is discussion of how to use pretexting as a social engineer. Finally, to tie it all together, this chapter explores some stories that show how to use pretexting effectively.

What Is Pretexting?

Pretexting is defined as the act of creating an invented scenario to persuade a targeted victim to release information or perform some action. It is more than just creating a lie; in some cases it can be creating a whole new identity and then using that identity to manipulate the receipt of information. Social engineers can use pretexting to impersonate people in certain jobs and roles that they never themselves have done. Pretexting is not a one-size-fits-all solution. A social engineer must develop many different pretexts over his or her career. All of them will have one thing in common: research. Good information gathering techniques can make or break a good pretext. For example, mimicking the perfect tech support rep is useless if your target does not use outside support.

Pretexting is also used in areas of life other than social engineering. Sales; public speaking; so-called fortune tellers; neurolinguistic programming (NLP) experts; and even doctors, lawyers, therapists, and the like all have to use a form of pretexting. They all have to create a scenario where people are comfortable with releasing information they normally would not. The difference in social engineers using pretexting and others is the goals involved. A social engineer, again, must live that persona for a time, not just act a part.

As long as the audit or social engineering gig lasts, you need to be in the persona. I "get in character" myself, as do many of my colleagues, some of whom even stay in character "off the clock." Anywhere you need to, you should be the pretext you set out to be. In addition, many professional social engineers have many different online, social media, email, and other accounts to back up a slew of pretexts.

I once interviewed radio icon Tom Mischke on this topic for a social engineering podcast I am a part of (hosted at www.social-engineer.org/episode-002-pretexting-not-just-for-social-engineers/). Radio hosts must be proficient at pretexting because they constantly have to release only the information they want to the public. Tom was so proficient at this that many listeners felt as if they "knew" him as a friend. He would get invitations to weddings, anniversaries, and even births. How was Tom able to accomplish this amazing kind of pretext?

The answer is practice. Lots and lots of practice is what he prescribed. He told me that he would actually plan out his "acts" then practice them—use the voice they would have, sit how they would sit, maybe even dress like they would dress. Practice is exactly what makes a good pretext.

A very important aspect to remember is that the quality of the pretext is directly linked to the quality of the information gathered. The more, the better, and the more relevant the information the easier it will be for the pretext to be developed and be successful. For example, the classic pretext of a tech support guy would utterly fail if you went to a company that either had internal support or outsourced to a very small company of one or two people. As natural as you are when you converse with someone about who you really are is how easy applying your pretext should be.

So that you can see how you can utilize this skill, the following section covers the principles of pretexting then shows how you can apply them to actually planning a solid pretext.

The Principles and Planning Stages of Pretexting

As with every skill, certain principles dictate the steps to performing that task. Pretexting is no different. The following is a list of principles of pretexting that you can use. By no means are these the only principles out there; maybe others can be added, but these principles embody the essence of pretexting:

» The more research you do the better the chance of success.

» Involving your own personal interests will increase success.

»   Practice dialects or expressions.

»   Many times social engineering effort can be reduced if the phone is viewed as less important. But as a social engineer, using the phone should not reduce the effort put into the social engineering gig.

»   The simpler the pretext the better the chance of success.

»   The pretext should appear spontaneous.

»   Provide a logical conclusion or follow through for the target.

The following sections discuss each of these principles in detail.

The More Research You Do, the Better the Chance of Success

This principle is self-explanatory, but it can't be said enough—the level of success is directly connected to the level and depth of research. As discussed in Chapter 2, it is the crux of successful social engineering. The more information a social engineer holds the more chances he or she has of developing a pretext that works. Remember the story I told in Chapter 2 about my mentor Mati Aharoni and how he convinced a high-level executive to visit his "stamp collection" site online? At first glance, the path inside that company might have seemed to be something to do with financial, banking, fund raising, or something along those lines because it was a banking facility. The more research Mati did, the clearer it became that the pretext could be a person who was selling a stamp collection. Finding out what the executive's interests were allowed Mati to find an easy way into the company, and it worked.

Sometimes those little details that are what make the difference. Remember, no information is irrelevant. While gathering information, looking for stories, items, or aspects of a personal nature is also a good idea. Using a target's personal or emotional attachments can enable you to get a foot in the door. If the social engineer finds out that every year the CFO donates a sizable sum to a children's cancer research center, then a pretext that involves fund raising for this cause could very likely work, as heartless as it sounds.

The problem is that malicious social engineers use pretexts that feed on emotions without a second thought. After the attacks on the Twin Towers in New York City on September 11, 2001, many malicious hackers and social engineers used the losses of these people to raise funds for themselves via websites and emails that targeted people's computers and fake fund raisers that obtained funds from those with a giving heart. After the earthquakes in Chile and Haiti in 2010, the same things occurred where many malicious social engineers developed websites that were positioned as giving out information on the seismic activity or the people who were lost. These sites were encoded with malicious code and hacked people's computers.

This is even more evident directly after the death of a movie or music star. Search engine optimization (SEO) and marketing geniuses will have the search engines pulling up their stories in a matter of hours. Along with marketers, malicious social engineers will take advantage of the increased search engine attention by launching malicious sites that feed off that SEO. Drawing people to these sites, they harvest information or infect them with viruses.

That people will take advantage of others' misfortune is a sad fact about this world, and one of those dark corners I said you would visit in this book. As a social engineering auditor, I can use an employee's emotions to show a company that even people with seemingly good intentions can trick a company's employees into giving access to valuable and business-ruining data.

All these examples solidify the point that the better a social engineer's information-gathering and research-gathering process, the better chance he has at finding some detail that will increase the chances of a successful pretext.

Involve Personal Interests to Increase Success

Using your own personal interests to increase the chances of a successful social engineering move seems very simple but it can go a long way in convincing the target that you are credible. Nothing can ruin rapport and trust faster than a person who claims to be knowledgeable about a topic and then falls short. As a social engineer, if you have never seen a server room before and have never taken a computer apart, trying to play the part of a technician can be a quick path to failure. Including topics and activities in your pretext that you are interested in gives you a lot to talk about and gives you the ability to portray intelligence as well as confidence.

Confidence can go a long way toward convincing the target you are who you say you are. Certain pretexts require more knowledge than others (for instance, stamp collector versus nuclear researcher) to be convincing, so again research becomes the recurring theme. Sometimes the pretext is simple enough that you can get the knowledge by reading a few websites or a book.

However you gain the knowledge, researching topics that personally interest you, as the social engineer, is important. After you pick up on a story, aspect, service, or interest that you have a lot of knowledge in or at least feel comfortable discussing, see whether that angle can work.

Dr. Tom G. Stevens, PhD, says, "It is important to remember that self-confidence is *always* relative to the task and situation. We have different levels of confidence in different situations." This statement is very important, because confidence directly links to how others view you as a social engineer. Confidence (as long as it is not overconfidence) builds trust and rapport and makes people feel at ease. Finding a path to your target that offers you the chance to talk about topics you are comfortable with, and that you can speak about with confidence, is very important.

In 1957 psychologist Leon Festinger came up with the theory of cognitive dissonance. This theory states that people have a tendency to seek consistency among their beliefs, opinions, and basically all their cognitions. When an inconsistency exists between attitudes and behaviors, something must change to eliminate the dissonance. Dr. Festinger states two factors affect the strength of the dissonance:

» The number of dissonant beliefs

» The importance of each belief

He then stated that three ways exist to eliminate dissonance (which should cause every social engineer's ears to perk up):

» Reduce the importance of the dissonant beliefs.

» Add more consonant beliefs that outweigh the dissonant ones.

» Change the dissonant beliefs so they are no longer inconsistent.

How does a social engineer use this information? Approaching a pretext with lack of confidence when your pretext says that you should be confident automatically creates dissonance. This dissonance raises all sorts of red flags and puts barriers up to rapport, trust, and forward motion. These barriers affect the target's behavior, who is then expected to balance out her feelings of dissonance, and kills any likelihood of your pretext working.

One of the methods to counter that is to add more consonant beliefs so that they outweigh the dissonant ones. What would the target expect of your pretext? Knowing that will allow you to feed their minds and emotions with actions, words, and attitudes that will build the belief system and outweigh any beliefs that might bring in doubt.

Of course, a skilled social engineer can also change the dissonant beliefs so they are no longer inconsistent. Although this is trickier, it is a powerful skill to have. It is possible that your appearance does not fit what the target might envision for your pretext. You might think back to the show *Doogie Howser, M.D.* Doogie's problem was that his "pretext" of being a top doctor never fit since he was so young. That was a dissonant belief, but his knowledge and actions often brought that into the consonant beliefs of his "targets." Just like the previous example, a social engineer can align his pretext with the target's beliefs by their attitudes, actions, and especially their knowledge of the pretext.

One example of this I recently saw in real life was at Defcon 18. I was part of the team that brought the Social Engineering CTF to Defcon. We saw many contestants who used the pretext of an internal employee. When presented with an objection like, "What is your employee badge number?" an unskilled social engineer would get nervous and either not have an answer or hang up, whereas a skilled social engineer would bring those dissonant beliefs into alignment for the target. Simply stating a badge number they found online or using another method they were able to convince the target that information was not needed, therefore aligning the target to their beliefs.

These points are very technical answers to a very simple problem, but you must understand that one can do only so much faking. Choose your path wisely.

Practice Dialects or Expressions

Learning to speak in a different dialect cannot be glanced over quickly. Depending on where you live, learning to speak a different dialect or with an accent can take some time. Putting on a southern drawl or an Asian accent can be very difficult, if not impossible. Once I was in a training class with an international sales organization and it had some statistics that said 70% of Americans prefer to listen to people with a British accent. I am not sure if that statistic is true or not, but I can say that I enjoy the accent myself. Now after that class, I heard quite a few people in the class practice their "cheerios" and "Alo Govenors," which were horrible. I have a good friend from the UK, Jon, who gets very angry when he hears Americans trying to use lines from Mary Poppins in an imitation British accent. If he had heard this group, he might have blown a fuse.

What that class taught me was that although the stats might say one accent is better than another for sales or just because you may be social engineering in the south or in Europe doesn't mean you can easily put on the accent to make you appear local. When in doubt, throw it out. If you can't make the dialect perfect, if you can't be natural, and if you can't be smooth, then just don't try. Actors use vocal coaches and training sessions to learn to speak clearly in the accent they have to portray. Actor

Christian Bale is from Wales, but determining that fact from listening to him is very difficult. He doesn't sound British in most of his movies. Actress Gwyneth Paltrow took on a very convincing British accent for the movie *Shakespeare in Love*.

Most actors have dialect coaches who will work with them to perfect the target accent. Because most social engineers cannot afford a dialect coach, there are many publications that can help you learn at least the basics of putting on an accent, such as *Dialects for the Stage* by Evangeline Machlin. Although this is an older book, it contains a lot of great tips:

» Find native examples of the accent you want to learn, to listen to. Books like *Dialects for the Stage* often come with audiotapes full of accents to listen to.

» Try speaking along with the recording you have, to practice sounding like that person.

» After you feel somewhat confident, record yourself speaking in that accent so you can listen to it later on and correct errors.

» Create a scenario and practice your new accent with a partner.

» Apply your accent in public to see if people find it believable.

There are innumerable dialects and accents, and I personally find it helpful to write out phonetically some of the sentences I will speak. This enables me to practice reading them and get the ideas sunk into my brain to make my accent more natural.

These tips can help a social engineer master or at least become proficient at using another dialect.

Even if you cannot master another dialect, learning expressions that are used in the area in which you are working can make a difference. One idea is to spend some time listening to people in public talk to one another. A great place for this is a diner or a shopping mall, or any place you might find groups of people sitting and chatting. Listen closely to phrases or key words. If you hear them used in a few conversations you might want to find a way to incorporate these into your pretext to add believability. Again, this exercise takes research and practice.

Using the Phone Should Not Reduce the Effort for the Social Engineer

In recent years, the Internet has come to dominate certain more "impersonal" aspects of social engineering, whereas in days past the phone was an integral part of social engineering. Because of this shift, many social engineers do not put the energy or effort into phone usage that can make it truly successful.

This topic is here to show that the phone is still one of the most powerful tools of the social engineer and the effort put into using it should not be diminished due to the impersonal nature of the Internet.

Sometimes when a social engineer plans a phone attack his thinking may differ because using the Internet might appear easier. Note that you should plan to put the same level of effort, the same level and depth of research and information gathering, and most importantly the same level of practice into your phone-based social engineering attacks. I was once with a small group that was going to practice phone presentations. We outlined the proper methods, the tone, the speed, the pitches, and the words to use. We outlined a script (more on this in a minute) and then launched a session. The first person made the call, got on the phone with someone, and messed up the first few lines. Out of complete embarrassment and fear he just hung up on the person. There is a very good lesson there—the person on the other end of the phone has no clue what you are going to say, so you can't really "mess up." Practice sessions can help you learn how to handle the "unknowns" caused by your accidentally altering something in your script that throws you off base.

If you are not as fortunate to have a group to practice or hone these skills with, you will have to get creative. Try calling family or friends to see how far you can get manipulating them. Another way to practice is to record yourself as if you were on the phone and then play it back later to hear how you sound.

I personally feel that using an outlined script is very important. Here is an illustration: suppose you had to call your phone company or another utility. Maybe they messed up a bill or you had another service problem and you are going to complain. After you explain yourself to the rep, telling her how upset and disappointed you are, and the rep does absolutely nothing for you, she says something like, "XY&Z is committed to excellent service; have I answered all your questions today?" If the drone behind the phone thought for one second about what she was asking she would realize how silly it is, right? This is what happens when you use a written-out script instead of an outline. An outline allows you "creative artistic freedom" to move around in the conversation and not be so worried about what *must* come next.

Using the phone to solidify your pretext is one of the quickest methods inside your target's door. The phone allows the social engineer to "spoof," or fake, almost anything. Take into consideration this example: If I wanted to call you and pretend I was in a bustling office to add to the pretext I was trying to use, I could simply grab the audio track from Thriving Office (www.thrivingoffice.com/). This site offers a track called "Busy" and another called "Very Busy." From the creators: "This valuable CD, which is filled with the sounds people expect to hear from an established company, provides instant credibility. It's simple, effective, and guaranteed!"

That sentence alone is filled with social engineering goodness—filled with what *people expect to hear* from an established company. Already you can see that the CD is geared to fill expectations and provide credibility (at least, in the target's mind, after his expectations are met), thereby automatically building trust.

In addition, spoofing caller ID information is relatively simple. Services like SpoofCard (`www.spoofcard.com`) or using homegrown solutions, allows a social engineer to tell the target you are calling from a corporate headquarters, the White House, or the local bank. With these services you can spoof the number to be coming from anywhere in the world.

The phone is a deadly tool for social engineers; developing the habits to practice using it and to treat it with utter respect will enhance any social engineer's toolset for pretexting. Because the phone is such a deadly tool and has not lost its effectiveness, you should give it the time and effort it deserves in any social engineering gig.

The Simpler the Pretext, the Better the Chance of Success

"The simpler, the better" principle just can't be overstated. If the pretext has so many intricate details that forgetting one will cause a social engineering failure, it is probably going to fail. Keeping the story lines, facts, and details simple can help build credibility.

Dr. Paul Ekman, a renowned psychologist and researcher in the field of human deception, cowrote an article in 1993 entitled, "Lies That Fail." In that article he says

> [t]here is not always time to prepare the line to be taken, to rehearse and memorize it. Even when there has been ample advance notice, and a false line has been carefully devised, the liar may not be clever enough to anticipate all the questions that may be asked, and to have thought through what his answers must be. Even cleverness may not be enough, for unseen changes in circumstances can betray an otherwise effective line. And, even when a liar is not forced by circumstances to change lines, some liars have trouble recalling the line they have previously committed themselves to, so that new questions cannot be consistently answered quickly.

This very salient point explains clearly why simple is better. Trying to remember a pretext can be almost impossible if it is so complex that your cover can be blown by a simple mistake. The pretext should be natural and smooth. It should be easy to remember, and if it feels natural to you, then recalling facts or lines used previously in the pretext will not be a task.

To illustrate how important it is to remember the small details I want to share a story with you. Once upon a time I tried my hand at sales. I was placed with a sales manager to learn the ropes. I can recall my first call with him. We drove up to the house, and before we left the car he looked at the info card and told me, "Remember, Becky Smith sent in a request card for supplemental insurance. We will present the XYZ policy. Watch and learn."

In the first three minutes of the sales call he called her Beth and Betty. Each time he used the wrong name I saw her demeanor change and then she would say quietly, "Becky." I feel we could have been giving away gold bullion and she would have said no. She was so turned off that he couldn't get her name right that she was not interested in listening to anything.

This scenario really drives home the point of keeping the simple facts straight.

In addition to remembering the facts, it is equally important to keep the details small. A simple pretext allows for the story to grow and the target to use their imagination to fill the gaps. Do not try to make the pretext elaborate, and above all, remember the tiny details that will make the difference in how people view the pretext.

On the other hand, here is an interesting tidbit: A popular tactic used by famous criminals and con men is to purposely make a few mistakes. The thought is that "no one is perfect," and a few mistakes make people feel at home. Be cautious with what types of mistakes you decide to make if you employ this tactic because it does add complexity to your pretext, but it does make the conversation seem more natural. Use this tip sparingly, however you decide to proceed, keep it simple.

Let me tie all this together with a few examples that I have used or seen used in audits. After some excellent elicitation on the phone, a nameless social engineer had been given the name of the waste removal company. A few simple Internet searches and he had a usable and printable logo. There are dozens of local and online shops that will print shirts or hats with a logo on it.

A few minutes of aligning things on a template and he ordered a shirt and ball cap with the logo of the waste company on it. A couple days later, wearing the logo-laden clothing and carrying a clipboard, the social engineer approached the security booth of the target company.

He said, "Hi, I'm Joe with ABC Waste. We got a call from your purchasing department asking to send someone over to check out a damaged dumpster in the back. The pickup is tomorrow and if the dumpster isn't repairable I will have them bring out a new one. But I need to run back there and inspect it."

Without blinking, the security officer said, "OK, you will need this badge to get onsite. Just pull through here and drive around the back and you will see the dumpsters there."

The social engineer had a free pass to perform a very long and detailed dumpster dive but wanted to maximize his potential so went in for the kill with this line. While looking at his clipboard he said, "The note says it is not the food dumpsters but one of the ones where paper or tech trash goes. Which block are those in?"

"Oh, just drive the same way I told you and they are in the third bay," replied the security guard.

"Thanks," said Joe.

A simple pretext, backed up by clothing and "tools" (like the clipboard), and the storylines were simple to remember and not complex. The simplicity and lack of detail actually made this pretext more believable, and it worked.

Another very widely used pretext is that of the tech support guy. This one only requires a polo shirt, pair of khakis, and small computer tool bag. Many social engineers employ this tactic to get in the front door because the "tech guy" is usually given access to everything without supervision. The same rules apply: keeping the storyline simple will help make this particular pretext very real and believable.

The Pretext Should Appear Spontaneous

Making the pretext appear spontaneous goes back to my point on using an outline versus using script. Outlines will always allow the social engineer more freedom and a script will make the social engineer sound too robotic. It also ties in to using items or stories that interest the social engineer personally. If every time someone asks you a question or makes a statement that requires you to think, and you go, "Ummmm" and start to think deeply, and you cannot come back with an intelligent answer, it will ruin your credibility. Of course many people think before they speak, so this is not about having the answer in one second, but about having an answer or a reason for not having the answer. For example, in one phone call I was asked for a piece of information I didn't have. I simply said, "Let me get that." I then leaned over and made it sound like I was yelling for a workmate: "Jill, can you please ask Bill to give me the order form for the XYZ account? Thanks."

Then as "Jill" was getting the paper for me I was able to obtain the data I needed and the paper was never brought up again.

I have compiled a small list of ways that you can work on being more spontaneous:

» **Don't think about how you feel.** This point is a good one, because often in a pretext if you overthink you will start to add emotion into the mix, which can cause fear, nervousness, or anxiety, all of which lead to failure. On the other hand, you might not experience nervousness or fear, but over-excitement, which can also cause you to make a lot of mistakes.

» **Don't take yourself too seriously.** Of course, this is great advice in life, but it applies wonderfully to social engineering. As a security professional you have a serious job; this is a serious matter. But if you're not able to laugh at your mistakes, you may clam up or get too nervous to handle a small bump in the road. I am not suggesting you take security as a joke. In your mind, though, if you view a potential failure as the pinnacle of failure in your life, the pressure you create can cause just what you fear the most. Minor failures can often lead to greater success if you have the ability to roll with it.

» **Learn to identify what is relevant.** I like to phrase this concept as, "Get out of your head and into the world," which is more great advice. A social engineer may be trying to plan three steps ahead and in the meantime miss a vital detail that can cause the pretext to fall apart. Be quick to identify the relevant material and information around you, whether it is the target's body language, words spoken, or microexpressions (see Chapter 5 for more on this topic), and assimilate the information into the attack vector.

Also keep in mind that people can tell when someone isn't really listening to what they are saying. Getting the feeling that even unimportant sentences are falling on deaf ears can be a massive turnoff for many people. Everyone has experienced being with someone who just didn't seem to care what he or she is saying. Maybe that person even had a legitimate reason to be thinking on a different path, but doing it is still a turnoff.

Be sure to listen to what your target is saying. Pay close attention and you will pick up the details that are very important to them and in the meantime, you might hear something to help you in your success.

» **Seek to gain experience.** This concept goes back to what you will probably see repeated four million times in this book—practice. Gaining experience through practice can make or break the pretext. Practice spontaneity with family and friends and total strangers with absolutely no goal in mind but to be spontaneous. Strike up conversations with people, but not in a scary stalker kind of way—simple little conversations can go a long way toward making you feel comfortable being spontaneous.

These points can definitely give a social engineer the upper hand when it comes to pretexting. Having the ability to appear spontaneous is a gift. Earlier in this chapter I mentioned my interview with Tom Mischke, who had an interesting take on spontaneity. He said he wants to give the illusion of spontaneity wrapped in practice and preparation. He would practice so much that his pretext would come out as a spontaneous generation of humor and talent.

Provide a Logical Conclusion or Follow-through for the Target

Believe it or not people want to be told what to do. Imagine if you went to a doctor and he walked in, checked you over, wrote some things on his chart, and said, "Okay; see you in a month." That would be unacceptable. Even in the event of bad news, people want to be told the next step and what to do.

As a social engineer, when you leave the target, you may need him to take or not take an action, or you may have gotten what you came for and just need to leave. Whatever the circumstance, giving the target a conclusion or follow-through fills in the expected gaps for the target.

Just as if a doctor checked you over and sent you home with no directions, if you engineer your way into a facility as a tech support guy and just walk out without saying anything to anyone after cloning the database, you leave everyone wondering what happened. Someone may even call the "tech support company" and ask whether he needed to do anything, or at worst you just leave the workers wondering. Either way, leaving everyone hanging is not the way to leave. Even a simple, "I checked over the servers and repaired the file system; you should see a 22% increase in speed over the next couple days," leaves the targets feeling as if they "got their money's worth."

The tricky part for a social engineer is getting the target to take an action after he or she is gone. If the action is vital for completion of the social engineer audit, then you may want to take that role upon yourself. For example, in the account in Chapter 3 of my information-gathering session at the chamber of commerce event, if I wanted that target to follow-up with me through email I could have said, "Here is my card; will you email me some details on Monday about XYZ?" He very well may have, or he could have gone to the office, forgotten about me completely, and the whole gig would have failed. What would be better is to say, "I would love to get some more information from you. On Monday could I perhaps call you or shoot you an email to get some more details?"

The requests you make should match the pretext, too. If your pretext is being a tech support guy, you won't "order" people around with what they must and must not do; you work for them. If you are a UPS delivery person, you don't demand access to the server room.

As mentioned earlier, more steps may exist for perfecting a pretext, but the ones listed in this chapter can give a social engineer a solid foundation to build a perfectly believable pretext.

You might be asking, "Okay, so you listed all these principles, but now what?" How can a social engineer build a well-researched, believable, spontaneous-sounding, simple pretext that can work either on the phone or in person and get the desired results? Read on.

Successful Pretexting

To learn how to build a successful pretext, take a look at a couple of stories of social engineers who used pretexts that worked and how they developed them. Eventually they did get caught, which is why these stories are now available.

Example 1: Stanley Mark Rifkin

Stanley Mark Rifkin is credited with one of the biggest bank heists in American history (see a great article about him at `www.social-engineer.org/wiki/archives/Hackers/hackers-Mark-Rifkin-Social-Engineer-furtherInfo.htm`). Rifkin was a computer geek who ran a computer consulting business out of his small apartment. One of his clients was a company that serviced the computers at Security Pacific Bank. The 55-floor Security Pacific National Bank headquarters in Los Angeles looked like a granite-and-glass fortress. Dark-suited guards roamed the lobby and hidden cameras photographed customers as they made deposits and withdrawals.

This building seemed impenetrable, so how is it that Rifkin walked away with $10.2 million and never held a gun, never touched a dollar, and never held up anyone?

The bank's wire transfer policies seemed secure. They were authorized by a numerical code that changed daily and was only given out to authorized personnel. It was posted on a wall in a secure room that only "authorized personnel" had access to.

From the archived article mentioned previously:

> *In October 1978, he visited Security Pacific, where bank employees easily recognized him as a computer worker. He took an elevator to the D-level, where the bank's wire transfer room was located. A pleasant and friendly young man, he managed to talk his way into the room where the bank's secret code-of-the-day was posted on the wall. Rifkin memorized the code and left without arousing suspicion.*
>
> *Soon, bank employees in the transfer room received a phone call from a man who identified himself as Mike Hansen, an employee of the bank's international division. The man ordered a routine transfer of funds into an account at the Irving Trust Company in New York—and he provided the secret code numbers to authorize the transaction. Nothing about the transfer appeared to be out of the ordinary, and Security Pacific transferred the money to the New York bank. What bank officials did not know was that the man who called himself Mike Hansen was in fact Stanley Rifkin, and he had used the bank's security code to rob the bank of $10.2 million.*

This scenario offers much to talk about, but for now, focus on the pretext. Think about the details of what he had to do:

» He had to be confident and comfortable in order to not raise suspicion for being in that room.

» He had to have a believable story when he called to do the transfer and have the details to back up his story.

» He had to be spontaneous enough to go with the flow with questions that might have come up.

» He had to also be smooth enough to not raise suspicion.

This pretext had to be meticulously planned out with the utmost detail being thought through. It wasn't until he visited a former associate that his pretext failed, and he was caught. When he was caught, people who knew him were amazed and some even said things like, "There is no way he is a thief; everyone loves Mark."

Obviously his pretext was solid. He had a well-thought-out, and one would guess, well-rehearsed plan. He knew what he was there to do and he played the part perfectly. When he was in front of strangers he was able to play the part; his downfall came when he was with a colleague who knew him, and that colleague saw a news story then put two and two together and turned Mark in.

Amazingly enough, while out on bail, Rifkin began to target another bank using the same scheme, but a government mole had set him up; he got caught and spent eight years in federal prison. Although Mark is a "bad guy" you can learn much about pretexting from reading his story. He kept it very simple and used the things that were familiar to him to build a good storyline.

Mark's plan was to steal the money and turn it into an untraceable commodity: diamonds. To do so he would first need to be a bank employee to steal the money, then a major diamond buyer to unload the cash, and finally sell the diamonds to have usable, untraceable cash in his pocket.

Although his pretext did not involve elaborate costumes or speech patterns he had to play the part of a bank employee, then major diamond buyer, then play the part of a diamond seller. He changed roles maybe three, four, or five times in this gig and was able to do it well enough to fool almost everyone.

Mark knew who his targets were and approached the scenario with all the principles outlined earlier. Of course, one can't condone what he did, but his pretexting talents are admirable. If he put his talents to good use he would probably make a great public figure, salesperson, or actor.

Example 2: Hewlett-Packard

In 2006 *Newsweek* published a very interesting article (`www.social-engineer.org/resources/book/HP_pretext.htm`). Basically, HP's chairwoman, Patricia Dunn, hired a team of security specialists who hired a team of private investigators who used pretexting to obtain phone records. These hired professionals actually got in and played the roles of HP board members and parts of the press. All of this was done to uncover a supposed information leak within the ranks at HP.

Ms. Dunn wanted to obtain the phone records of board members and reporters (not the records from the HP facilities, but the personal home and cell phone records of these people) to verify where she supposed the leak was. The *Newsweek* article states:

> *On May 18, at HP headquarters in Palo Alto, California, Dunn sprung her bombshell on the board: She had found the leaker. According to Tom Perkins, an HP director who was present, Dunn laid out the surveillance scheme and pointed out the offending director, who acknowledged being the CNET leaker. That director, whose identity has not yet been publicly disclosed, apologized. But the director then said to fellow directors, "I would have told you all about this. Why didn't you just ask?" That director was then asked to leave the boardroom, and did so, according to Perkins.*

What is notable about this account is what is next mentioned about the topic of pretexting:

> *The HP case specifically also sheds another spotlight on the questionable tactics used by security consultants to obtain personal information. HP acknowledged in an internal e-mail sent from its outside counsel to Perkins that it got the paper trail it needed to link the director-leaker to CNET through a controversial practice called "pretexting"; Newsweek obtained a copy of that e-mail. That practice, according to the Federal Trade Commission, involves using "false pretenses" to get another individual's personal nonpublic information: telephone records, bank and credit-card account numbers, Social Security numbers and the like.*

> *Typically—say in the case of a phone company—pretexters call up and falsely represent themselves as the customer; since companies rarely require passwords, a pretexter may need no more than a home address, account number, and heartfelt plea to get the details of an account. According to the Federal Trade Commission's Web site, pretexters sell the information to individuals who can range from otherwise legitimate private investigators, financial lenders, potential litigants, and suspicious spouses to those who might attempt to steal assets or fraudulently obtain credit. Pretexting, the FTC site states, "is against the law." The FTC and several state attorneys general have brought enforcement actions against pretexters for allegedly violating federal and state laws on fraud,*

*misrepresentation, and unfair competition. One of HP's directors
is Larry Babbio, the president of Verizon, which has filed various
actions against pretexters.*

(If you're interested in exploring it, the Telephone Records and Privacy Protection
Act of 2006 can be found at `http://frwebgate.access.gpo.gov/cgi-bin/getdoc`
`.cgi?dbname=109_cong_bills&docid=f:h4709enr.txt.pdf`.)

The end result was that criminal charges were brought not only against Dunn,
but against the consultants she hired. You may wonder, "How is that possible considering they were hired and contracted to perform these tests?"

Take a look at what avenues they used and what information they obtained to
help answer this question. The consultants obtained the names, addresses, Social
Security numbers, telephone call logs, telephone billing records, and other information of the HP board members and reporters. They actually used the Social Security
number to establish an online account for one reporter and then obtain records of
his personal calls.

Page 32 of a confidential document from Hewlett-Packard to its lawyer and internal legal staff (`www.social-engineer.org/resources/book/20061004hewlett6`
`.pdf`) lists a communication from Tom Perkins to the HP board members that
offers a little more insight about what pretexts were used. A few tactics used were:

» They represented themselves as the carrier company to obtain the
   records of calls illegally.

» The identities of the ones being investigated were used and spoofed to
   obtain their personal call records.

» Online accounts with carriers were generated using illegally obtained
   names, Social Security numbers, and other information to access their
   call records.

On September 11, 2006, the United States House of Representatives Committee
on Energy and Commerce sent Ms. Dunn a letter (see a copy of this letter at
`www.social-engineer.org/resources/book/20061004hewlett6.pdf`) requesting the information she had obtained. They listed in their requests the obtained
information as the following:

» All published and non-published telephone numbers

» Credit card bills

» Customer name and address info

- » Utility bills

- » Pager numbers

- » Cell numbers

- » Social Security numbers

- » Credit reports

- » Post office box information

- » Bank account information

- » Asset information

- » Other consumer information

All of this information was obtained through a very gray area of professional social engineering: is what they did ethical and moral, even though they were hired to do it? Many professional social engineers would not go to these lengths. The lesson to be learned from this very important case is that as a professional social engineer you might mimic the methodologies and the thinking of malicious social engineers, but never should you stoop completely to their levels. The problem with these consultants came in that they were authorized to pretext, social engineer, and audit Hewlett-Packard. They were not authorized to social engineer AT&T, Verizon, utility companies, and so on. When employing pretexting you must have it outlined and planned so you know what legal lines you might get near and what lines you must not cross.

HP's story lends itself to a discussion about policy, contracts, and outlining what you will be offering if you are a social engineer auditor, but these topics are not within the context of this chapter. Using the principles outlined so far in this chapter can help you make decisions that will keep you out of trouble.

The danger with malicious pretexting is the threat of identity theft, which makes it a very valid part of a social engineer pentest. Testing, checking, and verifying that your client's employees will not fall for the methods used by malicious social engineers can go a long way in safeguarding you from a successful pretexter.

Staying Legal

In 2005 *Private Investigator Magazine* was granted an interview with Joel Winston, Associate Director of the Federal Trade Commission (FTC), Division of Financial Practices. His office is in charge of regulating and monitoring the use of pretexting (see a copy of this valuable article at `www.social-engineer.org/resources/book/ftc_article.htm`).

Here are some of the key points from this interview:

>> Pretexting, according to the FTC, is the obtaining of *any information* from a bank or consumer, not just financial information, using fraud, deception, or misleading questions to obtain such information.

>> Using already-obtained information to verify that a target is a target, even while using false pretenses, is legal under the FTC's definition of pretexting, unless the social engineer is using this information to obtain information from a financial institution.

>> Acquiring toll phone or cellular records through deceptive business practices is considered illegal pretexting.

The FTC website provides some clarity and additional information to this interview:

>> It is illegal for anyone to use false, fictitious, or fraudulent statements or documents to get customer information from a financial institution or directly from a customer of a financial institution.

>> It is illegal for anyone to use forged, counterfeit, lost, or stolen documents to get customer information from a financial institution or directly from a customer of a financial institution.

>> It is illegal for anyone to ask another person to get someone else's customer information using false, fictitious, or fraudulent statements or using false, fictitious, or fraudulent documents, or forged, counterfeit, lost, or stolen documents.

Although the FTC's focus is on financial institutions, the guidelines outlined are a reminder of what is considered illegal in the United States. Looking into their local laws and making sure they are not breaking those laws is a good idea for professional social engineers. In 2006, the Federal Trade Commission moved to expand Section 5 of the FTC Act to specifically include a law banning the use of pretexting to retrieve telephone records.

HP's pretexting situation ended in one of the private investigators being charged with conspiracy and federal identity theft—very serious charges.

Keeping pretexting legal will entail some research on the part of the professional social engineer as well as a clearly defined and *signed-off* plan of what pretexts, if any, will be used.

Despite the legal matters mentioned earlier, using a solid pretext is one of the quickest ways into a company. Pretexting is a talent all its own and, as you can see from this chapter, is not simply putting on a wig or a pair of fake glasses and pretending you are someone you are not.

Additional Pretexting Tools

Other tools exist that can enhance a pretext.

Props can go a long way in convincing a target of the reality of your pretext; for example, magnetic signs for your vehicle, matching uniforms or outfits, tools or other carry-ons, and the most important—a business card.

The power of the business card hit me when I was recently flying to Las Vegas on business. My laptop bag usually gets scanned, rescanned, then swabbed for bomb dust or whatever. I am one of those guys who doesn't really mind the extra security precautions because they keep me from blowing up in the air, and I am happy with that.

Yet I realize that 90 percent of the time I am going to get extra attention by Transportation Security Administration (TSA). On this particular trip I had forgotten to take my lock picks, RFID scanner, four extra hard drives, bump keys (see Chapter 7), and plethora of wireless hacking gear out of my carry-on laptop bag. As it goes through the scanner I hear the lady working the x-ray say, "What the heck?"

She then calls over another gentlemen who stares at the screen and says, "I have no clue what the heck that stuff is." He then looks around, sees my smiling face, and says, "Is this you?"

I walk over to the table with him as he is emptying my RFID scanner and my large case of lock picks and he says, "Why do you have all of these items and what are they?"

I had nothing planned but decided at the last second to try this move: I pulled out a business card and said, "I am security professional who specializes in testing networks, buildings, and people for security holes. These are the tools of my business." I said this as I handed him a business card and he looked at it for about five seconds and then said, "Oh, excellent. Thanks for the explanation."

He neatly put all my items back in, zipped the bag up, and let me go. Usually I go through the bomb screening, the little dust machine, and then a patdown, but this time all I got was a thank you and a quick release. I began to analyze what I did differently than normal. The only difference was that I had given him a business card. Granted, my business card is not the $9.99 special from an online card printer, but I was amazed that what seemed to have happened was that a business card added a sense of license to my claims.

My next four flights I purposely packed every "hacking" device into my bags I could find and then kept a business card in my pocket. Each time my bag was examined and I was asked about the contents, I flipped out the card. Each time I was apologized to, had my items packed in neatly, and let go.

Imagine my experience was a pretext. Little details can add so much weight to what I am saying that I can appear valid, trustworthy, and solid with nothing more than a card that tells people that everything I say is true. Don't underestimate the power of a business card. One word of caution: getting a weak and pathetic-looking business card can actually cause the opposite effect. A business card that was "free" with an advertisement on the back will not add weight to a professional pretext. Yet there is no reason to spend $300 on a business card to use once. Many online business card printers can print a small amount of very nice cards for less than $100.

Another reason to take this chapter very seriously is that often times pretexting is the very first step used by professional identity thieves. Because identity theft is taking a front row seat in the crime industry of late, knowing what it is and how to identify it is important for consumers, businesses, and security professionals. If you are a security auditor you must help your clients become aware of these threats and test them for possible weaknesses.

Summary

In addition to extensively covering pretexting and providing real-world examples of pretexting in action, this chapter also continually brushed up against the psychological principles that affect different aspects of pretexting. The logical next stop on the framework covers just that—the mental skills that professional social engineers use that make them seem like mind control masters and that give each social engineer a huge leg up in success.

5

Mind Tricks: Psychological Principles Used in Social Engineering

It all depends on how we look at things, and not on how they are themselves.

—CARL GUSTAV JUNG

In Hollywood movies and television shows con men and law enforcement are portrayed with almost mystical talents. They have the ability to get away with anything; they seem to be able to just look into the eyes of a person and tell if they are lying or telling the truth. It is not uncommon to see situations like this: the cop looks into the eyes of his suspect and can automatically tell whether he is lying or telling the truth, or with just the power of suggestion the con man's targets are handing over their life's savings. Movies might have you believing that manipulation tactics and getting people to do anything you want is plausible or even easy. Are these scenarios really fiction? Is it possible to gain such abilities that are saved for fantasy in the movies?

This chapter could be a book unto itself, but I will condense this information down to principles that will truly change the way you interact with people. Some of the topics in this chapter are based on research done by the brightest minds in their respective fields. The techniques discussed in these topics were tested and put through the paces in social engineering environments. For example, the topic of microexpressions is based on the research of the world-renowned psychologist and researcher, Dr. Paul Ekman, who used his genius to develop techniques into reading facial expressions that can literally change the way law enforcement, governments, doctors, and everyday people interact with others.

Some of the principles of Richard Brandler and John Grinder, the originators of neurolinguistic programming, changed people's understanding about thought patterns and the power of words. These topics are subjects for much debate, and this chapter attempts to demystify this subject and explain how you can use them in social engineering.

Some of the best interrogators on the planet developed training and frameworks to help law enforcement learn how to effectively interrogate suspects. These principles have such deep psychological roots that learning the methods used can literally unlock the doors to the minds of your targets.

Using cues that people give in their speech, gestures, eyes, and faces can make you appear to be a mind reader. This chapter examines these skills and explains them in detail so they can be utilized by a professional social engineer.

Rapport is often a word used by sales trainers and salespeople, but it is a very important aspect of gaining trust and displaying confidence. Knowing how to instantly develop rapport with people is a skill that truly enhances the skill set of a social engineer, and this chapter shows you how.

This chapter finishes with my own personal research on how you can use these skills to hack the human mind. A *buffer overflow* is a program usually written by a hacker to execute code, of malicious intent normally, through the normal use of a host program. When executed the program does what the hacker wants. What if it were possible to run "commands" on the human mind that would cause the target to do what you ask, give over information you seek, and, in essence, prove that the human mind is able to be manipulated?

This powerful information, of course, can be used for very malicious intentions. My goal in releasing this information to the public in this way is to pull back the curtain from what the "bad guys" are doing by exposing their methods, thinking, and principles, then analyzing each one and showing what you can learn from it. Exposing these techniques makes identifying, defending, and mitigating against these attacks easier for everyone.

This chapter is truly a mind-altering collection of data and principles. Following, studying, and researching the methods will not just enhance any security endeavors but these principles can also alter the way you communicate and interact with others.

 By no means, though, is this chapter a complete collection that covers all aspects of each of these skills. I provide links and tips to where you can find more information and programs to help you enhance these skills. This chapter sets a foundation as well as acts like a guide, pointing you in a direction so you can learn to enhance each skill over time.

Learning social engineering skills is not a quick process, so don't be impatient. The methods of learning some of these skills can take years to perfect and a lot of practice to even become proficient. Of course, you may possess a skill for a certain aspect but if you do not, don't become impatient with trying to learn it. Keep on trying harder and practicing and you will get it.

Before you get into the meat of this chapter, the following section sets the stage for why and how these principles will work. You must understand the modes of thinking that exist. After you understand more clearly how people take in and process information you can begin to understand the emotional, psychological, and physical representations of that process.

Modes of Thinking

To alter someone's way of thinking you must understand the *way* people think and in what *modes* they think. This seems a logical first step to even attempting this aspect of social engineering.

You might think you need to be a psychologist or a neurologist to understand the many aspects of how a person can think. Although that can help, it is not necessary. With a little research and some practical application you can delve into the inner workings of the human mind.

In August of 2001 the FBI put out a law enforcement bulletin (`www.social-engineer.org/wiki/archives/ModesOfThinking/MOT_FBI_3of5.htm`) that made a few very profound statements on the modes in which people think:

> *Simply confirming your nonverbal behavior to the client, using language from the client's preferred representational system and matching speech volume, tone, and area of speech often overcomes client reluctance to communicate.*

This simple statement has a lot of depth in it. Basically it is saying that if you can first figure out the target's dominant mode of thinking and then confirm it in subtle ways, you can unlock the doors of the target's mind and help him actually feel at ease when telling you even intimate details. Logically you may ask then, "How do I figure out a target's dominant mode of thinking?"

Even asking people what their mode of thinking is will not offer a clear answer, because many people do not know what mode of thinking they often reside in. Due to that, as a social engineer you must have some tools to help you determine this mode and then quickly switch gears to match that mode. A clear and easy path exists to this answer but you need to know the basics first.

The Senses

For centuries philosophers have argued the value of perception. Some go so far as to say that reality is not "real" but just what our senses build into our perceptions.

Personally, I do not subscribe to that idea, but I believe that the world is brought to our brain by our senses. People interpret those senses for their perception of reality. In the traditional classification we have five senses: sight, hearing, touch, smell, and taste.

People tend to favor one of these senses and that is the one that is dominant. It is also the way people tend to remember things. As one exercise to determine your dominant sense, close your eyes and picture yourself waking up this morning—what is the very first thing you remember?

Was the *feeling* of the warm sun on your face? Or maybe you remember the *sound* of the voice of your spouse or children calling you? Do you remember clearly the *smell* of coffee downstairs? Or quite possibly the bad *taste* in your mouth, reminding you that you need to brush your teeth?

Of course, this science is not exact and realizing what your dominant sense is may take a few tries to figure out. I once talked to a couple about this concept and it was interesting to watch their expressions. The wife first remembered waking up and seeing the clock and then worrying that she was running late, whereas the husband first remembered rolling over and not feeling his wife next to him. After some more questions it became evident that the husband was a *kinesthetic*, or his dominant sense was his feeling, whereas his wife was very visual.

Of course, walking up to your target and saying, "Close your eyes and tell me the first thing you remember this morning," doesn't seem reasonable. Unless, of course, your pretext is the family shrink, you might meet with some opposition on this route.

How can you determine without going through an embarrassing interrogation about their morning rituals what a target's dominant sense is?

The Three Main Modes of Thinking

Although we have five senses, the modes of thinking are associated with only three of them:

- » Sight, or a visual thinker
- » Hearing, or an auditory thinker
- » Feeling, or a kinesthetic thinker

Each sense has a range within which it works, or a *sub-modality*. Is something too loud or too soft? Too bright or too dark? Too hot or too cold? Examples of these are as follows: staring at the sun is too bright, jet engines are too loud, and −30 degrees

Fahrenheit is too cold. Ivan Pavlov ran an experiment where he rang a bell every time he fed a dog. In the end the dog would hear the sound of the bell, then salivate. What most people don't know is that he was more interested in the physical and emotional aspects of sub-modalities. The interesting point is that the louder the bell rang the more the dog salivated. The range change of the sub-modality produced a direct physical change. Pavlov's research and all of his lectures are discussed in much detail at www.ivanpavlov.com.

Even though people are very different from dogs, Pavlov's research is very important in understanding how a person thinks. Many of us can think in all three modes, but we dominate in one—one "rings" the loudest. Even within our dominant mode, we might have varying degrees of depth for that dominant sense.

Following I will discuss some of the details of each of these modes in more depth.

Visual

The majority of people are usually *visual* thinkers, in that they usually remember what something looked like. They remember the scene clearly—the colors, the textures, the brightness or darkness. They can clearly picture a past event and even build a picture for a future event. When they are presented with material to decide upon they often need something to see because visual input is directly linked to decision making. Many times a visual thinker will make a decision based on what is visually appealing to him regardless of what is really "better" for him.

Although men tend to be visual, this does not mean that all men are always visual. That visual marketing or visual aspects normally appeal to men is true, but do not assume all men are visual.

A visual person often uses certain words in his speech, such as:

- »   "I see what you mean."
- »   "That looks good to me."
- »   "I get the picture now."

And the range that the dominant sense works in for a visual thinker can have certain characteristics, or sub-modalities, such as:

- »   Light (bright or dim)
- »   Size (large or small)
- »   Color (black and white or color)

» Movement (fast or slow)

» Focus (clear or hazy)

Trying to debate, sell, negotiate, manipulate, or influence a visual thinker with no visual input is very difficult if not impossible. Visual thinkers need visual input to make decisions.

Auditory

Auditory thinkers remember the sounds of an event. They remember that the alarm was too loud or the woman whispered too low. They recall the sweetness of the child's voice or the scary bark of the dog. Auditory people learn better from what they hear and can retain far more from being told things than being shown things.

Because an auditory thinker remembers the way something sounded, or because the sounds themselves help recall memories, he may use phrases such as:

» "Loud and clear…"

» "Something tells me…"

» "That sounds okay to me."

And the range of this dominant sense can be within these sub-modalities:

» Volume (loud or soft)

» Tone (base or treble)

» Pitch (high or low)

» Tempo (fast or slow)

» Distance (near or far)

It is imperative to choose your words carefully with auditory thinkers. The words they hear will make or break the deal. I have seen whole encounters go from great to a disaster with one wrong word spoken to an auditory thinker.

Kinesthetic

Kinesthetic thinkers are concerned with feelings. They remember how an event made them feel—the warmth of the room, the beautiful breeze on their skin, how the movie made them jump out of their seat with fear. Often kinesthetic thinkers feel things with their hands to get the sense of the objects. Merely telling them something is soft isn't as real as letting them touch it. But helping recall a soft item they touched before can recall emotions and feelings that are very real to a kinesthetic thinker.

The term "kinesthetic" relates to tactile, visceral, and sense-of-self sensations of the body—basically, where a person's body is in space and the self-awareness of how something made him feel. A kinesthetic thinker uses phrases such as:

>> "I can grasp that idea."

>> "How does that grab you?"

>> "I'll get in touch with you."

>> "I just wanted to touch base."

>> "How does this feel?"

And the range for this type can have the following sub-modalities:

>> Intensity (strong or weak)

>> Area (large or small)

>> Texture (rough or smooth)

>> Temperature (hot or cold)

>> Weight (heavy or light)

Helping a kinesthetic thinker recall a feeling or emotion tied to something can make those emotions reappear as real as the first time they occurred. Kinesthetic thinkers are probably the most difficult for non-kinesthetic thinkers to deal with because they do not react to sights and sounds and social engineers have to get in touch with their feelings to communicate with this type of thinker.

Understanding these basic principles can go a long way toward being able to quickly discern the type of person you are talking to. Again, without asking the target to picture his morning rituals how can you discern the dominant sense? Even more so, why is this so important?

Discerning the Dominant Sense

The key to determining someone's dominant sense is to try to introduce yourself, start a small conversation, and pay close attention to what is being said. As you walk up to the target and lean in to say good morning, maybe she barely looks at you. She might be rude, or she just may not be a visual. Visuals need to look at the person speaking to communicate properly, so this behavior would seem to lend to the fact she is not visual. Now ask a simple question such as, "Don't you just love the feel of a beautiful day like today?" and notice her response, particularly whether she seems to light up or not.

Maybe you wear a large, shiny silver ring. As you talk you gesture; maybe you see that the ring catches her eye. Does she reach out, interested, and need to hold the ring or get close to observe it? Kinesthetics are very touchy-feely when it comes to these things. I know a woman who is a strong kinesthetic and when she sees something she thinks is soft or high quality she *must* touch it. She will say, "Wow, that sweater looks so soft!" From that statement one might assume she is a visual, but what happens next is what solidifies it. She then walks up to the person and touches the sweater and feels it. This shows her dominant sense is kinesthetic. The same woman must touch everything in the grocery store when she shops, whether she needs it or not. By touching the objects, she makes a connection and that connection makes it real to her. Often she cannot remember things very well that she did not come into physical contact with.

Asking questions that contain some of the key dominant words, observing a target's reactions, and *listening* can reveal what dominant sense he or she uses. Listening for key words such as *see, look, bright, dark* can lead you to treat a target like a visual. As mentioned earlier this is not an exact science. There isn't a general rule that states if a person says, "I can see what you are saying..." then he is always a visual. Each clue should lead you down the path toward verifying your hunch with more questions or statements. One word of caution: talking to someone in a different mode than they think in can be irritating to some. Using questions to determine a person's mode of thinking can be off-putting. Use questions sparingly and rely more on observation.

Why Understanding the Mode Is Important

I once worked with a guy, Tony, who could sell a cup of water to a drowning man. Tony was a big believer in seeking out and then using a person's dominant sense in sales. He had a few methods that he used that you may learn from. When he first engaged the target he had a very shiny silver-and-gold pen he would hold in his hand. He would gesture a lot and notice whether the person followed the pen with her eyes; if she did slightly Tony would continually make the gestures bigger to see whether her eyes followed. If that didn't seem to work in the first few seconds he would click the pen open and closed. It wasn't a loud noise, but loud enough to disrupt a thought and draw someone's attention if she were an auditory. If he thought that was working he would click it with every important thought, causing the target to have a psychological reaction to the sound and what was being said. If that didn't seem to work he would reach out over the table and tap her wrist or forearm, or if he was close enough touch her shoulder. He didn't touch excessively, but enough to see whether she would shy away or seemed overly happy or disturbed by the touch.

With these subtle methods he could quickly discern what the person's dominant sense most likely was. This whole act would take under 60 seconds. After he found the information he was looking for, he would then start to move his conversation to that dominant sense, even taking on the traits of that sense in the words he spoke and way he acted and reacted to the conversation. One thing about Tony is that he outsold any person I have ever met. People would often say about him, "It is like he knew exactly what I needed."

Tony would talk to the person and treat the person the way they wanted to be talked to. If the person was a visual thinker, Tony would use phrases like "Can you see what I am saying?" or "How does this look to you?" He would use illustrations that involved "seeing" things or visualizing scenarios. He would put people in their comfort zone.

People feel at ease when they are in their comfort zone. The more you can do as a social engineer to put people in their comfort zone, the better chance you have at success. People gravitate towards those with whom they are comfortable; it is human nature. For example, if someone makes you feel "warm and fuzzy," or seems to understand what you are saying, or seems to see where you are coming from, you easily open up to, trust, and let that person in your circle.

I want to reiterate this point: finding and using someone's dominant sense is not an exact science. A social engineer should use it as a tool in the arsenal and not rely on it as something magical or scientific. Certain psychological aspects of human nature are based on proven science and can be relied upon. As a matter of fact, some of these aspects are so impressive that they can make you seem like a mind reader. Some of them have been a topic of serious debate and some accepted by psychologists, law enforcement, and social engineers for years. The next section of this chapter discusses these, starting with microexpressions.

Microexpressions

You are probably familiar with the idea of reading facial expressions. When someone is happy, sad, angry, or whatever, when someone feels it you can look at his or her face and see that emotion. What if someone tries to fake that expression, like a fake smile? We have all done it, walking through the market and bumping into someone we just don't like that much—we put on a "smile" and say, "Hey John, nice to see you. Say hi to Sally."

We may act very pleasant and cordial, but inside we are feeling nothing but irritation. The expressions that we show for longer periods of time on our face are called *macroexpressions* and are generally easier for people to see the emotion that is being conveyed. Similar to microexpressions, macroexpressions are controlled by our emotions, but are not involuntary and often can be faked.

A certain few pioneers into the study of human behavior have spent decades researching something, coined *microexpressions*, to understand how humans relay emotions.

Microexpressions are expressions that are not easily controllable and occur in reaction to emotions. An emotion triggers certain muscular reactions in a face and those reactions cause certain expressions to appear. Many times these expressions last for as short as one-twenty-fifth of a second. Because they are involuntary muscular movements due to an emotional response, they are nearly impossible to control.

This definition is not a new understanding either; Charles Darwin wrote a book in 1872 called, *The Expression of the Emotions in Man and Animals.* In this book Darwin noted the universal nature of facial expressions and how muscles were used in facial expressions.

In the early 1960s two researchers, Haggard and Isaacs, first discovered what today is called microexpressions. In 1966, Haggard and Isaacs outlined how they discovered these "micromomentary" expressions in their publication titled, *Micromomentary Facial Expressions as Indicators of Ego Mechanisms in Psychotherapy.*

Also in the 1960s, William Condon, a pioneer who studied hours of tapes frame by frame, discovered that humans had "micro-movements." He also heavily researched neurolinguistic programming (more on that later) and body language.

Probably one of the most influential researchers in the field of microexpressions is Dr. Paul Ekman. Dr. Ekman pioneered microexpressions into the science it is today. Dr. Ekman has been studying microexpressions for more than 40 years, receiving the Research Scientist Award as well as being labeled one of *Time Magazine's* most influential people on earth in 2009.

Dr. Ekman researched facial expressions with psychologist Silvan Tomkins. His research revealed that, contrary to popular belief, emotions are not culturally determined, but are universal across cultures and biological.

Working with Dr. Maureen O'Sullivan he developed a project called the Wizards Project. He began to pioneer the use of microexpressions in lie detection. He used a base of 15,000 people from all walks of life and all cultures and found out of that large number that only 50 had the ability to spot a deception without training.

In the 1970s Dr. Ekman developed FACS (Facial Action Coding System) to label and number each conceivable human expression. His work branched out to not only include facial expressions but also how the whole body was involved in deception.

By 1972, Dr. Ekman had identified a list of expressions that were linked with basic or biologically universal emotions:

» Anger

» Disgust

» Fear

» Joy

» Sadness

» Surprise

Dr. Ekman's work began to take on a following, and many law enforcement and corporate environments began to use this research in detecting deception. In 1990, in a paper entitled "Basic Emotions," Dr. Ekman revised his original list to include a range of positive and negative emotions (www.paulekman.com/wp-content/uploads/2009/02/Basic-Emotions.pdf). Dr. Ekman has published many books on emotions, facial expressions, and lie detection that can help each person to understand the value in being able to decode facial expressions.

This brief history indicates that the subject of microexpressions is not some fantasy; on the contrary, real doctors, researchers, and professionals in the field of human behavior have put countless hours into understanding microexpressions. As a social engineer, understanding microexpressions can go a long way toward protecting your clients and teaching them how to notice subtle hints of deception.

If you are a social engineer, or just a person interested in learning about microexpressions, I strongly suggest reading Dr. Ekman's books, especially *Emotions Revealed* and *Unmasking the Face*. He is truly the authority on this topic. The following sections describe the microexpressions in a simplistic format so you can see how you can use this later on as a social engineer.

As mentioned earlier, Dr. Ekman labeled six main microexpressions and later on added contempt to the list, making seven. The following sections cover these one by one.

Anger

Anger is usually easier to spot than some other expressions. In anger the lips become narrow and tense. The eyebrows slant downward and are pushed together—then comes the most noticeable characteristic of anger, the glare.

Anger is a strong emotion and can trigger many other emotions along with it. Sometimes when a person feels anger at something, what you see is a microexpression such as that shown in Figure 5-1. What makes it hard to see is that the facial movements may last only one-twenty-fifth of a second.

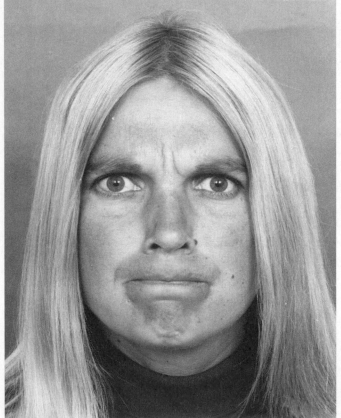

Dr. Paul Ekman

Figure 5-1 Notice the glare, tense lips and tightened brows.

Learning to see a specific microexpression can greatly enhance your understanding of people. To learn how to do so, Dr. Ekman recommends practicing that expression on yourself. He says follow these steps:

1. Pull your eyebrows down and together; pretend you are trying to touch your nose with the inner parts of your eyebrows.

2. While your brows are down, try to open your eyes wide, without adjusting your brow position.

3. Press your lips together tight. Do not pucker your lips, just tense them together.

4. Glare.

What emotion do you feel? The first time I did this, I was overwhelmed with anger. The following is a vital point to this chapter:

> *If producing the facial expression can cause the emotion, that must mean that our facial movements can affect the emotions we feel, and maybe even the emotions of those around us.*

Practice this emotion in a mirror until you get it right. Figure 5-2 shows a picture of a young woman showing us exactly how anger is displayed.

It is just as pronounced as in Figure 5-1 and the icy cold gaze gives it away too.

THEFINALMIRACLE (NIKHIL GANGAVANE) | DREAMSTIME.COM

Figure 5-2 Notice the definite expression of anger on her face.

Mastering the ability to reproduce microexpressions will go a long a way toward understanding the emotion behind them. When you can successfully reproduce and decode a microexpression, you can understand the emotion that is causing it. At that point you can understand the mental state of the person you are dealing with. Not only reproducing them on yourself but also being able to see and read them in others can be helpful in controlling the outcome of your social engineering engagements.

Disgust

Disgust is a strong emotion usually in reaction to something you really do not like. This "something" does not always have to be a physical object; it can also be something that is based on a belief or feeling.

A food that you truly hate can cause the feeling of disgust, which will trigger this expression. What is amazing is even in the absence of the actual smell or sight of the food, the thought of it can cause the same emotion.

When I was a teenager, I went to Disney World with a few friends. I am not, and I mean *not*, a fan of roller coasters. After much prodding I went on Space Mountain, an indoor roller coaster. About halfway through I had determined that I really didn't mind roller coasters when suddenly I was smeared with something very wet and chunky. I was then hit with an odor that I can only describe as stomach contents. Not only me, but many behind me had the same reaction and none of us could hold back our lunch, so to speak. Before you knew it, a simultaneous puking splattered the glass of the Tomorrowland Transit Authority, a slow-moving observation ride that offers a peek into the actual Space Mountain ride on part of its journey. What is amazing is that people in the Tomorrowland ride who sat there slowly going around the park saw the aftereffects hit the glass as they rode through, and saw all the other riders getting physically ill, which made them also vomit—yet they didn't smell the odor or have physical contact with the puke from the roller coaster riders. Why?

Disgust. Bodily fluids generally bring on feelings of disgust and this is one reason that while reading this paragraph you probably started to exhibit the expressions of disgust.

Disgust is often characterized by the upper lip being raised to expose the teeth, and a wrinkling of the nose. It may also result in both cheeks being raised when the nose is wrinkled up, as if to try to block the passage of the bad smell or thought into one's personal space.

What ever the man in Figure 5-3 just saw, it caused a very noticeable display of disgust.

Figure 5-3 Clear signs of disgust with his nose wrinkled and a raised upper lip

Disgust is one of those emotions, according to Dr. Ekman's research, that is in reaction to the sight, smell, or even thought of something distasteful. From a social engineering standpoint this emotion might not lead you down paths of success, but it can surely help you to see whether you are hitting the mark with your target or causing him or her to mentally shut down to your ideas.

The odds are that if you cause disgust for any reason in your target, you have lost. If your appearance, smell, style, breath, or other aspect of your person can make a person feel disgust, then it will most likely close the door to success. You must be aware of what is acceptable and unacceptable to your targets. For example, if your audit is for a prestigious law firm and you have many piercings or tattoos, a very strong negative emotion may rise in your target, which can close the door to your social engineering attempt. If you see a facial expression similar at all to Figure 5-4 then you know it is time to leave the scene.

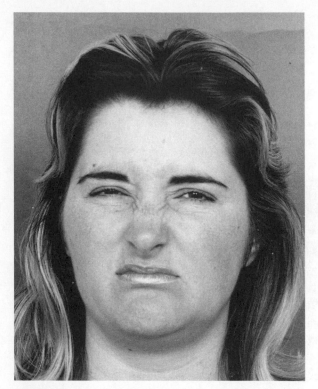

Figure 5-4 If you see this expression, something is wrong.

You must seriously consider your appearance when working on your pretext. If you happen to notice the strong negative emotion of disgust in your target, then backing down and politely excusing yourself to rework your pretext or find a different path in may be a good idea.

Contempt

Contempt is a very strong emotion that is often confused with disgust because it is so closely linked. Dr. Ekman didn't even include contempt on his first list of the base emotions.

In Dr. Ekman's book *Emotions Revealed* he says, "Contempt is only experienced about people or the actions of people, but not about tastes, smells, or touches." He then gave an example of eating calf brains, which might be disgusting to you as a thought, and will trigger disgust. Yet seeing someone eating them may trigger contempt for the person committing the act, not the act itself.

The fact that contempt is directed at a person rather than an object is crucial to understanding the microexpressions that go along with it. Being able to see whether the person you are dealing with is feeling contempt can help you to pinpoint more closely the reason for his or her emotion.

Contempt is distinguished by wrinkling the nose and raising the lip, but only on one side of the face, whereas disgust is the raising of the whole lip and the wrinkling of the whole nose. A very subtle contempt expression can be seen in Figure 5-5 whereas a more pronounced one is shown in Figure 5-6.

Figure 5-5 Notice the slight nose wrinkle and the raising of only the right side of Dr. Ekman's face.

Figure 5-6 Notice the signs of contempt are more prominent in this picture.

Try to mimic contempt, and if you are like me, you will quickly feel anger and contempt in your heart. Performing this exercise and seeing how these reactions affect you emotionally is interesting.

Contempt is often accompanied by anger, because the things that can cause contempt in a person can also trigger strong negative emotions. Contempt is one emotion you want to avoid triggering in anyone with whom you are dealing, especially if you are in a social engineering engagement.

Fear

Fear is often confused with surprise because the two emotions cause similar muscular reactions in the face. Recently while on a plane, I was about to write the section on happiness, but something amazing happened at that time that served as the impetus for writing this section on fear instead.

I am not a short man, being 6'3", and not a small build, either. While I sat on the plane with a few hours to kill I thought I would take advantage of the time to work. Let me add that coach seats aren't what they used to be. As I sat with my laptop open staring off into space I pondered how to start the section I had intended to write. I soon realized I was meant to start writing about fear, because the gentlemen next to me pulled out a water bottle and took a swig, but I didn't see him recap the bottle. Out of the corner of my eye I saw his bottle falling from his hands and toward my keyboard. My instant reaction was easily identified as fear.

My eyes opened wide, while my eyebrows crunched together inward. My lips pulled together and out towards my ears. Of course, I didn't realize all this as it was happening but afterward I was able to analyze what had happened and I knew I had felt fear. I then analyzed the way I felt my face move and determined that if I repeated the expression I felt that same emotion all over again. I am sure I looked similar to what is seen is Figure 5-7.

Try to see whether you can generate this emotion in yourself by following these steps:

1. Raise your eyebrows as high as they will go.
2. Drop your mouth open slightly and pull the corners of your lips back.
3. If you can, pull your eyebrows together while raising them as high as you can.

How did you feel? How about in your hands and arms and your stomach? Did you notice any semblance of fear? If not, try the exercise again but think back to a time when you were in a situation (something similar to my plane experience, or a car in front of you screeching to a halt) out of your control. See how you feel then.

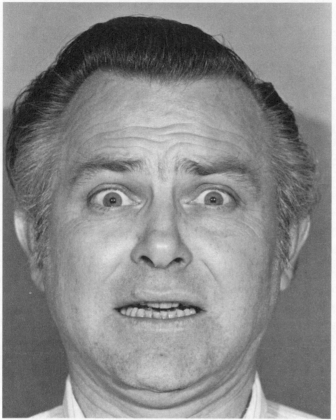

Dr. Paul Ekman

Figure 5-7 Clear signs of fear.

Most likely you will feel the emotion. A friend of mine sent me this picture of his daughter's first roller coaster ride (Figure 5-8). You can clearly see the raised eyebrows, eyes wide and the mouth open with lips pulled back.

From a social engineering standpoint, fear is often used to cause people to react a certain way. Malicious social engineers use fear tactics to get an unsuspecting user to click a banner or give up a valuable piece of information. For example, malicious banners might claim "Your computer is infected with a virus. Click here to get fixed now!!" These banners work against non-technical users who fear the virus and will click, only to be infected at that point.

Figure 5-8 This little girl is showing clear signs of fear on the roller coaster.

One company I worked with was hit by a malicious social engineer who used fear to gain access to the building. Knowing that the CFO was out of town on an important business meeting and could not be disturbed, the social engineer went into the company as a tech support guy. He demanded access to the CFO's office, which was promptly denied. He then played this line, "Mr. Smith, your CFO, called me and told me that while he was away at this meeting I better come down and fix his e-mail problem and that if it is not fixed while he is gone, heads will roll."

The secretary feared that if it didn't get fixed, she would be to blame. Would her boss really be angry? Could her job be at risk? Because she feared a negative outcome, the secretary let the phony tech support guy in. If he was a skilled social engineer he may have been watching her facial expressions and noticing whether she exhibited signs of worry or anxiety, which are related to fear. He then could have played on these signs more and more, getting her to cave in to her fear.

Fear can be a big motivator to do many things that you (or your target) would not normally consider doing.

Surprise

As mentioned earlier, Dr. Ekman and many other psychologists in the area of micro-expressions have concurred that surprise is closely linked to fear because of certain similarities. Even so, some marked differences exist, such as the direction the lips take and the way the eyes react.

Try this exercise to show surprise:

1. Raise your eyebrows, not in fear but with the goal of widening your eyes as much as you can.

2. Let your jaw unhinge and open slightly.

3. After you get the expression down pat try doing it quickly.

I noticed I almost was forced to gasp in some air when I did it, causing me to feel something similar to surprise. You should see an expression similar to Figure 5-9.

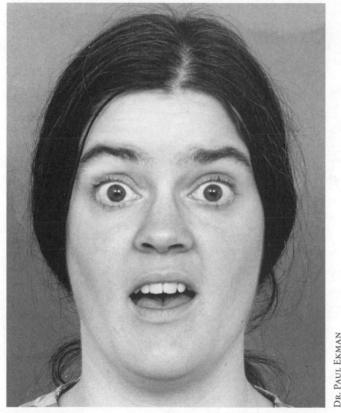

DR. PAUL EKMAN

Figure 5-9 Notice the way the eyes and lips appear similar to fear.

Surprise can be good or bad. Hearing your daughter's first words, of course, is a good surprise. Or the surprise can be one of an event, statement, or question that you didn't expect that causes this response.

As you can see in Figure 5-10 whatever that woman must have seen really surprised her. Maybe a gift is being presented or something one of her grandchildren said to her. Notice her eyebrows raised and her jaw is unhinged and open. This kind of surprise is easy to see because it is so pronounced and the expressions are easy to pick out.

© Stylephotographs (Robert Kneschke) | Dreamstime.com

Figure 5-10 Often confused with fear, surprise has some minor differences.

If the surprise is positive, it can often cause a smile or a jovial response after the initial shock wears off. A social engineer can sometimes use surprise to open the target's door, so to speak; following up with quick wit or a joke can quickly put the target at ease, causing the target to lower his or her guard.

Sadness

Sadness is an overwhelming and strong emotion. Sadness is one of those emotions that we may feel ourselves when we see other people who are expressing this emotion. Some people can feel sadness just by seeing others who are sad, even to the point of crying.

To show you how easily you can feel sadness, try this exercise:

1. Drop your mouth open slightly.

2. Pull the corners of your lips down.

3. Hold your lips in place, and while doing that try to raise your cheeks as if you are squinting.

4. While maintaining that tension, look down and let your upper eyelids droop.

Most likely you will begin to feel sadness. When I first did this exercise, it was overwhelming for me. I instantly felt sad and found I had to control the length of time I performed it because it caused me to be sad for quite a while. To see how this should look, notice the expression in Figure 5-11.

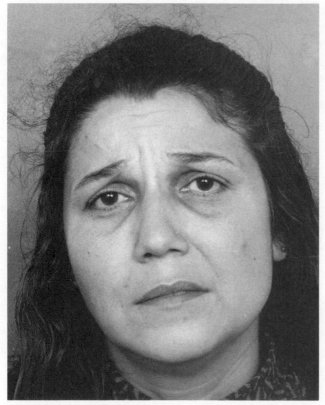

DR. PAUL EKMAN

Figure 5-11 Notice the lips and eyes drawn back and down, signifying sadness.

Another aspect of sadness that makes it an amazing emotion is that it does not always have to display as agony or extreme grief. Sadness can be very subtle. Sadness can also be displayed in just one part of the face. People may try to hide sadness by using a fake smile or what I call "stoic eyes," where they stare straight ahead, almost in a daze, but you can tell they are trying to control the emotion they are feeling.

Take a look at Figure 5-12. In this case you can see an example of sadness when half the face is covered. This woman is showing definite signs of sadness which can be noticed even though her face is covered. Notice her brow is slightly furrowed as well her eyelids dropping and you can see the corners of her mouth pointing downward.

Figure 5-12 Notice how the signs of sadness
are visible in her eyes, brows and lips.

The eyes are one of the best indicators to reading sadness. The expression is often
confused with tiredness and other emotions that can cause similar eye movements.
Tying in the body language with what is read on the face can also help to determine
if it is sadness or another emotion.

 This can be especially true if you are dealing with other cultures. Particularly
in cultures where much of the face is covered by clothing. In many Middle Eastern
cultures where women cover much of their face, you may only be able to see the
persons eyes. In these cases it will be very important for the social engineer to also
use body language to determine if what they are seeing is genuine sadness.

Sadness is often used in social engineering because it can trigger people to take
an action such as donate money or give out information. You have probably seen
it used in television commercials showing a very disadvantaged child. These children may be malnourished, poverty stricken, and seemingly unloved, but for just a
small donation you can bring a smile to the child's face. The images of sad, crying,
emaciated children will tug at your heartstrings. I am not suggesting that these
commercials are malicious social engineering, just that they use social engineering
to a degree, by using an emotional trigger to get a reaction out of the target.

Unfortunately, malicious social engineers often use this emotional trigger to obtain things from their targets. I once walked into a restaurant and overheard a young man telling a group of older folks who were leaving that he just ran out of gas on the highway and needed to get home because his wife was nine months pregnant. He had been out of work and had just walked a mile off the highway to use the phone to call his wife and wondered if they could give him $20. When I heard some of the story I slowed down and made believe I was on a phone call to observe the rest. He told his tale and then backed it up with, "Look if you give me your address, I will mail you a check for the $20," concluding with "I swear to God."

The story had some elements in it that could elicit compassion, especially when his face showed concern, anxiety, and sadness. He didn't get $20—he was given $20 by each of the three people in that group. He said "God bless you" a few times and gave the group a few hugs and said he was going to go in to call his wife and tell her he was on the way home. He hugged them and they left feeling as if they had done their good deed for the week.

A few minutes later as I'm eating my meal, I see him at the bar drinking a couple of fully paid-for drinks with his buddies. Mixing a sad story with some sad facial expressions, he had been able to manipulate the emotions of those around him.

Happiness

Happiness can have many facets to it—so many that I can probably make a chapter just on it, but that is not my focus. Dr. Ekman's books cover many excellent points about happiness and similar emotions and how they affect the person with the emotion and those around him or her.

What I want to focus on are just a couple aspects of happiness—most importantly the difference between a true smile and a fake smile. The true and the fake smile are an important aspect of human expressions to know how to read, and as a social engineer to know how to reproduce.

Has there been a time where you met someone who was very pleasant but after you parted ways your spouse or you yourself said, "That guy was a fake..."?

You might not have been able to identify the aspects of a true smile in your head but something told you the person wasn't being "real." In the late 1800s a French neurologist, Duchenne de Boulogne, did some fascinating research into smiling. He was able to attach electrodes to a man's face and trigger the same "muscular" response in the face as a smile. Even though the man was using all the right muscles for smiling, de Boulogne determined that the look of the man was still a "fake smile." Why?

When a person smiles for real, de Boulogne indicates, two muscles are triggered, the zygomaticus major muscle and the orbicularis oculi. Duchenne determined that the orbicularis oculi (muscle around the eyes) cannot be triggered voluntarily and that is what separates a real from a fake smile.

Dr. Ekman's research concurs with Duchenne's and although recent research indicates some can train themselves to think about triggering that muscle, more often than not a fake smile is all about the eyes. A real smile is broad with narrow eyes, raised cheeks, and pulled-up lower eyelids. It has been said that a real smile involves the whole face, from the eyes to the mouth, as seen in Figure 5-13.

Figure 5-13 Dr. Ekman demonstrates a fake smile (left) next to a real smile (right).

If you were to cover the top half of Dr. Ekman's face you would be hard pressed to tell a real from a fake smile. It is not until you examine the eyes that it becomes clear, side by side, which smile is fake and which is real.

When a person sees a real smile on another person's face, it can trigger that same emotion inside of them and cause them to smile. Notice Figure 5-14, this man is showing genuine happiness with a real smile. Notice how his whole face is involved in this smile.

From a social engineering standpoint, knowing how to detect and also create a real smile is a valuable piece of information. A social engineer wants a target to be put at ease, so as to have the greatest positive effect on the target. Social engineers in any form, whether they are salespeople, teachers, psychologists, or any other social engineer, often start off a conversation with a smile. Quickly our brains analyze how we feel about that visual input given to us and it can affect the rest of the interaction.

A lot of information is packed into the preceding section, yet you may be wondering how social engineers can train themselves not only to see microexpressions but also how to use them.

Figure 5-14 Notice how his whole face is involved in this smile.

Training Yourself to See Microexpressions

Hollywood often overstates the abilities of the characters that appear in movies and television. For example, in the new hit television show *Lie To Me* (based on Dr. Ekman's research) the main character, Dr. Lightman, can read microexpressions with seemingly no effort, and what is even more amazing is he usually can tell why the emotion is occurring.

Yet in real life, much of the research done by those in the field, like Dr. Ekman, meant sitting in front of prerecorded sessions and analyzing these sessions frame by frame. After many years of working on this task he is probably able to notice, pick up, and analyze microexpressions very quickly. In the 1970s he did a research project where he identified some who had a natural ability to notice and correctly analyze microexpressions.

Because many of us might not fall into that natural ability category we need a way to practice, train, and become proficient at performing, reading, and using microexpressions. I can tell you what works for me. I read the methods on how a particular microexpression is identified, then practice reproducing it using a mirror, comparing my expression to the notes from the professionals that describe how it is done. I usually have a picture that shows the emotion I am working on because having something to mimic helps me.

After I feel relatively good about reproducing the microexpression I focus on how it makes me feel, tweaking small areas until the muscular movements cause me to feel the matching emotions.

I then scour the Internet looking for pictures and try to identify the expressions in those pictures. Next, I record news or television shows and play certain parts in slow motion with the sound off to see if can determine the emotion, then listen to the story to see if I was close. All this leads up to working with live "subjects." I watch people interact with each other and try to identify the emotions they are feeling during their discussions. I try both with being able to hear the conversation and also without being able to.

The reason I chose this path before trying to read microexpressions in my own conversations is that I found that trying to do it in a live environment without having to also focus on making good conversation is easier. I just read the facial expressions and do not get confused by other sensory input. The preceding method is the one I used before I had a chance to meet Dr. Ekman and be introduced to his training methods. Of course, he has books that contain step-by-step instructions on recreating and reading these expressions. His books also include pictures showing the emotions as well as examples in the news that show those emotions. His book *Emotions Revealed* does this in a very professional format that is excellent for learning.

In recent years Dr. Ekman has developed and released training specifically for microexpressions. His website, `www.paulekman.com`, has three different types of training that have changed the way people can learn this powerful science.

Ekman's training gives the user a lesson on each type of microexpression via video and text. The user can replay the expression video to see how each part of the face is involved. After the user spends as much time as needed learning and watching the video sections, she can take a pretest. The pretest enables her to see how good she is at noticing microexpressions. When the user guesses at what microexpression is being displayed, she can get confirmation or correction. If correction is needed then she can take additional education and training.

After the user is confident in her abilities she can take the real test. In the final exam no correction is given. The user is shown a microexpression once for a brief one twenty-fifth of a second, and then she must select what the microexpression is and then wait to be graded at the end.

This type of training tool can take years off of your learning curve in becoming proficient at reading microexpressions. One caveat: Dr. Ekman, as well as his contemporaries, state that even though you may become proficient in reading microexpressions, a microexpression is limited. What does that mean?

One of the tricks actors use to be able to successfully show proper emotion is to remember and focus on a time when they truly felt the emotion they need to portray; for example, a moment of happiness that produced a real smile. As mentioned earlier, making a real smile is very difficult to fake if you aren't truly feeling happy, but if you can bring up a memory when you felt that emotion your muscles will remember and react.

Therefore, although you can become proficient at reading the emotion, you cannot read the *why* behind it. The *why* is often lost to science. I had a friend who had some bad experiences as a child with a person who closely resembled a good friend of mine. Whenever my friend would come around she had strong emotional reactions. If you were to read her microexpression you would probably see fear, contempt, and then anger on her face. She did not hate my friend, but she hated the person in her memory who resembled my friend.

This is a good point to remember when you are learning how to read microexpressions. The expression is linked to an emotion, but the expression doesn't tell you *why* the emotion is being displayed. I know when I first started learning about microexpressions and then became somewhat "proficient" at reading certain expressions, I felt like I was a mind reader. Although this is far from the truth, the caution is to not be assumptive. You may become very good at reading microexpressions; however, later sections discuss how to combine this skill with interrogation tactics, body language skills, and elicitation skills to not only figure out what targets are thinking, but also to lead them down the path you want.

The question you still may have is, "How can I use these skills as a social engineer?"

How Social Engineers Use Microexpressions

This whole section leads up to this: As fascinating as the research is, as amazing as the science is behind this psychology, how do you utilize microexpressions in a social engineer audit and how do malicious social engineers use them?

This section discusses two methods of how to use microexpressions in social engineering. The first method is using microexpressions (ME) to elicit or cause an emotion, and the second method is how to detect deceit.

Let me start with the first method, using your own ME to cause an emotional response in others. I recently read a research paper that changed my view of ME and opened my eyes to a new area of research. Researchers Wen Li, Richard E. Zinbarg, Stephan G. Boehm, and Ken A. Paller performed a study called "Neural and Behavioral Evidence for Affective Priming from Unconsciously Perceived Emotional Facial Expressions and the Influence of Trait Anxiety" that changes the face of microexpression usage in modern science.

The researchers connected dozens of mini-EKGs to muscle points on their subjects' faces. The devices would register any muscular movements in their face and head. They then played videos for them that had one-twenty-fifth-second flashes of microexpressions in frames. Li et al., found that in almost every case the subject's muscular movement would begin to mirror that which was embedded in the video. If it was fear or sadness, the subject's facial muscles would register those emotions. When interviewed about the emotion the subject was feeling it was the emotion embedded in the video.

To me, this groundbreaking research proves that a person can manipulate another person to a certain emotional state by displaying subtle hints of that emotion. I have started conducting some research into this from a security angle and I am calling it "neurolinguistic hacking," mainly because it takes much from microexpressions as well as neurolinguistic programming (discussed in the next section) and combines them to create these emotional states within a target.

Imagine this scenario. A social engineer wants to walk into a company with the goal of getting the receptionist to insert a malicious USB key into the computer. His pretext is that he has a meeting with the HR manager, but on the way in, he spilled coffee all over his last resume. He really needs this job and to help, would she print him out another copy of the resume?

This is a solid pretext that tugs on the receptionist's heartstrings and has worked for me in the past. Yet, if the social engineer allows his own emotional state to run rampant he might be showing signs of fear, which is linked to nervousness. That fear can translate to an uneasy feeling in the receptionist and failure or rejection of the request. Whereas if he were to control his emotions and flash subtle hints of sad microexpressions, which is closely linked with empathy, then he might have a very good chance at his request being honored.

Recall the previous discussion of the commercials that encourage people to donate "only a dollar a day" to feed a child in need. Before requesting money, before flashing a phone number and URL, before telling you that credit cards are accepted, many long images of very sad children flash across your TV screen. Those images of children in need and children in pain put your brain in the emotional state that is needed to comply with the request.

Do those commercials work on everyone? No, of course not. But although not everyone donates, it will affect almost everyone's emotional state. That is how a social engineer can use ME to the fullest. Learning to exhibit the subtle hints of these ME can cause the neurons in your target's brain to mirror the emotional state they feel you are displaying, making your target more willing to comply with your request.

This usage of ME can be malicious, so I want to take a moment to talk about a mitigation (see also Chapter 9). Being aware of how ME can be used doesn't mean you need to start training everyone in your company to be an ME expert. What it does mean is that good security awareness training does need to occur. Even when requests are designed to make you desire to help, desire to save, desire to nurture, the security policy must take precedence. A simple, "I'm sorry we cannot insert foreign USB keys into our computers. But two miles down the road is a FedEx Kinko's shop. You can print another resume there. Should I tell Mrs. Smith you will be a few minutes late?"

In this scenario, such a statement would have squashed the social engineer's plans as well as given the target the feeling of being helpful.

To utilize the power of ME, sometimes you have to combine it with other aspects of human behavior as well. The second method, how to detect deceit, describes how you can do this. The second method for using ME as a social engineer is in detecting deception. Wouldn't it be nice if you could ask a question and know whether the response was truth or not? This subject has been a source of heated debate among many professionals who claim that eye patterns, body language, facial expression, or a combination of all the preceding can indicate truth or deception. While some do not believe this to be the case, others feel these can be used as an exact science.

Although some truth may exist in each of those thoughts, how can you use microexpressions to detect deception?

To answer this question you must take into account more than just microexpressions because, as identified throughout this section, microexpressions are based on emotions and reactions to emotions. Keep this in mind while reading this section, which analyzes some causes and effects.

Four things can help you detect deceit in a target:

» Contradictions

» Hesitation

> » Changes in behavior
>
> » Hand gestures

The following sections discuss these items in more detail.

Contradictions

Contradictions are particularly tricky because they often can and do occur in factual accounts. I know in my case I often forget details, and my wife will fill them in quickly. After I get a little hint here or there I often can remember the full story. This doesn't mean that I am always lying at the beginning of a story or conversation, but I don't always remember all the details clearly enough to comment on them at first, or I think I do remember the details but I really don't. Even after I "remember" the details, the details may be my version of reality and not the way the story actually happened.

This inadvertent dishonesty is important to consider when evaluating contradictions as a clue to lying. What a contradiction should do is prompt you to dig more. Watching the person's microexpressions while you question him about a contradiction is also helpful.

For example, suppose you have developed a pretext as a visiting salesperson. You are going to try to gain physical access to the CEO to deliver a CD with a special offer. You know the CEO is very partial to a certain charity so you developed the pretext around that. As you walk into the lobby the front desk person says, "Sorry, he is not in, you can just leave it with me."

You know that if you leave the CD a greater chance exists that your "malicious" CD will never be used. You also feel he is in because you see his car in the parking lot and you know today was a normal work day for him. With those facts in mind and without wanting to embarrass the front desk person you say, "Oh, he's really not? I called the other day and asked when I could visit and was told today was a good day. Did I mix up my days?"

If you've played your cards right and your expressions are genuine, this can turn out two ways:

> » She may hold steady and again say, "Sorry, he's not in."
>
> » She may contradict herself (which can be a clue that she is not being truthful): "Let me check whether he is in or not."

What? She went from a stern "He is not in" to "Let me check." That contradiction is enough to signal that you should dig more. What was her ME when she did that? Did she show shame or maybe some sadness at lying? Was she angry at being caught in a lie? Was she embarrassed that she was wrong and maybe confused? You cannot automatically assume she is lying, because maybe she really didn't know, and when you rebutted she decided to really find out.

After she confirms whether he is in you can choose to dig a little deeper and probe more to determine truthfulness if needed. Again, playing your card of "Maybe I mixed up my days" and watching her facial expressions can be a good indicator of her truthfulness or not.

If in your first go-round you saw any hints of anger, continuing to enquire can cause her to be more angry and embarrassed and end your interaction. At this point, you may want to ask something like, "If Mr. Smith isn't in right now and I really mixed up my days or times, when can I stop in to see him? What time is the best?"

This type of question allows her to save face, as well as gives you another opportunity to read some facial expressions. If you didn't notice anger but maybe saw she looked a little sad or embarrassed then you might want to respond with empathy and understanding to open her up. "I could have sworn that he said today was a good time to drop it off, but you know, my memory is so bad, my wife tells me I am getting Alzheimer's. I bought one of these smart phones, but I'll be darned if I can figure it out. I don't want to be a bother, but when can I just drop this off for him? I want to make sure it gets right into his hands."

Be very observant of minor contradictions as they can be key indicators in deceit and help you get your foot in the door.

Hesitation

Similarly to contradiction, you can use someone's hesitation to detect a potential untruth. If you ask a question and the answer should have come quickly from the person, but he hesitates beforehand, it can be an indication that he was using the time to fabricate an answer.

For example, when my wife asks me how much my new electronic gadget costs, she knows I know the answer. A hesitation can mean either I am evaluating whether I want to answer truthfully or I might just be remembering the price.

When I get a progress report from my son's school that says he missed X number of days at school and I only know about two or three valid absences, I ask him where the rest of these missed days are from. If his answer was, "Dad, don't you remember I had that doctor appointment and then you kept me home that day to help you with that project?" Most likely that is full-on truth because it was quick and has facts in the response. However, if he hesitates and comes back with, "Wow, I don't know—maybe the report is wrong," then noting his microexpression during his response is a good idea. Does it indicate anger, maybe at being caught, or sadness at the imagined punishment? Either way, it is time for me to investigate more and find out where he was those days.

Another thing to look out for is a well-known hesitation tactic of repeating the question back to you as if asking for verification that the question is correct. Doing so allows for time to fabricate a response. The use of hesitation to detect deception is not an exact science, but it can be a good indicator. Some people just think before they speak. I am from New York, so I speak fast. If someone speaks slower than me it is not an indication of deceit. You must be able to use the ME to determine if someone is just slow at speaking or trying to fabricate a response.

If the emotion does not match the question asked then it might be worth looking into.

Changes in Behavior

During a discussion the target may change his behavior every time a certain topic is brought up. Maybe you notice an expression change or a shift in the way he sits, or a marked hesitation. All of these actions can indicate deceit. Whether these actions amount to deceit is not certain, but they should cause you to probe more on the topics being discussed in a way that does not alert suspicion. These behaviors can be signs that the person is using the time delays to generate a story, recall facts, or decide whether he wants to reveal those facts.

Hand Gestures

People often paint pictures with their hands using gestures. For example, someone may use his hands to show how big something is, how fast something was going, or to show how many times something was said. Many professionals feel that when someone is being untruthful he will touch or rub his face often. Some psychological connection exists between rubbing the face and generating a fabrication. Some of the cues used by psychologists and body language experts to detect deceit are discussed here: www.examiner.com/mental-health-in-new-orleans/detecting-deception-using-body-language-and-verbal-cues-to-detect-lies.

Taking note of a change in the size, frequency, or duration of hand gestures during a conversation is important. In addition, you should watch facial expressions during gestures that can raise a flag in your mind.

When you detect deceit, having a plan for how to respond is important and a good idea. In the earlier scenario with the front desk person and her "out-of-the-office" boss, calling her out on her lie would most likely have raised all sorts of red flags, embarrassing her, and ruining any chances of success. If your pretext is someone with authority, like a manager or department supervisor, and you catch someone in a lie you can then use that to your advantage. By "forgiving" the person you are now owed a favor in return. But in the same scenario, if the position you are in is lower (someone in a non-management position such as a secretary, receptionist, or sales position) than the target, playing that card can be dangerous. The authority action would not fit the pretext of someone in a non-management position.

What it boils down to simply is that as a social engineer auditor you must learn to use a person's microexpressions to determine whether he is presenting the truth or a lie and to determine whether you are affecting the target the way you want. In some cases you can even use certain expressions to manipulate the target into a certain state of mind.

Remember, microexpressions alone are not enough to determine *why* an emotion is occurring. Determining that someone is angry or sad, for instance, doesn't tell you why that person is angry or sad. Be cautious when using microexpressions to take into consideration all factors to determine, as closely as possible, the reason for the emotion.

Malicious social engineers employ these tactics of using microexpressions discussed in this section but their goals are completely different from those of a social engineer doing an audit. They often don't care about the residual effect on the target. If damaging a person's belief system, psychological stability, or even job stability can lead the malicious social engineer to a payday he will take that path.

Earlier in this book you read about some scams that came up during the attacks in New York City after 9/11. People who saw an opportunity to cash in on people's sympathy and the tragedy that occurred didn't seem to care whether their actions hurt others. Many came out of the shadows claiming to have family who were lost in those attacks. Some of these malicious people received money, gifts, sympathy, and even media attention only for it to be discovered down the road that the stories were all false accounts.

The malicious social engineer spends a lot of time learning about people and what makes them tick. This knowledge makes locating an acceptable target to attack easier.

This section just scratched the surface of microexpressions; the work of many professionals in the field has filled volumes. Seek out training, become proficient in reading and using microexpressions, and you will see an increase in your communication abilities with others. In addition, this proficiency will enhance your ability to have success in your audits.

Neurolinguistic Programming (NLP)

Neurolinguistic programming (NLP) studies the structure of how humans think and experience the world. It is very controversial in itself because the structure of NLP does not lend itself to precise, statistical formulas. Many scientists will argue or debate the principles of NLP due to this fact, but the structure does lead to models of how the principles work. From these models, techniques for quickly and effectively changing thoughts, behaviors, and beliefs that limit people have been developed.

As stated in Wikipedia (source: *Oxford English Dictionary*), neurolinguistic programming is "a model of interpersonal communication chiefly concerned with the relationship between successful patterns of behavior and the subjective experiences (esp. patterns of thought) underlying them," and "a system of alternative therapy based on this which seeks to educate people in self-awareness and effective communication, and to change their patterns of mental and emotional behavior."

This book is far from a self-help book, so although the principles in it can assist in changing deep-seated thought patterns and habits in yourself, its focus is on how you can use NLP to understand and then manipulate those around you.

If you are unfamiliar with NLP your first instinct may be to run to a computer and type the term into Google. I want to ask you not to do that just yet. You will find that similar to social engineering, what you will often find first are many videos and demonstrations that just seem very unrealistic, such as videos of someone touching another person's shoulder and changing that person's brain patterns to think brown is white or somesuch. These videos make out NLP to be some form of mysticism, and for those who are leery of these things, these types of videos discredit it.

Instead the following sections break NLP down into a few parts. Up next is a very brief history of NLP, which can help you to understand that its roots are not with street magicians; instead, it has deep psychological roots.

The History of Neurolinguistic Programming

Neurolinguistic programming (NLP) was developed in the 1970s by Richard Bandler and John Grinder with the guidance of Gregory Bateson. Its roots came from Bandler and Grinder's research into some of the most successful therapists of their time.

From this initial research they developed the "code" concepts of NLP. This early research led to the development of a *meta-model,* which recognizes the use of language patterns to influence change.

Both Bandler and Grinder were students at the University of California and used the principles of their research to develop a therapy model called the meta-model. After writing a few books based on this model they began to refine the core principles that would become what we call NLP today. This included things like anchoring, swish pattern, reframing, belief change, nesting loops, chaining states, and submodalities applications.

After graduating with degrees in psychology, Bandler and Grinder began hosting seminars and practice groups, which served as places for them to practice and test their newly discovered patterns while allowing them to transfer the skills to the participants. During this period, a creative group of students and psychotherapists who formed around Grinder and Bandler made valuable contributions to NLP, helping refine NLP even more.

In the recent years, NLP became the new buzzword again for managers, driving rapid growth of trainers, classes, and experts. Without any regulating body, the field grew as everybody wanted to learn to control others, lie without getting caught, or solve all their psychological problems. Practitioners were not licensed, so each group taught its own form and concept of NLP and issued its own certification as experts. All of this is what led to NLP being viewed somewhat unfavorably.

Despite its rocky history, the core foundation of NLP can enhance your abilities as a social engineer. The next section discusses some of the core codes of NLP so you can analyze them more deeply.

Codes of Neurolinguistic Programming

In the early 1970s NLP had a code comprised of the collective body of learning and investigation that generated the first books and the term *neurolinguistic program-ming*. As time went on John Grinder and others have continued to contribute to the field of NLP. The "new code of NLP" is an ethical and aesthetic framework for NLP development.

New Code of NLP

NLP's original ideas were born in the 1970s. As time passed, John Grinder began to realize that much of the old code must change to be brought into modern times. He began working with Gregory Bateson and Judith DeLozier and produced the "new code" that focused more on what the person thinks or believes will happen and changing that belief. Learning techniques for expanding your perceptions, overcoming old thought patterns, and changing habits all help in self-change.

The new code focuses on the key concepts of *states, conscious/unconscious relationships*, and *perceptual filters*, all of these pointing to states of your mind and your perception of those mental states. These new concepts are meant to move NLP forward and help practitioners think about it in new ways. Many of the basic tenets from the new code are being taught now as part of the standard NLP courseware. This new code is best understood by reading *Turtles All the Way Down* by Grinder and DeLozier. It's compiled from their seminar "Prerequisites to Personal Genius."

In essence, the new code states that to make a change the client must involve their unconscious mind, the new behavior must satisfy their original positive intention, and the change must occur internally at the state of mind rather than at the behavioral level. This new code suggests how NLP can create serious and drastic changes to a person's thinking.

This is a key concept for social engineers because, as you investigate and analyze the new code, you will begin to see how it can be used to manipulate others. Before doing that, though, you need to understand the scripts that the new code uses.

Scripts in the New Code

People tend to have common problems, so groups of scripts have been developed to help therapists use NLP in their practice. These scripts lead the participant through a series of thoughts that help guide the person to the desired end. Several good books on NLP scripts exist, with *The Big Book of NLP Techniques: 200+ Patterns & Strategies of Neuro Linguistic Programming* being highly recommended.

An example of one script is an outline of how to increase your sales by getting someone to start talking about their dreams. Once you have them talking about certain goals or aspirations, you can posit your product or service as answering one of the needs to reach those goals. By positively building on your product as fitting a need they have, you give your potential sale's brain a way to connect your product with positive sales.

If you take time to Google much of the information included here you will see that NLP can take on a life of its own. You can take many angles and paths when studying NLP. Despite all the plethora of information out there the question remains, how can a social engineer use NLP?

How to Use NLP as a Social Engineer

Many of the scripts and principles of NLP tend to lean toward hypnosis and similar avenues. Even though you will not use hypnosis to social engineer a target, you can use many of the principles of NLP as a social engineer. For example, NLP can teach you how to use your voice, language, and choice of words to guide people down the path you want.

Voice in NLP

You can use your voice to inject commands into people just as you would use code to inject commands into a SQL database. The way you say things is where the injection occurs; this single moment of injection is framed within regular conversation. Sometimes *how* you say something is more important than *what* you say.

NLP promotes the use of embedded commands to influence a target to think a certain way or take a certain action. Also, using the tones of your voice to emphasize certain words in a sentence can cause a person's unconscious mind to focus on those words. For example:

For instance, ask "Don't you agree?" Instead of putting an upswing on the word "agree," like you would normally at the end of a question, put a downswing to make the question more of a command.

Another one I have heard used effectively is, "My customers usually do the things I say. Do you want to begin?" The way that sentence is used and surrounded by other statements can make this a very commanding statement.

More on this in the next section, but this skill alone can change the way you interact with others; the principles for it are steeped in NLP.

Sentence Structure

In English, the sound of the person's voice at the end of sentence indicates whether what is being said is a question, statement, or command. A person's voice goes up at the end of a sentence for questions. The voice stays the same through the end of the sentence in statements, and the voice lowers at the sentence close for commands.

For the next few paragraphs, the **bold** font denotes to lower (deepen) your voice tone.

Try this exercise: When you ask a question such as, "Is that your dog?" your voice will rise at the end of that sentence. Yet you can embed subtle commands into sentences by just changing them to a downward point during the sentence, not at the end. Here are a few simple commands for you to practice. Notice how they have the command injected inside the sentence.

"Remember how **clean your room** looked last Christmas?" The embedded command is "clean your room," which includes a time shift to a happier time. This is an example of a pleasant, painless injection.

"**Buy now**, you can see the **benefits**!" This one starts with the voice low, then up to a normal tone, then back down for *benefits*.

"The **higher my company** goes in consulting, the more **nice people like you** we encounter." Implanting the *higher my company* with a pleasant comment has just increased your chance of being hired, partly because of the play on words (*Higher* sounds like *hire*—thus what the listener hears is ***hire my company***).

From a social engineering standpoint you can form sentences when performing an audit over the phone to maximize the potential for success, such as:

"This is Larry from tech support; we are **giving** all reps new passwords. **Your** new **password** is..."

The following are tips for using your voice in successful social engineering:

» **Practice.** You have to practice speaking in this manner so you don't sound like a teenage boy entering puberty. Your rising and falling tones can't sound canned; they must be subtle.

» **Have careful sentence structure.** Develop sentences that maximize your ability to accomplish your tasks. Don't go for the kill, so to speak. A command like "give me access to your server room now" is probably not going to work, but you can use these voice techniques to help a target be more open to the idea.

» **Be realistic.** Don't expect to speak and have people falling at your feet to do what you ask. These techniques can put your target in a frame of mind that will make getting what you want easier.

One technique, *Ultimate Voice*, if mastered, does have very powerful effects. I once interviewed an NLP practitioner on a podcast who had this gift. When he spoke it was as if you could not argue with him. He spoke with such control and technique that disagreement never even entered my mind. How can one master this technique?

Using Ultimate Voice in Social Engineering

You can master the Ultimate Voice but it takes lots of practice. The ability to embed commands into normal conversation is a skill that is very useful when mastered. Ultimate voice is the ability to inject commands into people's minds without their knowledge. It can sound very artificial when new people try it, until enough practice makes them sound natural.

Hypnotists often use this technique like so:

"You can feel **yourself relaxing** as you slip into **calmness**."

This standard therapy phrase can be adapted to nearly any command you like. Put extra emphasis on the vowels in the words you want to accent—for example, "yooouurseeelf reelaaxiing."

Planet NLP (`www.planetnlp.com/`) offers three exercises that you can use to work on mastering this technique.

1. **Move your voice around.** Press your hand on your nose and say "nose." Concentrate on your nose as you repeat the word until you can feel your nose vibrating. Now do the same exercise with your hand on your throat, saying "throat." Do the same on your chest, saying "chest." Keep practicing until you can really feel the vibration in each place. Notice how different each one sounds.

2. **Use your range.** Starting from a high note, say "ar" (as in the letter *r*). Keeping your mouth open, allow the note to drop down until your breath runs out.

   Repeat this exercise ten times.

   Then, starting from a low note, say "ou" (as in *you* without the *y*), allowing the note to rise until you cannot support the sound.

   Repeat this exercise ten times.

3. **Resonate.** To use your voice correctly, it must resonate in the *mask*, which is the facial area surrounding the nose and mouth.

   There are two ways to practice resonating:

   » Hum at whatever pitch is most comfortable for you. After you have found your pitch then hum "umm" followed immediately by the word "ready." Do this a few times, then try the words "now," "one," "two," and "three."

   » Hum and then allow your lips to vibrate. You are attempting to sound like a dove. Allow the pitch to rise and fall. This is very difficult if you have any tension in the jaw or face. Done correctly for a few minutes, your face will start to feel numb.

After a couple of minutes using these methods, you should notice that your voice sounds crisper. If you find it hard to notice, record yourself and listen back to see how it sounds to you.

The best way to improve is to spend about five minutes a day going through these exercises.

Practice can help you to learn to control this vocal technique. For example, I am generally a loud person. It seems like I don't have the ability to whisper. For me to control my tones, pitch, and volume, I need practice. Doing simple voice exercises like these can help you to control these voice characteristics.

When you speak a sentence in which you want to include a hidden command, and you want to lower your tone, being so subtle that the target doesn't realize it is imperative. Otherwise, you will alert that person's subconscious to trigger that something is amiss. If that occurs he may pick up on your attempts thereby shutting down your success.

Like most things in social engineering, if a technique doesn't come naturally, practice is essential. Try this voice technique on your family and friends before you ever attempt it in an audit.

From personal experience, when I first started working on the Ultimate Voice techniques I decided my goal was to embed commands into questions. This goal took a while to realize but I would try simplistic things like:

"Honey, what do **you want to eat** for dinner tonight, **steak** or something else?"

To conclude this section, consider three things a social engineer should focus on when studying NLP:

» **Vocal tones.** As stated previously, the tones of your voice as well as the emphasis you put on certain words can change the whole meaning of a sentence. Using tone and emphasis, you can embed commands inside of the subconscious mind of the target and allow the target to be more open to suggestion.

» **Chose your words carefully.** Learn to choose the words that have maximum impact. Match positive words with thoughts you want the target to think positively on and negative words with those you want them to not think of too highly. This technique can also help the social engineer make a target more pliable.

» **Create a list of command sentences that you can use in person or during a phone social engineering audit.** Writing out and practicing command sentences will help you be able to recall and use them when in need.

Most of all, practice. Controlling your vocal tones, the words you choose, and how you say them is not an easy task. Practice can make this become second nature.

NLP is a powerful topic, and, much like microexpressions, this section only scratched the surface. Once you start to master the techniques in NLP and the ability to read facial expressions, a next logical step is using these tools when interacting with a target. Next, this chapter analyzes the same tactics professional interrogators use.

Interview and Interrogation

Scenario 1: The door flies open and the perpetrator is noticeably nervous. Captain Bad-Mood comes over and grabs the perp by the collar and slams him up against the wall. Getting about an inch from his face he screams, "You'll tell me what I want to know, one way or another!"

Scenario 2: The bad guy is tied to a chair, already bruised from the previous 30 minutes of beatings, and as the interrogator grabs a pair of shiny pliers he says, "You'll be talking in no time...."

Scenario 3: The perp is sitting in a chair and two police officers enter the room. Calmly they walk over to the table and set a file labeled "Evidence" down on the table. Before they sit down they ask, "Do you need a coffee or a soda or something?"

Cracking open an ice-cold soda the first officer says, "Thanks for coming in today to help us out...."

Which one of the preceding scenarios is a real-life interrogation? If you guessed the third one, you're right. It is how a real interrogation often goes. The first two have been portrayed in Hollywood movies and television series so much that many of us might think they are real. Outside of wartime scenarios and nations that do not ban the use of torture, the third scenario is most likely the way most interrogations begin.

Rarely will you as a social engineer be in a situation where your target is waiting in a room for you to question him. With that in mind, you might ask, how can you use the tactics of professional interrogators and interviewers as a social engineer?

Before going further you should know the differences between an interrogation and an interview. The following table presents some of these differences, but this topic has many different angles, viewpoints, and opinions, so more could exist.

Interview	Interrogation
Subject talks, you listen.	You talk to subject about his statements.
Subject leads direction of conversation; you clarify his statements and listen, then apply NLP skills.	You lead direction. Apply NLP skills here.
Non-accusatory.	Accusatory.
Soft in nature.	Hard in nature.
Subject's location, subject at ease.	Interrogation room, subject is tense.
You gather information (who, what, when, where, why, and how).	If you reveal certain information, you can learn details.
Early in investigation.	Final questioning session.

The main difference between an interview and interrogation is that an interview is in an atmosphere where the target is comfortable both physically and psychologically, whereas in an interrogation the goal is to put some pressure on the target by creating discomfort with the location or the questions asked, with the goal of gaining a confession or some knowledge the target possesses.

Good interrogation is an art that you can master through experience. Many social engineering skills tie into to being a good interrogator. Skills like elicitation (see Chapter 3); reading people, faces, and gestures; and having insight into human behavior can all help you become a legendary interrogator.

Interviewing is a great skill to have, but as long as you can master the use of elicitation you can become great at conducting interviews.

Interrogation principles are used widely by successful social engineers. Putting a target in some psychological or physical discomfort to make gathering information from them easier is a skill most social engineers will spend a considerable time obtaining.

Professional Interrogation Tactics

Before conducting any interview or interrogation, the social engineer will need to have done thorough information gathering. You must obtain as much information about the target, the company, the situation, and details of each as possible. You must know how to approach a target and what to say, and have in mind the path you will take with the target. Be careful to observe your surroundings as well as any changes in the target during the conversation and initial approach.

One of the mistakes people new to interviewing and interrogation make is assuming every behavioral change has major meaning. A target's crossing her arms doesn't just mean a closed thought; she could also be cold, have underarm stink, or feel increased stress because of your questions.

Watch not for only one sign; watch for groups of signs. For example, a target crosses her arms, turns her head, and places her feet flat on the floor. This is a closed person; in other words, her body language indicates that she will divulge no more information or cooperate any longer—this door has been shut. A group of changes is the most important thing to watch for, so note the topic that was being discussed when the group of changes occurred.

When starting an interview or interrogation here are areas to observe for changes in the subject:

- » **Body posture:** Upright, slumped, leaning away
- » **Skin color:** Pale, red, white, changes
- » **Head position:** Upright, tilted, forward/back
- » **Eyes:** Direction, openness
- » **Hands/feet:** Movement, position, color
- » **Mouth/lips:** Position, color, turned up/down
- » **Primary sense:** Visual, aural, kinetic, feeling
- » **Voice:** Pitch, rate, changes
- » **Words:** Short, long, number of syllables, dysfunctions, pauses

Changes can indicate a question or line of questioning that needs more attention. For example, if the body posture is very relaxed when you ask, "Is Mr. CEO in? I would like to leave this information packet for his review," and then the body posture changes to a defensive posture—the torso pointing away and the eyes averting from looking at you—it may be a good indication that there is some untruth coming up and further questioning might reveal the truth on this topic.

Especially be sure to pay attention to the words a target uses. During the interview or interrogation process, pay particular attention to the subject's voice and how she answers questions. When you ask a question, how long does it take for her to answer? Blurting out answers quickly is believed to be a sign of practicing the answer. If she takes too long, maybe she was thinking up the answer. Response time depends on each person, though, because you have to determine what is "natural" for each person.

Determining what is natural in a target (that is, the *baseline*) is not a small matter in a social engineering gig and must be done very fast. Being very observant is the key to success with this skill. One method of creating a baseline involves asking questions that cause the suspect to access different parts of his brain. The interrogator asks nonthreatening questions that require simple memory and questions that require creative thinking. Then look for outward manifestation of his brain activating the memory center, such as microexpressions or body language cues.

Another area to listen for is changes in verb tense and pronoun use. These shifts from past tense to future tense show areas you might want to investigate further. Switching tense can indicate deception. When a target switches tense they may be fabricating an answer or thinking of a past statement to fabricate an answer. Further questioning can reveal the truth here also. Other areas of change you should listen to are the pitch of the voice (is it going up with stress?) and the speed of speaking.

You don't have to learn how to do all this at the same time. The more practice you get actively listening and observing people the easier it becomes for you to do it without thinking.

Professional interrogation is comprised of a number of parts. The following sections discuss each one, in the context of how it pertains to a social engineer.

Positive Confrontation

In law enforcement *positive confrontation* doesn't mean anything positive and good; on the contrary, it means the officer is telling the suspect he is the one who committed the crime; in other words, the officer is making a strong accusation. In a social engineering audit, though, you already have identified the "target" you want and now you are going to tell (maybe using the NLP tactics previously mentioned) that target that he will do what you are asking of him.

You confront the target with the objective of starting him on the path to doing what you want. For example, a social engineer may approach the receptionist and ask, "Is Mr. CEO in? I have a meeting with him." Or, to use a positive-confrontation angle, "I am here for my meeting with Mr. CEO at 11 am." Notice the second example positively states the meeting as being set, expected, and in such a way that you are sure it is happening.

Theme Development

Theme development in police interrogations is when the interrogator develops a story to postulate why the suspect may have committed a crime. Many times that story is relayed to the suspect during the interrogation. "So he insulted you and you got so mad, you grabbed the pipe and began hitting his windshield with it." While the officer is telling the story, he or his partner is watching the body language and microexpressions of the suspect to see if there are any clues that would constitute agreement.

Although social engineers can use this method, I also like to state that from a social engineering viewpoint, theme development needs to be seeing your pretext from the eyes of the target. What would a "tech support rep," "manager," or "fellow employee" look like, say, and do? How would he act?

Theme development for social engineers is when your supporting evidence that is displayed feeds directly into the theme of who you are portraying. Your approach to a target, whether on the phone or in person, often involves a pretext of some sort. The pretext, of course, supports your storyline or theme. This part of the interrogation is where you offer reasons or support for the pretext (see Chapter 4 for a refresher on pretexting).

For example, in one audit my pretext was very simple—I was just an employee who belonged. Armed with a trade publication I found in the trash, I followed a few employees through the door and past the security guard. As we approached the security guard I began a very simple conversation with one of the employees about an article in the journal. All of my actions contributed to theme development. Your goal is to give the people who would normally stop you justification for not doing their job.

The more you fit in, the less you stand out, and the easier it is for security guards and the like to justify not stopping you and letting you in.

Handling Denials and Overcoming Objections

Whether on the phone or in person, what is the plan of action if you are denied access to the place or information you are seeking? I like to call these conversation stoppers. People use them with salespeople all the time, "I'm not interested." "I don't have time right now." "I was just leaving...."

Whatever flavor of stopper targets throw out, you must have a plan to overcome it and handle the denial of access. I like to preemptively dismiss objections if I feel the situation warrants.

When I was in sales, I worked with a man named Tony who had a tactic that involved knocking on a door and introducing himself, and without pausing saying, "I know you might want to say you are not interested, but before you do, can you answer this one question: Is five minutes of your time worth $500?"

At this point, the person was much less likely say, "I'm not interested." By diminishing the possibility of denial and following up with a question, Tony was able to get the target to think about something else besides her objection.

In a social engineering engagement you can't walk up to the security guard and say, "I know you don't want to let strange people in the door but..." because it would raise way too much suspicion. Using this methodology to overcome objections is much more complex for social engineers.

You have to think about what objections might arise and organize your theme, story, dress, and person to pre-empt those objections. Yet you still have to have a good answer to give for when objections come up. You can't just run out the door or hang up the phone. A good exit strategy enables you to come back to attack later on.

An exit strategy can be as simple as, "Well, ma'am, I'm sorry you won't let me in to see Mr. Smith. I know he will be greatly disappointed because he was expecting me, but I will give him a call later and set up another appointment."

Keeping the Target's Attention

If you handled your social engineering move correctly up to this point and you are in front of the target, then the target may start to think about what would happen if she does not allow access, take the file, or do what you are asking. You need to feed off of that inherent fear and use it to continue to move the target to your goal.

A few short statements like, "Thank you for your help. I was so nervous about this interview that I obviously put the wrong date down in the calendar. I hope that Mrs. HR Manager is some place warmer than here?" Allow for a response then continue, "I want to thank you for your help. When will she be back so I can call to make another appointment?"

Presenting an Alternate Route

When you are interrogating the target in a social engineering audit, the possibility exists that your first path will not be greeted with smiles, so having a lesser but just as effective path of action ready is a good idea.

Maybe you have used all these tactics to try to get Sally, the receptionist, to let you in to see Mr. Smith. The tactics are all failing and you are being shut down. You should have an alternative path prepared, such as, "Sally, I appreciate you have to make sure things are done by appointment only. I am just not sure when I will be back through the area. Can I leave you with this CD of information for Mr. Smith and then I can follow up with a phone call tomorrow to see whether he will set up an appointment?"

Having a few CDs prepared with some maliciously encoded PDFs can help to make this path a reality, as well as having practiced and then using interrogation tactics quickly.

A contact I have sent me a document, entitled "Interview and Interrogation," that is used by the Department of Defense to train its staff in passing the polygraph. It outlines the different approaches that professional interrogators use, and I have provided them here. Looking at these different approaches one can learn a lot about different methods that might make sense for a social engineer.

» **Direct approach:** The interrogator assumes an air of confidence in this approach. The attitude and manner of the interrogator rules out that the suspect is innocent at all. Without threatening, the interrogator disarms the suspect by telling him anyone else would have done the same thing.

   As a social engineer, you can utilize this approach depending on your pretext. Maybe you are management, a consultant, or another person who has power over the target. This means you must have an air of confidence and assume that the target "owes" you the response you seek.

» **Indirect approach:** The suspect is allowed to tell his side of the story in detail and the interrogator looks for omissions, discrepancies, and distortions. The interrogator's job is to let the suspect know that the best course of action is to tell the truth.

   As a social engineer you can use this approach by not approaching the target in any role, but maybe as an elicitation, a question designed to elicit information from the target. The social engineer can gather information from the target by letting him do most of the talking.

» **Sympathetic approach:** The DOD manual offers some excellent thoughts on this approach. The interrogator drops his voice and talks in a lower, quieter tone that gives the impression he is an understanding person. He sits close to the suspect and maybe puts his hand on the suspect's shoulder or pats him on the arm. Physical contact at the right time is very effective.

   The social engineer can use this approach in the very same manner as the interrogator. Maybe you overhear some employees complaining about the boss as you are waiting to tailgate in the door. Or maybe you have followed the target to the local bar and get into a conversation where you can show empathy to a situation. You can use this approach all around, and it is very effective.

» **Emotional approach:** This approach plays on the morals or emotions of the suspect. Questions such as, "What will your wife or kids think about this?" are used in this interrogation tactic. The thoughts that are aroused emotionally upset him and make him nervous; as these emotions manifest themselves, the interrogator can capitalize on them.

You can use this approach in a similar manner to the preceding, in which you play on a weakness identified in the target. In one engagement, I knew the target was partial to charities for children who suffer from cancer. Playing on those emotions I was able to get the target to take an action he should not have taken, and it compromised his operation.

» **Logical approach:** This non-emotional approach presents strong evidence of guilt. The interrogator should sit erectly and be business-like, displaying confidence.

You can use this matter-of-fact approach when presenting evidence of your legitimate reasons for being present—for example, such as being dressed and armed as an IT repairman and having the air of confidence that you belong there.

» **Aggressive approach:** For an interrogator, a fine line exists between gathering information and infringing on the target's rights that must not be crossed. The voice should be raised, and the look and act should be aggressive, but the suspect's civil rights should never be violated.

The social engineer auditor needs to keep this fine line in mind. As in the case of Hewlett-Packard, discussed in Chapter 4, being hired to social engineer a company does not give you the right to break civil laws. Most of the time the company hiring you has no right to allow you to tap home phones, read personal e-mails, or invade people's privacy.

» **Combination approach:** One interrogator may combine two approaches to have maximum effect. This would be decided upon based on the suspect's personality.

As a social engineer you may use the same technique—combine your attacks and approaches for maximum effect. For instance, after you discover some personal details about a target—such as their favorite local bar—you can approach the target and start a conversation. Such a tactic, especially when employed in a relaxed atmosphere, can go a long way toward opening people up.

» **Indifferent approach:** This approach is very interesting because the interrogator acts as if he does not need the confession because the case is solved. At that point the interrogator may try manipulating the suspect into giving his side of the story.

  As a social engineer you may not be able to use this approach unless caught. If you're caught in an area or situation you should not be in, you can act indifferent instead of afraid that you are caught. Acting indifferent can cause the person who caught you to not be alarmed as much and afford you an opportunity to dispel any worries. Kevin Mitnick (see Chapter 8 for more on Mitnick) was great at this technique. He had the ability to think quickly on his feet. Also, acting indifferent when he was in a precarious situation allowed him to get away with a lot.

» **Face-saving approach:** The interrogator should rationalize the offense, giving the suspect a way out and an excuse to confess and save face. An interrogator should not make the excuse so good, however, that the suspect can use it in court as a defense.

  A social engineer can really utilize this approach. An interrogator does not want to give someone too good an excuse, but a social engineer does. You want the excuse to be so good the target doesn't even need to think before rationalizing it as an excuse for complying with you.

  One approach is to say a higher-level person asked you to be there. You can follow this up by saying, "I can understand how you might feel now, but I don't even want to imagine how upset Mr. Smith will be if I don't fix that massive e-mail blunder before he returns on Monday." This approach gives the target the ability to save face and comply.

» **Egotistical approach:** This approach is all about pride. For it to work you need a suspect who is very proud of an accomplishment. Bragging on good looks, intelligence, or the way the crime was performed may stroke his ego enough that he wants to confess to show that, indeed, he was that smart.

  In social engineering gigs this method is often used. Playing up someone's accomplishments gets them to spill their deepest secrets. In the case of the U.S. nuclear engineer in China (refer to Chapter 3), social engineers loaded the man with compliments, and he spilled the beans and divulged information he shouldn't have.

» **Exaggeration approach:** If an interrogator overexaggerates the case facts, the suspect may admit to what was real. One example would be if an interrogator accuses a thief of wanting to commit rape and saying, "Why else would someone break into a bedroom in the middle of the night?" This often causes the suspect to admit to only wanting to steal and not commit rape.

You can also use this approach by overexaggerating the task you are there to perform. By overexaggerating the reason for being there you can give the target a reason for providing you lesser access. For example, you can say, "I know Mr. Smith wanted me to fix his computer personally because he lost a lot of data, but if you don't feel comfortable with that, I can potentially fix his problem from another computer in the office."

» **Wedging the alibi:** A suspect seldom confesses his transgressions all at once. Getting him to make minor admissions, such as he was on the site, owned the weapon in question, or owned a similar car, can move him toward admitting more and more, eventually leading to a complete confession.

Maybe you get stopped at the door during a social engineering gig and the gatekeeper refuses you access to the building. See whether you can "gain access" by using a line like this: "I understand Mr. Smith is busy and can't meet with me. Would you mind giving him this CD of information about our products and I will follow up with a phone call later on today or tomorrow?"

It is a lesser admission, but nevertheless would get if not you, then one of your tools in the door.

The End Goal

To prepare to use proper interview or interrogation tactics, as a social engineer you may want to answer a few questions of your own. I encourage you to write these down in a notepad because doing so can help you prepare for your encounter with the target. Plus, writing down your answers makes them real and gives you a path to work on during the preparation for your interrogation.

Answer these questions:

» **Who:** With whom is the interrogation or encounter being conducted? What role does he play? List names, titles, and other information about him that is relevant to the interrogation.

» **What:** Exactly what preparation has been done and what is going to be your goal during the interrogation? You must have a definite aim.

» **When:** What is the timeframe of the interrogation? What time of day or night? What are the circumstances at the business that lead to this decision about when to make your move? Is there a party you overheard about? Is it a time when a large portion of the employees are on vacation? Is it during lunch time? Is it during the changing of the security staff?

» **Where:** What is the location of the interrogation? Are you going to be at the target's location? Are you tracking the person to his or her gym, local bar, or daycare? Where is the best place to try to obtain the information you need from the target?

» **Why:** People hear this question often enough from their kids, but it must be asked. What is the purpose of this interrogation? To make the target admit to the location of something? To make him give out information he should not? For you to gain access to a room or a server?

» **How:** What methods will you use in this interrogation? NLP? Embedded commands? Human buffer overflow (discussed at the end of this chapter)? Microexpressions?

Of course, in a criminal interrogation the goal is confession to a crime. With interrogation as a social engineer the goal is a confession of a different sort. You want people to feel comfortable giving you information, and using the interrogation tactics discussed earlier you can make that easier to do. In the end, your social engineering interrogations should be like smooth interviews. However, a social engineer can use some other techniques to help while using interview and interrogation tactics on a target.

Gesturing

Gestures have a wide variation due to the fact that they are very much culturally dependent. Unlike microexpressions, which are universal, gestures from the United States can actually be insulting in other parts of the world, or have no meaning at all.

Here is an exercise to help you better understand gesturing differences. If you want you can write down your answers to refer to in a few minutes. Depending on what culture you're from, the answers will be interesting to see.

Write down what you think this gesture means and whether it is rude in each case:

1. Holding your palm facing upward, point at someone with your index finger and beckon to him.

2. Make a "V" sign with your index and middle fingers.

3. Sit with the soles of your feet showing.

4. Make the "ok" symbol with your fingers.

5. Wave a hand with your palm facing outward.

6. Nod your head up and down.

If you wrote down your answers, compare them to some of the following interesting cultural differences:

1. In the U.S. this gesture simply means "Come here," but in the Middle or Far East, Portugal, Spain, Latin America, Japan, Indonesia, and Hong Kong, beckoning someone this way is considered rude or insulting. Beckoning someone with the palms facing down and using all the fingers to beckon is more acceptable.

2. In the U.S. this gesture is a "peace sign," but in Europe it means "victory." If you put the palm toward your face it actually means, "Shove it."

3. In the U.S. this is a comfortable way of sitting and doesn't denote any bad intent. Yet in other countries, such as Thailand, Japan, and France, as well as countries of the Middle and Near East, showing the soles of the feet demonstrates disrespect. Exposing the lowest and dirtiest part of your body is insulting.

4. In the U.S. this gesture means everything is okay. But in other parts of the world it has much different meaning. In Brazil and Germany it is an obscene gesture, in Japan it means "money," and in France it means "worthless."

5. In the U.S. this is a greeting, a way to say hello or good-bye. In Europe it can mean "no," and in Nigeria it is a serious insult.

6. In the U.S. nodding your head is a way of saying "yes." The same is true for many places, but in some areas, such as Bulgaria or Greece, it is a way of saying "no."

These are just a few examples of gestures that can have varying meanings depending on where you are or who you are talking to. Understanding the different meanings of gestures is important because communication is often much more than what is said.

This section is intended to show that, during an interaction with a target, not only can these principles be observed but they can also be utilized to manipulate the target into a path of least resistance. Understanding the culture of the targets you approach will also keep you from performing a gesture that can have undesirable results.

Anchoring

Gestures can have some powerful effects when used properly. Some of these principles come from the study of NLP but can have a lot of power when you're trying to set your target's mind on a path you control.

One such method is *anchoring*, which is a method of linking statements of a like kind with a certain gesture. For example, if you are talking to a target and he describes something positive and good, you can repeat it back while gesturing with your right hand only. If it is something bad you can gesture with your left hand only. After doing this gesture a few times you begin to "anchor" in your target's mind that right-handed gestures are linked to good things.

Salespeople use this method to further solidify that "their product" or "their service" is excellent and the competitor's is not. Some politicians use this method to anchor positive thoughts or thoughts they want their audience to think of as positive with certain gestures. Bill Clinton was a great example of someone who understood this. To see this in action (albeit not former President Clinton) visit `www.youtube .com/watch?v=c1v4n3LKDto&feature=player_embedded`.

Mirroring

Another tactic when it comes to gestures is called *mirroring*, where you try to match your gestures to the personality of the target. Of course, this is not as easy as it sounds. But what can you discern about the target from just observation? Is she timid? Is he loud and outgoing? If you approach a timid person with large, loud gestures you will surely scare her off and potentially ruin your chances of making your social engineering attempt. By the same token, if you are more timid you will need to mirror "louder" gestures when dealing with "louder" people. Mirroring not only involves mimicking a target's body language but also using gestures that make it easy for a person to listen to you.

You can take this principle to another level. Seeing gestures a target is familiar with can be comforting to him or her. However, you must strike a careful balance, because if your target has a particular gesture he seems to be using a lot and you use it exactly the same way, then you run the risk of irritating him. You want to mirror him, but not exactly. If the target ends a thought by placing his hand on his chin you can end a thought by placing your hand on another part of your face or raise a finger to tap your chin a couple times.

The following section analyzes the topic of gesturing a bit further by discussing the importance of the position and placement of a target's arms and hands.

Arm and Hand Placement

Law enforcement officers are trained to notice the placement and position of the arms and hands during both interviews and interrogations. An increase in movement or "fidgeting" during an interrogation can show an increase in stress levels, signifying that the interrogation is having the desired effect. This is, of course, in a law enforcement setting; in a social engineering setting you would watch for these same signs, but signs of stress in the target might indicate you need to back off (unless your goal is to stress him or her out).

Certain law enforcement officers are taught to pay attention to a couple of signs:

» **Elbows** generally hang free next to the body when a person is relaxed. When you feel threatened or scared your body's natural reaction is to pull the elbows in towards the rib cage. In essence this position serves as a layer of protection to one's internal organs that might be threatened.

» **Hand** gestures often can be very revealing, too. A target may describe something with his hands that he doesn't say. For example, in a crime interrogation suspects may make a gesture that describes the activity (that is, strangling, shooting, stabbing, and so on) but just say the word *crime* or *incident*. Watching for the subtle hand gestures your target may use is important.

Taking note of signs that the target is feeling threatened or scared can help you to adjust and put them back at ease. When you approach a target, much can be said with body language and arm and hand gestures before the first word is even spoken.

Other gestures to take notice of include:

» An open palm might indicate sincerity.

» Steepled fingers could indicate the person feels authoritative.

» Tapping or drumming fingers can indicate anxiety.

» Touching the face can indicate thought; touching hair can indicate insecurity; and touching ears can indicate indecisiveness.

Taking note of these gestures in your target can tell you a lot about his mindset. On the other hand, performing these gestures can help you to portray one of these images if this is your pretext.

From a social engineering standpoint here are a few key points about gestures, which can be imperative if you are a "big" gesturer like me:

» No one should remember the gesture, but only the message attached to it. If people tend to say, "Wow, that guy gestures a lot" you need to calm down a bit. The message is important, not the gesture.

» Avoid monotony. Even in gestures you can be so bland, boring, and repetitive that the gesture can adjust the target's perception of you to be negative.

» Be very concerned about exhibiting anxiety, such as tapping or drumming your fingers or making jerky movements. They tell the target you are nervous and detract from your message.

» Too much is too bad. Overgesturing can also detract from your message.

Remember that using facial expressions, gestures, and posture is a package deal. They must all blend together, be balanced, and support your pretext.

As good as all this information is, one tool in the interrogation arsenal can make or break the way you use this knowledge in your social engineering skills.

Listening Your Way to Success

Probably not one skill exists that can be as encompassing as listening. Listening is a major part of being a social engineer. What you have to realize is a major difference exists between *hearing* and *listening*.

It is commonly believed that people retain much less than 50% of what they hear. That means if you are talking to a person for ten minutes he will remember only a few minutes of what you said. Although people eke through life this way, it is not acceptable for a social engineer.

Often the little things that are said can make or break how successful you are in a social engineering endeavor. This area is where massively improving your listening skills comes in, and not just listening to what is said, but how it is said, when it is said, and with what emotion. All of these factors contribute to your perception of the information relayed.

Being a good listener might sound easy, but when you are in the heat of the moment, your end goal is to gain access to the server room, and you are listening to a story by a few employees out for a smoke break who you plan on following into the building, truly listening can be hard.

Yet it is during these times you might want to really listen. Maybe Susan starts to complain about her manager in HR, Mr. Jones. She tells a story about how short he has been with her lately and how she is fed up with it. Then her fellow smoker, Beth, says, "Well you should come over to the paradise of accounting. It is filled with jerks there, too."

Maybe this just sounds like the complaining chatter of two tired and ticked-off employees. Or is it more? You have both of their names, the name of a manager, the names of their departments, and some idea of the general demeanor of some of the employees. This information can be very valuable later on if you need to provide proof of your validity for being inside the building.

Often the way someone says something can tell you a lot about the person, but applying this will require a lot of listening. Is the person angry, sad, or happy? Did she speed up or slow down in her delivery? Did he get emotional or did his emotion trail off? Paying attention to these types of things can tell you a lot more than the words at times.

So how can you become a great listener?

The following steps can help you perfect your listening skills. These tips can assist you not only in social engineering but also in life, and when applied to a social engineering audit can make a world of difference.

1. **Pay attention.** Give your target your undue attention. Do not fiddle with your phone or other gadget. Do not drum or tap your fingers. Try to focus intently on what is being said, looking at the person speaking. Do this in a very inquisitive way, not in a scary, "I want to stalk you" way.

   Try hard not to think ahead and plan your next response. If you are planning your next response or rebuttal you will not be focused, and you may miss something important or give the target the impression you don't really care. This can be very hard to control, so perfecting this tendency will take some serious work for most people.

   Also try to not be distracted by environmental factors. Noise in the background or a small group laughing about something can shift your focus; do not allow that to happen.

   Finally, pay close attention to what the speaker is *not* saying, too. The body language, facial cues, and other aspects of communication should be "listened" to intently.

2. **Provide proof that you are listening.** Be open and inviting with your body language and facial expressions. Nod once in a while, not too often, but often enough to let the target know you are there. You don't want to look like a bobble head doll, but you want to let the target know you are "with him."

    Don't forget the all-important smile. Smiling can tell the target you are with him mentally and you understand what he's saying. As with paying attention mentioned earlier, add small smiles when appropriate. If the person is telling you her dog just died, nodding and smiling will most likely get you nowhere.

3. **Provide valuable feedback.** Letting your personal beliefs and experiences filter the message coming your way is all too common. If you do that you may not truly "hear" what the speaker is saying.

    Be sure to ask relevant questions. If she is telling you about the blue sky then you say, "So how blue was the sky?" will not be effective. Your questions must show you have been actively listening and have the desire to gain a deeper understanding.

    Every now and then mirroring or summarizing what you have heard can work well, too. Don't recite the conversation like a book report, but recapping some of the main thoughts can help the target see you are in tune with the message.

4. **Do not interrupt.** Not much more needs to be said on this tip. Interrupting your target shows a lack of concern for his feelings and stops the flow of thoughts. Letting him finish and then speaking is better.

    However, circumstances do exist where interrupting can be useful or even a tactic. If you want to see an example, watch the movie *Sneakers*. When Robert Redford is trying to gain access to a locked door that he must be buzzed into, he interrupts the doorman in a heated dispute over some delivery items. He does so a few times, eventually frustrating the doorman and causing him to unlock the door with no authorization. If you think it will get you somewhere, interrupting might be a good idea. Most of the time however, it is not.

5. **Respond appropriately.** This is the pinnacle of good or bad listening skills. If you were focused on your rebuttal or next statement, or you were thinking about the very attractive blonde that just walked by, you might put your foot in your mouth.

I was once training a group of people and was telling them some aspects of very detailed manipulation tactics. I could tell two guys were not listening. I put in a random thought like, "So then you bake the lion at 350 degrees for 15 minutes til crispy." The rest of the group broke out in laughter and I turned to one of the two and said, "What do you think, John?" He responded with a blank stare and a stuttered, "Um, yah, sounds perfect."

Do not ever do that to a target. It is a death blow to rapport (discussed later in this chapter). Be respectful, keep your emotions in check, and respond appropriately at all times when conversing with a target.

Paying attention, providing proof, giving positive feedback, being careful to never interrupt, and responding appropriately can make or break you when it comes to listening. They especially come into play during extended social engineering engagements, such as when I had to interact with the gentlemen at the Chamber of Commerce social gathering by "meeting" him at the bar and then talking to him about his business. Much of the information I was seeking would have been divulged in normal, mundane conversation. Make sure you practice these tips at home or the office before the time comes for the conversation to take place. You want good listening to become second nature as part of your arsenal of talents, not something you have to think about.

Your own emotions are another aspect of listening you must take into account. For example, I was raised in a strict, religious Italian family. I was taught that you didn't disrespect women, and I shudder to tell you of the one time I called my mom a disparaging name. I will tell you that it did not end too well for me. One day many years after that incident, I was working an engagement and was talking with a guy from whom I was trying to obtain some information. I approached him in a social setting and we started a conversation. He started to talk about a woman he worked with, in a very inappropriate way. Being raised the way I was, I found a lot of anger boiling up inside me. I had a hard time containing those feelings and it must have shown on my face and in my body language, leading to that particular vector being blown. In that failure I learned a very valuable lesson—when it comes to listening during social engineering engagements, you must try your hardest to not let the built-in filters you have get in the way.

Also, remember to react to the message, not the person. If you don't agree with a person's beliefs or stance, affording him or her dignity will go a long way in making that person feel comfortable with you. Even in situations where you might not agree you can find something empathic to say. For example:

Target: "This job stinks. They make me work this horrible shift and for low pay, too."

SE: "It sounds to me like you are overwhelmed by your situation here."

Although you might be thinking "Try Harder,"™ by responding this way you let the target know you were listening, as well as empathizing with her plight in life.

This technique is known as *reflective responding*. Reflective responding has some basic principles to it:

» Listen actively, as described earlier.

» When it's time to respond, be aware of your emotions. Knowing what you feel as the target is speaking can help you to react properly.

» Repeat the content, not like a parrot, but in your words.

» Start your response with a non-committal phrase such as, "It sounds like," "It seems like," or "It appears that." These phrases ease the message you are trying to deliver. If you need proof of this, the next time you get into an argument with your mate, boss, parents, or whomever say, "You are mad at me because…" and compare the person's reaction with what you get when you say "It appears you are mad because of…" instead. You will see which one is taken better.

Reflective responding used with active listening is a very deadly force in the trust and rapport-building skills arena.

As you learn to listen better and it becomes part of your nature you will enhance your ability to react to the message you hear. A social engineer's goal is to gather information, gain access to someplace or something you should not have access to, or cause the target to take an action he should not take. Thinking that you must be perfect at manipulation often stops people from learning and practicing great listening skills, but this is the exact reason you need to be a great listener.

Consider these two scenarios:

» One of your neighbors comes over and asks whether you have time to help him with a project in his garage for about an hour. This neighbor has a dog that has gotten into your garbage a few times and tends to like to use your yard as a bathroom. You are just about to sit down to relax at the end of a long day and watch some TV or read a book.

» Your childhood friend comes over and tells you that he needs some help moving some furniture. He just got a place about five miles from you and he can't get the couch up the stairs. You are just about to sit down to relax a bit.

For which scenario are you more likely to put aside relaxing? Most people will put aside relaxing for the second scenario, but will come up with an excuse or reason to not help out in the first scenario or at least try to postpone it to another day when they are not "busy."

Why? People are very open and free with friends. When you feel comfortable with someone, you have no boundaries and will put aside your own wants and needs at times to help them out. One naturally trusts the message coming from a friend, whereas with the stranger one might start to double-guess what's being said, trying to determine whether it is truthful or not. In the case of the relationship with the friend, this connection is called *rapport*.

For years rapport has only been talked about when it comes to salespeople, negotiators, and the like. Rapport isn't just for salespeople; it is a tool that anyone can use, especially the social engineer. If you are wondering how to build rapport instantly, then read on.

Building Instant Rapport

My former coworker, Tony, used to say that building rapport was more important than breathing. I don't really believe that to be true, but it does have a ring of truth in that rapport building is vital.

Wikipedia defines rapport as, "One of the most important features or characteristics of unconscious human interaction. It is commonality of perspective: being 'in sync' with, or being 'on the same wavelength' as the person with whom you are talking."

Why is rapport discussed in this chapter? It is a key element in developing a relationship with any person. Without rapport you are at an impasse. Within the psychological principles behind social engineering, rapport is one of the pillars.

Before getting into the aspects of how to use rapport as a social engineer you must know how to build rapport. Building rapport is an important tool in a social engineer's arsenal.

Imagine that you could make people you meet want to talk to you, want to tell you their life story, and want to confide in you. Have you ever met someone like that, someone you met recently but feel totally at ease telling him or her very personal things? Many psychological reasons may play into why that may be the case, but the case may be that you and that person just had good rapport.

The following sections outline important points about building rapport and how to use rapport in social engineering.

Be Genuine about Wanting to Get to Know People

How important are people to you? Do you enjoy meeting new people? It is a mindset about life, not something that can be taught. The prerequisite to building rapport is liking people. People can see through a fake interest.

To be a good social engineer and to be able to use rapport, people need to be important to you. You must like people and enjoy interacting with them. You have to want to learn about people. People can see through fake smiles and fake interest. Developing a genuine interest in your target can go a long way toward building rapport.

Take Care with Your Appearance

You cannot change some things that may affect your interaction with others. Unfortunately, people can still hold your skin color, gender, or age against you before you facilitate any interaction. You can't control those things, but you can control aspects of your appearance such as clothing, body odor, and cleanliness, as well as your eye contact, body movements, and facial expressions. I read a statement once that I have seen proven true too many times to ignore: "If a person is not comfortable with himself, others will not be comfortable with him either."

Be aware of your pretext and your target. If your pretext is the janitor, make sure your demeanor, dress, attitude, and words reflect someone in that position. If your pretext is a manager of a business, then make sure you act and dress appropriately. This takes research but nothing kills rapport easier than not looking the part. Your goal in some instances is to keep people in the autopilot mode that will let them not question you. Having your dress, grooming, or demeanor out of place removes the target from autopilot and hurts your chances at success.

Be a Good Listener

See the earlier section for more details. The importance of good listening can't be overstated.

Whether you are trying to make a friend or make a social engineering move, listening is a skill you need to master.

Be Aware of How You Affect People

One time I saw an older woman drop an item as she left a grocery store. I picked it up and followed her out to the parking lot. By the time I caught up with her she had her trunk open and was loading groceries into her car. I came up behind this short, little elderly woman and with all 6' 3" of me looming over her said, "Excuse me, ma'am." I was obviously too close for her comfort and when she turned around she screamed out, "Help! He's trying to mug me. Help!"

I obviously needed to think about how my presence might affect this woman during my interaction with her. I should have realized that an elderly woman all alone in a parking lot who was not expecting a huge man to walk up behind her might freak out. I should have come around and approached her from a different angle.

Be aware of how your appearance and other personal aspects might affect those you will be in contact with. Do you need a breath mint? Make sure no food is on your face or in your teeth. Try to be relatively sure that nothing is glaring in your personal appearance that will turn the person off.

UCLA Professor of Psychology Albert Mehrabian is known for the 7-38-55 Rule, which states that statistics show that only 7% of normal communication is the words we say, whereas much more lies in the body language and vocal tones. Try to be aware of yourself, but also pay attention to the first few seconds of interaction with a person. His or her reaction to your approach can tell you whether you possibly missed something, or whether you need to change something to be more effective.

As a social engineer, be aware of how you affect people. If your end goal is all that is on your mind you will affect the people you come into contact with negatively. Think about how your appearance, words, and body language may affect your target. You want to appear open and inviting.

Keep the Conversation off Yourself

We all love to talk about ourselves and even more so if we feel we have a great story or account to share—it is human nature. Talking about yourself is one way to kill rapport. Let the other person talk about himself until he gets tired of it; you will be deemed an "amazing friend," a "perfect husband," "great listener," "perfect sales guy," or whatever other title you are seeking. People feel good when they can talk about themselves; I guess we are all a little narcissistic, but by letting the other person do the talking you will leave that interaction with his liking you a lot more.

Keep the conversation off yourself. This point is especially cogent for social engineers. You have a definite goal in mind and sometimes your judgment and direction can be clouded by what "you" want. Taking that focus off of the target is dangerous as far as success goes. Let targets talk about their jobs, roles, and projects, and be amazed at how much information they release.

Remember That Empathy Is Key to Rapport

Empathy—defined by *Random House Dictionary* as "the intellectual identification with or vicarious experiencing of the feelings, thoughts, or attitudes of another"— is lacking in many people today and is especially hard to feel if you think you have the solution to someone's problem. However, really listening to what someone is saying, trying to identify and understand the underlying emotions, and then using reflection skills can make a person feel as if you are really in tune with him.

I felt it necessary to provide the definition of empathy because understanding what it is you have to do is important. Notice that you must "intellectually identify" with and then experience "the feelings, thoughts, or attitudes" of someone else.

These aren't always serious, depressing, or extreme emotions. Even understanding why someone is irritated, tired, or not in the best mood can go a long way. Imagine you go to the bank drive through and the teller lady gives you a monster attitude because you forgot to sign your check and she now has to send it back. You also forgot a pen and need to ask her for yet another favor. Your reaction might be similar to mine, especially if she gave you the eye roll and the irritated glance—you want to tell her that she is here to serve you. Instead, try saying this, "It appears you might be a little irritated. I understand that; I get irritated when I have to deal with my forgetful clients, too. I hate to ask this, but could I please get a pen?"

It's important to not be patronizing when attempting to show empathy. If your empathy seems to come off haughty or arrogant, you can make the target feel like you are patronizing them.

You acknowledged her being upset but without accusation, showed that you have the same feelings, and then made a request. Empathy can go a long way toward building rapport; one caveat is that rapport cannot be faked. People need to feel you are genuinely concerned to build that trust relationship. If you are not a natural at displaying empathy, then practice. Practice with your family, friends, coworkers, teachers, or classmates. However and wherever you do it, practicing being empathetic will greatly improve your relationship-building skills.

Empathy is a tool of the social engineer. Unfortunately, it is also used often in malicious social engineering. When a catastrophe hits somewhere in the world a malicious social engineer is often there to "empathize" with you. The thing that probably makes this tool so easy for malicious social engineers to use in many cases is because they truly are from bad, poor, or impoverished places. Being in bad straits themselves makes appearing empathetic to others' plights in life easy and therefore creates rapport automatically.

Nothing builds rapport more when people feel like you "get them." This is proven very true when someone is a victim of disaster. It's a scary thought, but those who have been victims of abuse, crime, rape, natural disasters, war, or other atrocities on earth often can "understand" the feelings of those who are experiencing them. This opens victims up to trusting the wrong type of people if that rapport is built.

As mentioned before, when the 9/11 attacks happened in New York City, many people claimed to have lost family or friends in terrorist attacks. That made people empathize and therefore these "victims" were given money, fame, or whatever they were seeking.

As a social engineering auditor, you must be able to have a broad range of emotions that you can tap. Being closed in your emotions makes being empathetic very hard. This point goes along with really liking people. If you do, you won't have a hard time getting to know them and their stories and empathizing with them.

Be Well Rounded in Your General Knowledge

Knowledge is power. You don't have to know everything about everything, but having some knowledge about some things is a good idea. It makes you interesting and gives you something to base a conversation on.

Knowledge is power. The old hacker mantra comes back to you as a social engineer. A social engineer should be a reader and a studier. If you fill your head with knowledge then you will have something to talk about when you approach a target. Don't neglect reading, researching, and studying about the topic of the target's occupation or hobbies. Your goal is not to be a "know-it-all" and become an expert on every topic, but rather to have enough knowledge that you don't look at the target with a blank stare when she asks, "Did you bring an RJ-45 connector with you to fix the server's network connection issues?"

Develop Your Curious Side

People normally feel a little self-righteous when it comes to their beliefs or thoughts on the way things should be done. That self-righteousness or judgmental attitude can change the way a person reacts to something being said. Even if you don't say anything you may start to think it, which can show in your body language or facial expressions. Instead of being self-righteous, develop a curiosity about how other people think and do things. Being curious keeps you from making rash judgments. This can be applied by being humble enough to ask for help or ask for more information. Be open minded enough to look into and accept another's thoughts on a topic, even if those thoughts differ from yours.

Curiosity did not kill the social engineer. This point doesn't change much from a non–social engineer perspective. When you become curious about others' lifestyles, cultures, and languages you begin to understand what makes people tick. Being curious also keeps you from being rigid and unbending in your personal judgments. You may not personally agree with certain topics, beliefs, or actions but if you can remain curious and nonjudgmental then you can approach a person by trying to understand why he is, acts, or portrays a certain way, instead of judging him.

Find Ways to Meet People's Needs

This point is the pinnacle of the list and is one of the most powerful points in this book. Dr. William Glasser wrote a book called *Choice Theory* in which he identified four fundamental psychological needs for humans:

- » Belonging/connecting/love
- » Power/significance/competence
- » Freedom/responsibility
- » Fun/learning

The principle behind this point is that creating ways for people to get these needs met by conversing with you builds instant rapport. If you can create an environment to provide those needs for people, you can create bonds that are unbreakable.

Let me tell you a brief story about how powerful meeting people's needs can be. I was in a minor car accident. A young driver pulled out in front of me and then decided to stop. I had a split second to decide between hitting him going 55 mph or veering off away from him then launching my car over a small ditch into the side of a mountain. I chose in a second to not kill the three young people in the car. My car went airborne until it was stopped by solid rock. I watched my beautiful little customized Jetta crumple under the weight, and my face smacked off the windshield. I barely nicked the other driver's rear bumper but I was moving fast enough that his car was sideways in the highway. When I was able to get my bearings we called the cops and an ambulance.

The young man had a different insurance company than I did. The next morning I got a call from my agent, who politely asked me questions. He told me that an adjuster would come out to see my now-crumpled Jetta, and within 48 hours I was handed a check and a letter stating they would cover all medical costs for my recovery.

I was then given a follow-up call from *his* insurance agent to see whether I was okay. How many calls from my insurance company do you think I got? I got one, just to tell me how to answer questions.

I understand that caring about each person is not the job of these large companies. But the other agent called me just see whether I was okay. I fought no battles to get paid and I was given a very fair price for my car.

Two days after that I cancelled my insurance and went to see Eric, the insurance agent who called me, from the young man's company. I told him I was so impressed that I wanted what he was selling. It has been 12 years now and I use Eric for every insurance need I have. About two years ago I got a call from an insurance company offering me rates that were substantially lower than what Eric and his company offer. I couldn't even think about doing that to Eric. Why? Rapport—plain and simple. Eric is my friend, my helper, someone I can call about questions on insurance, and someone who will always give me the best advice. He cares, he knows my family, and he never tries to hard-sell me. He doesn't have to, because I will buy whatever he has, because I trust him.

This is the power of rapport. I don't know, maybe Eric's end game in checking on me was to get me to move to his insurance practice, although I doubt it. Knowing him, he actually cares and anyone who knows him says the same thing. His brother and he run a solid business. Rapport can create bonds between people that transcend cost or loss.

Filling a need for the person you are talking to drastically increases the chances of building rapport. Do it without appearing to have an end game, do it with a genuine desire to help, and be amazed at the results. Perhaps no other avenue is more valuable for social engineers than being able to meet these needs. Learning how to create an environment that allows the target to feel comfortable and get one of the basic four fundamental needs met is a sure way to ensure unbreakable rapport.

Spies use this principle of filling a need or desire often. In a recent trip to a South American country I was told that its government is infiltrated all the time via fulfilling the basic need of "connecting or love." A beautiful woman will be sent to seduce a man, but this is no one-night stand. She will seduce him for days, weeks, months, or even years. As time continues she will get bolder with her requests for where they are intimate, eventually making their way to his office, where she gains access to plant bugs, Trojans, or clone drives. This method is devastating, but it works.

Social engineers fill desires through phishing emails also. In one test 125 employees of a very reputable company were sent fake image files labeled BritneyNaked.jpg, MileyCyrusShowering.jpg, and other such names, and each image was encoded with malicious code that would give the social engineer access on the user's computer. The results were that more than 75 percent of the images were clicked. What was found was the younger the star mentioned in the picture, the higher the click ratio.

These disgusting and devastating facts show how well fulfilling people's desires can work. In person, too, it is no different. Police interrogators use this tactic for building rapport all the time.

One time I interviewed a law enforcement agent for a podcast I did at social-engineer.org (`www.social-engineer.org/framework/Podcast/001_-_Interrogation_and_Interview_Tactics`). The guest told a story that proves this point about the power of rapport to make people comply with requests. The officers had arrested a man who was a peeping tom. He had a fetish where he loved to invade the privacy of women who wore pink cowboy boots. The agent, instead of judging him for the freak he is, used phrases like, "I like the red ones myself," and "I saw this girl the other day wearing short shorts and high cowboy boots, wow!"

After just a short time he began to relax. Why? He was among like-minded people. He felt connected, part of the crowd. Their comments put him at ease and he began to spill his guts about his "habits."

The preceding is a nice example of how to develop and build rapport, but how can you use it as a social engineer?

You can build rapport in a matter of seconds by applying the principles of building rapport discussed earlier. To prove this, imagine you need to grab some cash, you don't have your ATM card on you, and you forgot your account number, so you have to go in and ask someone for some help. Maybe you feel a little embarrassed about having to ask for your account number. You walk into a local branch of your bank you have never been into. No one is in the bank and you have your choice of tellers. Maybe you don't think about it, most people don't, but you will look over all the open lanes and choose the person who makes you feel the most comfortable. You will get the same results from each lane, but you will choose the one that makes you feel okay.

Maybe you choose the most attractive person, or the one with the biggest smile, or the one who greets you first—whomever you choose and however you choose them you make the choice either consciously or unconsciously, but a lot of it has to do with rapport. The same principle will prove true when it comes to you and your target. As you walk up to a target she will make instantaneous snap judgments of you based on your personal appearance, demeanor, facial expressions, and, of course, her mood. Most of these factors you can control, so take pre-emptive action on them to ensure success.

Building rapport properly creates a bond like strong glue that can withstand minor inconvenience and even some misunderstanding.

Rapport allows a person to say and do things that only close friends can do, because he or she is brought into that inner circle of trust. It is a powerful force without which salespeople, friendships, employment, and many other situations are much more difficult.

Remember Chapter 4 on pretexting? You learned that pretexting is more than just playing a part, it is living, being, and becoming the person you are portraying to the target. Having a strong pretext is imperative to building the right kind of rapport. In many social engineering engagements you will not have the time to build a storyline and use long-term seduction or rapport techniques, so your success will be based on many of the non-verbal things you will need to do.

Using Other Rapport-Building Techniques

Other rapport-building techniques exist that are based in NLP research. As you now know, rapport is basically connecting with someone and putting him or her at ease; some NLP techniques used by hypnotists and NLP practitioners can put people at ease instantly, as discussed next.

Breathing at the Same Rate as Your Target

Breathing at the same rate as someone doesn't mean you closely listen to every breath and try to breathe in and out when your target does. But some people have very defined breathing patterns: Some have fast and short breathing, and some have long and deep breathing. Notice how the target breathes and mirror that pattern, but without parroting (that is, doing it at the same exact time).

Matching Your Target's Vocal Tone and Speech Pattern

I was born in New York and raised in an Italian family. I talk fast, loud, and with my hands. In addition to being 75 percent Italian, I am 25 percent Hungarian. I am big, tall, and loud and gesture like a professional sign language translator on speed. If I approach a timid, shy, slow-talking southerner I can kill rapport if I do not slow down, put the hands away, and change my communication style. Listen to your target's vocal tone and match yours to his, whether he is a slow, fast, loud, quiet, or soft speaker. As for accents, a good rule is: Don't try. Unless you can do it very well don't even attempt it. A poorly done accent is a rapport killer.

Along these same lines, you can also try to listen for *key phrases.* People use terms like "okie dokie" or "yepper." Listen for any key phrases, and even if they are out there, you might be able to work them into a sentence.

Once I was talking with a target who would say things like, "It's six of one and half dozen of another." I don't use that phrase a lot and didn't want to screw it up, because that would create a lack of rapport. Instead, I would mix in some of the key words of that phrase and say things like, "I must have done that a *half dozen* times."

How someone talks is also an area where you should restrict your personal judgments. Some people are close talkers, some are whisperers, some are touchers—if you are not, you need to allow a person freedom to talk the way he or she is comfortable and then mirror it.

Matching Your Target's Body Language

Matching body language is a very interesting avenue of rapport building mainly because it can work to create very strong bonds but at the same time it can kill all your rapport in a matter of seconds in the case of a mismatch.

If you notice someone standing a certain way, maybe with both arms crossed, don't assume she is shutting you out—maybe she's just cold. Can you cross one arm across your body to mirror her stance, or fold your hands into a steeple?

When sitting across from someone who is eating a meal you can take a few sips from your drink while he eats to mirror him. Don't do everything he does, but make similar actions.

People like people who are like themselves. That is just human nature. It makes them feel comfortable. Bill Philips was the genius behind the Body-*for*-Life program that changed the way workout programs were developed. He promoted something that was heavily tied to the mirroring principle. If you are fat and you only hang out with fat people, the chance of your changing is slim to none. Why? The answer is that you are comfortable with being fat and with people who are also comfortable with it. If you want to change, then hang out with skinny people and a mental change will quickly happen.

This principle is the same in social engineering. You don't want your targets to make a change, so you need to be like them. You want them to feel good with you.

Testing Rapport

Using these alternative rapport-building techniques as well as matching energy levels, facial expressions, and the like can build strong rapport on a subliminal level.

After trying some of these tactics you can test your rapport by making a movement, like scratching your head or rubbing your ear, and if in the next minute or two you see your target make a similar movement you probably have developed some strong rapport.

These techniques can work wonders in many parts of your life when developing, building, and starting relationships with others. Learning how to use the psychological principles included in this chapter can make a huge difference in your social engineering practice.

For years, there has been a myth that the human mind can be overwritten like a program. Is it just a myth? Can the human mind be mastered?

The next section reveals some of the most mind-blowing information in this book.

The Human Buffer Overflow

A glass can only hold so much liquid. If you have an 8-ounce glass and you try to pour 10 ounces of liquid into it, what will happen? It will overflow and spill all over the place. If you try to force the container to hold more liquid than it is meant to you can eventually break the glass due to pressure.

Computer programs work in a similar manner. Imagine you have a small program that has only one purpose and two fields: User Name and Password.

When the program opens you see a little screen where you type in *admin* in the User Name field and *password* in the Password field. A little box appears that says "OK," signifying all is good.

The developer allocated a certain amount of memory space for the User Name field, enough to hold the word *admin* a couple times. What happens if you put 20 A's in that field and click OK?

The program crashes and gives you an error message. Why? The input entered is longer than the allocated space and without proper error handling the program throws an exception and crashes.

The goal of software hackers is to find the address that the program will call upon in a crash and insert malicious code into that address. By controlling the execution flow the hacker can tell the program to "execute" any program he desires. He can inject commands of any type into the memory space of that program because he now controls it. As a penetration tester few things are more exciting than seeing a program execute commands you tell it to.

The human mind runs "software" and over the years you build instruction sets, buffers, and memory lengths into your "software package."

Before applying this to the human mind, definitions of a few technical terms are necessary. A *buffer* is an area of space that is given for something to happen or to hold data. As in the simplistic glass-of-water example, the password field is given a buffer, which is the number of characters that it is allowed to have. If a larger number than the buffer is entered the programmer needs to tell the program to do something with the larger than necessary data set.

If he doesn't, the computer crashes and your program shuts down. Often what happens in the background is the program didn't know what to do with all the data so it overflowed the allocated space, crashed the program, and exited. Hence the term buffer overflow.

The human mind works in a similar way. Space is allocated for certain datasets. If a certain dataset does not fit the space we have for it, what happens? Unlike a computer, your brain doesn't crash, but it does open up a momentary gap that allows for a command to be injected so the brain can be told what to do with the extra data.

A human buffer overflow is basically the same principle. The goal is to identify a running "program" and insert codes into that program that will allow you to inject commands and in essence control the movement of thought to a certain direction.

To test this concept, take a look at a very simplistic example (see Figure 5-15).

Because the picture in this book is black and white, I have put a color copy up on the website at www.social-engineer.org/resources/book/HumanBufferOverflow1.jpg.

Here is the gist. Open that URL, and then as fast as you can try to read the *color* of the word, not what the word spells.

Figure 5-15 Human buffer overflow experiment 1.

This game is not as easy as it looks. If you successfully get through it, then try to do the exercise faster and faster. What will happen to most, if not all, of us, is that at least once you will read the word and not the color, or find yourself struggling through it.

Why do we have such a hard time with this exercise? It is because of injected commands. Our brains want to read the words not the colors. It is the way the human mind is wired. Our brain sees the color but it reacts to the word being spelled first. Therefore, the thought in our minds is the *word* not the color. This exercise shows that having "code" execute in the human brain that might be the opposite of what the person is thinking or seeing is possible.

Setting the Ground Rules

In a paper entitled "Modification of Audible and Visual Speech" (`www.prometheus-inc.com/asi/multimedia1998/papers/covell.pdf`) researchers Michele Covell, Malcolm Slaney, Cristoph Bregler, and Margaret Withgott state that scientists have proven that people speak 150 words per minute but think at 500–600 words per minute. This means that most people you talk to can jump around your conversations in their heads. So overflowing the brain through fast speech seems almost impossible.

You must also understand how people make decisions in life. People make most of their decisions subconsciously, including how to drive to work, get coffee, brush their teeth, and what clothes to wear without really thinking about it.

Have you ever driven all the way to work and when you get there, you can't remember what billboards you passed, what route you took or that traffic accident on the news? You were in a state of mind where your subconscious took over and did what you always do without you consciously thinking about every turn.

Most decisions people make are like this. Some scientists even believe people make decisions up to seven seconds earlier in their subconscious before making them in the real world. When people finally do make a decision consciously they do it from more than just what they hear—sight, feelings, and emotions become involved in the decision.

Understanding how humans work and think can be the quickest way to creating a buffer overflow, or an overflow of the natural programs of the human mind so you can inject commands.

Fuzzing the Human OS

In actual software hacking, a method called *fuzzing* is used to find errors that can be overwritten and give control to a malicious hacker. *Fuzzing* is where the hacker throws random data at the program in differing lengths to see what makes it crash, because it cannot handle the data. That gives the hacker a path to inject malicious code.

Just like fuzzing a program, you must understand how the human mind reacts to certain types of data. Presenting people with different sets of decisions or different sets of data, then seeing how they react can tell us the "programs" they are running. Certain laws in the human mind seem to be inherent that everyone follows.

For example, if you approach a building with two sets of doors (one outer and one inner) and you hold the first set open for a complete stranger, what do you think he will do next? He will either hold the next set open for you or make sure that set stays open until you get inside.

If you are in a line of merging traffic and you let a complete stranger merge in front of you, most likely if you needed to merge later on he would let you in without even thinking. Why?

The reason has to do with the *law of expectations*, which states that people usually comply with an expectation. Decisions are usually made based on what that person feels the requestor expects him or her to do. One way you can start sending your malicious "data" to the brain program is called *presupposition*.

By giving the target something first, the request you make next will be "expected" to be followed. A simple example for you to test is with the doors. Hold a door for someone and most likely that person will at least make an attempt to ensure the next set of doors is open for you. A social engineer can do this by first giving the target a compliment or a piece of information they deem valuable, before the request is made. Giving that over first creates in them the need to comply with a future request as it is expected.

Presupposition can be described best via an example:

"Did you know my next door neighbor, Ralph, always drives a green Ford Escort?"

In this sentence you presuppose:

» I know my neighbor.

» His name is Ralph.

» He has a driver's license.

» He drives a green car.

To use presupposition effectively you ask a question using words, body language, and a facial expression that indicates what you are asking is already accepted. The basic gist of this method is to bypass the "firewall" (the conscious mind) and gain access directly to the "root of the system" (the subconscious). The quickest way to inject your own "code" is through embedded commands, discussed next.

The Rules of Embedded Commands

Some basic principles of embedded commands make them work:

» Usually the commands are short: three to four words.

» Slight emphasis is needed to make them effective.

» Hiding them in normal sentences is the most effective use.

» Your facial and body language must support the commands.

Embedded commands are popular in marketing with things like:

» "Buy now!"

» "Act now!"

» "Follow me!"

In a real buffer overflow, exploit writers use padding, which is a method of adding some characters that do not interrupt the execution but allow a nice little "landing pad" that leads to the malicious code. Social engineers can utilize phrases that are like padding, to help the next command have a soft place to land when it is injected, such as:

» "When you..."

» "How do you feel when you..."

» "A person can..."

» "As you..."

All of these statements create an emotion or a thought that allows you to inject code into the subconscious.

Many examples of embedded commands exist, but here are a few to ponder:

» **Using quotes or stories:** The brain tends to process stories differently than other information. Some of the greatest teachers who have ever lived—Aristotle, Plato, Gamaliel, Jesus—all used stories and illustrations to teach those listening to them. Why?

The unconscious mind processes stories as direct instructions. Bandler, one of the fathers of NLP, taught that NLP practioners need to learn to use quotes. He knew the power of stories or quotes would give the speaker power over the thinking of his listeners. Reading quotes, using quotes, and then embedding commands into quotes can be a powerful use of this technique.

For example, in one situation I needed to manipulate a target to give me an old password so I could "change" it to a more secure password. My pretext was a support rep and they automatically questioned why there was a need to change old passwords. I used something like, "A recent study by Xavier Research Inc. stated that 74% of the people use weak passwords in corporate America. That is the reason we launched a program to change the passwords corporate-wide. I will perform that password change for you; I need for you to give me your old Windows password and then I will make that change now." By quoting a research facility it added weight to my words about why this change had to occur.

»   **Using negation:** Negation is much like reverse psychology. By telling the target to not do something too much, you can embed a command into the sentence. For example, if I tell you "Don't spend too much time practicing the use of embedded commands," I can slip the command "practice the use of embedded commands" into my sentence. I also can presuppose that you *will* practice it to some extent, and if you are stubborn you might say, "You can't tell me what to do, I will practice all I want."

Telling a person that something is not important or relevant makes his unconscious pay extra attention so he can determine whether it is relevant or not. You can embed commands in negative sentences like the earlier example that will leave the listener no option but to take action.

»   **Forcing the listener to use his imagination:** This method works when you ask the listener a question, using phrases such as "What happens…" or "How do you feel when…," for which he must imagine something to answer it. If you ask, "What happens when you become rich and famous?" The listener has to internally imagine the time he might be rich and famous to answer that question. If I ask you, "What happens when you master the use of embedded commands?" I am forcing you to imagine becoming a master and how you will feel when that happens. Think of it this way: If I tell you, "Do not imagine a red cow," you have to picture a red cow first to tell yourself to not think about it. Your unconscious mind is responsible for interpreting each word in a set of commands into something it can represent and then give meaning to.

By the time your brain has understood the sentence, your unconscious has imagined it. The unconscious mind processes statements directly, with no regard to the context. The other great part is that the unconscious can track body language, facial expressions, voice tones, and gestures, and then connect each of them to the message being spoken. While it is connecting the dots, so to speak, the unconscious mind has little option but to comply if an embedded command exists.

What's important when using embedded commands is to not mess up your tones. If you overemphasize the words then you will sound odd and scare the person off instead of embed commands. As with a software buffer overflow, the information must match the command you are trying to overflow.

Summary

As you probably have already imagined, embedding commands is a vast field with a lot of room for error. You must practice to be very successful at it. Although I do not promote using this information for seduction some decent videos exist about seduction that show how embedded commands can work.

Using these principles can create an environment where the target is very receptive to your suggestions.

Just because you tell the person, "You will purchase from me" does not mean he always will. So why use these commands?

It creates a platform to make social engineering easier. Using these types of commands is also a good lesson for companies you work with to educate them about what to look for and how to spot someone who may be trying to use this type of social engineering tactic against them.

If you were to write out this principle of embedded commands as an equation, you could write it this way:

Human Buffer Overflow = Law of Expectations + Mental Padding + Embedded Codes.

Start a conversation with a target using phrases, body language, and assumptive speech. Presume the things you ask for are already as good as accomplished.

Next, pad the human mind with some statements that make embedding commands easier, while at the same time embedding the command. In essence this is the equation for the human buffer overflow. Use this equation sparingly, but practice *a lot* before you attempt it. Try it at work or home. Pick a target at work that might not normally comply with simple requests and try to see whether you can get him to serve you coffee: "Tom, I see you are heading to the kitchen, will you get me a cup of coffee with two creams please?"

Escalate your commands to larger tasks to see how far you can get. Try to use this equation to get commitment from people. Eventually use this equation to see how much information you can get and how many commands you can inject.

This chapter covered some of the deepest and most amazing psychology principles in social engineering. This chapter alone can change your life, as well as your ability as a social engineer. Understanding how people think, why they think a certain way, and how to change their thoughts is a powerful aspect to being a social engineer. Next on the docket: how to influence your target.

6

Influence: The Power of Persuasion

If you would persuade, you must appeal to interest rather than intellect.

—BENJAMIN FRANKLIN

The epigraph sums up this entire chapter. You might be wondering why I didn't include this within Chapter 5's discussion of psychological principles of social engineering. Psychology is a science and a set of rules exists in it that, if followed, will yield a result. Social engineering psychology is scientific and calculated.

Influence and persuasion are much like art that is backed up by science. Persuasion and influence involve emotions and beliefs. As discussed in some of the earlier chapters, you have to know how and what people are thinking.

Influence and the art of persuasion is the process of getting someone else to *want* to do, react, think, or believe in the way *you* want them to.

If you need to, reread the preceding sentence. It is probably one of the most powerful sentences in this whole book. It means that using the principles discussed herein, you will be able to move someone to think, act, and maybe even believe the way *you want him to because he wants to.* Social engineers use the art of persuasion every day and, unfortunately, malicious scammers and social engineers use it, too.

Some people have devoted their life to researching, studying, and perfecting the art of influence. Those such as Dr. Ellen Langer, Robert Cialdini, and Kevin Hogan have contributed a very large repository of knowledge in this field. Mix this knowledge with the research and teachings of NLP (neurolinguistic programming) masters such as Bandler, Grinder, and more recently Jamie Smart, and what you have is a recipe to become a true artist.

True influence is elegant and smooth and most of the time undetectable to those being influenced. When you learn the methods you will start to notice them in commercials, on billboards, and when used by salespeople. You will start to get irritated at the shoddy attempts of marketing people and if you are like me, you will begin to rant and rave at terrible commercials and billboards while driving (which does not make my wife very happy).

Before getting into how social engineers will use in influence and persuasion, the chapter begins with a short tour of some of the key elements of persuasion and influence that I have compiled and used. This chapter will discuss things like reciprocation, manipulation, and the power of setting goals, just to name a few of these key elements.

Influence and persuasion can be broken down into five important aspects, as discussed in the following sections.

The Five Fundamentals of Influence and Persuasion

The five fundamentals of persuasion are crucial in obtaining any type of successful influence upon a target:

» Setting clear goals

» Building rapport

» Being observant of your surroundings

» Being flexible

» Getting in touch with yourself

The whole goal of social engineering is to influence the target to take an action that may or may not be in their best interest. Yet they will not only take the action, but *want* to take the action and maybe even thank you for it at the end. This type of influence is powerful and can make a social engineer who possesses these skills legendary.

World-renowned NLP trainer Jamie Smart once said, "The map is not the territory." I love that quote because it blends perfectly with these five fundamentals. None of them are the whole sum on their own, but individually they are like points on a map that show you the whole territory of what you want to accomplish. The following section delves deep into the first fundamental: why setting clear goals is very important.

Have a Clear Goal in Mind

Not only should you have a clear goal in mind, you should even go so far as to write it down. Ask yourself, "What do I want out of this engagement or interaction?"

As I discussed in Chapter 5, especially in relation to NLP, a human's internal systems are affected by his thoughts and goals. If you focus on something, you may be more likely to become it or get it. This doesn't mean that if you focus on the thought of getting one million dollars, you will get it. In fact, it is unlikely. However, if you had a goal of making one million dollars and focused on the steps needed to make that money, your goals, education, and actions would increase the likelihood of you achieving that goal. The same is true with persuasion. What is your goal? Is it to change someone's beliefs? To get him to take an action? Suppose a dear friend is doing something terribly unhealthy and you want to try and persuade her to stop. What is the goal? Maybe the end goal is to persuade her to stop, but maybe little goals exist along the way. Outlining all of these goals can make the path to influencing that person clearer.

After setting the goal, you must ask yourself, "How will I know when I have gotten it?" I once listened to a training program offered by Jamie Smart, one of the world leaders on NLP, and he asked each person in the classroom these two questions:

» What do you want?

» How will you know when you have it?

At this point, I paused the CD for the first question and answered for myself out loud what I wanted from this course. Then I pressed Play again and when he asked that second question, "How will you know you have gotten it?" I paused the CD again and was lost. It was clear to me that I didn't have a roadmap. I knew what I wanted out of that course, but I didn't know how to gauge when I had gotten it.

Knowing what you want out of your engagements is an important aspect of influence and persuasion tactics. When you approach a target knowing what your goals are and what the indicators are that you are getting what you want, then you can clearly identify the path you need to take. Clearly defined goals can make or break the success of the influence tactics used by a social engineer as well as make the next step much easier to master.

Rapport, Rapport, Rapport

Chapter 5 has a whole section on rapport building. Read it, study it, and perfect your rapport-building skills.

Developing rapport means that you get the attention of the person you are targeting and his unconscious mind, and you build trust within that unconscious portion.

Mastering the skill of building rapport can change the way you deal with people, and when it comes to social engineering, it can change your whole methodology.

To build rapport, start where the person you want to influence is mentally—try to understand their frame of mind. Are they suspicious? Are they upset, sad, or worried? Whatever emotional state you perceive them to be in, start from there. Do not focus on your goals as much as focusing on understanding the person. This is a very vital point. This means a social engineer must understand his target enough that they can imagine where they are consciously. What are the target's thoughts and state of mind?

For example, imagine you want to influence your dear friend to want to quit smoking or doing drugs or something else. Notice you don't want to convince her to quit, but convince her to *want* to quit. Your goal cannot be about *you*, right? It must focus on the target. You can't start your conversation with what her addiction is doing to *you* and how much *you* hate the smell, and so on. The argument has to be what is in it for *her*. You cannot start the conversation with a verbal attack about what the person has done to you with their habit, but you need to understand where that person's frame of mind is, accept it, and come into alignment with it.

Social engineering is much the same: you can't start where *you* are mentally. This is going to be struggle for many people. Do you know why she smokes? Do you understand the psychological, physical, or mental reasons why? Until you can really get into her shoes, you cannot build a strong rapport and your efforts at influence will fail.

In addition, you cannot always base the idea of building rapport on logic. I once was in the hospital with a dear friend who was dying from throat cancer. He had smoked for more than 40 years and one day he found out he had cancer. It spread fast, bringing him to the hospital to live out his last days. His children would come to visit and every now and then they would leave the room. I thought they were overcome with emotion. One time after they excused themselves I went out to comfort them and they were outside the hospital smoking! I was dumbfounded. I don't smoke and have no desire to, and although I can understand how strong an addiction can be, I couldn't understand how after seeing the pain their father was in, how they could raise a cigarette to their lips.

Logic would not win in this case. Telling my friend's children why smoking is bad and how it will kill them would do no good—this information was useless because it was combative and only made me feel good in saying it, but did not align with their present frame of mind. Until you understand the person you cannot successfully build a good enough rapport to influence him or her.

Getting someone to want to do something is a blend of emotion and logic, as well as understanding and humility in many cases. Once I walked into an office I was going to do some work for and I had heard a funny comment outside, so when I walked in the main lobby I was chuckling. The woman behind the desk must have just done something embarrassing because when she saw me she immediately got angry and yelled at me, "It's not very funny and you are a jerk."

Now I didn't know this woman and to tell you the truth I had a goal in mind that this interaction was not going to help. In addition, I felt insulted that she assumed I was laughing at her, and wanted to lash back at her. But instead, I saw she was upset. I got close to the counter so as not to embarrass her anymore, I looked her in the eye, and with sincerity said, "I am so sorry if you thought I was laughing at you. I was in the parking lot and some of your workmates were telling a story about a party over the weekend and I thought it was very funny."

She looked at me and I could tell she was now even more embarrassed, so to save face for her, I loudly said, "Ma'am, I am sorry for laughing and embarrassing you." This allowed her to save face to those around us. She understood that I "took one for the team" and she responded with extreme kindness. A minute later she apologized and it worked to my benefit as I was given all the data I asked for, data I normally would have had to work very hard to get.

A teacher I had once used to tell me to "kill them with kindness." That is a pretty powerful statement. Being kind to people is a quick way to build rapport and to establish yourself in the five fundamentals of persuasion and influence.

One method to influence people using kindness and rapport is to ask questions and give choices that lead them to a path you want. For example, once I was influenced to take a job I really didn't want as part of a team effort. The team leader was very charismatic and friendly and had the "charm factor" that allowed him to speak to anyone. He approached me and said, "Chris, I wanted to talk to you separately from the team. I need a right hand for a small project. But the person needs to be a go-getter, self motivated. I think this is you, but I don't want to assume; what do you think?"

I was excited and flattered by the compliments and the potential to be "important," so I responded, "I am a very self-motivated person. Whatever you need, tell me."

The team leader continued, "Well, I am a big believer in leading by example. And I think you have that leadership quality. The problem is, some on the team do not, and they need a strong person to show them how it is done."

Before the end of the conversation, what he wanted appeared as if it was my idea, which made it impossible to back out of. Powerful indeed, and all started with the power of persuasion.

Be in Tune with Yourself and Your Surroundings

Being aware of yourself and your surroundings, or *sensory acuity*, is the ability to notice the signs in the person you are targeting and yourself that will tell you that you are moving in the right direction or not.

Many of the principles discussed in the previous chapter apply to persuasion. Reading body language and facial signs can tell you much about your influence on the person.

To really master the dual art of influence and persuasion, you have to become a master watcher and master listener. Chris Westbury, a cognitive neuropsychologist at the University of Alberta, Canada, estimates that human brains process information at 20 million billion calculations per second. Those calculations are represented by facial expressions, microexpressions, gestures, posture, voice tones, eye blinks, breathing rate, speech patterns, nonverbal utterances, and many more types of distinguishing patterns. Mastering influence means to be aware of those subtle things in yourself and others.

I found, for myself, the ability to be observant proved to be easier for me after receiving some training from Dr. Ekman in microexpressions. I found afterward that not only did I become much more aware of what was going on with those around me, but also myself. When I felt a certain expression on my face, I was able to analyze it and see how it might be portrayed to others. This recognition of myself and my surroundings was one of the most enlightening experiences of my life.

NLP experts promote minimizing your internal dialog when trying to influence others. If you approach the target thinking about the next stage of the attack, the end goal, or comebacks for potential conversation stoppers, that internal dialog can cause you to miss a lot of what is going on around you. Being observant takes a lot of work but the payoff is well worth it.

Don't Act Insane—Be Flexible

What do I mean by not acting insane and being flexible? One definition of insanity that's been floating around for years is "doing the same thing over and over and expecting different results." Being willing and able to flex is one of the keys to persuasion.

You can think of this flexibility in terms of physical things. If you were tasked to persuade or bend something, would you rather it be a branch from a willow tree or a steel rod? Most people would say the willow branch because it is flexible, easier to bend, and makes the task accomplishable. Trying to persuade others while being unyielding and inflexible doesn't work, and neither does persuasion if you are not flexible.

Many times, an audit will not go as planned. A good social engineer will be able to roll with the punches and adjust their goals and methods as needed. This does not go against the idea of planning ahead; instead, it bespeaks the point of not being so rigid that when things do not go as planned you can move and adapt so the goal is not lost.

The way a person would view an insane person is the way a target would view the inflexible social engineer. The social engineer would look unreasonable and you would most likely never reach endgame.

Get in Touch with Yourself

By getting in touch with yourself, I am not suggesting some Zen meditation avenue, just that you understand your emotions. Emotions control practically everything you do, as well as everything your target does. Knowing your emotions and being in touch with yourself can help you lay the groundwork for being an effective social engineer.

Going back to the earlier example of you and your smoking friend—approaching your friend if you have a deep-seated hatred for those who smoke affects your approach. It can make you act, express, say, or do something that will close the door to persuasion. You may never compromise on certain things, and being aware of those things and your emotions about them can help you to develop a clear path toward influencing a target.

These five fundamentals are key to understanding influence and persuasion. Being able to create an environment where a target wants to do what you are requesting is the goal of persuasion, and these five fundamentals will help you create that environment. The next section examines how social engineers use these fundamentals.

Influence Tactics

As mentioned, social engineers must practice the skill of persuasion until it becomes part of their everyday habits. This doesn't mean that they must influence everyone in everything they do, but being able to turn this skill on and off at will is a powerful trait of a good social engineer.

Influence and persuasion have many aspects you can use and many that fit easily into an audit. Other aspects might not fit too easily, but hold a very powerful position in the world of influence. The following sections cover eight different techniques of influence that are used often by media, politicians, government, con men, scammers, and of course, social engineers.

Each section provides an analysis of each technique to see how it is used in other areas of influence besides social engineering, as well as takes a closer look at how it can apply to a social engineer.

Reciprocation

Reciprocity is the inherent expectation that when others treat you well you respond in kind. A simple example is when you are walking into a building—if someone holds a door open for you, he expects you to say thank you and then make sure that next door stays open for him as he comes in.

The rule of reciprocity is important because often the returned favor is done unconsciously. Knowing this means that you now have a step up on how you can use it as a social engineer. Before getting into that, though, here are a few examples where reciprocity is often used:

» Pharmaceutical companies will spend $10,000–$15,000 per doctor (yes, per doctor) on "gifts" that might include dinners, books, computers, hats, clothing, or other items that have the drug company's logo on it. When the time comes to choose a drug to support and buy, to whom do you think the doctors are more likely to go?

» Politicians are influenced in much the same way. It is no secret that many times politicians or lobbyists are more favorable to people who helped their political campaign than those who did not.

» Reciprocity is often used in business, especially when it comes to matters of contracts. Maybe the sales guy will pay for a meal, then later on ask for a concession in the contract. The client is compelled to give this concession.

» A fellow employee filled in for you one week when you needed a day off. Now she asks you to return the favor, but you have plans. In this situation, people will reschedule and honor the request.

All of these are examples of reciprocity. Sociologist Alvin Gouldner wrote a paper called, "The Norm of Reciprocity" (http://media.pfeiffer.edu/lridener/courses/normrecp.html) in which he states:

> *Specifically, I suggest that a norm of reciprocity, in its universal form, makes two interrelated, minimal demands: (1) people should*

help those who have helped them, and (2) people should not injure
those who have helped them. Generically, the norm of reciproc-
ity may be conceived of as a dimension to be found in all value
systems and, in particular as one among a number *of "Principal*
Components" universally present in moral codes.

Basically, his research led him to see that reciprocity works despite cultural
backgrounds. Reciprocity, used under the right circumstances, is all but impossible to resist.

Think of reciprocity as the process shown in Figure 6-1.

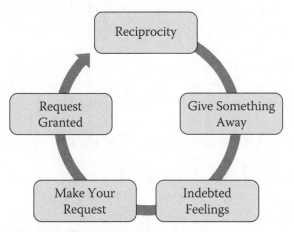

Figure 6-1 The cycle of reciprocity.

The following sections expand on some key points of the preceding idea.

Give Something Away

The thing you give away can't be some simple piece of junk. The thing given must
have value—to the recipient. Giving away a beautiful hardcover novel written in a
language the recipient does not read or collect is useless.

The item can be a service, a physical item, some valuable information, assistance,
or anything else that the receiver will deem as a value (even something as simple
as holding the door or picking up something dropped). Some sales organizations
promote this method but then fall short by offering something that has no value.
Imagine you are at a trade show and at each table is a giveaway. If you walk up to a
table and notice a pile of cheap-looking pens you might just walk by. The next table
has an interesting puzzle-like game. You are intrigued so you pick it up; after you

spend a few minutes playing with it a salesperson approaches and says, "You want a hint?" After showing you a small hint he asks whether you have a minute so he can show you a service you might really love.

How can you say no? You get an intriguing game and a free hint, and now all he wants is a minute of your time? It's a perfect setup.

Create Indebted Feelings

The more value the gift has to the recipient and the more unexpected it is, the greater the sense of indebtedness.

Not allowing the gift to be used in an obvious manipulation tactic is important. Don't say or act like, "I gave you this great gift now you owe me." Even thinking it can take away any feelings of indebtedness. The "gift" should be totally free and of great value to the recipient.

The Humane Society of the United States, for instance, gives away personalized mailing labels as a free gift. No strings are attached and many people use them for holiday cards or personal letters. They are attractive and good quality. You sign up for them, and many months later you will get a call asking for a donation to support your local Humane Society. The recipient's sense of obligation is usually too great to not contribute even a little.

By way of another example, *Fortune Magazine* offers college professors free issues of its magazine to try out in their classes with no strings attached at all.

Many examples of reciprocity like these exist. On the flip side, many companies fail at reciprocity by thinking things like the following are good gifts:

» Sharp-looking and colorful corporate brochures

» Useless and junky toys

» Sales literature about *your* products or company

These things do not build indebtedness. The recipient must deem the "gift" valuable. Another source of "gifts" that can build true indebtedness is information. Giving away a valuable, beneficial, or useful piece of information can literally be of more interest than a physical gift to some.

Ask for What You Want

On one occasion as I was entering a building, I saw a man who looked very much to be the "boss" get out of his car parked in the spot marked "For CFO Only," and he was on his cell phone. He was not a happy guy, and I overheard him telling someone that he was upset because he had to go inside and let some people go. I assumed from his tone that he was on with his wife or girlfriend and he didn't like the job he was about to do.

I walked past him and went to the front desk and as I walked up I saw that the girl behind the desk was playing Minesweeper. As I approached the counter she gave me the standard, "How can I help you?" She had a look on her face that said she was bored and not in the mood. I said, "Look, I am here for a meeting, but your boss is about to walk in and he is in a bad mood..." I then trailed off and just stood there with a folder in my hand. A few seconds later the boss stormed in the front door and I said loudly, "Thank you so much for your assistance."

She looked over and said to me, "Excuse me, sir," then said to her boss, "Good morning, Mr. Smith, I have your messages," and then handed him a small pile of paper as he walked by.

When he disappeared to his office she thanked me profusely. I just saved her and she knew it. The information I gave her was invaluable, and my next words would be imperative: "I need your help. I wanted to see the HR manager just for a brief meeting. Can you get me into her office real quick?"

She walked me back to the manager's office and introduced me as "her friend" that stopped in. Within minutes my plan was launched, and all thanks to reciprocity.

As a social engineer, look for little opportunities to give out information that will make you valuable to the recipient and more importantly, make the recipient indebted to you.

Be aware of your surroundings and what little things you can do to make your targets indebted to you. Remember it doesn't have to be something amazing, just something that they value. A good point to keep in mind is to not "stalk" the target. Standing and staring at him or her waiting for an opportunity to do or say something can be off-putting. These principles should be natural.

Naturalness means you start doing these principles in everyday life. Hold doors for people, be very polite, and look for opportunities to do good things for others. These actions will become second nature and you will have fewer struggles doing them in an audit.

Reciprocity is a powerful influence tactic, and the next two principles discussed are closely tied into it.

Obligation

Obligation has to do with actions one feels he needs to take due to some sort of social, legal, or moral requirement, duty, contract, or promise. In the context of social engineering, obligation is closely related to reciprocation but is not limited to it. Obligation can be as simple as holding an outer door for someone, which will usually make him hold the inner door for you. It can be escalated to someone giving you private info because you create in them a sense of obligation to you. Obligation is a common attack vector used when targeting customer service people.

You can also use obligation in small doses by utilizing smart complimenting. For example, compliment the person, then follow it up with a request. This technique is very easy to do wrong if you are new or inexperienced and can come across so fake that it alerts the target's inner sense and has the wrong effect. But if done properly, it can lead to obtaining even little pieces of valuable information.

An example of complimenting in the wrong way would be something like, "Wow, you have beautiful eyes, can I get into your server room?" Sounds stupid, huh? Be sure to say your method out loud to see how it sounds. If it sounds like a cheap pickup line then it has to go.

A small conversation like this, on the other hand, can be a proper way to compliment:

As you approach the receptionist's desk you see some pictures of a couple of little children at Disney World and after you introduce yourself you say, "Are those your kids? They sure are cute." Regardless if they are the receptionist's kids or her nephews, she will most likely enjoy your compliment. Then you follow up with, "I have a couple of my own. They keep us young, huh?"

"Yes, my two kids. And I am not sure about young," she chuckles, "but they do tire me out."

"I haven't taken mine to Disney yet," I say. "Did you find they enjoyed it at that age?"

"Oh yeah, they loved every second of it," says the receptionist. "As long as my daughter is with her Daddy, she is having fun."

"Ah, yeah, I have my little princess too," I reply. "Well, I could stand here and talk about my kids all day, but I am wondering if you can help me out. I called in and spoke to someone last week about a new HR software package and I said I would drop off this information packet, but I lost the paper I wrote her name on. I am terribly embarrassed."

"Oh, that's probably Mrs. Smith," offers the receptionist. "She handles all of that."

"You are a life saver. I owe you one. Thank you."

These types of compliments go a long way to opening the target up to be more agreeable to influence.

The golden rule—treat others as you would wish to be treated—is a key principle in creating obligation. Treating people kindly and giving them something they may need, even if it is as small as a compliment, can create a sense of obligation to you.

Psychologist Steve Bressert makes this point in his article "Persuasion and How To Influence Others," in which he states, "according to the American Disabled Veterans organization, mailing out a simple appeal for donations produces an 18% success rate. Enclosing a small gift, such as personalized address labels, nearly doubles the success rate to 35%. 'Since you sent me some useful address labels, I'll send you a small donation in return.'"

If you want to prove to yourself the power of this principle try this simple exercise. Even something as small as a question can create obligation. The next time someone asks you a question, say nothing. Just stay silent or ignore it and move on in the conversation. Notice how awkward that is; something as simple as a question creates a sense of obligation to answer. Simply asking the target a question can lead to amazing results.

If your first action creates a feeling that there is an expected follow-up, then ful-filling that expectation can lead to strong feelings of obligation. When the person with whom you are interacting expects a result, fulfilling it can create a strong sense of commitment in him or her to do the same for you.

This method can be used, for example, by sending the CFO of a company a piece of technology, maybe an iPod loaded with malicious software. When he gets the gift he is obligated to plug it in. One successful attack vector I saw in play was where the social engineer sent a small relevant gift to the CFO or CEO with a card that said, "Please accept a small gift from our company. All we ask is that you browse our prod-ucts at `www.products.com` and download our PDF catalog here at `www.products .com/catalog.pdf`. I will call you next week."

This method was successful every time.

Concession

A *concession*, or the act of conceding, is defined as "an acknowledgment or admis-sion," or "the act of yielding." Concessions are used often within the social engineer-ing context as a play on the reciprocation instinct of humans. Humans seem to have a built-in function that makes them want to "do unto others as they do unto" you.

A social engineer can use the "something for something" idea or the "I'll scratch your back if you scratch mine" principle.

There are basic principles to concessions and how to use them properly:

» **Label your concessions:** Make it known when and what you are conceding, which makes it difficult for your mark to ignore the urge to reciprocate. This will take balance because you don't want to blow a trumpet, so to speak, while you announce a concession, but a simple statement like, "OK, I'll give you this one," or "I will meet you halfway," show you are willing to concede.

» **Demand and define reciprocity:** You can start by planting the seeds of reciprocation and this increases your chances of getting something in return. An easy way to start planting these seeds is through nonverbal communication showing that you are flexible, and also by being a good listener. These little things can make a big difference when building feelings of reciprocation in your target.

» **Make contingent concessions:** You can use "risk-free" concessions when trust is low or when you need to signal that you are ready to make other concessions. What I mean by this is a concession that does not come with a "now you can do something for me" attitude. By giving in to something the target wants or needs with no counter demand, you can build a very strong bond with the target.

» **Make concessions in installments:** The idea of reciprocity is deeply ingrained in our minds. Most people feel that if someone does them a favor then they are socially contracted to eventually return that favor. Similarly, if someone makes a concession, say in a negotiation or bargaining agreement, then one instinctively feels obligated to "budge" a little bit, too. Since this is a fact, you do not have to feel that all your concessions must be at one time. You can make "installments" with your concessions, where you give in a little here and a little there over time to keep your target reciprocating.

Concessions are used daily by salespeople, negotiators, and social engineers. A successful social engineer can use and abuse this instinctual tendency by not only resisting the manipulations being placed on them by others but also by trying to take over the situation completely. Concession and reciprocation skills play well with many of the other social engineering techniques discussed within the pages of this book.

An example of how many people fall for concessions can be illustrated with telemarketers who call for donations. They use a strategy for gaining concessions after someone is first given the opportunity to turn down a large request. The same requester counteroffers with a smaller request that you are more likely to accept than the large request.

Large request: "Can you donate $200 to our charity?"

Response: "No, I cannot."

Smaller request: "Oh, I'm sorry sir, and I understand. Can you donate only $20?"

People who are not aware of this technique might feel like the burden is taken off of them and realize they can part with a mere $20 rather than the initial asking price of $200.

Another great example appeared in an article (`http://ezinearticles .com/?How-to-Negotiate-the-Salary-Using-the-Power-of-the-Norm-of-Reciprocity&id=2449465`) written by David Hill:

> *The power of this norm can be felt in most bargaining situations. Assume a buyer and a seller are haggling over the price of a car. The seller starts out with a bid at $24,000. The buyer finds this offer unacceptable and makes a counter bid at $15,000. Now, the seller lowers his bid to $20,000, i.e., he makes a concession. In this case, the buyer will most often feel inclined to increase his bid, maybe to $17,000. The reason why the buyer will feel this inclination is because of the presence of the norm of reciprocity. This norm now demands that the buyer responds to the seller's concession with another concession.*

As with most of the principles discussed so far, the concession must be valuable to the receiver. You can't concede something that is valuable only to you or you lose the power you gain with a good concession.

As a social engineer, not giving a concession that will cause you to lose face, rapport, or your position is also imperative. A delicate balance must exist between the concession and your standing with the target, and finding it is half the work. Find it, though, and concessions can be a very serious tool in your hands.

Scarcity

People often find objects and opportunities more attractive if they are rare, scarce, or hard to obtain. This is why you will see newspapers and radio ads filled with

"Last Day," "Limited Time Only," "Only 3-Day Sale," and "Going Out of Business Forever" messages that entice people to come from all over to get a share of the soon-to-be-never-seen-again product.

The use of scarcity in the sales context is best known with the catch phrase *"Act now! Supplies are limited!"* Other techniques are the common *"The first X callers get a free widget,"* or having an intentional short supply of a popular product. In recent times, this practice was most popularly alleged with the Nintendo Wii. Jason Dobson, a writer for Gamasutra, said, "But I think [Nintendo] intentionally dried up supply because they made their numbers for the year. The new year starts April 1, and I think we're going to see supply flowing" (www.gamasutra.com/php-bin/news_index.php?story=13297).

Where I live, a car dealership ran an ad on a Thursday stating it had to get rid of X number of cars due to new stock arriving. The prices were so low and some of the cars—wait for it—were no longer being produced, and that weekend was the last weekend ever that you could come in for a piece of auto-selling history.

The sales went through the roof that weekend, so the sale was over right? Nope, that ad ran every Thursday for more than three months. I often wondered how people just didn't catch on to it, but the dealership sold a lot of cars using this method.

Social events can often appear to be more exclusive if scarcity is introduced. The perceived social benefit of attending these events often goes up in these circumstances. In advertising, this point is driven home with ads for music events that point out how the last concert was quickly sold out.

Many popular restaurants have been known to close off sections of the restaurant to appear busier than they really are. The perception that they are extremely popular can often trigger a heightened desire to eat at that establishment. To see an ad that actually mentions the use of scarcity in promoting an event, go to www.social-engineer.org/wiki/archives/Scarcity/Scarcity-Advertisment.html. This ad played on four major components of scarcity:

» The launch is limited access.

» The application is not public and only limited.

» Promoters are handpicked and limited.

» The e-book is free to those lucky enough to be chosen to come.

All of these points use scarcity by making the would-be partygoers feel that getting into this event is so difficult that only the elite, the few, and the proud can even have a remote chance of stepping foot onto that hallowed ground.

The basics of economics are made up of the allocation of resources that have alternative uses. This allocation is driven by the scarcity of the objects that are being allocated. The rarer the resource, the higher the perceived value the object retains. This rarity is why gold is worth more than salt, which is worth more than clay.

Also, within daily interactions scarcity is often used. Scarcity can be introduced into social situations in an attempt to make something one has go up in value. For instance, one might act like he is very busy on a regular basis, and free time is hard to come by. This action may excuse him from not spending time with someone he may have an obligation to spend time with, and at the same time make time that is spent seem that much more valuable.

You can manipulate attention through the use of scarcity as well. Think of how many people complain about salesmen bothering them in a store when there is no scarcity of salespeople's attention, yet they are just as upset when they are ignored by salespeople when their attention is scarce. On the whole, people are driven to desire that which is hard to obtain, because it is viewed as having more value. This holds true for attention as well.

Scarcity is often used in social engineering contexts to create a feeling of urgency in a decision-making context. This urgency can often lead to manipulation of the decision-making process, allowing the social engineer to control the information provided to the victim. This is done commonly by using a mixture of authority and scarcity principles. For example, saying something like, "The CFO, Mr. Smith, called me before he left for the long weekend and told me to come down and fix his email problem. He said he was sick and tired of the crashes and wanted it fixed before Monday." This creates urgency alongside scarcity in that the CFO is not available to speak to and time is the scarce item.

Using scarcity mixed with other principles can also make the attack even deadlier. Either way, scarcity creates a desire and that desire can lead someone to making a decision he might regret later.

This was proven to me recently when a truck pulled into my driveway with a freezer in the back. This decently dressed young man approached my wife and explained that he is a meat salesman. He delivers meat to customers and was just about to head back to the office and saw her working in the yard. He began talking about meat prices and how expensive things are in the store. My wife is a very price-conscious shopper, so this built rapport. Plus he had a very pleasant southern accent and called her "ma'am" and was very respectful.

After a few minutes of talking, she blurts out the question that usually stops salesmen dead, "How much do you want?"

Without missing too much of a beat he says, "Listen, I have been selling these all day for $400 per box, but this is my last box. I would love to just go back to the office with an empty freezer and give you some high-quality meat in the meantime."

Oh no, the last box! He told her before he only comes through once every two months. The desire has been raised, but my wife is no dummy. She knew she was being manipulated. She excused herself and came to get me.

He went through his spiel and laid on the scarcity thick. Of course, this type of an account can be a lesson on how to not fall for this tactic. The problem is that emotion gets involved. He sees that I have a grill outside that looks *used,* so he knows I love to cook outside and he plays on that. He then talks about the quality of meat and quickly makes comparisons to restaurant quality and what is in his boxes.

Many people could easily fall for the emotional aspect of his sales pitch. "What if it is his last one?" "He is right, this is much cheaper than eating out." "He comes to me...I don't even have to drive to the store."

Instead, I whipped out a calculator and asked him for the amount for the two last boxes, divided by the weight and then asked my wife how much she normally pays per pound for a Delmonico or ribeye in the store. When her price came in lower by $3.00 per pound I simply just shut up. Now his emotions get involved. He scrambles to save face. He lowers his price by $150 off the bat. I again do the math and he is still $.50 more per pound.

He tries to talk about quality, convenience, and all those aspects that make it worth the $.50 more. I shift my posture and position to be away from him and to show disinterest. Without saying anything, he trails off at the end of a weak spiel and offers me another $50 off. I tell him, "Sorry, I just don't think it's worth it."

He then does the classic mistake that shows how his claims of scarcity were false—he caves in more. "How much do you want to pay for these boxes?"

"I probably could do $100."

"If you can give me $125 we can call it a deal."

Now mind you a little bit ago he was at $400 per box and they were the last two in this area for two to three months. This should have been a bidding war for that value, but instead, I sent him packing with his two boxes of meat and no cash.

The lesson in this story for social engineers is that for scarcity to work it either has to be real, or you have to stick to your guns to give the appearance of reality.

People will perceive the value higher when something is really in need. A malicious example of this is how the petrol companies raised the prices of fuel after Hurricane Katrina. The claim was that fuel was in shortage due to the destruction, which caused terrible price increases. Of course, if this were true then the fuel would be worth a lot more than it is; instead it was an example of the claim of scarcity used to make money. Yet at the same time, when BP's error caused millions of gallons of oil to be lost in the Gulf of Mexico, ruining the ecosystem, instead of fuel prices skyrocketing due to lack of supply, they dropped. How? Well I won't get into that here, but it proves the point that for scarcity to work, it has to be believable, and this where the oil companies fail and where social engineers can fail, too.

From a social engineer's standpoint, the more limited or difficult it is obtain an opportunity the more value it will have to people. If information is deemed as private, restricted, and hard to come by, and you are willing to share it with someone, you have just gained a lot of value in their eyes.

A social engineer can leverage scarcity with information by using a statement like, "I am not supposed to be saying this but..." or "I am not sure if you heard this news, but I overheard..." Statements like these spoken in hushed tones imply that this information is scarce.

Authority

People are more willing to follow the directions or recommendations of someone they view as an authority. Finding a person who has enough assertiveness to question authority directly, especially when that authority holds direct power over him or is face-to-face with him is uncommon.

Children, for example, are taught to obey adults such as teachers, counselors, priests, and nannies because they have authority over them. Often, questioning authority is deemed as disrespectful and abject obedience is what is rewarded. These principles carry over into adult life because we are taught to respect authority figures and not question rules or orders given to us by those whom we deem authorities.

Unfortunately, it is this principle leads many children into the hands of abusers and molesters. Of course, not this principle solely, but those who prey on children realize how children are taught about authority and often seek out those who appear to be more compliant. Similarly, malicious social engineers use this principle to manipulate their targets to take some action or inaction that can lead to a breach.

Understanding how authority is used from a social engineering aspect is important. German sociologist and political economist, Max Weber, defined authority into categories that I have adapted to fit more closely into the realm of social engineering.

Legal Authority

Legal authority is based upon government and law. This generally applies to law enforcement officers or others who enforce the laws of the land, area, or facility you are presently in.

As a social engineer, pretexts that involve law enforcement or other government officials are usually illegal. However, security guards, bank security, or other types of enforcement authority figures can be well represented and are often used by social engineers.

In one episode of the BBC television program *The Real Hustle,* Paul Wilson and his cohorts dressed up like the guards who collect the money. When someone shows up in the uniforms that look similar to the real ones and acts as a normal person in that authoritative position would act, targets have little reason to doubt the imposter is who he "says" he is. Acting as an authority figure is a major ploy used by social engineers to gain access to a company.

Another ploy that can be effective is posing as a lawyer who is seeking certain information. Playing a role that is generally feared or respected by the masses can be one way a legal authority ploy is used.

Organizational Authority

Organizational authority is quite simply any authority defined by means of an organization. Typically, this refers to a supervisory hierarchy. Someone within a position of power in an organization has more power and access to more information than someone at the bottom of the hierarchy.

In a social engineering audit, a consultant may impersonate the CIO or someone else with clearly defined organizational authority. The consultant may then be able to obtain passwords or other information from the help desk or any other employee who may perceive that the impersonated person has authority over him or her.

In a paper entitled "The 'Social Engineering' of the Internet Fraud" Jonathan J. Rusch of the U.S. Department of Justice writes, "People are highly likely, in the right situation, to be highly responsive to assertions of authority, even when the person who purports to be in a position of authority is not physically present" (www.isoc .org/inet99/proceedings/3g/3g_2.htm).

This ploy is used in other ways, by not acting as if you are the CFO, but instead sent or authorized by the CFO. The authority the name and title wields may be enough to grant that power to the attacker in the eyes of the target.

Rusch cites an experiment performed by Robert B. Cialdini and recorded in his book *Influence* (1993), which showed 95 percent of nurses within 22 stations from three different hospitals were willing to administer patients a dangerous dose of medication based upon a phone call from a researcher purporting to be a physician the nurses had never met.

This experiment clearly shows that based upon orders and the perceived notion of authority, people might take certain actions despite their better judgment. This type of authority can and is often used to exploit companies into giving away valuable data.

Social Authority

Social authority refers to the "natural-born leaders" of any social group. A social group could consist of co-workers, college friends, or any other gathering of people.

In *Influence*, Cialdini writes, "When reacting to authority in an automatic fashion there is a tendency to often do so in response to the mere symbols of authority rather than to its substance."

For social authority to occur, an extraordinary amount of time or structure may not be needed to define an authoritative figure. In any setting, a quick flash of *social proof*, where people are influenced by a group of people taking the same action, may help provide a person social authority.

Social authority can be used to an advantage in social engineering by asking or pressuring the target for information. If the target refuses and is therefore not liked by the leader of the group, the target may fall out of favor with the entire group. Complying with the leader's social authority is perceived to be advantageous.

Social authority is successfully used when either directly stated or implied that a previous person or group reacted the way that the attacker is asking. "Yesterday the CFO sent me down to take care of this problem and Joe let me through and he checked all my credentials, did he put them on file?" A simple statement like that utilizes a few forms of authority.

If you comply with authorities mindlessly, you may respond to *symbols of authority* rather than to reality. Three *authority symbols* are particularly effective in Western countries—you may reward people with any one of these (and no other evidence of authority) for their compliance:

» Titles

» Clothes

» Automobiles

In an interview I conducted with Dr. Ellen Langer, Harvard psychologist and researcher of persuasion and influence (www.social-engineer.org/episode-007-using-persuasion-on-the-mindless-masses), she talked extensively about mindlessness. She stated that people often do much of their work in a state where there is not much thought; in other words, they are in autopilot. In those positions, the abuse of the authority role is very dangerous. Perceived authority can make someone on autopilot react without limits.

Using the right clothes, body language, and even having a fake business card printed has worked for many social engineers in presenting an authority stance and keeping their targets in autopilot.

Other forms of authority may come into play for a social engineer than the ones outlined here, but these are the most commonly used. Authority is a powerful force when it comes to influencing others, and with a little bit of reasoning and information gathering a social engineer can effectively use an authority pretext to his or her advantage.

Commitment and Consistency

People value consistency in others, and they also want to appear consistent in their own behavior. Generally people probably want their words, attitudes, and deeds to be consistent and congruent. Consistency reduces the need to reprocess information and offers shortcuts through complex decisions.

Gut feelings—those moments where you sense that an action is good or bad, or right or wrong, based on past experience—are often indicators that a decision being made might be against previously committed feelings and beliefs. These signals often indicate that you feel pushed to agree to something that you don't want.

Gut feelings can also occur when it comes to making commitments. Gut feelings may indicate that you are uncertain of whether your commitment was a mistake. You can ask yourself, *"Knowing what I now know, if I could do that again, would I make the same commitment?"*

Before looking at how a social engineer can use consistency to gain someone's commitment, take a look at three examples that might help hit this point home.

» **Marketing:** Companies often spend extraordinary amounts of money to gain market share. There is no real return, but they fight to remain in that share that they believe to be profitable. Coca-Cola and Pepsi are great examples of using marketing throughout the decades in the fight to remain visible, yet often a commercial will not sway a person to switch from Pepsi to Coke. Because the two companies have been "committed" to the war against each other it seems that when one of them comes out with a new product or marketing idea, the other is not too far behind.

» **Auctions:** The increased popularity of online auction houses such as eBay has this principle more visible. People feel a level of commitment to something they place a bid on and if someone outbids them it is as if they are compelled to bid again. At times they will even increase the bid way past their comfort zone because they feel committed. One classic example of this is when Robert Campeau bought Bloomingdales. He paid $600 million dollars *more* than it was worth. Max Bazerman, author of *Negotiating Rationally* quoted a journalist from the *Wall Street Journal* as saying, "We are not dealing with price anymore, but with egos...."

» **Carnivals, game houses, and so on:** Anytime gambling or game houses are involved a greater risk exists of commitment and consistency being used to persuade people. One columnist, Ryan Healy, an online marketing consultant, wrote a story about when he took his daughter to a circus (www.ryanhealy.com/commitment-and-consistency/). He spent $44 on the tickets, $5 to park his car, then 40 minutes of drive time to get there. He was committed to being at the circus. His daughter wanted cotton candy so he committed to a yes by giving her $5. How could cotton candy cost more than that? When the vendor came by and said the bag was $12, how could he back out on his commitment now? He couldn't, and therefore ended up spending the $12 on a single cotton candy.

Consistency in this pretense is defined as what is expected based on previous experience or expectations. That experience or expectation can motivate a target to take an action that can cause a breach. For example, when the tech support guy comes it is expected he will go to the server room. That request is consistent with the previous experience and expectation. When access to the server room is requested, it is more likely to be fulfilled because it is consistent with what is expected.

Commitment and consistency can be strong influence factors upon most people to take actions, give information, or divulge secrets.

A social engineer can make commitment and consistency some of the most powerful tools in his or her arsenal. If a social engineer can get a target to commit to something small, usually escalating the commitment is not too hard.

In his book *Influence*, Robert Cialdini writes:

> *The key to using the principles of Commitment and Consistency to manipulate people is held within the initial commitment. That is— after making a commitment, taking a stand or position, people are more willing to agree to requests that are consistent with their prior commitment. Many compliance professionals will try to induce others to take an initial position that is consistent with a behavior they will later request.*

The social engineer hoping to employ the technique of commitment and consistency usually tries to get the target to divulge a small piece of information toward the overall intended goal. By getting the subject to remain consistent with things he or she has already said, the attacker may get the subject to reveal even more information.

On the other hand, the attacker must remain consistent with what he is asking. The attacker should start off small and escalate the information gathering.

To use an unrealistic example, an attacker should never start off asking for the nuclear launch codes. This request will be denied, and the attacker will be left few options but to backpedal the request. However, starting off small and escalating the value of the information requested with each new piece of gathered information will seem like a more natural progression and will not appear so obvious to the victim.

Going slowly and progressively can be hard as social engineers are often impatient and want to get the "password" right now. Playing it cool and remaining patient can make this avenue rewarding. Clearly defining, maybe even writing out, a path that you can use on each audit can help you go into the audit with clearly defined goals and a path to accomplish them.

I created a chart you can see in Figure 6-2 that shows how a social engineer may be able to visualize this path to obtain information using commitment and consistency.

Getting a target to verbally commit to a certain action can force the target into a certain path of action. Cialdini states, "The commitment and consistency rule states that once we make a decision, we will experience pressure from others and ourselves to behave consistently with that decision. You can be pressured into making either good or bad decisions depending on your past actions."

Maybe you have felt this if you ever verbally told your wife or spouse that you wanted to lose weight. That verbal "commitment" leads to a lot of pressure to hold up to your end of the "bargain."

Sometimes, ending up disagreeing with yourself can be hard and almost impossible. Everyone has, at one point or another muttered the phrase, "I'm sorry, I changed my mind," at least once in our lives. When we do, we hang our head in shame, our voice tones drop, and we sound sad. Why? We have just broken a commitment we made and we feel guilty for doing it.

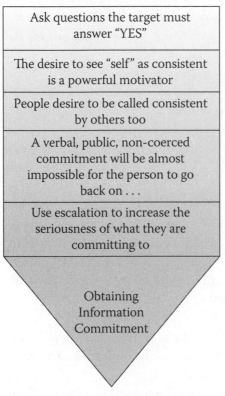

Figure 6-2 Clearly defining your goals can help you to obtain an information commitment.

Even small, seemingly insignificant commitments can lead to exploitation. For example, a phone conversation often used by solicitors goes something like this:

"Hello, how are you today?"

You answer, "I am doing great."

Now, prepare for the exploit: "That is good to hear, because some people who are not doing so great can use your help."

You can't go back on what you said now, because you are still doing great and committed to it.

This is not to say that you need to be so paranoid that you cannot even answer simple questions without the fear of exploitation, but being aware that one commitment does not mean you *must* commit to everything that follows is vital. I once worked with a guy who could literally get anyone to do the worst jobs and make them think it was their idea. Ensuring their commitment was one method he used.

If you committed to a path of agreeing with him on certain things, which was almost impossible not to do, because he got you to say "yes" upfront, then you had to continue to say "yes." Those yeses lead down one path, and that path was right to where he wanted, agreeing to the job he needed to get done.

Being aware that it is okay to say "no" can save you from committing to something that could be disastrous. Yet sometimes we convince ourselves that saying "no" is some form of cardinal sin that needs many prayers to be forgiven.

In the earlier example of the frozen meat salesman, my wife is a very self-aware person. Knowing she might be manipulated by a "seemingly good deal" she came inside to get me because I am a "jerk."

One of the best examples I have heard that really shows the power of commitment is a social experiment done by Dr. Thomas Moriarty in 1972. He sent an assistant to the beach as a "victim" with a portable radio. The victim sat in his chair listening to his radio for about 10 minutes, then he got up to go purchase a drink.

While he was gone, another assistant, the "criminal" who no one knew was working with him, came by to "steal" the radio. Only 4 out of 20 people—that's only 20%—stopped the thief from taking the radio.

The researchers then upped the ante in the next round. Before the "victim" would leave to buy the drink he would ask one of the neighboring sunbathers to watch his radio for him. What do you think the change was?

Now a staggering 19 out of 20 stopped the thief, some even resorting to violence. Why the staggering difference? Commitment and consistency. The researcher obtained commitment from the neighboring sunbathers and that caused them to have to act consistently with that commitment. In my opinion, these are amazing statistics that show the power of this influence method.

A social engineer can effectively use this method of influence to get a target to commit to even a small act or small "yes" and use that commitment to escalate it into a larger set of actions.

Liking

People like people who like them. As tongue twisting as that phrase is, it is a very true statement. Understanding the full depth of that statement gets you much closer to mastering persuasion.

When I say understand the depth, I really mean that because that sentence has much more to it than meets the eye.

This statement isn't saying that people who like you will respond well. Salespeople are often taught that people buy from people they like. That is true, but not the point. It also isn't saying that people must like you—it *is* saying you must like people and then they will like you in return.

This task is not as easy as it sounds because liking someone cannot be faked. As discussed in Chapter 5, smiles and happiness are very hard to fake. You must go into the circumstance genuinely caring for the person who you are trying to influence. Caring for people and their feelings is not a standard practice of the malicious social engineer; therefore, they often rely on charm. Charm can work on a short-term basis, but in the long term, liking people is a practiced and learned skill.

Liking is used in marketing extensively. In 1990 Jonathan Frenzen and Harry Davis published a study entitled, "Purchasing Behavior in Embedded Markets" (www .jstor.org/pss/2626820) that examined why Tupperware parties are so successful. All of their research led to this principle of liking.

The researchers concluded that most people bought because they wanted the hostess to be happy, to help a friend, and to be liked. How embarrassing to go to a party like this and not buy anything! That fear of not being liked is what will drive most people to purchase at these parties and it has little to do with wanting more Tupperware.

Other surveys and studies have compared the trust that people have in receiving "tips or advice" from those they consider friends to the trust they have in complete strangers or worse, people they don't like. A friend can give bad advice and one may be more prone to follow it than good advice from a person one doesn't like.

From a social engineering aspect the concept of liking is a powerful tool. Not only do you have to be likeable and win their trust, but you also have to genuinely be interested in people. This concept goes back to the discussion of pretexting in Chapter 4. When you pretext, you are not merely acting out an idea or belief—you must become the person you are pretexting; that role is what your life is about. If you can do that then the step of liking can become easier. Your pretext will be truly interested in helping, liking, or assisting that person.

One last aspect of liking that is important for you as a social engineer is physical attractiveness. Humans tend to automatically "like" those who we find attractive. As vain as that sounds, it is the truth. Some serious psychological principles back up this idea.

What is beautiful is good. In 1972 Berscheid, Walster, and Dion performed a study entitled just that, "What Is Beautiful Is Good," which unleashed some very profound findings. Participants were asked to rate photos of three individuals ranging from low, medium, and high attractiveness. Based on the photos alone they were to rate the people for personality traits, overall happiness, and career success.

They then compiled the ratings and averaged them and found that people who were deemed attractive were more socially desirable, had better occupations, were happier, and more successful. The study proved that people tend to link beauty with other successful qualities and it alters their opinions and ability to trust someone.

This study is an example of a phenomenon called the *halo effect*, where one particular trait influences or extends to the other qualities of the person. It has been proven to bias a person's decisions with a tendency to focus on the good traits of the other person. I have archived a copy of this amazing study at `www.social-engineer.org/wiki/archives/BlogPosts/BeautifulGood.pdf`.

In other words, if someone views you as beautiful, then that good trait extends to other judgments that person makes about you. This halo effect is often used in marketing. Beautiful people are given products to drink, eat, and wear, and other people will automatically assume these things are good, possibly thinking, "Well it must be good if this beautiful person is using it."

Recently I saw an ad on television that really hit this point home—the ad makes fun of marketing efforts but does it very intelligently. An attractive young female comes on the screen wearing beautiful clothing and says, "Hi, I am a believably attractive 18–24 year old female."

Using an attractive female who is not overly attractive, but believably real, someone we normal people can look up to is marketing genius. We can't really tell her age but her beauty can place her somewhere between the ages of 18–24.

"You can relate to me because I am racially ambiguous."

Again, this is another marketing genius tip. She is not black, white, or Native American—we can't tell, but she may be a mix, which may be attractive to many races and is non-offensive to most.

"I am in this commercial because market research shows girls like you love girls like me."

Her beauty and self-assuredness makes us like her; she is well dressed, well spoken, and we want to know her.

The camera then pans to different shots of her doing things like kickboxing, cheerleading, and playing with flowers. By showing viewers she can do all these things while being as beautiful as she is, we perceive her as strong and powerful, and all the things she's doing as good.

"Now I am going to tell you to buy something..."

She then goes on to sell tampons. This commercial is genius, because the advertiser actually outlines, uses, and educates the consumer on the methods used to make you want to buy. But despite all that, within this commercial lies this principle of liking and the halo effect.

Knowing all this about the importance of liking, what can you do? I have a hard enough time becoming an attractive male, let alone an attractive female. Because endless runs to my local plastic surgeon are out, is there anything a social engineer can do to capitalize on this principle?

Know your target. Know what is and isn't acceptable to him or her. How does he dress, and what does he consider bad and good? Too much jewelry, makeup, or other aspect of dress can turn off a target. Suppose you are auditing a doctor's office and your pretext is a drug sales representative. You know that most sales reps wear suits; have perfect hair; and look, smell, and act confident, a trait of many attractive people, so walking in with spiked hair and facial piercings would draw more attention to yourself than your goal.

You must know your target so you can successfully look the way the target would expect. Wear clothing, hairstyles, jewelry, and makeup that will not shock, surprise, or disgust the target. Putting her mind at ease can go a long way toward creating an atmosphere where she will like you, which will build trust and lead to success.

A social engineer can look for things to compliment a target on. When engaging a target, and when appropriate, starting the conversation with a simple complimentary question (such as "Those are nice shoes; where did you buy them?") is useful. People like positive reinforcement. When one receives compliments from another, he tends to stay engaged in order to receive more positive reinforcement. These compliments tend to reinforce a target's self image, making him feel as if you have a greater-than-normal understanding of him.

The University of Minnesota issued a paper (`www.cehd.umn.edu/ceed/publica-tions/tipsheets/preschoolbehaviortipsheets/posrein.pdf`) about reinforcement which states that too much positive reinforcement can have a negative effect. They call it satiation, which means that when reinforcement is given too much it begins to lose its effectiveness. To combat this effect, you can use positive reinforcement backed up by a question. This method reinforces positive behavior or attitudes but also makes people happy as they are asked about themselves.

Four steps can help you get people to like you:

1. Project a confident and positive attitude.

2. Establish rapport.

3. Synchronize, or get in tune with the target and surroundings using the methods mentioned earlier.

4. Effectively communicate.

In his book *How to Make People Like You in 90 Seconds*, Nicholas Boothman says that people decide whether they like someone in the first two seconds of meeting him or her. After an impression is made changing it can be hard. He promotes coming into an interaction with a good attitude. Having the ability to speak up and communicate effectively in many different situations can make you more likeable. What you project onto others is what they will feel. Your facial expressions, body language, dress, and so on must all project a good, positive attitude.

Boothman says some key things in his book about being likeable, including to ask lots of questions, actively listen, and be interested in what people are saying. Doing these things will help people like you.

A social engineer may need to practice it, but being likeable will go a long way toward succeeding in your audits.

Consensus or Social Proof

Social proof is a psychological phenomenon that occurs in social situations when people are unable to determine the appropriate mode of behavior. You can easily assume a behavior is appropriate if you see others acting or talking a certain way. Social influence in general can lead to conformity of large groups of individuals in either correct or mistaken choices. This behavior is common when people enter into unfamiliar situations and don't have a frame of reference on how to deal with the situation; they mirror their behavior off of others whom they assume are more familiar and therefore better informed.

In his book, *Influence: The Psychology of Persuasion*, Dr. Robert Cialdini states, "Social proof—people will do things that they see other people are doing. For example, in one experiment, one or more confederates would look up into the sky; bystanders would then look up into the sky to see what they were seeing. At one point this experiment is aborted, as so many people were looking up that they stopped traffic."

I will outline some excellent examples of social proof that will help you to see how powerful it is and if you have ever fallen for it.

Social proof is used heavily in marketing. Social proof is utilized in sales when high sales numbers are released, demonstrating to potential customers that the product is popular. Another example is when companies release shirts with logos or slogans printed on them, where the wearer then gives an implicit endorsement.

Social proof is not just influenced by large groups, but also by high-profile individuals. For instance, a single celebrity becoming associated with product will make others want to be associated with the celebrity's positive traits, and they will then use the same product.

Many examples exist of celebrity endorsements, here are a just a few:

» A major supplier of berets was able to get Samuel L. Jackson to endorse their product, The Kangol hat.

» Right through 2010 Maria Sharapova was paid millions in USD per year to endorse Canon products.

» Catherine Zeta Jones endorses T-Mobile Products in their TV commercials and print ads to the tune of $20 million in USD.

» In 2009, Tiger Woods was paid over $100 million in USD for his off-course product endorsements like AT&T, Gatorade, Gillette, Nike Golf and TAG HEUER to name a few.

» Michael Jordan still earns $45 million in USD per year for his Nike endorsements.

There are even some more unusual celebrity endorsements like:

» Ozzy Osbourne endorsing I Can't Believe It's Not Butter

» Mikhail Gorbachev endorsing Louis Vuitton

» Ben Stiller endorsing the alcoholic drink Chu High to Japanese Viewers

Why do companies spend so much just to have a celebrity endorse their products?

It is exactly how social proof works. When consumers see famous people they admire and adore wearing, using or even speaking about those products, it is as if they are being told directly by that person how amazing that product is. Many will view it as solid proof that these products are worth every penny.

In its marketing efforts the company said its hats were some of the hottest on the market and the proof was that Mr. Jackson can be seen wearing them.

Advertisers often say things like, "largest selling" or "hottest product" to convince their audience that they have the backing of many of our peers in these claims.

In addition, the Media-Studies.ca website posted an article on influencing its targets using social proof (www.media-studies.ca/articles/influence_ch4.htm):

> *Experiments have found that the use of canned laughter causes an audience to laugh longer and more often when humorous material is presented and to rate the material as funnier. In addition, some evidence indicates that canned laughter is most effective for poor jokes." The question is: why does it work, especially when the laugh track is often so obviously fake? To answer this question, Cialdini posits the principle of social proof: "One means we use to determine what is correct is to find out what other people think is correct...We view a behavior as more correct in a given situation to the degree that we see others performing it."*

As with the other "weapons of influence," social proof is a shortcut that usually works well for us: if we conform to the behavior we see around us, we are less likely to make a social faux pas. The fact that canned laughter provokes an automatic response in audiences suggests that auditory cues are powerful stimuli because they influence us at a level of consciousness that is difficult to critique.

Other examples are how bartenders or other establishments will "salt the tip jar," by placing a few bills in the jar. As a patron approaches to purchase food the implication is, "Many before you have tipped me, why don't you?" And it works, too!

One of the most profound bits of research in this field that really stands out was done by Dr. K. D. Craig in 1978. Dr. Craig devoted his life to the study of pain and its effect on people. In 1978 he published a paper entitled "Social Modeling Influences on Sensory Decision Theory and Psychophysiological Indexes of Pain" (www.ncbi.nlm.nih.gov/pubmed/690805?dopt=Abstract), in which he did an experiment that he described as:

> *Subjects exposed to social models dissimulating tolerance or intolerance generally exhibit matching behavior in their verbal ratings of painful stimulation. It has been unclear, however, whether these changes reflect voluntary alteration of evidence or genuine changes in distress.*

This study used alternative measures and controlled for method-ological limitations of earlier studies by examining non-palmar skin potential in addition to palmar skin conductance and heart rate indexes of psycho-physiological response to electric shock, and by evaluating verbal expressions of pain with sensory decision theory methodology.

Several indexes of non-palmar skin potential and heart rate reac-tivity exhibited lower reactivity in the tolerant group. Tolerant modeling was also associated with decreases in subjective stress. The results were consistent with the position that changes in pain indexes associated with exposure to a tolerant model represented variations in fundamental characteristics of painful experiences as opposed to suppression of information.

To boil this down, what he basically did was shock people and ask them to rate their pain level. Then using similar but varying shocks did the same test in the presence of a person who was "tolerant" to the pain; it was as if a magical cloak was over the subject, because they were now more tolerant to pain.

This experiment points to the fact that part of the motivation to show, exhibit, or feel pain is related to how others around you act. The people in the study weren't just acting like it hurt less: Their skin reactions and heart rate actually exhibited less pain reaction when a tolerant model was in place.

For a humorous example of the power of social proof, check out a video from the old television show *Candid Camera* at `www.social-engineer.org/framework/ Influence_Tactics:_Consensus_or_Social_Proof`.

This video shows subjects being influenced to face different directions in an elevator, even at one point facing toward the back because everyone else is doing it. There were four to five participants in the elevator acting as patrons. At set intervals, the participants would all turn to the left, to the right, or face backwards. After a few seconds, a hidden camera would catch the unsuspecting subject complying and facing the same direction, removing a hat, or taking some other action.

Using social proof as a social engineer can be a deadly tool. This principle can be used to stimulate a person's compliance with a request by informing him or her that many other individuals, perhaps some who are role models, took the action or behavior you are trying to get this person to do. Social proof can provide a shortcut for determining how to behave. But at the same time it can make targets vulnerable to the manipulations of others who seek to exploit such influence.

Social proof is most influential under two conditions:

» **Uncertainty:** When people are unsure and the situation is ambiguous they are more likely to observe the behavior of others and to accept that behavior as correct.

» **Similarity:** People are more inclined to follow the lead of others who are similar to themselves.

These conditions are where a social engineer can use social proof. Stating or even implying that many people before this target have taken a particular action can increase your chances of success.

In one social engineering situation where I was stopped by a leery security guard, I simply acted confused as to why I was stopped and said, "Yesterday, Jim let me in after checking all my credentials. I just figured I was still on record."

The present security guard, hearing that Jim approved me, allowed me to pass without question. Social proof won't always work so easily, but it is a very powerful force.

The principles outlined in this section are some of the deadliest influence tactics used today. These tactics can literally give a social engineer powers to motivate people, move them, and cause them to react in ways that will put them in the social engineer's control.

Remember that influence and the art of persuasion is the process of getting someone else to *want* to do, react, think, or believe in the way *you* want them to. Creating this motivation within a target is a powerful force; it is a social engineer's superpower. The principles outlined in this chapter can make that superpower a reality, but not without consequence and lots of work.

What do I mean by that? I have often found that after I practice a certain skill and become proficient at it, "turning it off" is very hard. This trait may sound attractive, but being cautious when it comes to who you are influencing, especially as a social engineer, is a good idea. To ingrain these skills into your personality, use them for helping others. For example, when you start to practice reading microexpressions and even using them to manipulate a target, the initial response might be to think you have some mystical power that allows you to almost read minds. This is where caution is wise. Practice the skill and work toward perfecting it, but don't assume you know it all.

If you can influence someone to stop smoking, to start working out, or to be healthier, then you will learn to tap into these skills at will to benefit others, and using them in your social engineering practice is not a farfetched idea.

Many of these skills require you to actually be interested in people, care about them, and empathize with them. If these are not natural abilities for you, then you must work hard to obtain those skills. I urge you to take that time, because the skills in the preceding section can lead you to being a grand master social engineer.

Imagine you could alter what you think to the extent that gaining these skills could be easier. Imagine now, too, if you could alter the thinking of your targets so what they experience is exactly what you want them to experience. Literally altering the reality of those you interact with, including yourself, is the next topic, and it will just blow you away.

Altering Reality: Framing

Framing has been defined as information and experiences in life that alter the way one reacts to the decisions one must make. From a non–social engineer point of view, framing is your own personal experiences and the experiences of others that you allow into your conscious mind to alter the way you make decisions.

Grocery stores use framing by putting "75% lean" on a package of ground meat as opposed to "25% fat." These terms mean the same thing (both have 25% fat content) but one sounds healthier and is more appealing to the buyer, and that is why stores use 75% lean as opposed to labeling the actual fat content.

The preceding example is simple, but it is also one that helps to show the power of framing. Simply presenting the facts in a different way can make something seem good that would normally be considered bad.

The following sections look at a few areas where framing is often used so you can see how powerful it is.

Politics

Framing has long been used in politics. Simply the way campaigns or messages are worded can make a huge difference in the way the public perceives a message.

Consider, for example, George Lakoff, a professional cognitive linguist. In an interesting observation on framing in politics, he states the difference in how people perceive the use of the phrases "Counterterrorism as law enforcement" versus

"Counterterrorism as war." When the 9/11 attacks occurred, Colin Powell argued that they should be treated as crimes. When the public demanded more action and stricter policies, then President Bush announced the "War on Terror" campaign.

Another example is the Social Security program in the United States. The name implies that this program can be relied upon to provide security for the future.

Yet another example is the difference in the terms *bailout* versus *economic stimulus*. *Bailout* met with lots of opposition because it can paint a word picture of bailing water out of a sinking boat. But *economic stimulus* paints the mental picture of helping the economy by stimulating the economy. Both programs did almost the same thing, but simple wording made the latter term more acceptable.

Judith Butler, Berkeley professor and author of the critically acclaimed book *Frames of War,* wrote about how framing is used especially in western cultures when it comes to political agendas and war. In her book she explores the media's portrayal of state violence:

> *This portrayal has saturated our understanding of human life, and has led to the exploitation and abandonment of whole peoples, who are cast as existential threats rather than as living populations in need of protection. These people are framed as already lost, to imprisonment, unemployment, and starvation, and can easily be dismissed. In the twisted logic that rationalizes their deaths, the loss of such populations is deemed necessary to protect the lives of "the living."*

These are just a few examples where framing is used in politics.

Using Framing in Everyday Life

The term *frame of reference* is defined as a set of ideas, conditions, or assumptions that determine how something will be approached, perceived, or understood. This definition can be helpful in understanding how framing is used.

Anything that can alter people's perceptions or the way they make decisions can be called framing. A friend tells you that last week she went to town and took a certain route that was backed up for 10 miles due to some construction. You might then take a longer route to avoid the potential delay, even though the news your friend shared is more than one week old.

Our minds are designed to not like "clutter" or chaos. When presented with things that are cluttered our brains will try to make order out of them. One interesting example of this is found in Figure 6-3.

Figure 6-3 Can you alter your reality frame to change what you see?

In your present frame, what is the background and what is the foreground? Your minds will insist on finding familiar patterns in things. We do it in clouds, space, and inanimate objects. Humans also tend to see faces in these things.

In Figure 6-3 can you alter your frame and change what is the image and what is the background? Try by focusing on the opposite of what you noticed first.

Another very interesting example of how human brains find order in chaos can be illustrated in an e-mail that circulated over the last few years that looked like this:

O lny srmat poelpe can raed tihs.

I cdnuolt blveiee taht I cluod aulaclty uesdnatnrd waht I was rdanieg. The phaonmneal pweor of the hmuan mnid, aoccdrnig to a rscheearch at Cmabrigde Uinervtisy, it deosn't mttaer in waht oredr the ltteers in a wrod are, the olny iprmoatnt tihng is taht the frist and lsat ltteer be in the rghit pclae. The rset can be a taotl mses and you can sitll raed it wouthit a porbelm. Tihs is bcuseae the huamn mnid deos not raed ervey lteter by istlef, but the wrod as a wlohe. Amzanig huh? yaeh and I awlyas tghuhot slpeling was ipmorantt! if you can raed tihs psas it on !!

I am not sure whether this is actually Cambridge research, but the interesting part in that forwarded e-mail is how many of us who use English as our main language or are very proficient in reading English are probably able to read that paragraph without much effort, because our brains are very efficient at making order out of chaos.

Many times the framing is more subliminal. Companies use this in marketing in hopes that the subliminal messages will alter the target's perception of their product. Many times companies will use subtle measures of framing to plant an idea.

For example, Figure 6-4 shows something you probably have seen many times.

Figure 6-4 Can you spot the frame?

After I show you this, you will never see the FedEx logo the same way again—there is an arrow in the FedEx logo. In an interview with the creator of the logo, he said he embedded the arrow in the logo to plant an idea about FedEx's services. It is there to communicate movement, speed, and the dynamic nature of the company.

Did you find it yet? Look at Figure 6-4 where I outlined and circled the arrow.

Figure 6-5 The arrow indicates quality service that is always moving.

FedEx is not the only company that utilizes framing. For decades companies have been embedding messages into logos in an effort to frame the thinking of the viewer to remember, think, and view their company in the way they want. The next few figures show more examples.

Did you ever notice Amazon's logo for its embedded framing message (see Figure 6-6)?

Figure 6-6 Do you see the smiling happy customer?

Amazon has two framed messages in its logo. One is the happiness you will feel as a customer, represented by the smile in the image, but the smile is also an arrow. That arrow points from A to Z, indicating the Amazon has everything from both points and in between.

Another great example is the Tostitos logo. This is a very social logo, as you can see in Figure 6-7.

Figure 6-7 Does this logo make you want to share a chip with someone?

The two T's in the middle are people sharing a chip over a bowl of salsa. In 2004, Tostitos issued a press release that said, "Tostitos plays a role as a 'social snack,' helping to create connections between friends and families, whether it's at a party, during the 'big game,' or at simple everyday get-togethers. The new logo brings to life this idea of making connections."

These examples are just a small subset of how framing is used in marketing. Framing is not all about images; mostly it is about the value that *the target perceives*. The perception that the target has of an item can increase or decrease its value. Take an expensive clothing store—when you walk in everything is hung neatly, pressed, and perfect. The perception can be that the clothing is worth the exorbitant amount of the price tag. Yet, if you were to take one of the ties, shirts, or other pieces of clothing off the rack; bring it to a discount store; and throw it into a large bin full of other clothes marked, "Discount 75% off" your perception of the value of that item of clothing would go way down.

Marketing gurus play off this phenomenon in an effort to frame the public's perception of value. Many companies have been successful at framing to such an extent that people actually have coined phrases to create a whole genre of words to describe products.

For example, everyone has probably said, "Will you make a Xerox of that?" even if the machine is not a Xerox but another brand. Xerox is the brand name, not the type of machine.

A more recent example is no matter what search engine you use, people often say, "Did you Google it?" because Google has become synonymous with searching on the Web. And people say, "Hand me a Kleenex please," when really they want a tissue.

Others that you might not even be aware were brand names (unless you are of the generation in which they were introduced) include:

» *Aspirin* is a trademarked product of Bayer.

» *Thermos* is a product name of Thermos GmbH Company.

» *Band-Aid* is a trademark of Johnson & Johnson.

» *Frisbee* was a trademark of Wham-O.

All of those names became so popular that people's frame of reference eventually encompassed any product similar to it. I never take aspirin—I usually use another brand—but I will always ask for "two aspirin," be given the brand I use, and be happy.

Volumes of information exist about framing, but boiling down this information to some main principles you can use as a social engineer is necessary. The preceding information set a very detailed stage for what framing is and how it is used in different areas of life. Before moving to the social engineering arena, take a look at the different types of framing alignments.

Four Types of Frame Alignment

Two researchers, David Snow from the University of Arizona and Robert Benford from the University of Nebraska, wrote a paper entitled, "Clarifying the Relationship Between Framing and Ideology in the Study of Social Movements" (`www.social-engineer` `.org/resources/book/SNOW_BED.pdf`).

Snow and Benford argue that when individual frames become linked in congruency and complementariness, that *frame alignment* occurs, producing *frame resonance*, which is key to the process of a group transitioning from one frame to another. Snow and Benford then outline four conditions that affect framing efforts:

» **"The robustness, completeness, and thoroughness of the framing effort":** Snow and Benford identified three core framing tasks, and the degree to which these tasks are attended to will determine how much each participant gets involved.

The three steps are:

1. Diagnose the frame for problems.

2. Analyze it for solutions.

3. If successful, a call to action.

The more effort put into the frame the better chance the person has to call those he is framing into action.

» **"The relationship between the proposed frame and the larger belief system":** People tend to discount frames or proposed frames if a link does not exist to a core belief or a value of their belief system.

Trying to convince a person who holds a belief that eating meat is cruelty to animals to go to the steak place down the road that has a great special will certainly fail. The frame must fall with the core of a person's beliefs to be successful (unless your goal is to use a frame to change his or her core beliefs); it is imperative to success.

A large-scale framing change attempt was made through the controversial anti-smoking commercials where volunteers pile up body bags in front of a tobacco industry building's front door. The body bags represent how many people die every minute, hour, or day from smoking. The hope is to alter the frame of those who support smoking to think about the death toll for those who smoke.

» **"Relevance of the frame to the realities of the participants":** The frame must be relevant to the person (target). It must be creditable and testable as it relates to the target's experience.

You can't expect to use a marketing frame that will encourage people to take a luxury cruise in a land where people cannot afford food for the day. No matter how good you are at using framing in marketing, it just would fail. For the frame to align, it must not just be relevant but must also be provable in order to hold value, even if that proof is just in the mind of the target.

For example, in 2007 a very popular and trusted news source, *Insight Magazine* (which is owned by the same company as *The Washington Times*) reported that then-presidential candidate Obama had attended an all-Muslim school that was known for teaching a very radical and fundamental form of Islam. When this news report was released many believed it right away—why? It fit into the frame of their reality, it seemed credible, and it came from a "trusted" source.

CNN, another reputable source for news, sent out investigators, discovered that story was false, and reported its findings.

This is a good example of altering people's frames on a matter using a very trusted source for "truth"—news media. People who wanted to believe that Obama was a radical Muslim ran with that story, and the news went wild. When research revealed the story to be false, many people's thinking was altered again.

» **"Cycles of protest; the point at which the frame emerges on the timeline of the current era and existing preoccupations with social change":** What is happening in the world can affect a social frame. Think back a few years ago; if the idea of full body X-ray scans were proposed to companies in the U.S. or other Western cultures, the idea would have been thrown to the wind.

Activists for privacy would have fought against the idea and won, simply by using the idea of someone being able to see your private areas and potentially saving that picture to mock or sexually harass you. This argument would have outweighed the sales efforts of the creators of the machines. Yet, after the attacks in America on September 11 and the subsequent rise of terrorist activity, those machines are being installed at airports around the globe despite the cries by activists, even arguing with the power of child pornography laws on their side.

Why? The social frame of how to remain safe has been altered, allowing a new breed of decision to enter.

Snow and Benford propose that when proper frames are constructed as described in these four points, large-scale changes in society such as those necessary for social movement can be achieved through frame alignment. Their studies focus on society as a whole, but these same principles are effective when dealing on a smaller scale or even one-to-one.

The preceding discussion is just the process to frame alignment; actually four different types of alignment can occur after these four conditions are met. Although many of these aspects are geared towards framing groups as a whole, the following sections discuss these four framing alignments on a personal level that will show how you can use them on a smaller scale both as a social engineer and/or just as a person wanting to align frames with others. Imagine trying to align your goal of entry to a building with the frame of the security guard designed to stop you. Bringing his frame into alignment with your pretext can ensure success.

One thing to remember about frames is that they are never constructed from scratch. Frames are always drawn on already-existing cultural codes that involve the core of a person's beliefs and experiences. Knowing this will affect how you use framing.

Frame Bridging

The Cathie Marsh Centre for Census and Survey Information defines *frame bridging* as the linkage of two or more ideologically congruent but structurally unconnected frames regarding a particular topic.

Bridging is not about tricking people into believing your frame as much as your understanding their frame so deeply that you find the connecting link. You then use that connecting link to bring a target into your frame.

The situation could be that you want to gain access to an area, building, or piece of information. Your frame is that you want that to happen. The frame of the person you are approaching is not necessarily to stop you; he may not even know what you are going to attempt. If you were to approach the situation in that frame you may alert him to a problem and thereby shut down your chances.

By understanding the target's job, role, and mental outlook you can understand his frame of mind and maybe find a link that will make his transition into your frame much easier.

What is your pretext? How would the person you are about to approach treat a person in your pretext? A good social engineer must understand this to be successful. The "gatekeeper" will treat a sales guy differently from the soda delivery guy. Understanding the frame of the target means knowing how he will treat you—not you as a social engineer, but you as the pretext.

A more personal example may be to think of how you want others to view you—maybe as cool, "together," intelligent, or confident. A professor wants to appear smart. A manager wants to appear in control. An athlete wants to appear calm and strong. A comedian wants the audience to view her as funny. All of these are frames that a person wants others to be in alignment with.

In the comedian's case, what if there is a heckler—a person who doesn't see her as cool, funny, intelligent, or confident? Because of the heckler's frame they are angry, not happy, put off, or just not interested? If the comedian persists in his frame he may convert some people around him, but until he delves deep and try to understand where someone is coming from he will not be able to align their two frames and bring that person into his frame. The comedian who can handle a heckler is able to put aside her fears about her frame and use the heckler to her advantage.

The frame bridging alignment technique can be one of the most powerful used by a social engineer, but involves some preparation to make sure you get it right.

A social engineer can utilize this particular form of frame alignment by helping a target bridge the gap of what they see and what they need to believe through a proper pretext. Again, recall the example of trying to gain access to the building as a tech support rep. Your dress, tools, and language must match the frame that the target expects of a support rep. If they do, the bridge is created and alignment occurs.

Frame Amplification

Frame amplification, according to Snow, refers to "the clarification and invigoration of an interpretive frame that bears on a particular issue, problem, or set of events." In other words, you will amplify, or focus on, the values or beliefs of the target. By focusing on those values you can find an area that will align your two frames, or at least drive the target to think there is alignment.

This form of alignment has been labeled as the most basic of the four because it is more of a maintenance method. It involves the accenting, augmenting, or punctuating of an event as being more important than others, which allows for this event to be linked with other events with greater ease.

An example of frame amplification can be revealed if we do further research into the earlier example about the full-body X-ray scanners. The scanners are being sold now as deterrents for terrorists. The frame that they are being sold under is how the recent terrorist activity caused a need for products like these, and here they are to fulfill that need. Yet research into these devices shows they were being built, marketed, and rejected long before the attacks of 9/11 and other recent attacks.

Using the events of 9/11 combined with the fear of flying many people have due to those attacks enables the scanner companies to link their frame with the frame of fear many people have, and thereby gain support for implementing these devices in airports around the globe.

One of the other strengths of frame amplification is that it can be successfully used to blur the frame and cause people with a certain belief to distance themselves from that belief. For example, many who believed in privacy and the freedom to choose how to be screened have been brought into a different frame by the x-ray scanner manufacturers focusing on certain aspects of other screening methods being unsafe or incomplete, and to prove their point they bring out stories like "the underwear bomber." Such tactics amplify their frame that the new x-ray scanners are better and safer, using widely held beliefs regarding the lack of security of other methods.

A social engineer can utilize this alignment technique in a few different ways. For instance, a social engineer may want to convince a security guard to give him access to an onsite dumpster area. The pretext of working for a waste disposal contractor is good and it very well may work alone, but it would work even better if you presented the idea that there is damage to one of the dumpsters, which represents a security liability for the company. Amplifying that frame can bring you to an alignment with the security guard that the best solution is allowing you onsite to check it out.

Frame Extension

"*Frame extensions* are a movement's effort to incorporate participants by extending the boundaries of the proposed frame to encompass the views, interests, and, more importantly, the sentiments of a group." In other words, by extending your frame's boundaries to encompass other subjects or interests of your target, you can bring them into alignment.

For example, the possibility exists that groups who support environmental or "green" initiatives will extend their frame to antinuclear movements, stating they are under the umbrella of a being concerned about the environmental risks.

However, a risk with using frame extensions is they can weaken the stance on the original frame and a certain level of appeal can be lost. This can be done by including too many frame extensions into a certain frame, eventually diluting the main frame and causing interest to be lost.

Even on a personal level, simple is best. When using this frame alignment tactic, keep it simple and easy to follow. Don't make the connecting web so convoluted you lose the interest of the target.

A social engineer may utilize this frame alignment technique through the elicitation skills discussed in Chapter 3. When a social engineer approaches a target, she can gather information about the target or their company by not acting interested in that but utilizing chit-chat at a party, or with a pretext as a reporter. This will give the social engineer the "right" to ask for information that they would normally have to work very hard to get.

Frame Transformation

"*Frame transformation* is a process required when the proposed frames may not resonate with, and on occasion may even appear antithetical to, conventional lifestyles or rituals and extant interpretive frames." In other words, a social engineer offers new arguments that point to why their frame is better in an effort to transform the thoughts or beliefs of a target from where they are to where the social engineer wants them to be.

When a frame transformation occurs, new values and new understandings are required to keep people involved and keep their support. This type of transformation was done on a large social level in the 1970s where the conservative movement was reframed or transformed into a more progressive environmentalist movement.

On a smaller, more personal scale, frame transformations occur every day through religious conversion, in which a person's frame or whole belief system is altered, changed, and transformed to be aligned with a new frame of thought, that of the new religion.

Transforming someone's frame is not easy; it is one of the most complicated alignment tactics to put into practice because it can take:

» **Time:** Changing someone's whole belief structure is not a quick process and can take the usage of other alignment techniques and lots of time to make it work.

» **Effort:** Knowing where the target is coming from and where you want him to be are just the initial steps. What will be his objections and mental blocks? Finding out these things will take some work.

» **Education:** Knowledge is power. You must help the target understand the new frame you want him to "convert" to.

»   **Logic:** The education must be logical and not all emotion. The target must be able to reason and rationalize the action he is about to take. The only way he can do that is with logic.

»   **Deep emotional ties:** Knowledge is what prepares a person for action, logic convinces him the action is good to take, but emotion is what makes the action happen. If you are emotional about your "cause" the target will feel that emotion. Just make sure the emotion you are expressing and feeling matches the pretext. If your pretext is a guidance counselor and you come in like a cheerleader you will offset the target's ability to align.

Being able to align others to your frame and align yourself with theirs can give people incentive to do the things you ask. Although using any of the four framing methods is powerful, a social engineer who is successful in frame transformation has endless power.

Read on to find out how to apply these framing techniques as a social engineer.

Using Framing as a Social Engineer

Throughout this section I mentioned many ways a social engineer might use framing as a technique. Some of these methods are so powerful that perfecting them can turn you into a master influencer.

To truly use framing as a social engineer you must understand four things about framing. These four things will help you to understand clearly how framing works and how to use it as a social engineer.

Remember what a frame is. A frame is a conceptual structure that our minds use in thinking. This is a vital piece of information because your goal is either to create a new frame, align with a person's frame, or bring the target into your frame.

One of those three goals needs to be outlined with the following four rules in order to master framing as a social engineer.

Rule 1: Everything You Say Will Evoke a Frame

People's minds work by picturing things. This natural fact cannot be altered, but you can use it to your advantage.

If I start to talk to you about your boss, your mind will picture him. If I paint a picture with words about how he was outside on the cell phone and he was angry, your mind will start to picture his angry face, body language, and words. You will not be able to control this and that mental frame will cause emotions and reactions.

Painting a picture with words is a powerful way to use framing. By choosing your words carefully you can cause a target's mind to picture things you want him to picture and start moving him to a frame you want.

Have you ever heard someone who you thought was a great storyteller? Why? What made her great? She was able to paint a mental picture, make you see things in your mind, which intrigues you and gets you involved. This skill is very important for a social engineer. It doesn't mean you talk as if you are telling a great story all the time, but you want to keep in mind the words you choose because those words hold the power to paint pictures in the minds of the targets.

Here is a simple example: I can tell you that I had spaghetti for dinner last night. If you are not a foodie or not Italian, maybe the last time you had spaghetti it wasn't that pleasurable. Your mental frame is not that strong and you might be turned off.

What if I told you that last night my wife made a sauce of vine-ripened tomatoes and basil she grew in the garden? It also had chunks of fresh garlic and oregano in it, as well as a hint of red wine flavors. She served it over a plate of perfectly cooked spaghetti noodles and with homemade garlic bread.

Whether or not you are a pasta fan, you are picturing a restaurant-quality dish. This is how you should plan your words with your targets. They should be descriptive, robust, and full of pictures. Yet the caution is not to be overly theatrical as a social engineer. Your goal should be to build a picture with your words, not to draw attention to yourself or your delivery.

Rule 2: Words That Are Defined Within a Frame Evoke the Mental Frame

You don't have to use the exact words to make a person picture the frame you want. For example, what do you think of when you read the following sentence?

"I saw the insect struggle to get free from the web, but he could not. Moments later he was wrapped up in a cocoon and saved for dinner."

Notice, I didn't have to mention a spider to make you think of a spider. If I want to frame you into thinking about a spider, I can do it without having to mention the word *spider*. This powerful rule of influence and framing gives a social engineer the ability to control the target's thoughts using indirect speech.

Toastmasters, the international organization focused on people's speaking abilities, teaches its members to move people with their speech by getting their audience's emotions involved. Delivering a story that causes the target to picture the frame you want while involving them emotionally will solidify your standing in leading that conversation.

Again, using this method of framing will take planning. A powerful aspect to this frame rule is that while a target's brain is processing the information you are feeding it and generating the mental pictures you are painting, there is a time when you can plant thoughts or ideas. Unlike where I painted a direct picture of a beautiful pasta dish, this rule allows the target the freedom to picture something else.

I could have ended my earlier spaghetti dinner story with, "My wife then served it on a plate of perfectly cooked pasta. What kind of pasta? I am not telling you, you have to picture it," and when your brain starts to picture it then I can say, "As I twirled it on my fork, the sauce was so thick and perfect it clung to each noodle."

This description paints the mental picture of spaghetti. What other pasta do you twirl? (I know there are others, but you get the point.)

Rule 3: Negating the Frame

If I tell you to *not* picture a spider in a web, your brain has to picture the spider first to tell yourself to not picture it.

This technique of negating the frame is powerful. Telling a target to be careful, watch out, or be cautious about something automatically puts them in the frame you may want. This technique is often used by professional social engineers. In one interview I did with a panel of social engineers, everyone agreed that this technique works great.

During one audit, I dropped a few USB keys that were laden with malicious code that I wanted someone in the company to run without thinking. I approached one of the employees who I had gained the trust of and said, "John, I heard a memo was issued to be on the lookout for a few USB keys that have been dropped. They are looking for them now."

It just so happens that you are in there as a janitor and you dropped the USB keys laden with malicious files, and now by telling people to look out for them, you are in essence planting the seed for them to do your bidding. This kind of a phrase negates the worry they may feel when finding a rogue USB key and cause them to plug it in to see whose it is.

Rule 4: Causing the Target to Think About the Frame Reinforces That Frame

Every time the brain focuses or thinks about something it is reinforced. The more you can make the target think about or picture the frame you want him in, the easier it will be to reinforce and move him to that frame.

Look back at Chapter 2 on communication modeling and analyze how the messages a social engineer will develop can have amazing effects on your targets.

I was once traveling in India. I don't remember the exact incident in the news, but all I know is that President George W. Bush had lost favor with people in Europe. I was flipping through the news stations and saw how people in certain European countries where hanging dolls that looked like George W. Bush in the streets. After wrapping American flags around the dolls they were lighting them on fire.

It was a shocking scene and while I was on the phone with my wife that evening I said, "Wow that news story on what's happening in Europe is crazy, huh?"

She hadn't heard anything about it. Why? News media and news stations are masters when it comes to framing and manipulation.

A social engineer can learn a lot from looking at how media utilizes this skill. By using omissions, or leaving out details of a story or the whole story itself, the media can lead people to a conclusion that seems like their own, but really is the media's.

Social engineers can do that, too. By omitting certain details and only "leaking" details that they want leaked, they can create the frame that they want the target to think or feel.

Labeling is another tactic used by the media. When they want to frame something positive they may say things like, "the strong defense of..." or "our healthy economy." These phrases paint mental pictures of stability and health that can help draw positive conclusions. The same rules can apply for negative frames, too. Labels such as, "Islamic terrorists" or "conspiracy theories" paint a very negative picture.

You can utilize these skills to label things with descriptive words that will bring a target into the frame you want. Once, approaching a guard booth that I wanted to gain access to, I walked right through as if I belonged. I was instantly stopped abruptly. I looked at the guard in shock and apologetically I used a phrase like, "Oh, yesterday that extremely helpful security guard, Tom, checked out all my creds and let me pass. That is why I assumed I was still on the list."

Labeling the previous guard as "extremely helpful" automatically puts the present guard in a frame I want. If he wants to receive such a prestigious label, he better be as "extremely helpful" as Tom was.

Framing is effective because it bends the truth but not so much that it becomes false, so it remains believable. A social engineer can create a desired impression without departing too far from the appearance of objectivity.

I read a white paper called "Status Quo Framing Increases Support for Torture," written by Christian Crandall, Scott Eidelman, Linda Skitka, and Scott Morgan, all researchers from different universities. In the white paper they supplied a very interesting data set that intrigued me on this topic. In the U.S. it seems many people are against the use of torture in wartime as a tactic for gaining intelligence information. The purpose of this study was to see whether the researchers could get a subset of people to agree that torture is less disagreeable by framing the message differently.

They took a sample group of roughly 486 people and asked them to read two paragraphs.

The first one read:

> *The use of stress by U.S. forces when questioning suspects in the Middle East is in the news. This kind of stress interview is new; according to some reports, it is the first time it has been widely used by the U.S. military. American forces have used many different methods, including strapping detainees to a board and dunking them underwater, stuffing detainees face-first into a sleeping bag, and long periods of hanging detainees by ropes in painful positions. Detainees are also kept awake and alone for days at a time.*

This paragraph paints the thought that these are *new* techniques being employed by the U.S. Government to obtain data.

The second paragraph read:

> *The use of stress by U.S. forces when questioning suspects in the Middle East is in the news. This kind of stress interview is not new; according to some reports, it has been used for more than 40 years by the U.S. military. American forces have used many different methods, including strapping detainees to a board and dunking them underwater, stuffing detainees face-first into a sleeping bag, and long periods of hanging detainees by ropes in painful positions. Detainees are also kept awake and alone for days at a time.*

The status quo version of the paragraph was identical, except that the second sentence in the paragraph was replaced with "This kind of stress interview is not new; according to some reports, it has been used for more than 40 years by the U.S. military."

What were the results in just changing one frame—a frame that these are brand-new methods or that these are tried-and-tested methods that have been used for decades?

The paper describes the researchers' measures. Seven items formed the basic set of dependent variables. These items corresponded to a seven-point "button" scale, with the point labels of very much disagree, moderately disagree, slightly disagree, uncertain, slightly agree, moderately agree, and very much agree. All items were reverse scored so that higher scores reflected greater agreement with each item.

The conclusion? "The status quo manipulation had an effect on overall evaluation of torture—when described as a long-standing rather than new practice, torture was evaluated *more positively;* [m]aking torture appear to be the status quo for interrogations increased individual support and justifications for using it as a tactic."

By changing just one little part of the frame the researchers were able to bring a sizeable group of people into alignment and make them agree (for the most part) that torture can be an acceptable policy.

That paper's remarks continued, "They can apply across many, many domains, and can affect judgment, decision making, aesthetics, and policy preferences," concluding with, "relatively modest changes in the way ethical choices and value dilemmas are presented, framed, or put in context can have profound effect on political choice and policy."

This experiment proves how powerful framing is because it can change even core beliefs, judgments, and decisions that people may have had for years. As a social engineer that is not even the goal most of the time. You are not trying to convert people; you're just trying to get them to take an action that with a little thought they would reason is not that good to take.

Applying the four framing rules and doing a lot of planning can make framing a devastating force to be reckoned with, which is why, unfortunately, malicious social engineers use this technique every day. In the U.S. and "westernized cultures," especially, people are trained to accept being framed, to accept being told what to think and how to think it.

If I told you 15 years ago that almost every program on television would be about watching real people do real things, you might have laughed at me. Why? Because watching shows like that sounded boring and silly. Yet in 2006, the *Los Angeles Times* stated that the number of reality TV programs jumped up 128% (`http://articles.latimes.com/2010/mar/31/business/la-fi-ct-onlocation31-2010mar31`), and it hasn't slowed down much since then, and it's because watching them is what's new and hip, and we are told that watching them is good and fun, and everyone does it. These shows are an example of how one thing can be made to look good that most people would have considered silly just a few years earlier.

Framing is definitely an art form that when mixed with the science of communication and influence can become a formidable force on a personal level in the hands of a skilled social engineer, through presenting information in a way that can make aligning with the social engineer "easy" for the target, can make him take action that will not leave him feeling guilty, and alter his perception of reality.

Framing and influence are key parts of social engineering, although another skill is often associated with the "dark corners" of social engineering. The book's introduction mentioned peering into these corners; the following section presents the information that will alter the way you look at influence.

Manipulation: Controlling Your Target

Manipulation is considered by many to be a very dark topic, a topic that creates a sense of fear because of the way it is often portrayed.

Taking a look at a few definitions found on the Internet may help to explain:

» "exerting shrewd or devious influence especially for one's own advantage"

» "influence or control shrewdly or deviously"

» "control (others or oneself) or influence skillfully, usually to one's advantage"

You can clearly see why many social engineers drool over this topic. Can you imagine being able to use your skills to control or influence someone to your advantage?

From something as dark as brainwashing to the subtle hints of a salesperson, manipulation tactics are something every social engineer should study and perfect. The aim of manipulation is to overcome the critical thinking and free will of their target. When the target loses his ability to make a decision based on informed processes, they can be fed the ideas, values, attitudes, or reasonings of the one manipulating them.

Manipulation is used in six ways that hold true whether the topic is brainwashing or something less insidious. I will quickly go through each one before we get into this very deep section.

» **Increasing the suggestibility of your target.** At its most extreme, sleep or food deprivation increases a target's suggestibility. On the lighter side, subtle hints that build in intensity over time to make your target more suggestible.

» **Gaining control over the target's environment.** This technique can involve everything from controlling the type and quantity of information to which a target has access to much subtler things like gaining access to a target's social media websites. In a social engineering context, having access to social media allows you to view your target's communications as well as exert control over the information he receives.

» **Creating doubt.** Destabilizing and undermining your target's belief system can go a long way toward manipulating your target to take an action you want. From a social engineering viewpoint, this must be done subtly. You can't just barge in and start degrading your target; instead, questioning the rules they follow, their job, or their beliefs can affect the target's ability to make rational decisions.

» **Creating a sense of powerlessness.** This truly malicious technique is used in wartime interrogations to make a target feel a lack of confidence in their convictions. A social engineer can utilize this tactic by taking away the target's agency by presenting the "facts" you received from someone with authority, thus creating a powerless feeling.

» **Creating strong emotional responses in the target.** Strong emotional responses include everything from doubt to guilt to humiliation and more. If the feelings are intense enough, they can cause the target to alter their whole belief system. A social engineer must be careful not to create damaging negative emotions, but using tactics that create an emotional response based on fear of loss or punishment can prove beneficial to your SE goal.

» **Heavy intimidation.** Fear of physical pain or other dire circumstances can be used to make a target crack under pressure. Again, most social engineers will not go this route unless they are using corporate espionage as a tactic, but in normal social engineering, this tactic utilizes perceived authority to build strong fear and feelings of potential loss.

Most times, however, manipulation is not so extreme. On its very basic level, imagine you're in a crowded room and someone calls out your name. What is your reaction? Usually it is to turn around or respond with a "Yes?" You have been manipulated, but not necessarily in a bad way.

On a psychological level, being manipulated is even more profound. Notice what happens to make that preceding interaction happen: Your brain hears your name, and you automatically formulate an answer ("Yes?"). The connection between that answer and your vocal response is very short. Even if you made no vocal response or if the name-calling is not targeted to you personally, if a question is asked your mind will formulate an answer.

Just being in close proximity of two people conversing and overhearing a question will cause your mind to formulate an answer. The answer can be an image or sound in your mind. If a target overhears two people talking about what someone looks like his mind will form a mental picture. If you hear two people telling a joke about a chicken crossing the road, you may picture the chicken, the road, or the whole scene.

This type of manipulation is just the beginning of what you can do. Another manipulation tactic is that of *conditioning*.

People can be conditioned to connect certain sounds or actions with feelings and emotions. If every time something positive is mentioned a person hears a pen click, after a short time the target can be conditioned to associate a positive feeling with this sound.

One of the most classic examples of conditioning was Ivan Pavlov and what we call Pavlov's dog, which was discussed in Chapter 5. The question then becomes whether you can use this type of conditioning on people. Although making targets salivate is not on most social engineers' priority list (although it would be humorous), are there ways to condition a target to react to certain sets of input the way you want them to react?

To find the answer, read the following sections, which provide a few examples of manipulation in business and marketing to set a foundation for discussion and an analysis of how to use manipulation on a personal level.

To Recall or Not To Recall

In May 2010 *The Washington Post* reported an interesting story (www.washingtonpost .com/wp-dyn/content/article/2010/05/27/AR2010052705484.html). The maker of children's Tylenol, Motrin, Benadryl, and Zyrtec, among other liquid over-the-counter medicines, discovered a defective batch of Motrin and didn't want to perform a recall due to the costs of such an action. What was the company's answer?

It used manipulation. The company hired a slew of contractors to go from store to store and buy back all the Motrin in the store, which would then be destroyed. Unfortunately, its plans were foiled when a contractor dropped a paper in one store that outlined the plot, which was then reported to the Federal Drug Administration (FDA).

On a side note, the FDA did make that company recall 136 million bottles in just one out of four recalls. Unfortunately, it was too late because 775 cases were reported of children and infants who had adverse reactions to this tainted batch, with 37 ending in death. The reports are not conclusive whether the deaths were a result of the bad Motrin or a reaction to the Motrin. That is not the focus here.

This is a very dark example of manipulation, or at least attempted manipulation. To protect this company's image it was willing to forgo the proper procedures and the safety of children all over the world. It attempted to manipulate the system and in the process people lost their lives. The documentation that was dropped in the store discussed how the contractors were under orders to buy the product back and not mention "recall" at any point in time.

When the company was caught it deployed many interesting manipulation tactics. It deflected the situation by saying the reason for the action was its experts didn't think a significant risk existed to children.

It followed this statement by a formal apology and the firing of six top executives. Then the real manipulation came in. While being questioned, the company stated that they were not trying to do a "phantom recall," as it was being called. The company was testing the alleged damaged batch by having the contractors buy it back to be tested. If it was found faulty the company would have taken the proper procedures. This company attempted to use a manipulation technique called *diversion*, to divert attention from what they were really doing to make it seem better than it was. In addition, it used a cover-up technique to manipulate the thinking of those who disagreed with their actions by issuing statements that the company was trying to do testing to determine if there was need for a recall.

This type of manipulation is worth discussing because a diversion tactic can work on a much smaller scale in a personal setting, too. If you are caught in an area or place you should not be, then having a good cover story that is believable can go a long way toward manipulating the target to allow you safe passage. Diverting the target's attention to something other than the problem at hand can give you enough time to redirect his or her concern. For example, if you are caught by a security guard, instead of getting nervous, you could simply look at him and say, "Do you know what I am doing here? Did you hear that some USB keys have been lost with very important data on them? It is imperative we find them before everyone comes in tomorrow. Do you want to check the bathrooms?"

Many of you probably never heard about the Motrin recall story, showing that the company did a good job of manipulating (so far) the media and justice system to keep the limelight off of it. Regardless, this situation outlines how diversion and cover-up can be used in manipulation.

Anxiety Cured at Last

In 1998 SmithKline Beecham, one the largest pharmaceutical companies in the world, launched an ad campaign designed to "educate" the masses about something it called "social anxiety disorder." It planted 50 press stories and surveys with questions like, "Do you have social anxiety disorder?" These quizzes and surveys were geared to "educate" people on this disorder and how to tell whether they suffer from it.

Later that year it changed its marketing campaign copy in medical journals from "Paxil means peace...in depression, panic disorder, and OCD" to "Show them they can...the first and only approved treatment for social anxiety disorder." This change cost the company about $1 million to make.

In 1999, a $30 million campaign was launched on print and television announcing that SmithKline Beecham found the cure for social anxiety disorder, and its name is Paxil. Using the data from the surveys and quizzes the company bought spots in some of the "hottest" television shows at that time and spouted statistics that 10 million Americans suffer from SAD (social anxiety disorder), and now there is hope.

By 2000, Paxil sales accounted for half of the increase in the entire market: The company "became number one in the U.S. selective serotonin reuptake inhibitor market for new retail prescriptions in 2000." In 2001 it won FDA approval to market Paxil for both generalized anxiety disorder and posttraumatic stress disorder.

The 9/11 attacks resulted in a dramatic increase in prescriptions for all antidepressants and anxiety drugs. During this time Paxil's advertising positioned it as an answer to the uncontrollable feelings of fear and helplessness that many people felt in the aftermath of the attacks.

I am not saying that these drugs do not work, or that the company's motive is malicious, but I find this case particularly interesting in that the manipulation of the market started with education and ended with a massive increase in sales, while creating new disorders along the way.

This type of case-building manipulation is often used in marketing, but is also used in politics and even on a personal level, presenting a problem that is terrible, but then presenting "facts" that you have derived as proof of why what you say is true. On one episode of *The Real Hustle*, Paul Wilson set up a scenario where he had to extract a famous star they were using in a scam to steal some CDs from a store. The store clerk detained the star and waited for the cops to arrive. Paul walked in, identified himself as a cop, flashed his wallet with nothing more than a picture of his kids in it, and was able to "arrest" the star, take the CDs and the money in the cash register as evidence, and leave unquestioned. This story is an excellent example of this type of case-building manipulation. Paul had a problem (the thieving star) and presented himself as the solution (the cop) to the problem. Whatever the scenario, build the case for what a good person you are before presenting your request, and that case makes the request more palatable to the person you're trying to manipulate.

You Can't Make Me Buy That!

Kmart. I felt like just leaving this section at that, but I think I should explain more. Kmart developed an idea it called the *planogram*, which is a diagram that shows retailers how to display their products based on colors, sizes, and other criteria to manipulate their customers to want to buy and spend the most.

Planograms are designed to create optimal visual and commercial product placement.

The use of these planograms is a form of manipulation because researchers have studied how people shop, think, and buy. Understanding these things helped them develop mechanisms to control the visual input to increase shoppers' desire to buy.

Software, as well as whole companies, are devoted to planning and executing these planograms for the maximum effect on keeping shoppers shopping.

Three different layouts are used to manipulate shoppers:

> » **Horizontal product placement:** To increase a customer's concentration on a certain article, a multiple horizontal placement side by side of one product is applied. Some retailers found that a minimum placement range between 15 and 30 cm of a single product is necessary to achieve an increase in customer attentiveness (see Figure 6-8).

> » **Vertical product placement:** A different method used is the vertical product placement. Here one product is placed on more than one shelf level to achieve 15–30 cm placement space (see Figure 6-9).

Figure 6-8 Placing the same or similar items in a horizontal row, as shown in this computer generated planogram, increases customer focus.

Figure 6-9 Products are grouped together to drawn the eye to items they want to sell.

» **Block placement:** Products that have something in common are placed in a block (brands). This can be done side by side, on top of each other, centered, or using magnetized hangers (see Figure 6-10).

Figure 6-10   Another example of a few different types of planograms being used at once.

Planograms are not the only method of manipulating shoppers. One test done involved a shopping mall running specifically designed music loops. The result was that those shoppers stayed in the mall an average of 18% longer than when the music was not running.

In the *Journal of Business Research*, Jean-Charles Chebat and Richard Michon published a study they performed in a Canadian shopping mall (`www.ryerson .ca/~rmichon/Publications/Ambient%20odors.pdf`). The researchers pumped specially designed aromas into the air that were supposed to trigger happiness and the desire to buy. The result there was that an average of $50 more per shopper was spent in that week-long study.

Your trips to the shopping malls and grocery stores will never be the same now. However, you can learn a lot from these methods and experiments. Knowing how people group things in their brains can affect how you organize your shelves to manipulate the feelings, emotions, and thoughts of your targets.

On the topic of colors, they are a major way to manipulate the emotions of a target. Many of the same principles apply to colors as they do to product placement. The colors you choose to wear or use can affect the target. A lot of research has been done on colors and their effects. The following is a short list of some ways a particular color could affect the thinking or emotions of another person:

» **White:** White is often associated with purity, light, and cleanliness. It gives feelings of safety and neutrality as well as goodness and faith. This is why white is often used in weddings or as the color of surrender.

» **Black:** Black often denotes power, elegance, mystery, and strength. It is used to denote authority, depth, and stability. Black gives the feeling of calmness and tranquility. Because it contrasts with other colors, it can also be used to enhance other colors.

» **Red:** Red is associated with excitement and joy. It is a color filled with celebration, action, and energy. It can denote good health, speed, passion, desire, and love. Red can stimulate emotions as well as increase heart rate, respiration, and blood pressure.

Red can trigger strong emotions—use caution when using red. Even though it can denote power and impulsiveness, it can denote force, intimidation, and conquest, even violence and revenge. Be careful how you use red.

» **Orange:** Orange gives warmth, enthusiasm, attraction, determination, strength, and endurance. It can stimulate a person to feel invigorated and even stimulate his or her appetite.

Orange is another color to be cautious with. Although using orange has many good benefits, like making the viewer feel warm and attracted to you or your product, too much or the wrong combination can create feelings of insecurity, ignorance, and sluggishness.

» **Gold:** Gold is usually associated with illumination, wisdom, wealth, and prestige.

» **Yellow:** Yellow is associated with energy and optimism, joy and cheerfulness, loyalty and freshness. It can cause a person to feel focused and attentive.

Yellow also has an impact on a person's memory (why are so many sticky notes yellow?). Used in small amounts, it can trigger positive emotions, but too much can cause a target to lose focus or feel criticized.

» **Green:** Green is often associated with nature, harmony, life, fertility, ambition, protection, and peace. It can produce a very calming effect, making someone feel safe.

Green is another power color but can also make one feel greedy, guilty, jealousy, and disordered if used in the wrong setting or used too much.

» **Blue:** Blue is associated with the color of the sky and ocean. It can be linked to intelligence, intuition, truth, tranquility, health, power, and knowledge. It is very calming and cooling and has been known to slow down the metabolism.

Blue is the easiest color for the eyes to focus on. It can have many positive effects, but be careful not to make the target feel cold or depressed.

»   **Purple:** Purple is associated with royalty, nobility, luxury, creativity, and mystery.

»   **Brown:** Brown is associated with earth, reliability, approachability, convention, and order. It can create emotions of being rooted or connected, or having a sense of order.

How can you use all this information? I am not suggesting that with a simple blue outfit you can make someone feel calm enough to hand you her password. Yet you can use this information to plan your attack vectors, ensuring you have the best opportunity to succeed, which includes how you look and how you are dressed.

A social engineer would want to analyze the target they will be calling on and make sure the colors they choose to wear augment their ability to manipulate the target and not turn them off. For example, knowing that green may elicit feelings of greed or ambition can help a social engineer decide not to wear green to a meeting with a charity where it might conjure feelings and emotions contrary to the charity's mission. Wearing something blue to a lawyer's office, on the other hand, can have a calming effect, allowing the lawyer to open up more. Careful planning and sensible use of these tactics can help ensure the success of your social engineering audits.

Conditioning Targets to Respond Positively

Conditioning is used in everything from normal conversation to marketing to malicious manipulation. Just like Pavlov's dog, people have been conditioned to respond to certain items. Human nature is often used to manipulate the majority of people to take actions the manipulators want.

When the majority of people think of babies they will smile, we will find talking animals "cute," and we might even be manipulated to sing a jingle for a popular product in our head.

These tactics are so covert that many times we don't even know they are working. Many times I find myself wondering what a scantily clad, bikini-wearing woman has to do with beer.

One example of how conditioning is used is Michelin Tires (see Figure 6-11). For years this company has used babies in its ads. Why? "Because so much is riding on your tires." But these ads have more to them. You see a baby, you smile, and you are happy. That emotion triggers a positive response, and that response conditions you to be agreeable to what is told to you next. When you see the baby you smile; when you see it enough you are conditioned to think of warm, happy feelings when you see Michelin tires.

Figure 6-11 Aren't babies cute?

Seeing the baby next to the tire makes you equate positive happy feelings with that brand. This is an example of classic manipulation.

Another advertisement (see Figure 6-12) that might have had many people wondering from Budweiser—remember those popular frogs belching out "Bud" "weis" and "er"? What do frogs have to do with beer? Along those same lines, think of the more recent Clydesdale horse and his gang of animal friends. These ads are catchy, even funny the first time, but not really explaining why you want to buy their beer.

Figure 6-12 Frogs selling lager.

This form of manipulation, conditioning, is subtle. You laugh at that commercial, and then later on you pull into your local beer distributor, see a cardboard cutout of the frogs or horse, and smile to yourself, which creates that positive feeling that makes you feel agreeable to buying the product.

These conditioning tactics are used often in the world of sales and marketing firms with the goal of manipulating the consumer to buy their products over the competition. Social engineers aren't really selling a product, but they do want their targets to "buy" the lines they are selling, the pretext they are putting out there, and the actions they want the target to take. But why use manipulation? What are the incentives to utilizing this powerful form of control? The next section covers that very topic.

Manipulation Incentives

What are the incentives to manipulate someone? This question gets to the root of the methods, thinking, and tactics used in any manipulation. Not all manipulation is negative, but is related to the incentives behind it. But each *incentive* can be positive or negative.

What is an incentive? An incentive can be labeled as anything that motivates you to take an action. It can be money, love, success, or anything—even negative emotions like hatred, jealousy, and envy.

The main reasons why people chose to manipulate others can be broken down into three categories: financial, social, and ideological incentives. The following sections look at each of these incentives and how they apply to manipulation.

Financial Incentives

Financial incentives tend to be the most common, as in the cases mentioned earlier related to increasing sales. Many scams have a financial incentive behind their tactics.

How many people play the lottery every day with the hopes of getting that winning ticket? They may spend hundreds of dollars over time, and winning a $20 payoff makes them happy and keeps them coming back for more.

A non-malicious example of financial incentive is coupons. If you buy this particular product at this particular store you will get X dollars or cents off. If you are a thrifty shopper or want to try that product you will go to that store.

Many commercials that promote furthering your education, career, or skill set use financial incentives by painting a picture that your income will increase after their course or education.

The malicious attacker's incentive for using manipulation is his own financial gain and therefore his motivation and his technique will reflect that. For example, if the malicious social engineer's goal is to get his target to part with some of his hard-earned money, the social engineer will utilize pretexts that will be "allowed" to ask for money—pretexts like charity organizations are suitable in this scenario because asking for donations or financial information is not out of the ordinary.

Ideological Incentives

Ideological incentives are the most difficult to describe. Each person's ideals are different and those ideals can affect the incentive. If your dream in life is to run a restaurant then that is your passion. You will work longer hours and put in more effort than any of your employees. You will also work for less money, because it is your dream or your motivation; for everyone else it is just a job.

Dreams and beliefs can be so ingrained in a person that separating them from the person can be almost impossible. When you hear the phrase, "I have a dream," did you think of Martin Luther King? Some people's dreams and goals are who they are, not what they think about.

People tend to be drawn to those with similar dreams and goals, which is why the phrase, "Birds of a feather flock together" applies so well in this discussion. But it is also why so many people can be manipulated.

Look at Christian televangelists, for example. People who have a faith and desire to believe in God flock together. Like-minded people can strengthen each other's faith and desire to do the right thing, but a televangelist can use that ideology to convince people that God's desire is for that particular church to prosper, therefore also lining the televangelist' pockets with cash.

The televangelist gives a few motivating sermons and sheds some tears and suddenly people are sending in the checks. These televangelists use the tools of both financial and social ideals (see the following section, "Social Incentives") to convert their listeners to their ideals so those people part with their hard-earned cash. What is interesting is that if you ask a follower how he feels about the preacher being way richer than he is, he believes it is God's will. His ideal set has been changed or manipulated.

Ideological incentives can also be used for the good by educating people about morals, and even resorting to using fear as the incentive can have great effects on people. Ideological incentives are often taught to children through stories and fables that have meanings behind them. The Brothers Grimm are an excellent example of this type of incentive. Stories that often end in the bad characters suffering physical harm or even death and the good characters, persevering through all forms of hardship, getting a massive reward at the end builds on fear that being bad leads to death or some terrible punishment.

Ideological incentives are used in marketing, too, through placing ads where "like-minded" ideals often "meet." For example, diaper companies market in family magazines, animal shelters market at zoos, athletic gear companies market at sporting events, and so on. This type of incentive gives a greater chance that the goods or services being advertised will be bought by those who share the same ideals.

Ideological incentives are used to bring one's ideals in alignment with those of a like mind. Often, once people are sympathetic to a cause is when the manipulation tactics start. Again, not all manipulation is bad, but it has to be used in the proper way.

Social Incentives

Social incentives are probably the most widely used and the most complex set of incentives out there, especially when it comes to social engineering.

Humans are social by nature; it is what we do in normal daily life. Social incentives also encompass all the other types of incentives. The right relationship can enhance your financial needs and can also adjust, align, or augment your ideals. It could be argued that social incentives are stronger than the other two types of incentives.

The power that peer pressure holds over many people is easy to see. For young and old alike, the draw of conformity is powerful. Many times, that which is acceptable is directly linked to a social incentive. One's outlook on life and self can be greatly affected by his or her social surroundings. In essence peer pressure can exist even in the absence of direct peers.

Am I good looking? Well, that depends. If I am in the United States where a supermodel is a size zero and the guys have muscles in places I didn't know muscles existed, probably not. If I am in ancient Rome where maybe being larger meant I was rich and powerful, then I am. Your whole inner self is framed by your social view of the world.

In 1975, the U.S. Air Force ran a study entitled "Identification and Analysis of Social Incentives in Air Force Technical Training" to try to see the power of social incentives on creating leaders during its training drills. It ran four different scenarios with a group and analyzed what effects they had on the students.

The end results were that a certain social incentive, usually involving praise or positive reinforcement from peers or authority figures, created a strong bond between the students and instructors:

> The major conclusion of this entire research effort is that the management of social incentives is a particularly difficult art. While social incentives can be identified and scaled with considerable ease, manipulation and management of the same incentives requires considerably greater effort. The scaling data show high attractiveness

value for various social incentives. The results of the field experiment show the positive influence of the acquaintanceship and psychological contract exercise on attitudes toward fellow trainees. Both of these findings underline the importance of social factors.

In other words, increasing or decreasing the attractiveness of the social incentive is not too difficult once you know what motivates a person. This phenomenon is particularly evident in groups of teenagers. When they find out what bothers someone, it is often used as a weapon to force compliance. The larger the group that provides the pressure, the greater the chance the target will comply.

This is a powerful statement. I wonder how that research would have gone if the researchers had been able to use the plethora of social media sites that exist today. Peer pressure is a strong influence and everyone wants to fit in and be part of the crowd.

Social incentives work. In 2007 a group of researchers (Oriana Bandiera, Iwan Barankay, and Imran Rasul) wrote a research paper entitled, "Social Incentives: The Causes and Consequences of Social Networks in the Workplace" (www.social-engineer.org/wiki/archives/Manipulation/Manipulation-Social-Incentivespdf.pdf).

The report is an interesting study along the lines of the Air Force study, but set in 2007. Basically the researchers analyzed how those who have "friends" at work handle their jobs when they work in groups with their friends. Their conclusion:

Our findings indicate there are social incentives—the presence of friends affects worker productivity, despite there being no externalities of worker effort onto their co-workers due to the production technology or compensation scheme in place. Due to social incentives, workers conform to a common norm when working together. The level of the norm is such that the presence of friends increases the productivity of workers who are less able than their friends and decreases the productivity of workers who are more able than their friends.

Social incentives are a quantitatively important determinant of a worker's performance. As workers are paid piece rates based on individual productivity, the strength of social incentives is such that (i) workers who are more able than their friends are willing to forgo 10% of their earnings to conform to the norm; (ii) workers who have at least one friend who is more able than themselves are willing to increase productivity by 10% to meet the norm. Overall, the distribution of worker ability is such that the latter effect dominates so the net effect of social incentives on firm performance is positive.

The presence of friends meant that a person would actually work harder or less hard depending on their normal work level. Peer pressure with the absence of the actual pressure can affect people's work. The pressure is perceived by what is standard. Why? Maybe if a person could work faster or better, she probably didn't want to appear to be a know-it-all or brown-noser, as these people can be called. Maybe if he is normally more of a slacker, he didn't want to appear lazy so he pushed up the pace a little. In either case their work ethic was affected by having friends.

A good point for management is to always put the hardest workers and natural leaders over the group. But there is so much to learn in this research.

This method is how social engineers use "tail-gating." Being in a large crowd of people coming back from break or lunch and looking like one of the employees minimizes the chance that the security guard will stop you while you walk through the front doors.

It is also how whole groups of people can be manipulated into thinking a certain action or attitude is acceptable. You can see this in the entertainment industry as each year the standard of what is acceptable or moral seems to get lowered, yet this drop in standards is sold as "freedom."

These three incentives are not the only types that are used. They can branch off into other aspects beyond the scope of this book, but the question still arises of how you can use them as a social engineer.

Manipulation in Social Engineering

Manipulation is less about making others think like you do and making them feel comfortable, and more about coercing them to do what you want.

Coercion is not a friendly word. It means "to force to act or think in a certain manner" or "to dominate, restrain, or control by force."

Manipulation and coercion use psychological force to alter the ideology, beliefs, attitudes, and behaviors of the target. The key to using them is to make the steps so small they are almost invisible. The social engineer doesn't want to alert the target he is being manipulated. Some of the following methods may be very controversial and downright horrible, but they are used each day by scammers, identity thieves, and the like. One of the goals of manipulation can be to create anxiety, stress, and undue social pressure. When a target feels that way he is more likely to take an action the social engineer is manipulating them to take.

With that in mind, you can see why manipulation is often thought of in a negative light, but it is used in social engineering and therefore must be discussed.

Increasing a Target's Suggestibility

Increasing a target's suggestibility can involve using the neurolinguistic programming (NLP) skills discussed in Chapter 5 or other visual cues. Earlier you read about conditioning people with the use of pen clicks or other noises or gestures that can elicit an emotion even when words are not spoken.

I once saw this in action when I was with a person who was manipulating a target. He used a pen click to indicate a positive thought. He would say something positive and then smile and click his pen. Literally, I saw the person begin to smile after about four or five times of hearing the pen click. He then brought up a very depressing subject and clicked his pen, and then the target smiled and felt instantly embarrassed. That embarrassment was the open door he needed to manipulate the target to do what he wanted.

Creating a situation where the other person feels susceptible to suggestion can be through repetition of ideas or other means that will soften the target to the ideas you are trying to present.

A social engineer can make sure the whole setup is geared towards this manipulation—the phrases used, the word pictures painted, the clothing colors chosen to wear. All of it can make the target more susceptible.

William Sargant, a controversial psychiatrist and author of the book *Battle for the Mind*, talks about the methods by which people are manipulated. According to Sargant, various types of beliefs can be implanted in people after the target has been disturbed by fear, anger, or excitement. These feelings cause heightened suggestibility and impaired judgment.

A social engineer can use this device to their advantage by offering the target a suggestion that causes fear or excitement and then offering a solution that turns into a suggestion.

For example, in the hit BBC TV show *The Real Hustle*, the cast ran a scam to show how this works when they set up a booth in a mall that allowed people to buy raffle tickets. People would buy a ticket for a chance to win three prizes worth much more than the ticket they just bought.

One woman bought the ticket, and, of course, she won the biggest prize. Her excitement was extreme because she had never won anything like this before. At this point, Paul Wilson gave the suggestion to manipulate her: At the height of excitement he told her she had to call a phone number and provide her bank info to claim her prize.

She did it without a second thought. The suggestion made sense, especially in the light of her excitement.

Knowing the target and his likes, dislikes, kids' names, favorite teams, and favorite foods, and then using this to create an emotional environment will make creating a susceptible atmosphere so much easier.

Controlling the Target's Environment

Controlling the target's environment is often used in online social engineering, scams, and identity theft.

Becoming part of the same social networks and groups gives the attacker the chance to have "face time" to be able to manipulate targets into acting or thinking the way the attacker wants. Being able to use a target's social networks to find out what triggers they have is also a powerful tool.

I used this method once when searching for an illegal scammer for a client who wanted to get the scammer's contact details. I was able to gain an account on a forum he used to post his "achievements." Using this tactic of getting into his environment, then befriending him, I was able to gain his trust, use his social networks to know what he was doing, and eventually get his contact info.

Any method used to control the environment of the target can be used in this manipulation technique. Controlling the environment can be as simple as approaching when you know you have the least chance of interruption, or allowing a target to see or not see something that will cause a reaction.

Of course, unless you plan on bringing your target to a dark closet, you can't really control his whole environment, so controlling as much as you can will take planning and research. After you locate your target's social circles, whether online or in the real world, you will need to spend time planning how you will get an in to control that environment. Once inside, what elements do you want to control? A good social engineer will not come in running for the "kill shot" but will take time to build a relationship and gather information before the final blow is administered.

Environment control is often used in police or war-time interrogations. The environment where the questioning will take place will have a certain atmosphere to make the target feel at ease, nervous, scared, anxious, or any other emotion the attacker (or lead officer) wants the target to feel.

Forcing the Target to Reevaluate

Undermining a target's beliefs, awareness, or emotional control of a circumstance can have a very unsettling effect on him or her. This tactic is very negative because it is used to make a target doubt what he or she has been told to be true.

Cults use this tactic to prey upon those looking for guidance through life. Many times, people who feel lost or confused are convinced that their whole belief system needs to be reevaluated. When the cults have control they can be so convincing that the victims can be thoroughly convinced that their family and friends do not know what is best.

On a personal social engineering level you can make a person reevaluate the beliefs he has been taught about what is safe and what is not, or what is corporate policy and what is not.

Each day social engineers use similar tactics by presenting one well-thought-out question that can cause the target to reevaluate his stand on a topic and cause him to falter.

For example, in this economy, salespeople are hungry to make sales, and you could call the sales department of a company that happens to have a strict policy about downloading PDFs from the web without proper scans and precautions. Yet you can still place this call:

"Hi, I am with ABC Company and I want to place an order for your product that could be more than 10,000 pieces. My employer wants me to get three quotes to see whether we can do better. I have uploaded the quote package to our website; can I give you the URL? I am going to a meeting in two hours. Could you look over the package and get me a preliminary quote before then?"

Do think this tactic would work? Most likely the salesperson would download and execute that file with little to no thought. You have caused him to reevaluate the policy he has been taught.

Making the Target Feel Powerless

Making the target feel vulnerable or powerless is another very dark, but effective, tactic. It is often used in social engineering when the pretext is an angry executive or someone who should have power over the target. Angry by the lack of response or the inability of the target to give quick answers, the attacker berates or threatens the target, causing him to doubt his position and feel a loss of power.

Another more subtle way this is used is to undermine the belief system using social incentives. In one audit, I was stopped by a custodian while doing scans of the internal network. When she did the right thing for stopping me, I reacted with something like, "Did you know that each year this company deals with a constant battle against network breaches? I am trying to secure you, and you are trying to stop me from doing my job!"

My overpowering demeanor caused her to feel powerless and she backed down.

Giving a target the impression he has no time to think or there is serious urgency can also make him feel powerless. He cannot take the time to think about how to handle a problem and therefore must make a decision in a way he knows he shouldn't.

This tactic was used after the recent earthquakes in Haiti. A website was launched that claimed to have information on loved ones who might have been lost. Because their claim was that no one was able to provide information on their loved ones but this group who set up the site, they could demand certain criteria be met to obtain this information. Many people, feeling hopeless and powerless, entered too much information and clicked things they knew they shouldn't and in the end were damaged by it. The BBC issued a story about this and lists some tips to stay protected: `http://news.bbc.co.uk/2/hi/business/8469885.stm`.

Dishing Out Nonphysical Punishment

Closely linked to making the target feel powerless is making them feel guilt, humiliation, anxiety, or loss of privilege. These feelings can be so strong that a target might possibly do anything to "regain favor."

Guilt over not giving what was expected can cause humiliation and doubt, which can cause the target to react the way the attacker wants.

I don't suggest using humiliation in most social engineering settings, but I have seen it used on a target in a team effort to open the door, and on another social engineering team member to soften the face of the target, making them more pliable to suggestion.

The first attacker approached the target in a public setting trying to get information; he was playing the role of someone important.

In the middle of the conversation an underling, who happened to be female (and on the team), came up and asked a question that angered the first attacker. He reacted by saying, "You have to be the dumbest person I have ever met." In a fit of anger he walked away. The female attacker looked dejected and hurt and was quickly comforted by the target, who fed into her act. The target's empathy allowed him to be manipulated to give out way more information than he wanted.

Intimidating a Target

Intimidation is not a tactic that you might think of using in a traditional sense in social engineering. You are not going to tie up your target and go all "Jack Bauer" on him, but you can use intimidation in subtle ways.

Suggesting that failure to comply can lead to being laid off or other adverse consequences can intimidate the target to react a certain way. Governments often use this tactic to manipulate society to believe that the economic system is collapsing. This way they can control the emotions of those they govern.

You can use it in a social engineering audit even by having an intimidating appearance. Looking busy, upset, and on a mission can intimidate many. Talking with very authoritative expressions can also intimidate people.

In business, sending things by certified mail or courier connotes a level of intimidation. Making the person sign for a package whose contents are unknown can make some people intimidated. The goal with this manipulation tactic is to make the target feel uneasy and anxious, which can cause him to react in a way he will later regret, but by then it is too late.

These darker manipulation techniques are used successfully by social engineers and professional auditors. Manipulating a person to feel completely helpless causes him or her to feel that giving in to the attacker makes sense.

That really is where manipulation differs in a social engineering practice from other forms of influence. With negative manipulation the social engineer leaves and doesn't care how the target feels later on. Even if a target realizes he has been hacked, it doesn't matter because the damage is done and the company or person is already infiltrated.

Other aspects of social engineering manipulation are just as powerful but not so dark.

Using Positive Manipulation

Positive manipulation has the same goals in mind as negative manipulation—in the end the target is in alignment with your thoughts and desires. The differences are in how you get there. But in positive manipulation, the target doesn't need therapy when you are done.

Over my years of research, I have compiled some tips about how parents interact with their children to get them to comply with the parents' wishes. A few of its points on positive manipulation are useful for social engineers. The following sections cover some of these positive techniques.

Disconnect Your Emotion from Their Behavior

Keeping your emotions separate from your target's behavior is important. As soon as you let your emotions get involved the target is manipulating you. You can feel emotion, of course, but be in control of what you feel and how you display what you are feeling.

You do not want to be the one out of control. You also want to control the negative emotions as much as possible so you can remain *in control* at all times.

Disconnecting your emotions can also put people at ease. This doesn't mean being devoid of emotion; that is not comforting to people. But if someone is really upset, showing the proper level of concern is good, but if your display of emotion is too much you can offset the target and ruin the gig.

Keep your emotions in alignment with the pretext you are trying to achieve. If you do not allow your emotions to get involved you can remain in control at all times. A good social engineer is able to do this despite the actions or attitudes displayed by the target. If the target is upset, mad, belligerent, rude, or if any other negative emotion is displayed, a good social engineer remains calm, cool, and collected.

Look for the Positive to Mention

Whenever you can, find something to make a joke about or compliment, but without being creepy. You don't want to walk up to the security guard and say, "So two nuns walk into a bar...." This method probably won't go over too well. At the same time you can't walk into the front office and say to the girl behind the counter, "Wow, you're pretty."

Finding something positive to mention puts everyone at ease, but it must be balanced, controlled, and in good taste. Using the example of approaching a security guard, after introducing yourself, complimenting the picture of her children by saying something like, "Wow, she is really cute; how old, four or five? I have a little girl at home, too," can go a long way toward opening the door.

Assume, Assume, Assume

You have probably heard what they say about people who assume, but in this case, *assume it all.* Assume that the target will act the way you want, assume he will answer the way you want, and assume he will grant you all your requests.

Assume with the questions you ask and the statements you make.

"When I come back from the server room..."

This statement assumes you belong there and you are already granted access. In the security guard situation mentioned earlier, after the compliment maybe offer a follow-up: "When I get back from checking the servers, I will show you a picture of my daughter."

Assuming that what you want will occur is a strong point, too, because it affects your mental outlook. You must have the mental outlook that you are getting what you came for; that belief system will create a new body language and facial expressions that will feed your pretext.

If you go in expecting failure you will fail or at best it will affect your body language and facial expressions. If you have the mental outlook that this deal is done, the same will occur. A word of caution, though—don't take this step so far you become arrogant.

For example, going in thinking, "Of course I have this in the bag because I am amazing and the best," can affect the way you come off and turn off the target quickly.

Try Different Opening Lines

Starting a conversation with the standard why/what/when is common but try a different approach and see what happens. The research group that runs a popular dating site (www.okcupid.com) compiled data that shows the value of starting out with non-traditional openers.

Remember the discussion about compliments? Well, the OkCupid guys found that starting off with too "big" of a compliment had the reverse effect than what one would think. Words like *sexy, beautiful*, and *hot* had terrible effects on people, whereas words like *cool, awesome*, and *fascinating* had a better effect.

In usual greetings these guys found that saying things like "hi," "hey," and "hello" left the target feeling blah and unmotivated, whereas "How's it going?," "What's up?," "howdy," and "hola" were strong openers to use.

Of course, these stats are about dating, but the point to be learned is that people react better to nontraditional greetings.

Similarly, in a social engineering situation, vary your approach and you may notice an increase in the way the target reacts to the message.

Use Past Tense

When you want to address anything negative that you do not want the target to repeat, put it in past tense. This technique puts the negative attitudes and actions in the past in his mind, presenting him with the new and improved "clean slate" on which to do good things for you. For example:

"When you *said* I couldn't get in to meet with Mr. Smith..."
as opposed to: "When you *say* I can't get in to meet Mr. Smith...."

Only verb tense changed, but the effect is very important. It gives the impression that the negative statement is so far in the past, let's move on to something new and improved. It also makes the target feel that you feel it is in the past.

Seek and Destroy

Identify, map, and plan how you will handle any disruptive or negative attitudes and actions. Imagine if your pretext is to be a tech support guy who will gain access to the server room. In your previous calls you knew that every day at 10 am a large group goes out for a smoke break. You decide this is a good time as people are shuffling in and out. You go all prepared, but as you enter the building the receptionist has just received some bad news and is an emotional mess. You should have a plan for handling this disruption.

If you wait to think about how you will handle potential conversation stoppers, or disruptive influences, until the first time you hear them you will most likely fail to handle them. That presents an interesting thought then. You have to sit back and think like the target: what objections would he raise? When a person he does not know calls or approaches him, what might he say? What objections might he raise? What attitudes would he portray? Thinking through these things can help you to make a game plan for these potential problems.

Write down your thoughts and the target's potential objections and then role play. Have your spouse or friend play the mean gatekeeper or security guard. Of course, he or she cannot imitate elements such as facial expressions and so on. But you can give him or her a small list of conversation stoppers to choose from to test your comeback.

Practice until you feel comfortable, but not scripted. Remember the comeback is not to be structured so stiffly that you cannot alter it at all.

Positive manipulation can have a very strong effect on the target. Not only does it not leave him feeling violated but if done properly he can feel accomplished and as if he did something good for the day.

Summary

Manipulation is a key component to social engineering as well as influence. This chapter covered areas of human behavior that spanned decades of research from some of the smartest minds on earth.

Common reactions to the thought of manipulating others might be:

»   "I don't want to manipulate people."

»   "It feels wrong to be learning this."

These comments represent the way most people think when they hear the word *manipulation*. Hopefully, you're now convinced that manipulation isn't always a dark art and can be used for good.

The world of influence has been dissected, researched, and analyzed by some of today's brightest psychologists and researchers. This research served as the basis of my own research to develop the information in this chapter. The section on framing, for instance, can truly change the way you interact with people, and the concept of reciprocation can shape your thinking as a social engineer and how you utilize influence. Influence is such an amazing topic, though, that volumes of books are devoted to that topic alone.

Understanding what triggers a person to motivate him to want to do a certain action and then having that action seem good to the target—that is the power of influence.

This chapter illuminated the science and psychology of what makes people tick, and clarified how influence is used by social engineers.

Remember, influence and the art of persuasion are the processes of getting someone else to *want* to do, react, think, or believe in the way *you* want them to.

The power in this statement transcends social engineering and manipulation. It is the key to altering any frame, the key to unlocking any door of manipulation, and the pathway to becoming a master at influence.

Social engineers also use many physical tools, some of which might look like they were taken out of a page of a James Bond movie, and they are discussed in the next chapter.

7

The Tools of the Social Engineer

Man is a tool-using animal.
Without tools he is nothing, with tools he is all.

—Thomas Carlyle

When it comes to social engineering having a decent toolset can make or break the ability of the social engineer to be successful. In addition, it is not so much having the tools but also possessing the knowledge on how to use them that can bridge the gap between success and failure.

This chapter discusses the differences between physical tools, phone tools, and software-based tools. Note that simply possessing the most expensive or best tools will *not* make you a social engineer. Instead, tools can enhance your security practice the way that the right blend of spices can augment a meal—too much or too little can make the meal bland or overpowering. You do not want to look like Batman wearing a utility belt going into a social engineering gig, nor do you want to be at the target's front door without the proper toolset to gain access.

The social engineer's tools category has the potential to be huge, but this book isn't trying to become a manual on how to pick locks or spoof a phone number. Instead it is an attempt to give you enough information to decide what tools would augment your practice.

The first section of this chapter, "Physical Tools," focuses on things like lock picks, shims, and cameras. Some new and exciting tools are on the market that will make the average social engineer feel like James Bond. This chapter covers some of these tools and how to use them, and even shows some pictures of the tools. In addition, this chapter provides some information on using phone spoofing in a social engineering attack, continues with a discussion of some of the best software-based information-gathering tools on the market, then ends with a discussion about password profiling tools.

Physical Tools

Physical security is comprised of the measures that companies or people take to remain secure that do not involve a computer. It often involves locks, motion cameras, window sensors, and the like. Understanding physical security and how it works is part of being a good social engineer. You don't have to be an engineer of these devices but having a clear understanding of the security mechanisms a target has in place can help you overcome obstacles that might stand in the way of a successful social engineering audit.

Lock Picks

Before getting into the topic of picking locks you have to know a bit about how a lock works.

Figure 7-1 shows a very rough image of a simple lock.

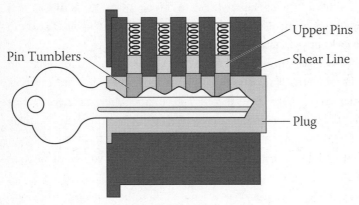

Figure 7-1 A simple view of a lock.

Basically the way a lock works is that it has tumblers that are manipulated by the key. The key pushes up the tumblers and upper pins, and when they line up it allows the key to turn and unlock the door, server room, cabinet, and so on.

A lock pick simulates the key in moving all the pins into the correct position one by one, allowing the lock to turn freely and open the door. You need two main tools to pick a lock: picks and a tension wrench.

Picks are long pieces of metal that curve at the end, similar to a dentist's tool. They reach inside the lock and move the pins up and down until they are in the right position.

Tension wrenches are small flat metal devices that allow you to put pressure on the lock while using the pick.

Rakes look like picks but are used in a "raking" motion over the lock in an attempt to catch all the pins. It is the quick motion of moving the rake in and out of the lock that many lock pickers find attractive because it usually makes quick work of most locks.

To pick a lock, follow these steps:

1. Insert the tension wrench into the keyhole and turn it in the same direction you would turn the key. The real skill here is knowing *how much* tension to add—use too much or too little, and the pins won't fall into place, thus allowing the lock to turn. Providing just the right amount of tension creates a small ledge that offsets the plug enough to catch the pin shafts.

2. Insert the pick and use it to lift the pins one by one until you feel them lock in place. You can hear a slight click when an upper pin falls into position. When you get all the pins into position the plug will rotate freely, and you will have picked the lock.

The preceding is the $2 tour of lock picking and barely scratches its surface. If you want some great information on lock picking visit any of the following websites:

» `http://toool.us/`

» `http://home.howstuffworks.com/home-improvement/household-safety/security/lock-picking.htm`

» `http://www.lockpicking101.com/`

These are just a few of the many sites devoted to lock-picking education. As a social engineer, spending time practicing picking locks is wise. Carrying a small lock-pick set with you can be a lifesaver when you're in front of a server cabinet, desk drawer, or other locked obstacle containing juicy information.

Lock pick sets can be as small as those shown in Figure 7-2, which are the size of a normal business card.

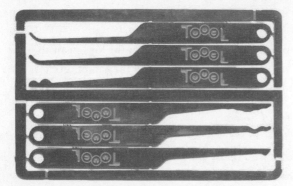

Figure 7-2 This business card–sized lock-pick set fits easily into a wallet or purse.

They can also be bulkier, as shown in Figures 7-3 and 7-4.

Figure 7-3 This set is about the size of a pocketknife.

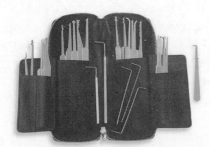

Figure 7-4 This lock-pick set is bulkier but contains everything you would need.

A good recommendation is to not let the first time you play with a lock pick be in a critical situation. Personally, I went out and bought a few Master padlocks of differing sizes. After I was able to successfully pick all of them I then bought a set of practice locks, something like those shown in Figure 7-5. These come in many different pin types. Locks contain varying pin types, which can add to the level of difficulty in picking. Having practice locks of varying pin types and sizes maximizes the effectiveness of your practice sessions.

Figure 7-5 These see-through locks allow you to see how you are doing.

I have even seen some very nice setups at different conferences that would be excellent for learning, like a homemade lock wall. Of course, as you gather intel on your target, taking pictures or just making mental notes of the types, makes, and models of the locks that might block your path to success is a good idea. Knowing this information can help you prepare before you engage in your social engineering attempt.

Practical Usage

Lock picking in the movies and on TV is portrayed such that one just puts the lock pick in and a few seconds later the door magically opens. Sure, some people pick locks that well, but the majority of people will find success slowly, after countless times applying too much tension, getting frustrated, and then at last learning how to truly rake and pick a lock. *Raking* is a talent in itself. This is where you use a rake tool and gently slide the rake in and out of the lock while applying light pressure to the tension wrench. This technique works on many types of locks, enabling them to be "picked" using this simple method. Learning to rake efficiently teaches a social engineer a lot about how to use the tension wrench properly and what it feels like when the lock is picked.

Many companies are starting to use RFID, magnetic badge cards, or other types of electronic access, which may lead one to believe that lock picks are obsolete. They are not, and neither is the skill of lock picking. It is a good skill to have that can save you in a pentest.

Here is an example of the benefit of carrying lock picks with you: On one engagement I came upon an obstacle that could not be social engineered—a door. Pulling out a trusty pocket-sized lock pick set and using the raking method, I gained access in about 30 seconds. Many social engineers have stories like this one, where understanding a little about locks and having the right tools meant success in the end. It is too often the case that companies will spend thousands or even millions of dollars on their hardware, firewalls, IDS systems, and other protection methods, and then put them all in a room with cheap glass and a $20 lock protecting it.

Practice is essential because picking a lock always carries the risk of being seen or caught. You must be quick about picking a lock to reduce that risk. Some places install cameras to catch people in the act, but in the end, unless the camera is manned by a live person, it will only record a person breaking in and stealing the servers.

In addition, many cameras can be easily rendered useless by using simplistic methods of LED lights shined right into the lens or wearing a hat or hood to cover your face.

Picking Magnetic and Electronic Locks

Magnetic locks have become more popular because they are very inexpensive to run and provide a certain level of security because they are not a traditional lock that can be picked. Magnetic locks come in all shapes, sizes, and strengths. Magnetic locks, however, also offer a level of insecurity: If the power goes out most magnetic locks will disengage, unlocking the door. This is, of course, if the lock is not hooked up to a backup power source.

Johnny Long, world-renowned social engineer and hacker who created the Google Hacking Database and author of *No Tech Hacking*, tells a story of a how he bypassed a magnetic lock using a coat hanger and washcloth. He noticed the locks were disengaged based on the motion of an employee walking toward the door. He also noticed a gap in the doors that was large enough to slide a cloth attached to a hanger through. Waving the cloth around released the lock and gave him access.

I recently had a chance to test out this technique. Sure enough with a little effort and testing different lengths of hanger, I gained access in under two minutes. What amazed me the most about this is that despite how much money was spent on the professional, commercial-grade lock and metal doors with bulletproof glass windows in them, with backup power sources to the locks and autolocking bolt locks if the power goes out, it was all thwarted by a hanger with a rag.

Of course there are higher-tech ways of picking these locks. Some have created *RFID cloners*, a small device that can capture then replay the RFID code unlocking the doors. There are machines to copy magnetic key cards as well.

Miscellaneous Lock-Picking Tools

In addition to tension wrenches and picks, a social engineer may want to employ some other tools, such as shove knives, bump keys, and padlock shims, to gain physical access. Some of these tools, when mastered, can make the job of physical access effortless.

Shove Knives

The *shove knife*, shown in Figure 7-6, is hailed as the quickest way to gain access to office doors or any door with a knob lock, such as server rooms or office doors. Basically this knife can slip into a position where it can release the latch without damaging the door.

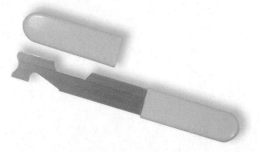

Figure 7-6 A typical shove knife.

Bump Keys

Bump keys have been around for ages, but have been getting a lot of notice in the news because they have been used in crimes. Bump keys are specially designed keys that allow the user to "bump" the key into the lock with light force that when done right, puts all the pins in proper alignment and allows the plug to be turned without damaging the lock. The basic technique is that you put the key inside the lock and pull it out one or two notches; then you put light tension on the key and use a screwdriver or other small object to "bump" the key into the lock using light force. This action forces the pins into the proper position and then allows the plug to turn. Figure 7-7 shows a bump key.

Figure 7-7 A typical bump key for a door.

Padlock Shims

A *shim* is a small piece of thin metal that is slid into the base of the padlock and used to release the locking mechanism. The shim is shoved in at the base of lock shaft, separating the locking mechanism from the shaft and unlocking the padlock. This is shown in Figure 7-8.

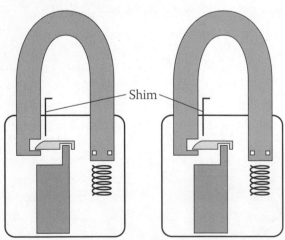

Shim

Figure 7-8. How a shim works.

Figure 7-9 shows professional-grade shims but you can also make a pair out of an aluminum can.

Some recent stories (www.youtube.com/watch?v=7INIRLe7x0Y) show how easy it is to bypass a hotel or other door with a chain lock. This particular video shows how an attacker can tie a rubber band around the lock and, using the natural tension of the rubber band, get the chain to slide right off. As well, MIT has a freely distributed guide (`www.lysator.liu.se/mit-guide/MITLockGuide.pdf`) on lock picking that is much more in-depth than the brief introduction included in this chapter.

Figure 7-9 Professionally made shims.

You might be wondering whether locks that are impossible, or at least hard to pick, exist. The Bump Proof BiLock (`www.wholesalelocks.com/bump-proof-bilock-ult-360.html`) is just such a lock. Its two cylinders make it near-impossible to bump or pick easily.

One of the problems I have seen in my career is not the lock choice but rather the security supporting the lock. Very often, a company will buy a heavy-duty lock that requires biometrics and key access to get to the server room, but right next to the door is a small, single-paned glass window. Who needs a lock pick then? A thief will break the glass and gain access without much effort.

The moral of the story is that a lock alone won't make you secure. Security is a mindset, not a simple piece of hardware.

Not every social engineer must be an expert locksmith, but having some basic knowledge on how locks work and a bit of experience picking locks might make the difference between a social engineering success and failure.

This discussion just scratched the surface of the topic of the lock-picking tools a social engineer can use. One of the other toolsets that is invaluable for a social engineer is recording devices, as discussed in the next section.

Cameras and Recording Devices

Cameras and recording devices seem so "peeping Tom-ish" that many times the question arises, "Why? Why use hidden cameras and covert recording devices in an SE gig?" Good question. It has a simple two-part answer: for proof and protection.

Let's discuss the concept of *proof*. As already mentioned, a social engineering audit is where you are testing people. It is trying to help a company patch the human infrastructure to be more secure. Unfortunately, these same principles are used when malicious social engineers do their deeds too. Many people are reluctant to admit they can be duped unless they see the proof or one of their colleagues being duped. The embarrassment from being tricked through a simple social engineering attack or the fear of employer repercussions can cause people to say it never happened. A recording device can provide that proof, but it can also be used to train both you as an auditor and your client on what to watch for.

You must never use these devices with the intent of getting an employee in trouble or to embarrass him or her. However, the information you get from these devices provides a great learning tool afterward for showing the staff who fell for the social engineer's pretext and how. Having proof of a successful hack can go a long way toward educating the company and its staff on how they should react to malicious social engineering attempts—in other words, how to notice and then either avoid or mitigate these attacks.

The second reason to use recording devices in an SE gig is for protection, mainly for the professional social engineers. Why? Seeing every microexpression, facial gesture, and little detail that you can use later on is impossible. Capturing this information on camera gives you something to analyze so you do get all the details needed for the attack. It can provide protection in that you have a recording of the events to prove what was and was not done, but also in that it doesn't leave everything to your memory of the situation. It also is a good educational tool for analyzing failed or successful SE attempts.

This principle is used in law enforcement. Police and federal agents record their traffic stops, interviews, and interrogations for protection, education, and proof to be used in court.

These principles also apply for audio recording. Capturing a phone call or conversation on a recording device serves all the same purposes as the ones mentioned previously for video. An important point to mention here is that recording people without their consent is illegal in many areas of the world. Make sure your ability to use recording devices is part of the social engineering contract you have signed with the company.

Audio recording devices come in all shapes and sizes. I own a small voice recorder that is a real working pen. This device sits nicely in my front pocket and records sound clearly up to 20 feet away. With 2 GB of internal storage I can easily record a couple hours of conversation without worry and then analyze it later on.

Cameras

Nowadays you can find cameras shaped like buttons; pens; hidden in the tips of pens; inside clocks, teddy bears, fake screw heads, smoke alarms; and basically any other device you can imagine. Locating a camera like the one shown in Figure 7-10 isn't too hard.

Figure 7-10 The camera is hidden in the knot of the tie.

Yes, believe it or not, this tie is hiding a full-color camera that runs on a 12-volt battery and connects to a mini recording device. Wearing this tie into a social engineering audit ensures you capture everything within a 70-degree angle.

Using a recording device like this gives an advantage. The social engineer can focus on the pretext or the elicitation that he or she practiced beforehand without having to worry about trying to remember every detail.

One story I like to tell is how I used an audio recording device in an audit where I was testing a theme park that sells tickets online. This company operates a small ticket window with one woman behind it manning a computer with a Windows operating system on it. The pretext was that I bought tickets online in the hotel but couldn't print them out. To assist I printed them to PDF and emailed the document to myself. I then used a line similar to this: "I know this is an odd request, but my daughter saw your ad at a restaurant. We went back to the hotel and bought the tickets online with the discount code and then I realized I couldn't print them out. The hotel printer was on the fritz and I didn't want to lose the tickets. So I printed them to a PDF and sent it to my email account. Could I just log in or have you log in to my email to get the document? " Of course, the "kids" were waiting in the sidelines and as a dad I didn't want to disappoint. Sure enough as the employee clicked the PDF, she wasn't presented with our tickets but a malicious piece of code that was scripted to give me access to her computer and start autocollecting data. Recording the conversation, the method used, and the heart strings that were pulled helped to educate the company so this attack could not be repeated, costing it thousands or more dollars.

One device that is available uses a "pay-as-you-go" cellular card to send audio content via a cellular signal to any number programmed. Or the social engineer can call in and hear what is going on at any time. This device can save the social engineer dozens of hours in obtaining passwords or personal information that she can use in a social engineering attack.

One can spend literally dozens of hours (and I could write dozens of pages) talking about all the neat and cool cameras out there. Figures 7-11 and 7-12 show a few pictures from a popular law enforcement provider of "spy equipment" (www.spyassociates .com). All of these pictures *are* hidden cameras or audio recording devices, believe it or not. You can use each of these devices to covertly record a target for later inspection.

Figure 7-11 All of these devices capture audio and color video from a hidden camera except for the pen, which is an audio recorder.

Figure 7-12 These devices also capture audio and video from hidden cameras.

Using the Tools of a Social Engineer

The preceding section outlines some of the different types of recording devices out there, but the question is still how to use them. Amazing as it seems, using cameras or recording devices follows the same principles as any other tool of the social engineer, such as pretexting or elicitation.

Practice is essential. If you don't determine the proper placement for a body-worn camera or audio recording device, you might end up capturing video of the ceiling or audio of a muffled voice. Setting up the appropriate outfit and gear you might carry and finding the right location for the camera or audio device is a good idea. Try sitting, standing, or walking and see how these movements affect the sound and video quality.

From a professional social engineer standpoint I must stress again the seriousness of getting the contract to outline your ability to record. Doing it without a contract can be a legal nightmare. Checking the local laws to make sure you cannot get in trouble for use of these devices is also a good idea.

Never would a social engineer use these devices to record people in embarrassing situations or to capture people in personal circumstances.

Discussion on this topic can go on and on, but hopefully this brief overview of the tools that are available and how to use them can open up the options out there to social engineers.

In the next section I will give a few examples of the usage of certain tools that can be very useful to a social engineer.

Using a GPS Tracker

Social engineers often want to track targets before or after they leave the office. What stops the target makes on the way to the office can tell a lot about him. Compiling and analyzing this information can help to develop a proper pretext or good questions to use to elicit the right response from the target. Knowing the start and end times for his day can also be valuable for physical red team attacks, where the goal of the team is to actually break in and recover valuable assets to show the company their physical weaknesses.

You can track people in many different ways, but one way is to use a device designed to help track a target. One such device is a GPS Tracker; for example, the notable SpyHawk SuperTrak GPS Worldwide Super TrackStick USB Data Logger available from www.spyassociates.com. One type of many, these devices can range from $200 to $600. SpyHawk SuperTrak magnetically sticks to a vehicle and can store days' worth of data on the target. The following sections provide a walkthrough from setup to usage of this little device.

The SpyHawk SuperTrak GPS TrackStick

Installing the software needed to make the device run is painless. Just clicking the software that came with the device and following the on-screen steps will install all the software needed. It installs without any problems and the setup afterwards is equally as painless. The TrackStick screen, shown in Figure 7-13, is very intuitive to use and easy to set up.

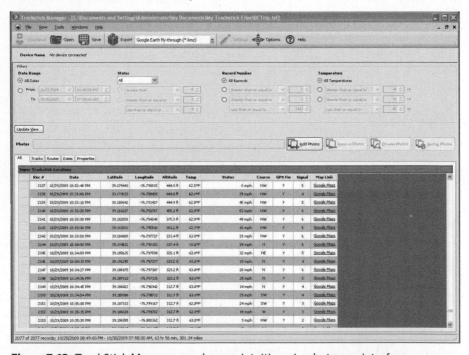

Figure 7-13 TrackStick Manager employs an intuitive, simple-to-use interface.

As you can see, it provides options to chose log times, time zones, and more custom options.

Using the SpyHawk TrackStick

The SpyHawk SuperTrak GPS Worldwide Super TrackStick device itself is lightweight and easy to use and hide. It comes with an on/off switch but has some neat technology. When it feels movement it turns on and starts logging. When the movement stops for a period of time, it stops logging.

The directions say to hide the device somewhere with the powerful magnets against metal but the device pointing up or toward plastic. Losing the device on its first run is always a concern, so finding a nice secure place under the hood can ease those worries and give easy access to the sky view. Once you have access (either internal or external) to the target's car, find a secure location in a wheel well, under the hood, or in the back of the car by the trunk. Anywhere that there is metal will work. If you have internal access, popping the hood and putting it somewhere in the engine compartment can ease concerns over discovery and/or loss.

In my first tests, I found a place in the engine compartment to place the device. Even through the metal of the hood the device logged perfectly. Another placement idea is to wait until the target's car is unlocked and then place it in the trunk under the carpet or by the rear lights. On a personal side note, when I ran this test, the device stayed on five days collecting data, some of which you can see in the following figures. As shown in Figure 7-14, it looks like the target likes to speed.

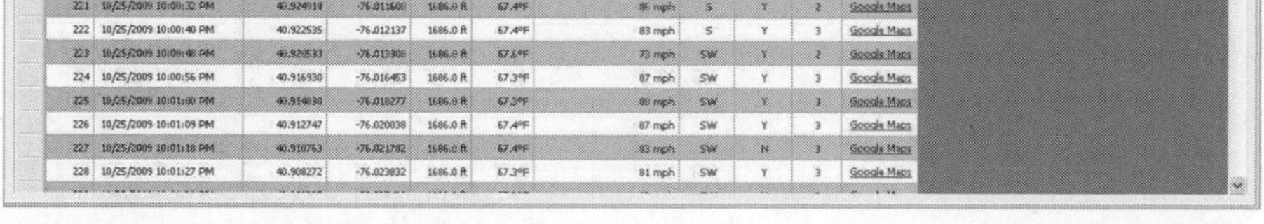

Rec #	Date	Latitude	Longitude	Altitude	Temp	Status	Course	GPS Fix	Signal	Map Link
212	10/25/2009 09:59:18 PM	40.944602	-76.026045	1558.4 ft	67.7°F	84 mph	S	Y	3	Google Maps
213	10/25/2009 09:59:27 PM	40.942353	-76.024832	1561.0 ft	67.7°F	86 mph	S	Y	2	Google Maps
214	10/25/2009 09:59:36 PM	40.940060	-76.023738	1593.2 ft	67.4°F	88 mph	S	Y	4	Google Maps
215	10/25/2009 09:59:45 PM	40.937853	-76.022563	1626.0 ft	67.6°F	81 mph	S	Y	4	Google Maps
216	10/25/2009 09:59:54 PM	40.934282	-76.019210	1675.5 ft	67.4°F	65 mph	SE	Y	3	Google Maps
217	10/25/2009 10:00:00 PM	40.932855	-76.017590	1686.0 ft	67.4°F	68 mph	SE	Y	3	Google Maps
218	10/25/2009 10:00:08 PM	40.931225	-76.015792	1686.0 ft	67.4°F	81 mph	SE	Y	3	Google Maps
219	10/25/2009 10:00:16 PM	40.929418	-76.013792	1686.0 ft	67.6°F	83 mph	SE	Y	2	Google Maps
220	10/25/2009 10:00:24 PM	40.927317	-76.012177	1686.0 ft	67.4°F	85 mph	S	Y	3	Google Maps
221	10/25/2009 10:00:32 PM	40.924918	-76.011608	1686.0 ft	67.4°F	86 mph	S	Y	2	Google Maps
222	10/25/2009 10:00:40 PM	40.922535	-76.012137	1686.0 ft	67.4°F	83 mph	S	Y	3	Google Maps
223	10/25/2009 10:00:48 PM	40.920533	-76.013308	1686.0 ft	67.6°F	73 mph	SW	Y	2	Google Maps
224	10/25/2009 10:00:56 PM	40.916930	-76.016453	1686.0 ft	67.3°F	87 mph	SW	Y	3	Google Maps
225	10/25/2009 10:01:00 PM	40.914830	-76.018277	1686.0 ft	67.3°F	88 mph	SW	Y	3	Google Maps
226	10/25/2009 10:01:09 PM	40.912747	-76.020038	1686.0 ft	67.4°F	87 mph	SW	Y	3	Google Maps
227	10/25/2009 10:01:18 PM	40.910763	-76.021782	1686.0 ft	67.4°F	83 mph	SW	N	3	Google Maps
228	10/25/2009 10:01:27 PM	40.908272	-76.023832	1686.0 ft	67.3°F	81 mph	SW	Y	3	Google Maps

Figure 7-14 The target likes to speed.

Time, date, and duration stamps help you outline a target's movement, as shown in Figure 7-15.

	Date	Time Period	Record #'s	Total Duration	Distance
▶	10/25/2009	08:49:00 PM – 12:00:54 AM	2 – 919	3 hr 11 min	175.59 mi
	10/26/2009	12:00:00 AM – 12:00:40 AM	920 – 1373	13 hr 54 min	61.42 mi
	10/27/2009	12:00:40 AM – 12:00:00 AM	1373 – 1610	15 hr 13 min	13.02 mi
	10/28/2009	12:00:00 AM – 12:00:00 AM	1610 – 1908	14 hr 35 min	16.85 mi
	10/29/2009	12:00:00 AM – 10:54:45 PM	1908 – 2244	14 hr 24 min	27.79 mi
	10/30/2009	05:19:00 AM – 07:58:00 AM	2245 – 2343	2 hr 39 min	6.51 mi

Figure 7-15 Tracking the target's movements.

Figure 7-16 shows the icons on a Google Earth map—they show speed, times, time stopped, and more.

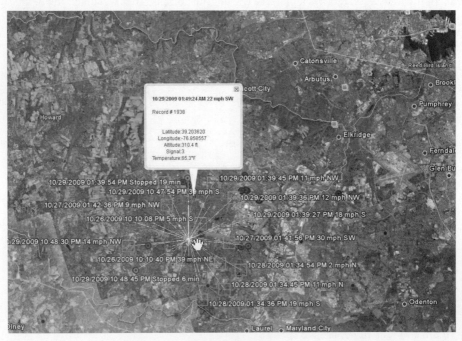

Figure 7-16 Device output rendered in Google Earth.

As you can see in Figure 7-17, the software creates nice maps of the whole route.

Figure 7-17 Mapping the target's route with SuperTrack.

Using Google Earth or Google Maps you can even get close-ups (see Figure 7-18).

Figure 7-18 Zeroing in on the target's travels.

Reviewing the GPS Tracker Data

The data collection is where a social engineer will see the most benefit. Being able to track every time the CEO of the target company stopped for coffee, what his favorite shop is, and what gym he attends can enable the social engineer to plan an attack with the highest rate of success.

Knowing the locations and stops can tell the attacker where he or she will have the best opportunities for cloning an RFID badge or making an impression of a key. The bonus is that you can get this information without having to stalk the target by being the creepy guy next door. The following figures show how these details can give the attacker the upper hand.

Notice the detail in Figure 7-19. You can see the speed the target drove, and the time and date he stopped. If you want to see the location in more detail, click the Google Maps link. Click the Export button to export the whole data set to a clickable Google Map or Google Earth Map.

Figure 7-19 The data set.

After you open the data set in Google Earth you can see the points he stopped, the route he took to and from his destination, and the times he stopped, as shown in Figure 7-20.

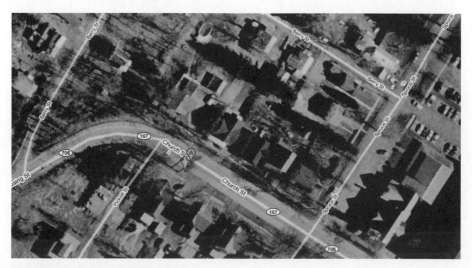

Figure 7-20 Stops along the way.

If you want to see his whole route, it's no problem—just export his whole route to one of many formats, as shown in Figure 7-21.

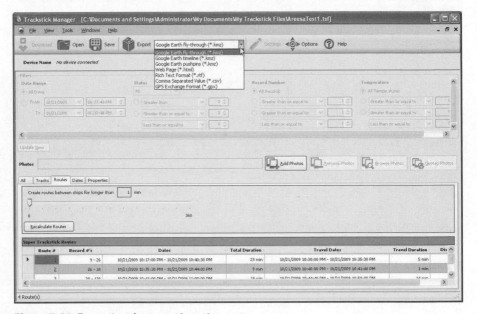

Figure 7-21 Exporting the target's entire route.

Figure 7-22 shows the data exported and displayed in Google Maps.

This short section could not possibly cover all the tools available to a social engineer. The keys to success are practice and research. Knowing what tools are available to social engineers can make or break the audit. That is just half the battle, though, because then as a professional social engineer, you must practice, practice, practice. Knowing how to properly use the tools will make a huge difference.

On the Social Engineer Framework located at www.social-engineer.org, I will be reviewing many tools that social engineers can use to enhance their practice.

Physical tools are just one part of being a successful social engineer though. All the physical tools on Earth are backed up by quality and thorough information gathering as discussed in Chapter 2. The next section covers some of the most amazing information-gathering tools in the world.

Figure 7-22 The target's route rendered in Google Maps.

Online Information-Gathering Tools

As previously discussed, information gathering is a key aspect of social engineering. Not spending enough time on this point alone can and will lead to failure for the social engineer. Nowadays many tools are available to the social engineer that can help collect, catalog, and utilize the data that is collected.

These tools can literally change the way a social engineer views and uses data. No longer are social engineers limited to what they can find in routine searches; these tools open every resource on the Internet to them.

Maltego

Collecting and cataloging information is probably a weak point for many people. What if a tool existed that enabled you to perform dozens of searches specific to a domain, IP address, or even a person? What if it gave you the weightings of those findings, showing what was more likely to be important or not? What if this tool then had a GUI interface that showed everything in color-coded objects that you can export and utilize? On top of it all, what if a free version of this amazing tool was available?

Enter Maltego. Maltego is a social engineer's dream tool. This amazing tool is made by the guys at Paterva (`www.paterva.com`). Maltego has a community edition available for free download from their website, which is also included in every edition of BackTrack4. If you want to remove the limitations of the free edition—like the number of transforms you can run and saving data—spending around $600 will get you a full license.

The best way to show the power of Maltego is to tell a story of an audit I was involved in. I was tasked with auditing a small company that had a very small web presence. The target was to get to the CEO but he was heavily guarded, paranoid, and didn't use the web much. As the owner of a printing company he was all about his business and didn't use technology to its fullest. Surely this task was going to be a difficult one.

I whipped out Maltego first. Using just the company's domain and pulling up all e-mail addresses linked with Whois info and the domain itself gave me a nice base of information to start searching with. I then delved deeper to see whether the CEO's email that came up was used on any other sites or URLs. I found he had written a couple of reviews for a local restaurant and linked his email address publicly. He also used it in a review he did for a restaurant in a different state. Reading his review fully revealed that he had visited that restaurant when he was visiting family in that state, even naming his brother in the review. With a few more searches in Maltego I located his parents and brother in that area. A few more searches with the family name and I found a few links that spoke about using another email he had from a business he started there to discuss a problem he had had with a local church and his switch to a new one. Later on, I found a blog post linking his Facebook page with pictures of his family after they left a ball game where their favorite team played. Here is what I was able to find in less than two hours of searching using Maltego:

>>   His favorite food

>>   His favorite restaurant

>>   His kids' names and ages

>>   That he is divorced

>>   His parents' names

>>   His brother's name

>>   Where he grew up

>>   His religion

>>   His favorite sports team

>>   What his whole family looked like

>>   His past business

A day later I mailed a package to the target containing information about a raffle for local businesses. The offer was that if he wins he gets a free dinner at the restaurant he listed as his favorite, and three free tickets to a Yankees game. All the business has to do is agree to have a short meeting with a sales rep to talk about a local charity. If the business agreed to that meeting its name would be entered into the raffle for a chance to win the Yankees tickets. My pretext's name was "Joe" and I prepared an outline for a call to the CEO. My goal was to get him to accept a PDF from me that outlined what we want and entered him in the drawing. By the time I called, he should have received my "mailed" package and I could easily use the line, "Yes, he is expecting my call."

While on the phone with "Joe," the CEO accepted and opened an email containing all the raffle details as well as a maliciously encoded file, ensuring the delivery of the reverse shell, giving me access to his network.

Of course, he got nothing on his screen and was frustrated that Adobe kept crashing. I told him, "I'm sorry you are having problems opening the file; we will include your name in the raffle and mail out some additional info to you today." But before that package went into the mail and arrived I called a report meeting to discuss how the target was completely compromised.

The majority of this success was due to the use of one tool—Maltego. It helped collect, organize, and categorize data for the best use.

How did Maltego help me succeed in this gig?

Think of Maltego as a relational database of information, finding links between bits of information on the Internet (referred to as entities within the application). Maltego also takes a lot of the hard work out of mining information such as email addresses, websites, IP addresses, and domain information. For example, you can search for any email address within a target domain or domains automatically with a few clicks. By simply adding the "EMAIL" transform on the screen then clicking in the box and typing the email I want to search for, I was given a view like what is seen in Figure 7-23.

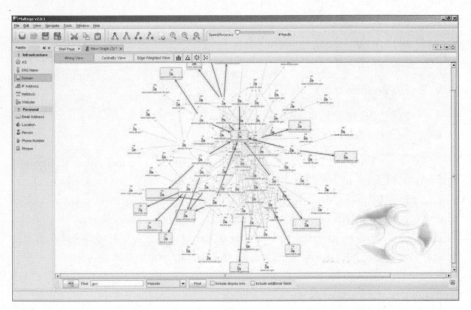

Figure 7-23 A representation of the information you can glean from Maltego.

Why Use Maltego?

Maltego automates much of the information gathering and large data correlation for the user, saving hours of Googling for information and determining how all that information correlates. Finding these data relationships is where the real power of Maltego comes into play. Although the mining is useful, discovering the relationships between the information is what will help the social engineer.

At www.social-engineer.org/se-resources/, I have posted a few videos outlining how to use Maltego to get the most out of it. In the earlier story Maltego contributed largely to the exercise's success, but the compromise came with another amazing tool.

SET: Social Engineer Toolkit

Social engineers spend much of their time perfecting the human aspect of their skills, yet many attack vectors call for the ability to produce emails or PDFs embedded with malicious code.

Both of these things can be done manually using many of the tools that exist in BackTrack, but when I was starting the www.social-engineer.org website I was talking to a good friend of mine, Dave Kennedy. Dave is the creator of a very popular tool called FastTrack that automated some of the most common attacks used in a penetration test using Python scripts and a web interface. I told Dave that I thought it would be a neat idea to develop something like FastTrack but just for social engineers—a tool that would allow a social engineer to create PDFs, emails, websites, and more with a few clicks and then focus more on the "social" part of social engineering.

Dave thought it over and decided that he could create a few easy Python scripts that would allow the social engineer to create PDFs and send emails with malicious code embedded in them. This was the birth of the Social Engineer Toolkit (SET). At the time of writing, SET had been downloaded more than 1.5 million times, and had quickly become the standard toolkit for social engineering audits. This section walks you through some of the main points of SET and how to employ them.

Installation

Installation is simple. All you need to have installed are Python and the Metasploit framework. Both of these are installed in the BackTrack distribution and there is no setup to worry about—in BackTrack 4 even the SET tool is installed. In case it is not or you are starting from scratch, installation is simple. Navigate to the directory you want it in and run this command in a console window:

```
svn co http://svn.secmaniac.com/social_engineering_toolkit set/
```

After executing this command, you will have a directory called set that will contain all the SET tools.

Running SET

Running SET is, again, an easy process. Simply typing ./set while in the set directory starts the initial SET menu.

sThis shows you exactly what the SET menu looks like. A comprehensive, in-depth tutorial about each menu option is available at www.social-engineer.org/framework/Computer_Based_Social_Engineering_Tools:_Social_Engineer_Toolkit_%28SET%29, but the following sections explain two of the most widely used aspects of SET.

First up is discussion the spear phishing attack, and following that is discussion of the website cloning attack.

Spear Phishing with SET

Phishing is a term coined to describe how malicious scammers will "cast a wide net" using targeted emails to try to draw people to websites, open malicious files, or disclose information that can be used for later attacks. Being able to detect and mitigate these attacks is essential for survival in the Internet world today.

SET allows the auditor to test their clients by developing targeted emails and then logging how many employees fall for these attacks. This information can then be used in training to help employees see how to spot and avoid these traps.

To perform a spear phishing attack in SET, chose option 1. After pressing that number you are presented with a few options:

» 1. Perform a Mass Email Attack

» 2. Create a FileFormat Payload

» 3. Create a Social-Engineering Template

The first option is where you actually launch an e-mail-based spear phishing attack. The second option is where you create a malicious PDF or other file to send in your emails. Finally, option 3 is where you can create templates for use later on.

Launching an attack in SET is as simple as choosing the right options in the menus then clicking Launch. For example, if I wanted to launch an e-mail attack that would send a victim a malicious PDF disguised as a tech report, I would chose option 1, Perform a Mass Email Attack.

Next, I would choose an attack vector (option 6) that was present in many versions of Adobe Acrobat Reader: `Adobe util.printf() Buffer Overflow`.

The next few choices set up the technical side of the attack. Using Metasploit to receive the reverse shell, or connection back from the victim's computer, and the port to come back on to avoid IDS or other systems, choose option 2, Windows Meterpreter Reverse_TCP.

Select port 443 so the traffic looks as if it is SSL traffic. The SET makes the malicious PDF and sets up the listener.

After doing so, SET asks you if you want to change the name of the PDF to something more devious like `TechnicalSupport.pdf` and then asks you to fill in the email information for both sending and receiving. Finally, SET sends out a professional-looking email that will try to trick the user into opening the attached PDF. A sample of what the victim receives is shown in Figure 7-24.

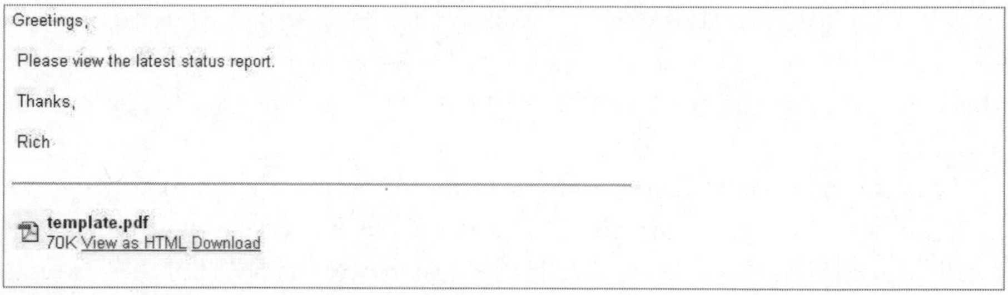

Greetings,

Please view the latest status report.

Thanks,

Rich

---

template.pdf
70K View as HTML Download

Figure 7-24 An innocuous email with a simple attachment.

After the e-mail is sent, SET sets up the listener and waits for the target to open the file. Once the target clicks the PDF, the listener responds by handling the incoming malicious code and giving the attacker access to the victim's computer.

Surprisingly (or perhaps not, depending on your outlook), all of this was done in maybe six or seven mouse clicks, and it leaves the auditor with the freedom to focus on the actual social engineering aspect of these attacks.

This is a devastating attack because it exploits a client-side piece of software, and many times there is no indication onscreen that anything bad happened.

This is just one of the many attacks that can be launched using SET.

Web Attack Vector

SET also allows the auditor to clone any website and host it locally. The power of this type of attack is that it allows the social engineer to trick users into visiting the site under the pretense of being a developer making changes, or even using the trick of adding or deleting one letter in the URL but pointing people to the new site that is cloned.

Once at the cloned website, many different parts of this attack can be launched—information gathering, credential harvesting, and exploiting are just a few.

To run this attack in SET you would choose option 2, Website Attack Vectors, from the main menu. Upon choosing option 2, you are presented with a few options:

» 1. The Java Applet Attack Method

» 2. The Metasploit Browser Exploit Method

» 3. Credential Harvester Attack Method

» 4. Tabnabbing Attack Method

» 5. Man Left in the Middle Attack Method

» 6. Return to the previous menu

A particularly evil attack vector is option 1, a Java Applet Attack. Basically, the Java Applet Attack presents the user with a Java security warning saying that the website has been signed by ABC Company and asks the user to approve the warning.

To perform this attack chose option 1, and then option 2, Site Cloner.

Upon choosing Site Cloner, you will be asked which website you want to clone. Here, you can chose anything you want—the client's website, a vendor they use, or a government website—the choice is yours. As you might imagine, though, choosing a site that makes sense to the target is essential.

In this exercise, imagine you cloned Gmail. You would be presented with the following on the screen:

```
SET supports both HTTP and HTTPS
Example: http://www.thisisafakesite.com
Enter the url to clone: http://www.gmail.com
[*] Cloning the website: http://www.gmail.com
[*] This could take a little bit...
[*] Injecting Java Applet attack into the newly cloned website.
[*] Filename obfuscation complete. Payload name is:
DAUPMWIAHh7v.exe
[*] Malicious java applet website prepped for deployment
```

Once you are done with this, SET will ask you what type of connection you want it to create between you and the victim. To use a technology discussed in this book, choose the Metasploit reverse shell called Meterpreter.

SET gives you the option to encode your payload with different encoders. This is to help you avoid getting caught by antivirus systems.

Next, SET launches its own built-in web server, hosts the site, and sets up a listener to catch your victim browsing the website.

Now it is up to the social engineer to either craft an email or a phone call to draw the target to the URL. In the end, the user would see what is shown in Figure 7-25.

The end result is the victim is presented with a Java Applet stating the site has been signed by Microsoft and that the user needs to allow the security certification to be run in order to access the site.

As soon as the user allows the security certification, the attacker is presented with a prompt to their computer.

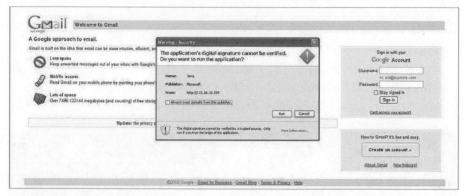

Figure 7-25 Who wouldn't trust a digitally signed applet from Microsoft?

Other Features of SET

SET was developed by social engineers with social engineers in mind, so the toolset that it gives the user is based around the common attacks needed by those in the auditing business.

SET is constantly growing and expanding. In recent months, for instance, SET has become capable of handling other attacks besides website cloning and spear phishing; it also houses an infectious media generator. An infectious media generator is where the user can create a DVD, CD, or USB key encoded with a malicious file that can be dropped or left at the target's office building. When it is inserted into a computer it will execute that malicious payload and cause the victim's machine to be compromised.

SET can also create a simple payload and proper listener for it. If the social engineer just wants to have an EXE that is a reverse shell that will connect back to his servers, he can carry this in a USB key for use on an audit. If he finds himself in front of a machine to which he wants remote access, he can put in the USB key and drop the payload file on the computer then click it. This will give him a quick connection back to his machines.

A newer attack vector is the Teensy HID attack vector. Teensy devices are tiny programmable circuit boards that can be embedded into things like keyboards, mice, or other electronic devices that get plugged into computers.

SET produces the programming needed to tell these tiny boards what to do when they are plugged in; commands like giving reverse shells or setting up listening ports are common.

One of the newest features of SET is a web interface to the tool. This means that a web server will start automatically to host the SET on a webpage for easier use. Figure 7-26 shows what this web interface looks like.

Figure 7-26 The new web interface of the Social Engineer Toolkit.

SET is a powerful tool made to help a social engineer auditor test the weaknesses that usually exist in a company. The SET tool developer is always open to suggestions and help in creating new parts of the tool to continue growing it to become a more popular toolset. Again, www.social-engineer.org has a full explanation of every menu option for review if you want to delve deeper into this amazing tool. Continue to check both www.social-engineer.org www.secmaniac.com for updates to the Social Engineer Toolkit.

Telephone-Based Tools

One of the oldest tools in the book for social engineers is the telephone. Nowadays, with cell phones, VoIP, and homemade phone servers, the options of how a social engineer can utilize the phone have grown considerably.

Because people are inundated with telemarketing calls, sales pitches, and advertisements, a social engineer needs to be skilled to use the phone successfully in an audit. Despite these limitations, using the phone as a social engineering tool can lead to total compromise of a company in a very short period of time.

In an era where everyone has a cell phone and people carry on personal and deep conversations on the bus, subway, or in any public place, the phone can be used in many ways. Eavesdropping or calling a target on their cell phone allows for additional vectors that were not available in days past. With the increased numbers of smart phones and computer-like phones on the market more and more people are storing passwords, personal data, and private information on their phones. This opens up the ability for the social engineer to be able to access the target and their data in many different situations

Also, being connected 24/7 makes people more ready to give out information quickly if the caller passes a certain set of "criteria" that makes him believable. For instance, if the caller ID on the cell phone indicates that the person is calling from corporate headquarters, many people would give over information with no verification. Both the iPhone and Android smart phones have applications that can be used to spoof your caller ID number to any number you want. Apps like SpoofApp (`www.spoofapp.com`) allow the social engineer to make calls that look as if they originate from anywhere on earth for a relatively low cost per call. All of this goes to building credibility of your pretext.

Using the phone for social engineering can be broken down into two different arenas: the technology behind it and planning out what you say.

Caller ID Spoofing

Caller ID has become a commonplace technology in both business and home use. Especially now with cell phones replacing many of the land-based phone lines people use, caller ID is part of daily life. Being aware of this fact and how to use this to your advantage is a must for a successful social engineer.

Caller ID spoofing basically is changing the information that appears on the target's caller ID display. In other words, though you are placing the call from one number, a different number appears on the target's caller ID.

One way to leverage this information is to spoof the number you found in a dumpster dive of a vendor used by your target. If the social engineer finds out that they use ABC Tech for computer support, the social engineer can find their number, and spoof that when a call is placed to set up an afternoon appointment. Using caller ID spoofing, you can "originate" calls from the following places:

» A remote office

» Inside the office

» A partner organization

» A utility/service company (telephone, water, Internet, exterminator, and so on)

» A superior

» A delivery company

So how do you spoof? The following sections discuss some of the methods and equipment available a social engineer can use to spoof numbers.

SpoofCard

One of the most popular methods of caller ID spoofing is by using a SpoofCard (www.spoofcard.com/). Using one of these cards, you call up the 800 number given to you on the card, enter your PIN, the number you want the caller ID to display, and then the number you want to call.

Some new features of the SpoofCard offer you the ability to record the phone conversation and mask your voice to be male or female. These features maximize the ability to hide who is calling and trick the target into divulging information the social engineer seeks.

On the plus side, SpoofCard is simple to use, it needs no extra hardware or software other than your phone, and it has proven service with thousands of customers. The only real negative to SpoofCard is the cost involved to purchase it.

SpoofApp

With so many people using smart phones like the iPhone, Android, or the Blackberry there has been an influx of apps created to assist in caller ID spoofing. SpoofApp uses SpoofCards (see the preceding section) but bundles the features into a package on your cell phone.

Instead of having to call a toll free number you simply enter the number you want to call into the application, then enter the number you want to display, and

SpoofApp connects you to the target displaying the information you requested to the target. All of this is as simple as a click of a button.

Asterisk

If you have a spare computer and a VoIP service you can also use an Asterisk server to spoof caller IDs. You can find some information about this method at `www.social-engineer.org/wiki/archives/CallerIDspoofing/CallerID-SpoofingWithAsterisk.html`. An Asterisk server is very similar to how SpoofCard works, with the exception of the server used to spoof the ID. In this case, you own the server. This is attractive because it allows for more freedom and there is no fear of being cut off or minutes running out.

The positive aspects of Asterisk are that it is free, it's easy to use and flexible after setup, and you alone control it. Minuses include that an extra computer or VM is needed, Linux knowledge is required, and you need a current VoIP service provider.

The great part about this option is that all the information about the caller and the person called resides with the social engineer. Personal and account data are not in the hands of a third party.

Using Scripts

The telephone is a favorite tool of the social engineer. It offers anonymity as well as the ability to practice on numerous targets by changing just slight parts of the pretext.

One aspect of using the phone in social engineering that you must consider is the use of scripts. Scripting can be an essential part in ensuring that all the needed elements are covered and touched on; however, a script should not be a word-for-word speech to be given. Nothing irritates the target more than to be presented with a person who sounds like he is reading a script.

After you write a script you should practice it over and over so you sound real, genuine, and believable,

This is where your information-gathering sessions will become vital. The better the information the social engineer gathers the clearer the script will become. I find it useful to read a few facts on the hobbies and interests of the target so I can use that to build rapport.

Once you have all the information laid out it can be helpful to then outline a plan of attack. In the case discussed previously—the CEO of the printing company—I had to develop an outline that would allow me to utilize the key parts of my pitch, high points I wanted to hit, as well as notes to myself like, "speak clearly," "don't forget to push the charity," "slow down," and so on, which kept me focused during the call.

Using a script or outline versus a fully written out manuscript will keep you fluid and natural and allow creative freedom when presented with things you didn't plan for.

The telephone is still a deadly tool for the social engineer and when used with the principles mentioned so far in this book, it can lead a social engineer down the path of success.

Password Profilers

Another set of tools that bear mentioning help you profile targets and the passwords they may use. After you have all the information on a target you can gather, your next is to develop a profile. A profile is where you plan out a few attack vectors you feel will work and also where you can start to build a list of potential passwords to try in brute force attacks. From a tool perspective, having a list of possible passwords can assist in expediting a hack if you are presented with that option. This section covers a couple profilers that are available.

Password profiling tools can take hours or even days off the work that you need to do.

Each year the number of people falling prey to simple attacks increases, despite the many warnings that are issued. The number of people who list all sorts of information about themselves, their families, and their lives on the Internet is amazing. Combining a profile built from their social media usage, what is found elsewhere on the web, and using the tools discussed subsequently, a social engineer can outline a person's whole life.

One of the reasons this works so well is the way that many people chose their passwords. It has been proven that many people will use the same password over and over again. What is worse is that many people choose passwords that can be easily guessed with little to no skill.

Recently, BitDefender, an Internet security firm, performed a study that proved this fact. BitDefender analyzed the password usage of more than 250,000 users. The results were amazing: 75% of the 250,000 used the same passwords for email as well as all social media accounts. This should be especially scary considering the recent story of how 171 million Facebook users had their personal information released on a torrent. The full story can be found at www.securityweek.com/study-reveals-75-percent-individuals-use-same-password-social-networking-and-email.

In 2009 a hacker by the nickname of Tonu performed a very interesting bit of research. With no malicious intent he obtained a recently dropped URL of a popular social media site. He spoofed the page, then for a brief period of time logged the attempts of people trying to log in.

You can view the results at `www.social-engineer.org/wiki/archives/BlogPosts/MenAndWomenPasswords.html`.

Some of this data will shock even the most seasoned security professionals. Out of 734,000 people, 30,000 used their first name as a password and almost 14,500 used their last name. Although those numbers are shocking what was found next was mind blowing—the top eight most commonly used passwords are outlined in the following table.

Password	Gender	Number of Users
123456	M	17601
password	M	4545
12345	M	3480
1234	M	2911
123	M	2492
123456789	M	2225
123456	F	1885
qwerty	M	1883

17,601 males used the password 123456? Staggering statistics.

If this isn't shocking enough, Tonu posted statistics that more than 66% of the users on that list used passwords that were six to eight characters long. With the information that most people have simple passwords, using a popular password-cracking tool, like Cain and Abel shown in Figure 7-27, to crack a simple password is not unreasonable for a social engineer to do.

You will notice that the Time Left box says 3.03909 days. To most hackers, three days is a short time to wait to be given clear access to the servers. Is three days really that long to wait for the administrator password?

To make this information really hit home, look at Figure 7-28, which shows the difference made if the same user were to use a 14–16 character password containing upper and lower case as well as non-alphanumeric characters.

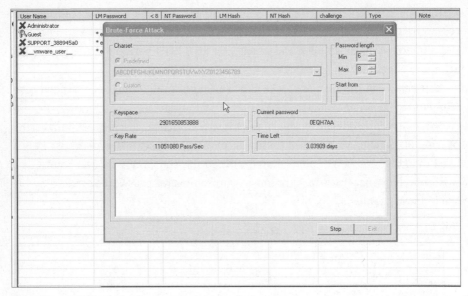

Figure 7-27 Only three days to crack a simple password.

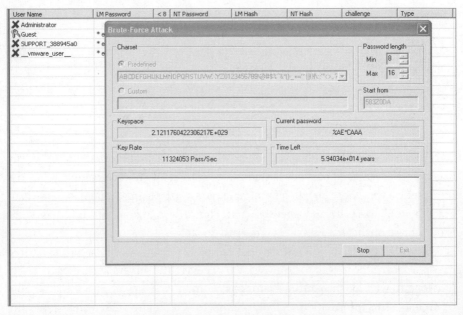

Figure 7-28 The Time Left box has increased to trillions of years.

Does more than 5 trillion years seem a little long to wait? By just increasing the characters to 14 and using some non-basic characters (that is, *, &, $, %, and ^) the odds of a hacker obtaining the password through brute force become next to impossible.

Because many users don't use this level of complexity, identifying the weakness in many users' passwords is not difficult. Certain tools (a couple of which are described in the next section) help profile potential passwords a user may have chosen.

Common User Password Profiler (CUPP)

Profiling a person is one of the main aspects of a successful social engineering audit. As previously discussed, Tonu's research shows that out of 734,000 people, more than 228,000 of them used only six characters in their passwords. More than 17,000 of those chose to use the password of "123456" and close to 4,600 chose the word "password" as their password.

Common User Password Profiler (CUPP) is a tool that was created to make password profiling an easy task.

Muris Kurgan, also known as j0rgan, created this amazing little tool. It runs as a script in the leading penetration testing distribution, BackTrack, or you can download it from www.social-engineer.org/cupps.tar.gz.

The most common form of authentication is the combination of a username and a password or passphrase. If both match values stored within a locally stored table, the user is authenticated for a connection. Password strength is a measure of the difficulty involved in guessing or breaking the password through cryptographic techniques or library-based automated testing of alternate values.

A weak password might be very short or only use alphanumeric characters, making decryption simple. A weak password can also be one that is easily guessed by someone profiling the user, such as a birthday, nickname, address, name of a pet or relative, or a common word such as God, love, money, or password.

Because most users have weak passwords that can be easy to guess, CUPP is a perfect tool for profiling. It can be used for legal penetration tests or forensic crime investigations.

The following is a copy/paste from a session using CUPP in BackTrack 4:

```
root@bt4:/pentest/passwords/cupp# ./cupp.py -i
[+] Insert the information about the victim to make a dictionary
[low cases!]
[+] If you don't know all the info, just hit enter when asked!
;)
> Name: John
```

```
> Surname: Smith
> Nickname: Johnny
> Birthdate (DDMMYYYY; i.e. 04111985): 03031965
> Wife's(husband's) name: Sally
> Wife's(husband's) nickname: Sals
> Wife's(husband's) birthdate (DDMMYYYY; i.e. 04111985):
05011966
> Child's name: Roger
> Child's nickname: Roggie
> Child's birthdate (DDMMYYYY; i.e. 04111985): 05042004
> Pet's name: Max
> Company name: ABC Paper
> Do you want to add some key words about the victim? Y/[N]: Y
> Please enter the words, separated by comma. [i.e. hacker,
juice, black]: christian,polish,sales person
> Do you want to add special chars at the end of words? Y/[N]: N
> Do you want to add some random numbers at the end of words? Y/
[N]n
> Leet mode? (i.e. leet = 1337) Y/[N]: Y
[+] Now making a dictionary...
[+] Sorting list and removing duplicates...
[+] Saving dictionary to John.txt, counting 13672 words.
[+] Now load your pistolero with John.txt and shoot! Good luck!
```

Notice at the end that a dictionary file of 13,672 passwords using the information provided was created. The power of this type of tool is that it can take a lot of the guesswork out of the password-guessing aspect of social engineering.

CeWL

As described by its authors, CeWL is a Ruby application that spiders a given URL to a specified depth, optionally following external links, and returns a list of words that can then be used for password crackers such as John the Ripper. For more information about CeWL see their website at www.digininja.org/projects/cewl. php. Take a look at a session using CeWL in BackTrack4:

```
root@bt:/pentest/passwords/cewl# ruby cewl.rb
 --help cewl 3.0 Robin Wood (dninja@gmail.com)
(www.digininja.org)
Usage: cewl [OPTION] ... URL --help, -h: show help --depth x, -d x:
depth to spider to,
default 2 --min_word_length, -m: minimum word length, default 3
--offsite, -o: let the
spider visit other sites --write, -w file: write the output to the file
--ua, -u user-
```

```
agent: useragent to send --no-words, -n: don't output the wordlist
--meta, -a file:
include meta data, optional output file --email, -e file: include email
addresses,
optional output file --meta-temp-dir directory: the temporary
directory,default /tmp -v:
verbose URL: The site to spider.

root@bt:/pentest/passwords/cewl# ./cewl.rb -d 1 -w pass.txt http://www.
targetcompany.com/about.php
root@bt:/pentest/passwords/cewl# cat passwords.txt |wc -l 430
root@bt:/pentest/passwords/cewl#
```

Using CeWL against a target company, this session generated 430 potential passwords to try from just one page on their web presence.

CUPP and CeWL are just two tools at your disposal to help profile and generate lists of potential passwords. An interesting exercise is to run one of these tools using your own information and see if any passwords you use are in the lists generated. It can be very sobering and make you want to take password security very seriously.

Summary

Tools are an important aspect of social engineering, but they do not make the social engineer. A tool alone is useless, but the knowledge of how to leverage and utilize that tool is invaluable.

If one overwhelming theme in this chapter resounds, it is that practice makes perfect. Whether you are using the phone, software-based tools, the web, or other spy gadgets, practicing how to utilize them is essential to success. For example, when using the phone for social engineering, you can use spoofing technologies or even voice-changing technologies, and while having all this great technology is amazing, if you make a call and sound too scripted, nervous and jittery, or unprepared and unknowledgeable, then all hope for social engineering success is lost and most likely any credibility, too. This principle goes back to being very well versed in pretexting. How would the person you are trying to impersonate talk? What would he say? How would he say it? What knowledge would he possess? What information would he ask for?

Whether the social engineer uses a software tool, hardware tool, or both, taking the time to learn the ins and outs of each tool and each feature can make or break the success of the audit.

Tools can take substantial time off audits and they can also fill in any deficiency gaps an auditor may have. This dynamic becomes apparent as you analyze the case studies in Chapter 8.

8 Case Studies: Dissecting the Social Engineer

The best security is through education.

—Mati Aharoni

Throughout this book I go through each aspect of what makes a great social engineer. Putting the information in these pages into play can make a social engineer a force to be reckoned with.

In school, students review history to learn what should or should not be done. History is a great tool for educating us about what things have worked in the past and why. It can tell us where we are going and how we can get there.

Social engineering history is not so different. Throughout the history of business, people have been there to scam and steal. People have devoted their lives to helping secure against those bad forces.

Discussing the aspects of professional social engineer attacks is often difficult because they were either done illegally or cannot be openly discussed due to client contracts. Fortunately, Kevin Mitnick—world famous social engineer and computer security expert—has published many of his stories for our reading pleasure. I have taken some of these stories from his book *The Art of Deception*.

In this chapter I pick two of Mitnick's most famous stories from his books and give a brief recap of what Kevin did, analyzing what aspects of social engineering he used and discussing what everyone can learn from it.

After dissecting those two accounts I do the same with two of my own accounts that demonstrate the ease with which you can obtain information and how easily you can use the information to compromise an entire company. Finally, I will disclose two "top-secret" stories whose sources I can't even mention, but as you will see, you will learn a lot from these accounts. What I am aiming to accomplish is to show you how dangerous even little bits of information can be, and how devastating they can be in the hands of a skilled social engineer. At the same time, you will see where a social engineer can learn from past successes and failures to enhance their own skill set.

Let's get started with the first case study.

Mitnick Case Study 1: Hacking the DMV

Kevin Mitnick is widely known as one of the world's most notorious social engineers. He has performed some of the boldest and most famous exploits in the world—and the exploit examined here is especially so.

A driver's license can often come in handy for obtaining information on people. Having the target's driver's license number can allow a social engineer to gain all sorts of personal information. However, no free services exist that allow a person to gain access to this personal information. A social engineer or private investigator must go through some lengths to be able to obtain and then use this information on a target.

Kevin Mitnick, in his book *The Art of Deception*, has a story he called "The Reverse Sting." The following sections provide some background information and analysis of this account.

The Target

In one of Mitnick's greatest stories, he discusses how "Eric" wanted to use the non-public Department of Motor Vehicles (DMV) and police systems to obtain people's driver's license numbers. He regularly needed to obtain license information on targets. Eric had a method of obtaining this information but feared repeated social engineering calls would render calling the DMV useless or alert the police to his ways.

He needed a different method to access the DMV's network and with some knowledge of the how the DMV works he knew just how to do it. His target was twofold—not only the DMV but also the police would assist him (of course, without knowing it) in accomplishing his goal of obtaining this information.

The Story

Eric knew that the DMV could give privileged information to insurance agencies, private investigators (PIs), and certain other groups. Each industry has access to only certain types of data.

An insurance company is privy to different information than a PI, whereas a law enforcement agent can get it all. Eric's goal was to get all the information.

Obtaining an Unpublished DMV Phone Number

Eric took a few steps that really proved his excellent social engineering skills. First he called telephone information and asked for the phone number for DMV head-quarters. Of course, the number he was given was for the public and what he wanted was something that would get him deeper.

He then called the local sheriff's office and asked for Teletype, which is the office where communications are sent to and received by other law enforcement agencies. When he reached the Teletype department, he asked the person for the number that law enforcement would use when calling the DMV headquarters.

Now I don't know about you, but that seems like it would fail. It just about did: "Who are you?" he was asked

He had to think quickly and responded, "This is Al. I was calling 503-555-5753."

All he did was give a random number with the same area code and base number and made up the last four digits. Then he just shut up. The officer made some assumptions:

» He was internal and already had the number for a non-public area (Teletype).

» He had almost all the number for the DMV.

With those two facts firmly in the officer's mind he assumed that Eric was allowed in and gave him the number. Eric wanted more than one number, though; he wanted as many as he could get his hands on.

Accomplishing this goal would require an even deeper hack—a multi-level, multi-faceted attack with many different avenues. It would be of epic proportion.

Gaining Access to the State's Phone System

Eric called the number he was given to get into the DMV. He told the DMV repre-sentative he was from Nortel and needed to speak to a technician because he worked with the DMS-100, a much-used switch.

When he was on with the technician he claimed to be with the Texas Nortel Technical Assistance center and explained he was updating all switches. It would be done remotely and the technician wouldn't need to do anything except provide the dial-in number to the switch so Eric could perform the updates directly from the Technical Assistance center.

This story sounded completely believable, so the technician complied, giving Eric all the info he requested. Armed with this information he could now dial directly into one of the state's telephone switches.

Getting a Password

The next hurdle was one that could have stopped this whole hack dead in its tracks—getting passwords. The Nortel switches that the DMV used were password protected. From past experience in using Nortel Switches Eric knew that Nortel uses a default user account, NTAS. Eric then dialed in several times trying the standard passwords he has encountered:

»   NTAS—fail

»   Account name—fail

»   Helper—fail

»   Patch—fail

»   Update—SUCCESS

Wow, really? The password was *update*. He now had full control over the switch and all lines connected to it. He queried the telephone lines that were his target. He quickly found out that 19 phone lines went to the same department.

After checking some of the internal setup of the switch he found out that the switch was programmed to hunt through the 19 lines until it found one that was not busy. He picked line 18 and entered the standard forwarding code that added a call forwarding command to that phone line.

Eric bought a cheap, pre-paid cell phone that could be disposed of easily. He entered that number as the number to forward to when line 18 was rung. Basically, as soon as the DMV got busy enough to have people on 17 lines, the 18th call would not ring to the DMV, but to Eric's cell phone.

It wasn't too long until that started happening. Around 8:00 a.m. the next morning the cell phone started to ring. Each time, it was a police officer looking for information on a person of interest. He would field calls from police at his house, at lunch, in the car—no matter where he was he pretended to be the DMV representative.

What made me personally get a good laugh was how the calls are reported as going:

The cell phone would ring and Eric would say, "DMV, may I help you?"

"This is Detective Andrew Cole."

"Hi Detective, what can I do for you today?"

"I need a Soundex on driver's license 005602789."

"Sure, let me bring up the record." While he simulated working on a computer he asked a couple questions: "Detective Cole, what is your agency?"

"Jefferson County."

Eric would then launch the following questions: "What is your requestor code?" "What is your driver's license number?" "What is your date of birth?"

As the officer would give all his personal information, Eric would pretend to be verifying it all. Then he would feign confirmation and ask what details he needed on his call. He would pretend to look up the name and other information then say, "My computer just went down again. Sorry, detective, my computer has been on the blink all week. Would you mind calling back and getting another clerk to help you?"

This would be a little irritating, I am sure, for the officer, but it would tie up all the loose ends. In the meantime, Eric now owned the identity of that officer. He could use this information for many things, but mostly to obtain information from the DMV whenever he needed.

He did his DMV information gathering for a few hours then called back into the switch and disabled call forwarding; he now had a juicy list of information in his possession.

For months after this hack, Eric could easily dial back in, enable the call forwarding switch, collect a number of officer information facts, disable call forwarding, and then use those police credentials to obtain valid driver's licenses that he would sell to private investigators or others who would not ask how he obtained this information.

Applying the SE Framework to the DMV Hack

In the story, Kevin identified some things that Eric did and attitudes he had that made him successful, such as not being afraid or uncomfortable talking to police and being able to find his way around unfamiliar areas.

You can also identify what part of the social engineering framework Eric used and how he used it.

For example, the first step in any successful social engineering audit or attack is information gathering. In this account you can see that Eric must have really done his homework prior to the attack. He knew a lot about the phone system, the way the DMV operates, and the general workings of the process he wanted to infiltrate. I am not sure how long ago this attack occurred, but nowadays making an attack like it is even easier due to the Internet. It is a goldmine for information gathering. Just a couple of years ago someone figured out a hack for a Tranax ATM, and within a few weeks manuals containing step-by-step processes of how to perform the attack were available on the Internet.

Also, as mentioned previously in this book, choosing a pretext that mimics what you do in real life or things you did in the past can increase your chance of success. The power lies in the fact that because the pretext is more "realistic" to you it helps you gather information as well as breach the target. Eric seemed to have a very intimate knowledge of this field.

As you may recall, the next part of the framework is elicitation, or being able to cleverly craft questions to obtain information or access to something you want. Eric elicited information masterfully. When on the phone with the police, Eric's use of elicitation served as the proof that he was who he said he was and knew his "job" well. He knew the lingo and asked routine questions that had to be answered. As a matter of fact, not asking those questions would have probably caused more of an alarm than by asking them. That is the power of good elicitation tactics.

Early on Eric knew he had to obtain certain phone numbers to perform the attack. Instead of trying to explain why he needed certain information, he used an assumptive close as mentioned in Chapter 3, and asked questions that basically stated, "I deserve these answers now, so tell me what I am asking." This is another example of powerful elicitation; you can learn a lot from analyzing his methods closely.

Most good attacks also include a very high amount of pretexting. This account was no exception. Eric had to develop a few pretexts in this attack vector. He had to switch gears many times to accomplish his goals. As impressive as it is that Eric had to impersonate law enforcement (which he did very well), keep in mind that this practice is highly illegal in the United States. You can learn much from the process and methods Eric used, but be cautious how you apply them. Even in a paid social engineering audit, impersonating a law enforcement agent is illegal.

Know your local laws—that is the lesson—or don't be afraid to be caught. Despite the fact that it is illegal, you can learn a lot from analyzing Eric's attitude in this hack. He was always collected. When he put on the pretext of the DMV agent he was able to use elicitation that served as the proof. When he put on the police pretext, his demeanor, voice, and phrases all backed up the pretext. Switching gears can be hard for many people, so it is best to practice before you go "live" with this.

Eric's pretexts were solid and he did a masterful job at holding them together, especially when he had to act as a DMV agent and field real calls from police. In many circumstances he could have easily fallen out of character but he seemed to hold it together quite well.

Many of the techniques used for the psychological aspects of social engineering, such as eye cues and microexpressions, were not used in this attack because it happened mostly over the phone. Eric did have to utilize certain aspects of the framework, though, such as rapport building, NLP (neurolinguistic programming), and modes of thinking.

Eric seemed to be a natural at building rapport. He was personable and easygoing, he seemed to not be afraid of the "what ifs," and was able to be and act confident in his abilities. He posed his voice and his conversation in a way that gave the person on the other end of the phone all the reason to trust him and no reason to not believe him.

Eric used impressive interrogation and interview tactics, even using them on law enforcement agents who are experienced in interview tactics. He used those tactics so successfully that he was undetected in his methods and obtained all the information he wanted.

Eric also seemed to have an excellent grasp of and ability to use influencing tactics. Probably one of the most noticeable in the attack was when he asked the police officer to call back to get a different DMV agent. This was probably annoying for the officer, but what made the tactic successful is that Eric "gave" the office something *first*. That is, he "verified" the data the officer needed and when he was supposed to give the officer final piece of info is when the "computer" froze.

Applying some rules of influence Eric was easily able to get the officers to comply.

Closely linked to Eric's pretext was his ability to use framing successfully. To refresh your memory, *framing* is bringing the target inline with your thinking by positioning yourself and your stories to make them believable. It is an important piece of the pretext puzzle that makes you stand out and prove to the target you certainly are who you say you are. Eric's pretexts were great and believable, but what really sold them were the frames that he used. His frame changed depending on who he was talking to. At one point he had to make sure the officer on the other end would give him the Teletype number; on the other call he had to be a knowledgeable and skilled DMV agent.

Eric made himself believable using framing by assuming he would get the information he asked, showing no fear in his dealings, and confidently asking for information he "felt" he was owed. All these attitudes framed the target to accept his pretext and allow for natural responses.

As you can see, you can learn much by analyzing Eric's social engineer attack. One can only assume that Eric either had practiced all these methods or had a few dry runs to know all he did about the internal systems used in the attack.

Eric's methods worked out for him and were successful, but I would have taken a couple extra precautions. For example:

» When he was fielding DMV calls, I would have made sure I forwarded the number only when I was in the "office." I would have set up an office area with some background office noises and had the proper supplies to take down all the information I needed to avoid the risk of a waitress or friend blowing my cover.

» Although a disposable cell phone is a good idea for tracing purposes, another technique is to have that number forward to a Google Voice or Skype number. I tend not to trust cell signals, and nothing could have ruined the gig faster than having the call drop or having a weak, static-filled signal.

Besides these items one can't improve much in this hack. Eric did a superb job at making sure it was done right by using many of the talents and skills in the framework to accomplish his goal.

Mitnick Case Study 2: Hacking the Social Security Administration

Mitnick mentions a man he called Keith Carter, a less-than-honorable private investigator hired to do some digging into a man who was hiding funds from his soon-to-be-estranged wife. She had funded his venture, which had grown into a multimillion-dollar company.

The divorce was almost settled but the woman's attorneys needed to find the "hidden assets." This attack vector is interesting because, as in the first case study, the story follows a very shady method of gathering intelligence.

The Target

The target was to find the assets of the husband, "Joe Johnson," but that wasn't the target used for the actual social engineering attack. To obtain information on Joe, the private investigator, Keith, had to hack the Social Security Administration (SSA).

Many times in a social engineering audit this option will present itself. This section covers some of the methods he used to accomplish this goal, but suffice it to say that hacking the SSA is a very slippery slope. As the story unfolds you will see how dangerous this particular hack was.

The Story

Joe Johnson was married to a very wealthy woman. He had knowingly used tens of thousands of her dollars to invest in one of his ideas. That idea grew into a multimillion-dollar organization.

As things happen, their marriage was not too solid, so they decided to divorce. During the divorce proceedings, soon to be ex–Mrs. Johnson "knew" he was hiding his money, trying to keep it out of the divorce settlement.

She hired Keith, the private investigator who was a less-than-ethical guy who didn't mind riding the edge of what was legal and what was not to obtain the information he needed to make the case.

As Keith sat down to analyze the case he determined that a good starting point was the Social Security Administration. He thought that if he could just obtain Joe's records he would be able to find some discrepancies and then nail his coffin shut. He wanted to be able to freely call Joe's banks, investment firms, and offshore accounts pretexting as Joe. To do so he needed some detailed information, which is what led him to the path of hacking the Social Security office.

Keith began with basic information gathering. He went online and found a guide describing the SSA's internal systems and their internal terminology and jargon. After studying that and having the jargon down pat he called the local public number of the Social Security office. When he got a live person he asked to be connected to the claims office. The conversation went like this:

"Hi, this is Gregory Adams, District Office 329. Listen, I am trying to reach a claims adjuster who handles an account number that ends in 6363 and the number I have goes to a fax machine."

"Oh, that is Mod 3, the number is…"

Really? That easy? Wow. In a few moments' time he gets the number of the internal office phones that the public normally cannot get. Now comes the hard part.

He has to call Mod 3, change his pretext, and obtain useful information on Joe. Thursday morning comes around and it looks like Keith has his plan well laid out. He picks up the phone and dials the Mod 3 number:

"Mod 3. This is May Linn Wang."

"Ms. Wang, this is Arthur Arondale, in the Office of the Inspector General. Can I call you 'May'?"

"It's 'May Linn'," she says.

"Well, it's like this, May Linn. We have a new guy who doesn't have a computer yet, and right now he has a priority project to do so he's using mine. We're the government of the United States, for crying out loud, and they say they don't have enough money in the budget to buy a computer for this guy to use. And now my boss thinks I'm falling behind and doesn't want to hear any excuses, you know?"

"I know what you mean, all right."

"Can you help me with a quick inquiry on MCS?" he asked, using the name of the computer system for looking up taxpayer information.

"Sure, what do you need?"

"The first thing I need you to do is an alphadent on Joseph Johnson, DOB 7/4/69." (*Alphadent* means to have the computer search for an account alphabetically by taxpayer name, further identified by date of birth.)

"What do you need to know?"

"What's his account number?" Keith asks (this is Joe's Social Security number he is asking for).

She read it off.

"Okay, I need you to do a numident on that account number." (*Numident* is similar to alphadent, only it's a numerical search instead of an alphabetical one.) This was a request for her to read off the basic taxpayer data, and May Linn responded by giving the taxpayer's place of birth, mother's maiden name, and father's name. Keith listened patiently while she also gave him the month and year Joe's Social Security number was issued, and the district office it was issued by.

Keith next asked for a DEQY (pronounced "DECK-wee"; it's short for "detailed earnings query.")

"For what year?"

"Year 2001."

May Linn said, "The amount was $190,286, and the payer was Johnson MicroTech."

"Any other wages?"

"No."

"Thanks," Keith said. "You've been very kind."

Keith then tried to arrange to call her whenever he needed information and "couldn't get to his computer," using a favorite trick of social engineers of always trying to establish a connection so that he can keep going back to the same person, avoiding the nuisance of having to find a new mark each time.

"Not next week," she told him, because she was going to Kentucky for her sister's wedding. Any other time, she'd do whatever she could.

At this point it seemed like game over. Keith had all the information he set out to obtain and now it was just a matter of calling the banks and offshore accounts, which, armed with the information he had, had now become a much easier task.

A well-executed and truly awe-inspiring attack.

Applying the SE Framework to the SSA Hack

The SSA attack just described leaves your mouth ajar and eyes wide. You can learn much from this particular attack, which used the social engineering framework.

Keith started the attack with information gathering. You are probably really tired of hearing me say this over and over again, but having information is truly the crux of every good social engineer attack—the more you have, the better.

Keith first found a truly amazing piece of intel on the Web, which dumbfoundingly enough, is still online at `https://secure.ssa.gov/apps10/poms.nsf/`.

This link directs you to an online manual for Program Operations of the Social Security Administration. It contains abbreviations, lingo, and instructions as well as what SSA employees are allowed to tell law enforcement. Armed with this information, Keith knew what to ask, how to ask, and how to sound like he belonged, as well as what information would raise red flags.

Although the link provided a wealth of information, he decided to take his information gathering a step further using the pretext of an Inspector General Office employee and calling his local SSA office. He really thought outside the box, by using his local office to obtain the internal numbers needed to complete his pretext as an internal employee.

Keith switched pretexts a couple of times and did so masterfully. He was able to obtain much of the information he needed by using the online SSA manual to develop the right questions. This manual proved to be an elicitation developer's dream. Armed with the right words and language, he sounded like he fit right in. He built rapport and a frame that fed the pretexts perfectly. Building rapport is not an easy task, but Keith did it well and in a way that indicated he was well practiced in this technique. He used many influence tactics to make sure the target felt comfortable and at ease. For example, he mixed obligation and reciprocation artfully. When he was able to get May Linn on his side by describing the lack of good tools and the lack of support from his management, she felt obligated to help him out.

He also used keywords and phrases that commanded empathy and yet showed his authority, such as "my boss is not happy with me," which gives an indication that he is in trouble and that the SSA employee, May Linn, can save him. People have a moral obligation to save those in need. Not many can walk away when someone is asking for help, and May Linn couldn't either. She felt compelled to not only help, but to even tell Keith about her personal schedule.

In the end, Keith used a number of important skills in the framework that do not involve personal onsite, in-person action.

The fact that governmental systems are run by people make them fallible to the hacking methods used in this story. This is not an argument for the invention of robotic or computerized systems to do these jobs; it merely points to the fact that many of these systems rely so much on overworked, underpaid, overstressed people that manipulating them is not a very hard job.

To be honest, improving upon this particular attack is difficult because it is not one I would ever perform myself and Keith did a superb job of applying the principles of the framework.

So many people are used to being mistreated, abused, and yelled at that a little bit of kindness can make them go to extraordinary heights to help out. This particular attack as relayed in Mitnick's *The Art of Deception* shows how vulnerable systems that rely on people truly are.

Hadnagy Case Study 1: The Overconfident CEO

My experience with an overconfident CEO is interesting because the CEO thought he would be impervious to any social engineering attempt for two reasons: First, he did not utilize technology much in his personal life, and second, he felt that he was too smart and protected to fall for what he called "silly games."

With that being said to his internal security team they decided to ask me to focus on him as the goal of the audit. They knew that if he did fail the audit it would be easier to get approval to implement many of the fixes that would help their security.

The Target

The target was a decent-sized printing company in the U.S. that had some proprietary processes and vendors that some of its competitors were after. The IT and security teams realized the company had some weaknesses and convinced the CEO an audit was needed. In a phone meeting with my partner, the CEO arrogantly said that he knew that "hacking him would be next to impossible because he guarded these secrets with his life." Not even some of his core staff knew all the details.

My job as the SE auditor was to infiltrate the company to obtain access to one of the company's servers where this proprietary information was held and retrieve it. The difficulty, as the CEO had mentioned on the phone, was that the passwords for the servers were stored on his computer and no one had access to it, not even the security staff, without his permission.

The Story

Apparently, the way in would have to involve the CEO, which presented a challenge because he was ready and waiting for an infiltration attempt. I started off as I did with any gig—by information gathering. I researched the company using online resources and other tools such as Maltego. I was able to harvest information such as locations of servers, IP addresses, e-mail addresses, phone numbers, physical addresses, mail servers, employee names and titles, and much more.

Of course, I documented all this information in a fashion that made it easy to use later on. The structure of the e-mail was important because as I searched the website I saw that it was `firstname.lastname@company.com`. I could not locate the CEO's e-mail address but many articles listed his name (let's call him Charles Jones) and title on their site. This would be information a standard, non-informed attacker would be able to obtain.

Using the `firstname.lastname@company.com` format, I tried to send an e-mail to him. It didn't work. I was actually disappointed at this moment, because I was sure that the e-mail method would yield a lot of juicy details.

I decided to try a nickname for Charles, so I tried `chuck.jones@company.com`. Sweet success! I had a verified e-mail address. Now I just had to verify it was the CEO's and not some other guy with the same name.

I spent some more time on Google and Maltego to harvest as much information I could. Maltego has this great transform that allows me to search a domain for any files that would be visible to a normal search engine.

I ran the transform against the company's domain and was greeted with an amazing number of files for my browsing. Maltego doesn't stop with just providing filenames with this transform. Many files contain metadata, which is the information about the dates, creators, and other little juicy tidbits about the file. Running Maltego's metadata transform showed me that the majority of these files were created by a "Chuck Jones." Much of the content in the files talked about him as the CEO.

This was the confirmation I needed, but during my browsing one file had caught my eye—InvoiceApril.xls. Upon reading that file I discovered it was an invoice from a local bank for a marketing venture Chuck was involved in. I had the bank name, the date, and the amount, but I didn't have the event the company was a part of.

I did a quick search of the bank website but because the event was six months earlier it was not listed on the site. What could I do?

I decided to place a call to the marketing person from the bank:

"Hi, this is Tom from [CompanyName]. I am trying to organize our books and I see an invoice here from April for $3,500 as a sponsorship package. I don't see the event name—can you please tell me what that invoice was for?"

"Sure, Tom," she said and I heard some clicking noise in the background. "I see that was the bank's annual Children's Cancer Fund Drive and you were part of the Silver Package."

"Thanks a lot; I am new here and I appreciate your help. Talk with you later."

I was beginning to see a picture of a possible attack vector that I could use, but I needed some more research and I needed to make a very carefully planned phone call.

I found a few articles on the Web about this fundraiser and how many companies came from all over the community to support it with money for cancer treatment research. In addition, the more digging I did into the CEO the more I found out about him. I had his parents' names, his sisters' names, pictures of his kids that he has on Facebook, the church he went to when he lived near his parents, a review he wrote of his favorite restaurant, his favorite sporting team, his oldest son's favorite sporting team and where he attended college, where his kids go to school, and the list goes on and on.

I wanted to find out why the company donates to the Children's Cancer Fund. Although many malicious social engineers exploit others' emotions, and I realized I might have to go down that path as well, I wanted to know whether the fund was something he was involved in because one of his sons has cancer. I placed a call to the marketing director of the company:

"Hello, this is Tom from XYZ. I was hired by First National Bank in town to call those who took part in the April Children's Cancer Fund and I was wondering whether I could take a few minutes of your time to get some feedback?"

"Sure," Sue, the marketing director, said.

"Sue, I see that you were part of our Silver Package in April. Did you feel the marketing you received was worth the price you paid?"

"Well, this is something we do every year and it does get us a lot of press time in the local area. I guess I wouldn't mind seeing a little more on the website for the Silver Package."

"Excellent; I will note that. Every year—yes, I can see you do this every year. I am wondering personally, with so many fundraisers out there why did you choose this one?"

"I know Chuck has always been particular to this one. He is our CEO and I think someone in his family battled cancer."

"Oh my; I am sorry to hear that. It isn't his own children is it?"

"No, I think a nephew or cousin. We didn't really talk about it."

"Well, we certainly appreciate your donations and support."

I finished up with a few more questions and then left it at that, thanking her for her time, and we parted ways.

I got the information I needed—it wasn't one of his kids who had cancer. Again, I knew this wouldn't stop a malicious social engineer, but I was very curious. Armed with this information I was ready to plan my attack vector.

I knew the CEO was originally from New York and his favorite restaurant was a place called Domingoes. He would bring his kids in often for a Mets game and then they would go eat at Domingoes.

He wrote some ratings on the place and talked about his top three favorite dishes. I knew his parents still lived close by and he visited often from some other things he wrote on Facebook.

I planned my attack vector to be a fundraiser for cancer research. It was for the tri-state area and for a small donation one's name would be entered into a raffle. The raffle prize would be two tickets to a Mets game and a choice of three restaurant coupons, one of which was Domingoes.

I would pretend to be from New York myself, but relatively new, in case he threw things at me I didn't know.

My end goal would be for him to accept a PDF from me that would be maliciously encoded to give me a reverse shell and allow me access to his computer. If he did not use a version of Adobe that would allow me access, then I would try to convince him to download a zip file and execute an enclosed EXE that would have the malicious file embedded.

I practiced the phone conversation I would use for my pretext, I tested my PDF and EXE files, and I had Google Maps open to the location of Domingoes so I could talk about that area openly. After I had my computer ready and waiting to receive the malicious payload from the victim, I was ready to place the call.

I placed the phone call around 4:00 p.m., because I found out through the company website that the office closes at 4:30 on Fridays. Because I wasn't on the initial meeting phone call to set up this audit, (my partner was), the CEO would not recognize my voice.

"Hello, is Mr. Charles Jones available?"

"Sure one second." The voice on the other end sounded tired and was ready to transfer me.

"Hello, Chuck speaking."

"Hello, Mr. Jones, my name is Tony from the Cancer Research Institute of America. We are running an annual fund drive to support our research into cancers that plague men, women, and children."

"Please, call me Chuck," he interrupted.

This was a good sign because he didn't give me any excuses or try to end the phone call saying he was busy; he took it upon himself to personalize the conversation. I continued, "Chuck, thank you. We are running a fund drive for companies who supported cancer funds before and are asking for small donations of $50–$150 dollars. The great part is that everyone who helps us out is being entered into a drawing for two great prizes. If you win you get two tickets to a Mets game in NYC and then a free dinner for two at one of three great restaurants. We are giving out five of those packages."

"Mets game, really?"

"I know, if you don't like the Mets the prize might not appeal to you, but the restaurants are good."

"No, no, I love the Mets, that's why I said that. I was happy."

"Well think about this—not only are you helping out a great research fund but you get a good game in and you get to eat at Morton's, Basil's, or Domingoes."

"Domingoes! Really! I love that place."

"Ha, that is great. You know I just went there the other night for the first time and had their Chicken Portabella. It was awesome." This was his third-favorite dish.

"Oh, if you think that is good, forget it, you need to try the Fra Diablo. It is really the best dish in there. I eat it all the time."

"I am going there again over the weekend, I will definitely try it out. Thanks for the tip. Look, I know it is getting late. Right now I am not even looking for money, I don't take money over the phone. What I can do is send you the PDF; you can look at it and if you are interested you can just mail the check in with the form."

"Heck yeah, send it over."

"Okay just a couple questions. What is your e-mail?"

"`chuck.jones@company.com`."

"If you can, open your PDF reader, click the Help menu and About, and tell me the version number please."

"One minute; it is 8.04."

"Excellent; I don't want to send you a version that you can't use. Just one second while we are on the phone I am going to send this to you—okay, it's sent."

"Great, thanks. I hope I win; I really love that place."

"I know; the food is good. Before I let you go, could you just check to see whether you got the e-mail and let me know if it is working?"

"Sure, I am logging out in about five minutes, but I can check. Yep, it is here." When I heard the sound of double-clicking, I looked over on my BackTrack computer saw my malicious payload collector, Meterpreter (see Chapter 7), reacting. I was holding my breath (because this part never gets boring) and bam, the shell appeared. My Meterpreter scripts changed the ownership to something like `Explorer.exe`.

Chuck then said, "Hmm, all I got is a blank screen. It's not doing anything."

"Really? That's odd. Let me check here." What I was really checking was that I had access to his drive and the ability to upload a reverse shell that would run on reboot in case he shut down. I said, "I am sorry, I don't know what happened. Can you give me a minute or do you need to go?"

"Well I need to go empty this coffee mug, so I will put the phone down and be back in a minute."

"Excellent, thanks." That minute was all I needed to make sure I had unlimited and returning access to his computer. He came back.

"Back."

"Well, Chuck, I'm really embarrassed but I don't know what happened. I don't want to hold you up, so why don't you go and I will e-mail this to you when I make you another PDF. We can touch base Monday."

"Okay, no problem. Have a great weekend."

"You, too, Chuck."

We parted ways and to my surprise and extreme joy his computer remained on and active. Yes, he kept everything in a secure drive that only he had access to, but in Word documents. I promptly downloaded those Word documents and within a few hours I had access to the servers and printed out all the internal processes he wanted to protect.

We did touch base on Monday morning, not as Tony the fund-raiser, but as his security consultants with printouts of his "secrets," his passwords, and recordings of the phone calls that were made to him and his staff.

This first meeting after a successful attack is always filled with the client's initial shock and claims that we used unfair tactics and personal weaknesses to gain access. When we explain that the bad guys will use the exact same tactics, the look of anger turns to fear, and that fear turns to understanding.

Applying the SE Framework to the Overconfident CEO Hack

As in the previous examples, applying the case to the social engineering framework and seeing what was good and what could have been improved upon can be beneficial.

As always, information gathering is the key to any social engineering effort, and this particular story shows it. Information gathering from many sources—the Web, Maltego, the phone, and more—is what made this attack successful. Insufficient information would have led to a miserable failure.

Proper and plentiful information makes all the difference, even information I never needed, like his church, and his parents' and siblings' names. These things were useful to have in case I needed them, but what proved to be invaluable was the information found about the e-mail naming convention and the files on the servers using Maltego. This was the pathway to getting my foot into door of this company.

Keeping the information you find cataloged into BasKet or Dradis, as discussed in Chapter 2, and ready to use is also important; otherwise, you just have a text file with a jumble of information you can't make use of. Organizing the information is just as important as gathering and using it.

Thinking like a bad guy—that is, looking for ways to exploit the weaknesses and desires of the target—isn't a great part of the job, but if a professional auditor wants to protect clients, he will show them how vulnerable they are. The more information you gather, the easier finding vulnerabilities becomes. You begin to see pathways that can lead to success.

Developing realistic pretexts and themes that will have the maximum effect also contributes to an attack's success. One must develop power questions and keywords to use that will attract the target. By gathering a lot of information I was able to develop good questions and a frame that involved keywords and neurolinguistic (NLP) power words, which I then used in influence tactics that I was fairly sure would work.

My pretext had to change often, from calling the company's vendors to calling internal employees for information. I had to plan out each pretext, get into that character, and successfully follow through. This, of course, took a lot of planning to make sure each pretext sounded right, flowed properly, and made sense.

Practice makes perfect. Before the attack was launched my partner and I practiced everything. I had to make sure the PDFs worked and that the vector made sense. I also had to have good enough knowledge to be believable to whatever target I was speaking to at the time.

The importance of practicing cannot be understated. Practice enabled me to figure out what tactics would work and what wouldn't, as well as ensure that I could stick to the plan and go with the flow, even if that flow was in a direction in which I wasn't planning on going.

In hindsight, I discovered a couple small improvements that would have made this attack more efficient. For one, it is always a risk to rely solely on a malicious PDF; I should have set up a small website that mimicked the real cancer research website and had the PDF on there. Both the website and the PDF could have been malicious. This would have doubled my chances of success and given me backup in case one avenue failed.

Another large risk I took was that the CEO would leave his computer on when he left the office. If he did not, I would have had to wait till Monday to try to gain access. To keep him at his computer, I should have had a "real PDF" with information in it he could read that I would send after the malicious PDF worked in exploiting his machine. This would have kept him working at his machine long enough to make good use of the exploit.

This audit took about a week's worth of time to investigate, gather, and organize information for, practice, and then launch. One week and this company's secrets could have been owned by its competitors or by the highest bidder. Read the story a few times and try to understand the subtle methods used and the way the conversations flowed. Picking up on the voice, tone, and conversation pace is difficult in written form, but try to imagine yourself in this conversation and decide how you would handle it.

Hadnagy Case Study 2: The Theme Park Scandal

The theme park scandal case was interesting to me because it involved some onsite testing. I used many of the social engineering skills mentioned throughout this book and thoroughly tested them during this case.

It was also interesting because of the nature of the business and the potential for a successful scam. If successful, the social engineer could potentially have access to thousands of credit card numbers.

The Target

The target was a theme park that was concerned about having one of its ticketing systems compromised. Where patrons checked in, each computer contained a link to the servers, client information, and financial records. The park wanted to see whether the possibility existed for an attacker to use malicious methods to get an employee to take an action that could lead to a compromise.

The goal wasn't to get an employee in trouble, but rather to see what damage would result from an employee check-in computer being compromised. In addition, the goal was not to compromise the computers through hacking but through purely social engineering efforts.

If such a compromise could occur, what were the ramifications? What data could be found and what servers could be compromised? They didn't want to go deep, just really find out whether the first stage, a social engineering compromise, could work.

To figure out whether a successful SE attack was possible, I had to understand the theme park's processes and methods for checking in customers and what the employees would and wouldn't do at their terminals—or more importantly, could and couldn't do.

The Story

As mentioned earlier, the goal for this particular job wasn't really complex; I just had to find out whether the person behind the counter would allow a "customer" to get the employee to do something obviously not allowed. Before I could even think of what that was I had to understand their business.

I browsed the park's website and used Maltego and Google to research articles and other information about the organization. I also did some onsite research. I then went to the park and went through the process of buying a ticket at the ticket counter. During this process I started a small conversation with the teller, and spent some time observing the layout, their computer nodes, and other aspects of the "office" area.

This area was where I started to see a clear picture. During the conversation I mentioned I was from a small town with a huge name. When she asked where, and I told her, she issued the normal response:

"Where the heck is that?"

"Do you have Internet access here?"

"Yeah, I do."

"Oh you'll love this. Go to `maps.google.com` and type in the zip code 11111, and put it on satellite view. Look how small that town is."

"Oh my gosh; that is tiny. I don't think I've ever heard of this place before today."

In this short amount of time I knew the following:

» The layout of the space a teller has to work in

» How employees check in each patron

» That the computers have full web access

I went back to the park's website and started browsing with a new enlightenment on their processes. I needed a way in to their computer systems. My pretext was a reasonable one—I was a father who was going to take his family to the theme park for the day.

My story was that the family and I didn't have plans to do it, but we came to the hotel and were browsing the web for things to do and saw a great discount for the park. We went down to the lobby and inquired about getting tickets but the price we were given there was substantially more than what we saw on the web.

When we double-checked the price we had found, we discovered it was a web-only price. We paid and then realized the tickets needed to be printed so they can be scanned. I tried to get the hotel to print them but the printer was down. I had already paid and was nervous about losing the tickets so I printed them to a PDF and then e-mailed them to myself. Sounds like a reasonable story, doesn't it?

One more step was needed before I could launch my evil plot. I had to make a quick phone call:

"Hello, is this XYZ Theme Park main office?"

"Sure is; how can I help you?"

I needed to get to an internal office person to ask my question and make sure I had the right answer. After requesting the purchasing department, I was directed to the right person. I said, "Hi, my name is Paul from SecuriSoft. We are giving away a free trial of a new software to read and even print PDFs. I would like to send you the URL for the free download, is that okay?"

"Well, I'm not sure whether we are interested, but you can send me some information."

"Okay; excellent. Can I ask what version of Adobe you use now?"

"I think we are still on 8."

"Okay; I will send you out a comparative information packet today."

Armed with the version information, all I needed to do was create a malicious PDF embedded with a reverse shell (which would give me access to their computer once they opened the PDF), call it Receipt.pdf, and then e-mail it to myself.

The next day I roped my family into a little social engineering action. As they stood off in the distance I approached the woman behind the counter and started a friendly conversation.

"Hi there, how are you...Tina?" I said, reading her name tag.

"Doing okay, what can I help you with?" she said with a friendly customer service smile.

"See, we decided to take a little weekend getaway trip and I am at the Hilton over here with my family," I say, pointing to my beautiful family a few feet away. "My daughter saw the ad for your theme park and begged us to come. We told her that we would take her. We found a great deal on tickets on the website..."

"Oh, yes, our web-only deal—very popular right now. Can I have your tickets?"

"Yeah, you see this where I need your help so I don't get the 'Loser Dad of the Year' award." My nervous laughter was covered by her smile. I explained, "Tina, I saw that deal and my wife and I said, let's save the 15% and we bought the tickets at the hotel computer. But after I got done paying, I couldn't print them because the hotel printer was down. But I was able to save it as a PDF and I e-mailed it to myself.

I know this is an odd request but would you log into my e-mail account and print it out for me?" Now this account was a generic one filled with e-mails titled "Pictures of the kids," "Dad and Mom's Anniversary" and things like that.

I could tell she was really struggling with this decision and I was unsure whether the silence would be to my benefit or if I should help her to think it through. I said, "I know it is a weird request, but my little girl is just dying to go and I hate to tell her 'no.'" I point again to my daughter who was doing a great job at being cute but impatient.

"Okay, how do I do it?"

"Go to gmail.com, log in with `Paul1234@gmail.com` and a password of B-E-S-M-A-R-T." (I know, using this password is terrible in a way, but a little last-minute warning never hurt. It went unfollowed.)

Moments later Tina was double-clicking on my PDF and getting a blank screen. "Are you kidding me—did I print it out wrong? Wow, I am definitely getting the Loser Dad award now."

"You know what, sir? I feel so bad for you, what if you just paid for the adult tickets and I will let your daughter in for free today?"

"Wow, that is so generous of you." With a smile I forked over the $50 and thanked her for all her help and asked her to log out of my e-mail. We part ways with me having a happy daughter and the park having been compromised.

Moments later my partner text messaged me and told me that he was "in" and "gathering" data for the report. After enjoying a few hours of relaxation, we left the park to go back to work to compile the report for the Monday meeting.

Applying the SE Framework to the Theme Park Hack

Information gathering, as shown in this case study, is not always majorly Web based; instead, it can be done in person. The juiciest information in this case was gathered during an in-person visit. Finding out what computer systems were used, feeling out the target to know how he or she would react to certain questions, and knowing how the ticketing system worked were major components of the information gathering stage.

The real takeaway from this particular hack is that a good pretext is more than just a story; it's more than just some made-up costume and phony accent. A good pretext is something you can easily "live" without too much effort.

In this scenario I was easily able to speak, act, and talk the father, because I am one. My concern about being a "loser" dad was real, not made up, and comes across as real and then is transferred to the target as genuine. This makes everything that is said more believable.

Of course, having a cute child in the distance looking longingly at the ticket lady helped, and so did a believable storyline about a hotel printer not working. Chapter 2 touched on this, but sometimes a social engineer will promote that pretexting or social engineering in general is just basically being a good liar. I do not believe that is the case.

In a professional sense, pretexting involves creating a reality that will manipulate the target's emotions and actions to take a path you desire him to take. People are not often motivated by a simple lie. A social engineer must "become" the character in the pretext for a gig, which is why using pretexts that are something you can closely follow, live, and act with ease is a good idea.

The pretext of the "free PDF software giveaway" had a lot of room for error. The pretext was solid, but a quick rejection would have meant a couple-day lag in the next attack attempt. It was also a "lucky guess" that the same version of Adobe would be used companywide and that the particular teller I chose had not updated her particular version of Adobe Reader to the newest edition, which would have in essence nullified my exploit attempts.

Banking on inherent human laziness is not a gamble I usually like to take, but in this case it worked out. Sometimes the best bet is to move forward as if what you are asking for is already a done deal. That attitude promotes a feeling of confidence and comes across to the target that what you are saying or doing is legit.

Using words and phrases such as, "I really need your help…" is a powerful tool, as mentioned in Chapter 5. Humans inherently want to help each other, especially when asked.

When asked, complete strangers will go to extraordinary lengths to "help out" even, as in this case, opening a unknown file from someone else's email account. The plea to help a "poor dad" get his cute daughter into the park lead to a compromised system.

Once compromised, the software that stores all the credit card information for each guest was wide open to an attacker. The ability to collect that data with very little effort could have left the park open to massive loss, lawsuits, and embarrassment.

Top-Secret Case Study 1: Mission Not Impossible

Every now and then my colleague and I are either involved in a situation or hear of a story that we would love to see turned into a movie, but for security reasons we are not allowed to write about or even speak of it. For those reasons, I cannot mention who was involved or what was taken in the story that comes to us from a social engineer named "Tim."

Tim's goal was to infiltrate a server that housed information that could be devastating if it fell into the wrong hands. The particular high-profile company involved had a lot to protect. When Tim was contracted to get this company's information he knew he would have to pull out all the stops; this job would test the very limits of his social engineering skills.

The Target

The target is a high-profile organization with certain corporate secrets that should never be revealed to its competitors. These secrets had to be guarded on servers that did not have outside access and were only routable from the internal network.

Tim was contracted to help the company test its security against a "rogue person" being able to infiltrate and walk out with the goods. Tim met one person from the company at an offsite location to sign the deal they worked out over the phone and e-mail.

The Story

Tim had a huge challenge in front of him. The first stage, as with any social engineering gig, was the information gathering. Not knowing what information he would and wouldn't use, Tim went full bore, collecting information such as the e-mail layout scheme, open requests for quotes, all employee names he could find, plus any social media sites they belong to, papers they wrote and published, clubs they were part of, as well as service providers they used.

He wanted to do a dumpster dive but when he scoped out the place he noticed that security was very strong around the dumpster area. Many of the dumpsters were even enclosed in small walled areas, so he couldn't see the logos on the dumpster unless he breached the perimeter. After finding out the department that handles waste services, he decided to place a well-planned-out phone call to the company:

"Hello, this is Paul from TMZ Waste Disposal. We are a new waste disposal service in the area and have been working with some of the large corporations in the area. I am part of the sales team that handles your region. Could I send you a quote for our services?"

"Well, we are pretty happy with our present supplier, but you can submit a quote."

"Excellent; may I ask you just a few quick questions?"

"Sure."

"How many dumpsters do you have?" asked Tim. After asking whether they used special dumpsters for paper and technology such as USB keys and hard drives, he then laid on a few finishing touches.

"What day is your normal pickup?"

"We have two pickups per week; Set 1 is Wednesdays and Set 2 is Thursdays."

"Thank you. I can prepare this quote and have it sent over by tomorrow afternoon. What e-mail should I use?"

"Send it to me personally at `christie.smith@company.com`."

At this point a little friendly chitchat ensued and before you know it they were laughing and exchanging pleasantries.

"Thanks a lot. Hey, before we hang up can I ask you who you presently use? I like to do a comparative quote."

"Well, you know…" she hesitated, but then said, "Sure, we use Wasters Management."

"Thanks Christie, I will make sure you are happy with the quote. We will talk later."

Armed with this information, Tim went to the website for the present waste management company and copied the logo to a JPG file. He then visited an online shirt printer and in 72 hours had a shirt with the logo in his hands. Knowing that the garbage is picked up on Wednesday and Thursday he wanted to go Tuesday night.

He then placed another call to the security department:

"Hello, this is John from Wasters Management, your dumpster disposal people. I was called by Christie Smith's office stating that you have a damaged dumpster. I know the pickup is on Wednesday so I wanted to come out and check it tomorrow night. If there is a damaged unit I will have the truck bring out a new one. Is it okay if I come out Tuesday night?"

"Sure, let me check—yes, Joe is on tomorrow. When you pull up just stop in the security booth and he will give you a badge."

"Thanks."

The next day Tim wore his "company" polo shirt and had a clipboard. The pre-text was genius because he knew the dates and internal names. Now, looking like a company employee, he approached the security booth.

"Joe, I'm John from Wasters and I called in yesterday."

The guard interrupted with, "Yes, I see your name right here." He handed him a badge and a paper map telling him how to get to the dumpsters. "Do you need one of us to tag along?"

"Nah, I do this all the time."

Tim was buzzed in and drove over to the dumpsters.

Armed with a perfect pretext and a badge he had the time to do some digging. He knew that Set 2 holds the non-food garbage, so he started his digging there.

After just a little while he loaded a few hard drives, USB keys, some DVDs, and some clear bags full of paper in his trunk. After about an hour or so he drove back out, thanked the security guys, and assured them all is good. Back at the office he dug through the "garbage" and was greeted with some of the juiciest details he couldn't have found in his wildest dreams.

Many times companies will dispose of hard drives and USB media by destroying them completely. They will erase all data and then send them to special disposal units. Every now and then, though, employees who don't think through their disposal procedures will just throw away a USB key they say is broken or a hard drive that no longer boots. What they don't realize is that there are many programs that can strip data off of even non-bootable drives and media. Even if the media has been formatted, data can still be recovered in many situations.

One of the bags contained what looked like the contents of an office. As he emptied the bag he noticed some papers that had not passed through the shredder. He sat down to read them and saw one was a contract for some IT services that went out for bid. The job was supposed to start in just a few days, but it looked like this particular copy was used to sop up some spilled coffee and then discarded.

This would be a great find, but he had so much more to search through. The DVDs were blank or unreadable, but surprisingly enough he located files on the USB keys. From this information he discovered the names and private lines of the CFO as well as some other key personnel.

The value of what he gathered was immense but I want to focus on what he did next. The next morning, armed with the contract for the IT services in hand and knowing the type of work that was to be performed, he placed a call to the contract point of contact during the lunch hour and prayed the contact was out to lunch.

"Hello, is Sebastian available?"

"No, he is out to lunch. Can I help you?"

"This is Paul from XYZ Tech. I wanted to confirm that our team will be coming to start the project tomorrow evening."

"Yes, just remember we can't have any interruption of service so please do not get here any earlier than 5:30 p.m."

"Yes sir, you got it. See you tomorrow."

The next day Tim knew that he couldn't arrive with the rest of the "team." But if he timed it right he would not be caught by the IT company or the target. Sitting across the dark parking lot he watched the IT contract company arrive. After a good 30 minutes he approached the front door and explained how he just ran out to get some paperwork from his car. He got buzzed in and now had free reign of the office.

He needed to do some reconnaissance, and he figured the best way was to approach the IT company as one of the internal employees. He walked around until he heard some talking and found one of the guys in a shirt identifying him as one of the IT team.

Armed with the names of the upper-level management from the USB key files and from the point of contacts from the contract, he began, "Hi there, I'm Paul and I work Mr. Shivaz [the CFO]—did someone explain to you about the prod23 production server ?" Tim had the server name from his information gathering; Tim knew that was the server he was attacking.

"Yes, we know that server is off-limits in this work. The CFO explained to us the encryption and how we are not to mess with that server. No worries."

After a few more minutes of conversing, Tim had discovered some valuable pieces of information:

>> The IT team is not to touch the server.

>> The server has full disk encryption.

>> The techs were "bragged" to by the in-house IT guy about how the target company use a keyfile on a USB key that only the admins carry.

Tim knew this last point would make his task harder, and because the admins were not in, he would not be able to access the server now. In addition, the physical security around this server was very intense and may have been too hardened to take the risk. He did know that the admins would have access to this server so he thought maybe he would try that avenue.

He visited the first office of the admin, but it was locked. He checked the second office, then the third. The third one was shut but had not been closed all the way and it merely opened when he pushed a little. He was in.

By shutting the blinds and leaving the lights off, he felt he would be protected a bit from the potential of being caught. In his social engineer kit he carried a wide variety of tools and clothing. One of the tools he always had with him on these types of gigs was a USB key that was loaded with a bootable Linux distribution such as BackTrack. In the BackTrack install is a preloaded version of Virtual Box, a free open source virtual machine tool.

He loaded the admin's computer, using a rear USB port, into BackTrack. After he was in BackTrack, he connected to his own servers via SSH, set up a listener, then connected back to it using a reverse shell he initiated from the admin machine. Then he started a keysniffer (to log all keystrokes typed on the computer) in BackTrack and set up the log file to be dumped through the SSH connection to his computer.

Then he did something truly pernicious. He opened Virtual Box and created a Windows virtual machine (VM), using the local hard drive as the physical media to boot from, and loaded the VM. Automatically, it loaded the admin's user profile and OS. At the login screen he loaded the VM to be in full screen mode, hid all bars, and made the existing hot key to exit VirtualBox some ridiculously long combo. This protects the user from mistakenly hitting that combo and revealing they are hacked.

A risk still existed that he could be caught at any moment using this method of a rear USB key loading a virtual machine using their own hard drive, but if it worked he would get every keystroke the admin typed and a shell on the poor guy's computer, giving Tim access to everything. Even though the shell would be on the virtual machine, he would be logging all his keystrokes and then gain access to the victim's machine using his captured username and password.

Tim did a few other things in the office such as set up a connection on another machine, which gave him network access remotely. He also set up a remote listening device, the kind that uses a cell phone SIM card. He could call its number from any phone on earth and listen to conversations from anywhere in a 20-foot radius.

After just a few hours Tim left the target's company and went back to his office. He was excited to see whether this all worked, but he still had a few more ideas to try.

Early the next morning he made sure his remote connections were still alive and he dialed into his listener to hear the early morning buzz of people coming into the office. The anticipation built as he waited to see whether first computer logs were coming through, capturing the admin's username and password.

About one hour later Tim saw some logs coming through. He knew that he didn't want to do anything that would compromise his connection, so he waited. Around 12:15 the logs stopped, so he figured the admin must be at lunch. He quickly checked his reverse shell and began to create a tunnel from the admin's machine to the server back to his machine using the password he captured from the admin for the server

After the tunnel was connected he made a mad dash to copy as much as he could before 1:00 p.m. At that time he didn't notice any logs, so he called into the listener and overheard someone asking, "Do you know how long this meeting is supposed to last?"

Figuring the admin might be at a meeting he made another attempt at a larger transfer. After about 30 minutes he noticed some activity so he stopped data collection and decided to wait until later. He didn't want to alert the admin to anything fishy going on by slowing down his connection through a large transfer. He started to sift through what he grabbed from the server, knowing he hit the jackpot.

His job wasn't over yet. That evening he did one more massive transfer, taking as much as he could get and then headed over to the company's office again, social engineering his way in as he did before. Once in he headed over to the admin's office, which was locked this time and pulled shut: he used a shove knife (see Chapter 7) to get in:

Once inside he turned off the virtual machine, then rebooted the machine after removing the USB key, and then he left the admin's office the way he found it. He collected his listener and made sure his tracks were covered.

He exited the building to go back to his office and compile his findings. Of course, at the report meeting he walked in with a stack of printed documents and a hard drive full of what he was able to copy. This was enough to drop the jaws of every person in the room.

Applying the SE Framework to Top Secret 1

This story offers many lessons. It is an example of a perfect social engineer. It can be summed up as practice, preparation, and, of course, information gathering. All the skills he used we can imagine he practiced, from using a shove knife and creating tunnels to effective pretexting and information gathering.

I cannot reiterate enough the importance of information gathering. I know I have said it a thousand times, but this whole deal would have fallen through without Tim having the appropriate information.

Being prepared through phone calls and onsite visits, and having the right hardware, led to success. Analyzing this hack, you can see some of the fundamental principles of social engineering at play.

Tim was a master at information gathering, using web resources to pull up all sorts of nuggets, expert elicitation skills while on the phone, as well as masterful persuasion skills in person. These techniques allowed him to gather data that probably would have been left behind by an unskilled hacker.

Information gathering gave Tim the foundation for what types of pretexts and questions to develop.

The dumpster dive was planned with surgical precision. Does a chance exist that he would have been let in without the shirt and appointment? Sure. Yet how much more powerful was the way he did it? He never left a doubt in their minds and he enabled each person he interacted with to go about their business and never think twice. That is a perfect pretext, when a person can interact with you without any red flags or warning signs going up. Tim did that and it gave him freedom to move around as if he belonged.

The best part of the story is what happened after he got in the building. Such a large margin for error existed, and he could have been caught so many ways. Sure he could have run in, grabbed the data off the server, and left, and probably no one would have stopped him, but doing it the way he did meant the company never knew how their secrets got out and would never have known they were compromised.

Tim took a huge risk when he left the admin's computer running a VM. That particular maneuver could have failed in many ways. If someone had ever rebooted the computer or it had crashed, or if by mistake the admin pressed that crazy key combo, it could have spelled the end to the hack and alerted the company that it had been compromised.

I might have taken a different, less-risky route, one where I could have created a reverse tunnel from his computer back to my servers using a custom EXE that would not be detected by antivirus software and in the startup scripts of the computer, something with less chance of failure, but Tim's method had the flair of being a very sexy social engineering hack.

Probably more than one lesson can be learned from this particular hack, but if anything, the old hacker adage of "trust no one" can be applied to some extent. If someone calls to say that Christine authorized a dumpster inspection and you didn't hear it from her or a memo, call her and ask. Turn your computers off at night and definitely make your important machines not able to boot from USB without a password.

Sure, these extra precautions will mean more work and longer load times. Whether they're worth doing depends on how important the data that sits behind those machines is. In this case, the data was able to ruin this company, so the protection should have been extreme. Although the company took many excellent precautions, like using full disk encryption, cameras, biometric locks, and so on around the server area, it did not secure the computers that had access to the most important data, and that is what led to the company's demise.

Top-Secret Case Study 2: Social Engineering a Hacker

Thinking outside the box and having to think fast is standard fare for a social engineer, so it is rare to be in a situation that will challenge the professional social engineer to the point of being stumped. What happens when a penetration tester is called on to put on a social engineering hat without prior warning?

This next account shows exactly what happens when this situation arises. It is a good example of how having certain social engineering skills practiced beforehand can be very useful when called on to use them without warning.

The Target

"John" was called on for a standard network penetration test for one of his bigger clients. It was a no-thrills pentest as social engineering and onsite work were not included in the audit outline. Still, he enjoyed the work of testing out the vulnerabilities on his clients' networks.

In this particular pentest nothing really exciting was occurring. He was doing his normal routines of scans and logging data and testing out certain ports and services he felt might give him a lead inside.

Near the end of a day he ran a scan using Metasploit that revealed an open VNC server, a server that allows the control of other machines in the network. This is a nice find, because overall the network was locked down so this sort of easy-in is especially welcome.

John was documenting the find with the VNC session open, when suddenly in the background the mouse started moving across the screen. This was a huge red flag, because with this client at this time of the day, no user would be connected and using the system for a legitimate purpose.

What could be happening? He noticed that instead of acting like an admin or normal user, this person appeared to be not very knowledgeable about the system. He suspected there was an unwanted intruder in the network. He didn't want to scare the intruder away but he wanted to know whether he was an admin or another hacker who found his way into the very same system.

Quickly the target went from being the company he was hired to pentest to a rogue hacker inside the organization.

The Story

John decided quickly that he would have to social engineer this hacker and get as much information as possible to help safeguard his client. He didn't really have time to think through every step and plan out properly. He didn't have time to do the appropriate information gathering.

He takes a big risk and opens Notepad. Quickly he develops the pretext that he is a "n00b" hacker, a newbie, someone unskilled, and he found this box open and is hacking it, like this guy. He was able to obtain some screenshots of the conversation. Take a look and notice how the pentester had to social engineer the hacker, as shown in Figure 8-1. John starts the conversation and every other line is the hacker.

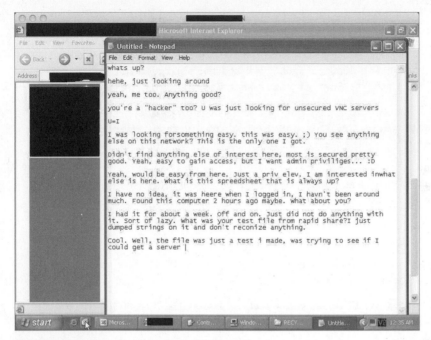

Figure 8-1 An actual screen shot of the event.

Following is the verbatim transcript of the conversation that took place. It is long, and all typos and jargon appear in the original, but the transcript shows exactly what transpired in this hack. John speaks first.

» whats up?

» hehe, just looking around

» yeah, me too. Anything good?

» you're a "hacker" too? U was just looking for unsecured VNC servers

» U=I

» I was looking forsomething easy. this was easy. ;) You see anything else on this network? This is the only one I got.

» Didn't find anything else of interest here, most is secured pretty good. Yeah, easy to gain access, but I want admin priviliges... :D

» Yeah, would be easy from here. Just a priv elev. I am interested inwhat else is here. What is this spreedsheet that is always up?

» I have no idea, it was heere when I logged in, I havn't been around much. Found this computer 2 hours ago maybe. What about you?

» I had it for about a week. Off and on. Just did not do anything with it. Sort of lazy. What was your test file from rapid share?I just dumped strings on it and don't reconize anything.

» Cool. Well, the file was just a test i made, was trying to see if I could get a server (trojan) running. But the firewall didn't allow it.

» lol. I had the same problem. I did metasplit shell and no-go. Thats why I kept using this. You in the us? or out of country? I know some people in denmark.

» I'm from Norway actually, hehe, I have relatives in Denmark.

» You hang in any boards? like I used to like some but they have been going away

» I mostly hang in some programming boards, but not much else. Have you been into hacking for a long time or what? What's your age btw? I'm 22.

» I have been on this for like fun for around a year or so. Still in school. 16. Just something to do. You ever go to evilzone?

» Haven't been there. I too mostly do this for fun, just trying to see what I can do, test my skills. I wrote the "VNC finder" myself btw, I have found a lot of servers, but this is the only one where I could actually have some fun

» Wow. What did you write it in? Can I dl it? Do you have a handle?

» It's written in a language called PureBasic, but it's kinda not ready for release yet, it's only for my own use. But maybe I can share it anyway, I could upload the code somewhere and let you compile it. That is if you can find some PureBasic compiler on some warez site :P

» Thats cool. you can put it in that pastebin site from irc. That lets you anon post I have not done purebasic before. just python and perl

» Let me see, I'll look for that pastebin site and upload it, just give me some minutes, I'll be around.

» Ok cool! do you have a handle?I I go by jack_rooby

»   Handle, for what? I don't chat on irc much or anything like that, but I could give you an email you could reah me on.

»   Thats cool. I mean handle like for irc and boardz and the such. heay e-mail works too.

»   Yeah, at the programming board I share my full name, etc. Maybe not too smart to share just yet. My email is: intruder@hotmail.com

»   Send me a message or whatever and I can add you on msn maybe.

»   I will send you a note. It is good to have someone that can program to know for this sort of stuff for when I get stuck or find something good

»   Hehe, yeah, we could be a team :P

»   Cool! let me know when you did the pastebin

»   http://pastebin.ca/1273205

»   btw... that is kinda very in the "alpha" stage, the GUI is not really finished. but it can be configured through some viariables.

»   Cool. I will test it and see what I can do with it. Thanks for sharing. if I do something cool, should I e-mail you?

»   Yeah, please do. If you run this program for some hours you'll find a lot servers, I even tried to make some code to detect servers that has no security and even some that has a bug which can let you log in even if it has a password. These servers will show up in the result (the "found tab") as "insecure". But sometimes it does a mistake and says some are insecure which are not, but that's not many, it's just to test them.

»   Wow. I saw some other vnc servers here too, but they all wanted passwords. Does your tool let us in to that?

»   Just a very few has the bug which can let you in, but you must use the special client for them, more info here btw:

»   http://intruderurl.co.uk/video/

»   Download the zip file.

»   Olol, k, soI wrry

»   sorry. Ok, I will dl that and have a look. Thats cool. Did you write the backdoor from rapid share too? or did you get that from someplace?

»   I try to write most of my tools myself, this way I learn. So yes, I wrote it myself, but it was not finished, I was just wanna see if I could run a server, but it didn't doo anything yet, hehe.

»   I see. I sort of gave up, but I thought I would come back and try some more.I figure there has to be some stuff around but I don't have a botnet of myown to use, this guy named Zoot54 tried to sell me one, and some people vouched for him, but I did not trust him at all. And I don't know how to write my own tools at all other then some perl and python which wont work for most windows hosts like this so I have been tryingthe metasploit but getting the firewall error. Do you have plans for this? Like something cool to do? or just moveon to the next?

»   Perl and python is a good start btw, I haven't been using them myself, but when you know some languages you can easily learn more :P Maybe you should give PureBasic a try, it's really easy actually. Hehe, a bot-net would be cool, I was thinking about making one, but it's kinda hard to make it spread, at least on Vista. But nah, I can't give up this server just yet, I have to try some more, there has to be a way to get more priviliges ;D

»   thast cool. You can have the server as I have had it for a while and don't know what to do next. let me know what you are doing if you would so I can learn some more though. That would be cool. Do you have a myspace or facebook or anything? Or just use the e-mail?

»   E-mail works for now, when I trust you more maybe I can add you on facebook, I don't have myspace. Yeah, I'll keep you updated :)

»   Cool that works for me. Do you have a shell or do you have this same gui? Is it just a multi connection vnc?

»   Yeah, I just used ThightVNC or whatever and made it not disconnect other users. I'm not a shell fan really, hehe :S

»   Cool. When I get a shell a lot of times I makes mistake tand dissconnect on accident

»   Good you didn't dissconnect me :D Btw, when I first saw you messing around I was like "damn, the administrator is here", hehehe...

»   Hah, no I looked up the time zone and they are in the middle of the US so it is the middle of the night for them.

»   Yeah, I did the same thing. Even did a speed test of the internet connection, hehe.They seem to have faster upload speed than download speed, weird... But handy for a DoD attack maybe.

» DoS, i mean.

» weird I woner what type of line it is its says it it from co. which I thought was a funny name.. Did you ever get any other systems here? I wonce saw a warez server but that was a long time ago and it is gone now.

» Haven't found any other systems. But I would sure like to access all these network computers they have... damn many, it's some kind of university. Hehe, I printed out "hello world" previous today.

» Haha did you send it to a printer or to the screen? these people would more then likkely freak out if they saw the mouse start mooving on them in the middle of the day whith tht weird spreadsheet

» Haha, they probably woold, but what silly idiots runds a VNC server without a password?! I printed to some of the printers, I hope somebody saw it.

» Haha thats is true, i bet som.. well they cant run it with out admin privs right? So it cant be just some user that did it, someone with admin would have to do it or else our backdoors should work on it and they are not going at all. Or do you think some one just changed the config?

» Hmm, well, i think you're right, maybe some admin or prankster..

» Do you do this work for a living? I keep hearing you can make money with it, and I think if I do this for a while and get to be good I might be able to get a job with it. Is that what you did?

» I have earned money on programming, but never on hacking or security stuff. But that's a good idea, people would pay to get their security tested and if we get good enough we could probably earn a lot this way.

» Thats what I hope. I bought a book on the ethical hacker and think that they have some good programs in there. I don't know what the age is to take the test, but if I do take it that might be a good start to do this work. And there are some good tools in there like the metasploit. You should take a look at it if you have not yet.

» Yeah, thanks, I should check that out :) But I'm getting a little tired now btw, hehe. Can't sit here chatting in bloody notepad all day, hehehehe. So cya later man, cool meeting you, very fun.

» Yeah I was scared when I saw the rapid share up on the screen. Cool to meet you and I will e-maiul you and let you know how the program works. Tht is exciting to try that out and see what happens. You stay safe and don't like the bad guys find you!

» Hehe, thanks, the same for you btw! :) This was interesting, I think I'll save this notepad log btw, give me a sec,lol...

» there, lol, sorry

» goodbye

» bye

This chat reveals how quickly John had to pretext and become someone else. This is not an easy task, as usually it takes a lot planning, but to secure his client and find out who this intruder was he had to play whatever role the "hacker" was going to put him in.

In the end, John ended up getting his picture, e-mail, and contact info. He reported this malicious hacker to his client and the problem was fixed to not allow such free reign in and out of its systems.

This top-secret case shows just how social engineering used in a professional sense can go a long way toward securing the clients.

Applying the SE Framework to the Top Secret Case Study 2

What I find interesting in this account is how the company wasn't really a target for the hacker. He was merely scanning the Internet for "low-hanging fruit" and that is exactly what he found. Open machines with full access are dangerous and this account shows just how much damage could have occurred if the pen tester was not sitting there just at the right time.

There is, of course, a lot one can learn about social engineering from this story, too. John did not come into this project with the idea of using his social engineering skills. Instead it was a straight out pentest. Sometimes you are called on to use your skills without being able to plan first.

What might have enabled John to be able to do this without having to go home and have a practice session? Most likely these skills were something that John used daily or that he at least practiced often enough to make him agile in his use of them.

The main lesson in this case study is probably practice makes perfect. Realistically, John could have confronted the hacker, told him he was an admin and that he was being logged, and that his life was over. All sorts of threats could have flown back and forth and he could have tried to use fear as his main tactic.

Most likely, the hacker would have fled the scene only to return later and try to format the system or do even more damage to cover his tracks. Instead, thinking very fast, John was able to farm a lot of usable information on his target. John later used the target's e-mail address and name and a good copy of Maltego to get a very clear picture of this individual's activities.

Another minor lesson one can learn from analyzing this story is how to be fluid. What I mean by that is learning to go with the flow. When John started "gathering information" from the hacker he really didn't know whether this person was a hacker or an admin. John's first line, "Hey what's up," could have been answered by the attacker in many ways. Without knowing exactly the response he would get, John had no time to really prepare. He had to try to use lingo and react the way he imagined a hacker would.

John took it even a step farther. Realizing that the best avenue was a submissive one, John put on the pretext of a "n00b," or new hacker who didn't know much and wanted a wonderful and intelligent real hacker to educate him. Feeding into the hacker's ego, John got him to spill his guts about all sorts of things, including all his contact information and even a picture.

Why Case Studies Are Important

These case studies are just a few of the stories that are out there, and these are by far not the scariest. Every day governments, nuclear power plants, multibillion-dollar corporations, utility grids, and even whole countries fall victim to malicious social engineering attacks, and that doesn't even include the personal stories of scams, identity theft, and robbery that are occurring by the minute.

As sad as reading all these stories is, one of the best ways to learn is by reviewing case studies. Experts from all fields utilize this methodology. Psychologists and doctors review countless hours of tapes and interviews to study the microexpressions people use when feeling certain emotions.

Persuasion experts review, analyze, and study accounts of positive and negative persuasion. Doing so helps them to pick up on the subtle areas that affect people and see how they can be used to learn and to protect their clients.

Law enforcement reviews case studies as part of their everyday lives to learn what makes a criminal tick. Along those lines, criminal investigators analyze and dissect every aspect of a malicious person, including what he eats, how he interacts with others, what he thinks about, and what makes him react. All of this information helps them to truly understand the mind of the criminal.

These same methods are how professional profilers target and catch the "bad guys." In the same fashion, professional social engineers learn a lot by studying not only their own case studies but also cases in their own practice and malicious accounts they can find in the news. By reviewing case studies a social engineer can truly start to see the weakness of the human psyche and why the tactics in the social engineering framework work so easily. That is why I have been working hard to make sure the framework on `www.social-engineer.org` will include updated web stories and case studies that you can use to enhance your skills.

In the end, all of these exploits worked because people are designed to be trusting, to have levels of compassion, empathy, and a desire to help others. These are qualities that we should not lose as we have to interact with our fellow humans every day. Yet at the same time, these qualities are the very things that are more often than not exploited by malicious social engineers. It may seem that I am promoting each of us to become a hardened, emotionless creature that walks around like a robot. Although that would definitely keep you protected from most social engineering attempts, it would make life dull. What I am promoting is being aware, educated, and prepared.

Summary

Security through education is the mantra of this book. Only when you are aware of the dangers that exist, only when you know how the "criminal" thinks, and only when you are ready to look that evil in the eye and embrace it can you truly protect yourself. To that end, the final chapter of this book discusses how to prevent and mitigate social engineering attacks.

9 Prevention and Mitigation

The preceding chapters show you all the methods and ways that social engineers trick and scam targets into divulging valuable information. They also describe many of the psychological principles that social engineers use to influence and manipulate people.

Sometimes after I give a speech or security training, people will look very paranoid and scared and say something like, "It just seems there is no hope to even attempt security. How do I do it?"

That is a good question. I promote having a good disaster-recovery plan and incident response plan because nowadays it seems that it is not a matter of "if" you will get hacked, but "when." You can take precautions to give you at least a fighting chance at security.

Social engineering mitigation is not as easy as ensuring hardware security. With traditional defensive security you can throw money into intrusion detection systems, firewalls, antivirus programs, and other solutions to maintain perimeter security. With social engineering no software systems exist that you can attach to your employees or yourself to remain secure.

In this chapter I present the top six steps I tell my clients they can take to prevent and mitigate social engineering attempts:

>> Learning to identify social engineering attacks

>> Creating a personal security awareness program

>> Creating awareness of the value of the information that is being sought by social engineers

>> Keeping software updated

>> Developing scripts

>> Learning from social engineering audits

These six points all boil down to creating a security awareness culture. Security awareness is not about a 40-, 60-, or 90-minute program once every year. It is about creating a culture or a set of standards that each person is committed to utilizing in his or her entire life. It is not just about work or websites deemed to be "important," but it is the way one approaches being secure as a whole.

This chapter covers the aforementioned six points and how creating a security awareness culture can be the best defense against a malicious social engineer.

Learning to Identify Social Engineering Attacks

The first stage in social engineering prevention and mitigation is to learn about the attacks. You don't have to dive so deep into these attacks that you know how to recreate malicious PDFs or create the perfect con. But understanding what happens when you click a malicious PDF and what signs to look for to determine whether someone is trying to trick you can help protect you. You need to understand the threats and how they apply to you.

Here's an illustration: You value your home and the things in it, but especially the people in your home. You do not wait to have your first fire to figure out how to plan, prevent, and mitigate its danger. Instead you install smoke detectors and plan out an escape route in case of a fire. In addition, you might train your children with the phrase to, "Stop, drop, and roll" if they are on fire. You teach them how to feel the door for heat and to stay low to avoid smoke inhalation. All of these methods are ways to prevent or prepare for a fire before you have a real fire and have to deal with the devastation it brings.

The same principle applies to protecting yourself and your company from social engineering attacks. Do not wait for the attack to occur to learn about how devastating they can be. Don't think I'm self-serving, but I promote social engineering audits to regularly test your employees' ability to withstand these attacks, and following up with training.

Teach yourself and your employees how to "stop, drop, and roll," so to speak, when it comes to these types of attacks. What are the latest news stories on how social engineers are attacking companies? Knowing them can be a first line of defense, the same as knowing what a fire can do to your home. Learn the different methods that modern social engineers and identity thieves use. You can find an archive of news stories and examples of social engineers, con men, identity thieves, and the like at www.social-engineer.org/framework/Social_Engineering_In_The_News.

Another good step is reading this book. It is full of all the methods and principles that social engineers use to manipulate their targets. This book is more than just a compilation of stories and wonderful hacks; it offers an analysis of the thinking and tactics used by the malicious social engineer.

Also check out the videos on the www.social-engineer.org site, in the Resources area, which demonstrate exploits in action. The average user does not need to watch them with the intent of understanding how to perform these attacks himself, but to understand how an SE performs the attack.

Basically, the more you know about how these attacks occur, the easier you can identify them in the "wild." Being aware of the body language, expressions, and phrases used in an SE attempt will make your ears perk up when you hear or see someone utilizing these methods.

You don't need to spend tons of time learning about SE methods. However, spending a few minutes now and then reading the news and reading stories on www.social-engineer.org or other sites can help you see the methods being used now against companies.

After you have a good basis of knowledge and an audit under your belt, the next step, creating a security-minded culture, will seem simple to develop.

Creating a Personal Security Awareness Culture

In July of 2010 I was part of a small team of security professionals that held one of the first organized and professional-level social engineering contests at Defcon 18. Some of the best and brightest minds from around the globe come to Las Vegas, Nevada, once a year to speak, teach, and learn.

My team and I decided it would be a great opportunity to hold a contest that would showcase whether corporate America is vulnerable to this attack vector (responding to a "contest"). We organized the contest by having interested people sign up to take part in two stages of social engineering : information gathering and active attacks.

To keep the contest legal and moral we did not want any person victimized, and no Social Security numbers, credit cards, and no personal identifying information would be gathered. Our goal was not to get any of these people fired. In addition our goal was not to embarrass any particular company, so we decided also no passwords or other personal security–related information from the companies. Instead we developed a list of about 25–30 "flags" that ranged from whether the company had an internal cafeteria, to who handles its trash disposal, to what browser it uses, and to what software it uses to open PDFs. Finally, we chose target companies from all sectors of business in corporate America: gas companies, tech companies, manufacturers, retail, and everything in between.

Each contestant was assigned one target company in secret, on which he had two weeks to do passive information gathering. That meant contestants were not allowed to contact the company, send it emails, or in any way try to social engineer information out of it. Instead they had to use the web, Maltego, and other tools to gather as much information as possible and enter all they found into a professional-looking report.

From the information gathered we wanted contestants to develop a couple of plausible attack vectors that they thought would work in the real world. Then contestants had to come to Defcon in Las Vegas, sit in a soundproof booth, and make a 25-minute phone call to their target to implement their attack vector and see what information they could obtain.

I could spend the next 20–30 pages telling you what happened at that contest and what the outcome was, but one thing we found was this: Every contestant obtained enough information out of the targets that the company would have failed a security audit. Regardless of the experience level of the contestant and the pretext, the contestants were successful in accomplishing their goals. For a full report about the CTF and what occurred, visit www.social-engineer.org/resources/sectf/ Social-Engineer_CTF_Report.pdf.

Now on to what applies here—security awareness. Corporations that care about security have programs where they train their employees how to be aware of potential security risks via phone, Internet, or in person. What we found was that security awareness in those companies was at failure stage. Why? How could it be that these Fortune 500 companies that spend millions or more on security, training, education, and services designed to protect their employees could be failing at security awareness?

That is my point in the title to this section—security awareness is not personal to employees. Often in my professional practice when I talk with employees about their feelings about an attack they respond with something like, "It is not my data; what do I care?" This attitude shows that the security awareness that these companies were trying to instill never hit home; it was not important, effective, and most importantly, not personal.

In reviewing much of the material and methods available for so-called security awareness, what I have found is that it is boring, silly, and not geared to make the participant interact or think. Short DVD presentations that cover a ton of things in a shotgun approach that blasts the participant with a lot of tiny little facts are not designed to sink in too deep.

What I challenge you to do as a company or even as an individual is to create a program that engages, interacts, and dives deep into security awareness. Instead of just telling your employees why having long and complex passwords is a good idea, show them how quickly one can crack an easy password. When I am asked to help perform security awareness training for a client, sometimes I ask an employee to come up to my computer and type in a password that she feels is secure. I do this before I release any information about passwords. Then as I start my presentation on that section I start a cracker against that password. Usually within a minute or two the password is cracked and I reveal to the room the password that was secretly typed into my computer. The immediate and drastic effect it has on each person has an extreme impact. But after numerous demonstrations like that employees will comment on how they now understand how serious having a good password is.

When I discuss the topic of malicious attachments in email, I do not have to show employees how to craft a malicious PDF but I do show them what it looks like from both the victim's and the attacker's computers when a malicious PDF is opened. This helps them understand that a simple crash can lead to devastation.

Of course, this teaching method produces a lot of fear, and although that is not the goal, it is not a terrible side product, because employees will remember it better. But the goal is to make them think not just about what they do not only at work and with their office computers, but also their own bank accounts, home computers, and how they treat security on a personal level.

I want each person who hears a security presentation or reads this book to review how he interacts with the Internet as a whole and make serious changes to reusing passwords, storing passwords or personal information in non-secure locations, and to where they connect to the Internet. I cannot tell you how many times I have seen a person sitting in the center of Starbucks on her free Wi-Fi checking a bank account or making an online purchase. As much as I want to go up and yell at that person and tell her how quickly her whole life can be turned upside down if the wrong person is sitting on that same network with her, I don't.

I want people who read this to also think of how they give out information over the phone. Con men and scam artists use many avenues to steal from the elderly, those having hard economic times, and everyone else. The phone still remains a very powerful way to do this. Being aware of the vendors', banks', or suppliers' policies on what they will and will not ask for over the phone can help you avoid many of the pitfalls. For example, many banks list in their policies that they will never call and ask from a Social Security number or bank account number. Knowing this can safeguard you for falling for a scam that can empty your life savings.

Calling security awareness a "program" indicates that it is something ongoing. A program means you schedule time to continually educate yourself. After you obtain all this useful information, then you can use it to develop a program that will help you to stay secure.

Being Aware of the Value of the Information You Are Being Asked For

Referring to the Defcon 18 social engineering contest again, in it we learned another valuable lesson—when the information is perceived as having no or little value, then little effort is placed on protecting it.

This is heavy-duty statement, but was proven true with how many targets willingly handed over information on their cafeterias, waste removal, and so much more. You must realize the value of the data that you have and be aware of a tactic a social engineer might use to reduce the value of this information in your eyes.

Before giving out information to someone, determine whether the person who is calling or interacting with you deserves it. Humans have this built-in desire to want to help and to be helpful to those whom we perceive need it. It is a major way a social engineer manipulates a target into handing over valuable information. Analyzing the person with whom you are interacting and determining whether she deserves the information she is asking for can save you the embarrassment and damage of falling victim.

For example, in the social engineering contest at Defcon one contestant had a pretext that he was a customer of a major antivirus company. He called in with a serious problem—his computer couldn't get online and he felt it was due to something the antivirus was doing and wanted the technical support representation to do one simple thing—browse to a website.

Malicious SEs often use this attack vector. By driving a victim to a website embedded with malicious code or malicious files they can gain access to a target's computer and network. In the case of the contest, the website was not malicious at all, but it was to show that if this were a malicious attack it would have been successful.

The first attempt was laid out like this by the contestant: "I cannot browse to my website and I think your product is blocking me. Can you check by going to this site so I know for sure whether it is your software or not?"

The technical support representative answered well by saying, "Sir, our product would not block you from going to that site; it wouldn't matter if I can go there or not." He declined the request.

The contestant did not give up there; after talking a bit more he again tried, "I know you said your product would not block the site, but it worked until I installed your software, so can you please check for me?"

Again he was declined his request: "Sir, I am sorry for that inconvenience but again our product would not block you and my going to the site will not help you fix the problem."

It seemed as if the request was going to be rejected for good when the contestant tried one last-ditch effort and said, "Sir, it would make me feel better if you would just try going to this site for me. Please, can you help me out?"

This simple request put our technical support rep over the edge and he opened his browser and went right to the site. He had the right idea, he even had the right security awareness answer, but in the end he wanted his "customer" to "feel better" and honored his request. This could have led that company to a major pitfall if it were a malicious attack.

The technical support representative knew that this information was not relevant to that particular call. Like him, you must be determined to analyze whether the information being asked for is deserved and relevant to the person with whom you are interacting. Approaching this scenario from the other angle, what if the contestant were a legitimate customer and the rep had declined to go to that website—what is the worst that could have happened?

The customer might have been a little upset at being declined the request he wanted but it still would not have changed the outcome. The product he had was not the cause of his woes.

A social engineer often uses charm to start a conversation about the weather, work, the product, anything at all, and uses it to reveal the information sought. This is where a good security awareness policy comes into play—educating your employees about what tactics might be used against them can save them from acting out of fear.

In one audit the pretext I used was being the assistant to the CFO. The call center employees had a fear of losing their jobs for rejecting the requests from such a high-level management. Why? They are not given the proper education to know that rejecting that request would not cost them their jobs. At the same time protocols should be in place for the employee to know when a request for information is proper.

The perceived value of the information being asked for closely ties in with an educated and aware person knowing that even minor tidbits of data can lead to a massive breach. Knowing that the person on the other end of the phone doesn't really need to know what the name of the food preparation company for the cafeteria can help an employee to answer appropriately. If you are an employer then help your employees develop answers to these requests. In most cases a simple, "Sorry, I don't have that information; please contact our purchasing department if you want that." Or "I'm sorry I am not allowed to divulge that information but you can send an email to info@company.com to request some of this info," can go a long way toward quashing many social engineering efforts.

I mentioned earlier that creating an atmosphere that makes information seem less valuable is also a tactic used by social engineers to get people to freely divulge this "unimportant" information.

Using the contest example again, one contestant was asked to provide some identifying information. His pretext was a company that was hired to do an internal audit and when the target wanted to verify who he was he asked for something off of the requisition form. Our contestant pretended to lean over to an imaginary co-worker and said, "Jane, the gentlemen from Your-Target-Company wants the ID number from the requisition, can you do me a favor and grab it from Bill's desk?"

As "Jane" went to get the form the contestant engaged the target in idle chitchat. "How's the weather in Texas?" and "Have you ever been to Charlie's Pub?" escalated into things like, "Who handles the food for the cafeteria?" and "Want to see a cool website we are working on here?"

All this happened while he was "waiting" for the ID number. Social engineers use this tactic every day. Diversion and charm are key tools in many pretexts. Information that is asked for during "chitchat" is perceived as having less value because of the time in the conversation it is asked for. If the SE had asked that same question when he was "verifying his audit findings" it would have been met with a different attitude, but because he asked it during a friendly conversation so much information was given freely.

Mitigation for this SE tactic is to ponder the value of the information that you are planning on releasing despite of when in the conversation it is asked for. In the earlier example, the target's simply waiting for that ID number before continuing any conversation would have been very appropriate and saved him from being duped.

This particular point is not always easy to implement because employees, especially those facing the customer, must be able to release some information without fear of attack. Simply being aware of the value of information cannot alone stop an attack.

Keeping Software Updated

In most businesses you must be able to release information to the public and to clients. Even in my business I must be able to give out my phone numbers, emails, and web addresses. I must be able to send and receive PDF files and I have to be able to freely talk on the phone with clients, suppliers, and vendors.

However, the points discussed so far indicate that releasing any of this information can be the end of one's business and possibly privacy. What can you do to have the freedom to release certain information and not fear the end?

Keep updated. In our contest, more than 60% of the companies that were called were still using Internet Explorer 6 and Adobe Acrobat 8. Those are staggering statistics.

Dozens if not hundreds of public vulnerabilities exist in those two applications alone. Knowing that a target uses those two applications opens them up for an enormous number of attacks that can be so malicious that all the IDs, firewalls, and antivirus systems cannot possibly stop them. But do you know what can stop them?

The answer is updates. The newest versions of software generally have patched their security holes, at least the majority of them. If a particular piece of software has a horrible track record, don't use it; switch to something less vulnerable.

The problem that comes up is that companies are very slow when it comes to upgrades. IE 6 is very old, almost to the end of its life on Microsoft Support. Adobe 8 has dozens of exploits publicly available. That is just two of the many pieces of information we found out in the contest. The reality of the matter, though, is that you have to be able to release information. You must be able to freely tell people what is going on. To do that with less worry, you must make sure you and your employee use updated software.

In the contest calls, if an employee divulged that the company used Firefox, Chrome, or another secure browser, or FoxIt or the most up-to-date Adobe software, contestants would have been shut down. I am not saying those pieces of software do not experience any problems at all. Exploits for certain versions certainly exist, but this software is significantly less vulnerable. The possession of that information is still valuable but if no exploits are available then the next phase of the attack cannot be launched.

Keeping software updated is the one tip that seems to get the most flack because it takes the most work and can cause the most overhead. Changing internal policies and methodologies that allow very old software to still be in play can be very difficult and cause all sorts of internal shifts.

However, if a company is committed to security and committed to creating a personal security awareness then committing to these changes will become part of the business culture.

Developing Scripts

One more beneficial thing bears mentioning: develop scripts. Don't cringe; I don't mean scripts in the sense that the employee must say X if a situation equals A plus B. I am talking about outlines that help an employee be prepared to use critical thinking when it counts the most. Consider these scenarios:

What is the proper response when someone who claims to work for the CEO calls and demands your password? What do you do when a guy who has no appointment but looks and acts the part of a vendor demands access to a part of the building or property?

Scripts can help an employee determine the proper response during these circumstances and help them feel at ease. For example, a script may look like this:

If someone calls and claims to be from the management office and demands compliance of either handing over information or internal data, follow these steps:

1. Ask for the person's employee ID number and name. Do not answer any questions until you have this information.

2. After getting the identifying information, ask for the project ID number related to the project he or she is managing that requires this information.

3. If the information in steps 1 and 2 is successfully obtained, comply. If it's not, ask the person to have his or her manager send an email to your manager requesting authorization and terminate the call.

A simple script like this can help employees know what to say and do in circumstances that can try their security consciousness.

Learning from Social Engineering Audits

If you have ever broken a limb you know that as you recover your doctor may send you for therapy. As therapists rehabilitate you, you may undergo some stress testing. This type of testing enables your doctors to see whether you have weaknesses that need to be strengthened. The same applies for your business, except instead of waiting for the "break" to occur before you "test," social engineering audits enable you to stress-test your company before a breach occurs.

The following sections answer a few key questions when it comes to social engineering audits and how to choose the best auditor. Before getting into the depth of social engineering audits, you should know what an audit really is.

Understanding What a Social Engineering Audit Is

In the most basic terms a social engineering audit is where a security professional is hired to test the people, policies, and physical perimeter of a company by simulating the same attacks that a malicious social engineer would use. The two main differences between a malicious social engineer and a professional auditor are:

» Usually, moral and legal guidelines exist that a professional auditor will follow.

» The goals of the professional auditor are always to help and not to embarrass, steal, or harm a client.

» Professional audits generally have scope limitations that are not imposed upon real attackers.

The professional auditor will spend a lot of time analyzing and gathering data on a "target" or client and will use that information to develop realistic attack vectors. While doing this the professional auditor always keeps in mind the goals that are set forth in writing for each audit. This is an essential piece of the puzzle, because going down a path that can have very bad repercussions on both the SE and the target might be tempting. Clearly defined goals can keep a social engineering auditor from making that mistake.

Setting Audit Goals

The professional social engineer must engage in moral and ethical behavior while still stretching across that line that allows him or her to put on the true "black hat" of a malicious social engineer. This means taking note of things that he or she can use to gain access and expose a hole or weakness in a company's defenses, no matter how low it may seem.

Finding the security gaps has to be balanced with a concern for the individual employees. Companies who are hacked with a social engineering audit often think that firing the employee(s) who fell for the attack fixes the problem and plugs the "hole." What the client fails to realize is that after an audit, those employees who did fall for the attacks are probably *the* most secure people in the building at that time.

The professional social engineer must take extra precaution to ensure that the employees are not put into the line of fire. Personally I make it a key point to tell clients that the audit is not about the employees and, as far as I can help it, I do not include names of the employees who were used. In cases where that cannot be helped and I need to include those names, I focus the report on the flaws the company has in its training, policies, and defenses that allowed the employee to falter.

Throwing an employee under the bus, so to speak, or ruining his or her character or life should never be an option for a routine social engineering audit. When outlining the goals of an audit with an auditor I outline the level of intensity from 0 to 10 for these key areas:

» To determine whether employees will click on links in emails or open files from people they do not know well, leading to compromise

» To determine whether an employee would go to a website and enter personal or business-related information on that site

» To determine how much information can be obtained via the phone or in-person visits of employees at work or personal places (that is, bars, gyms, daycares)

» To determine the level of security in the office perimeter by testing locks, cameras, motion sensors, and security guards

» To determine the ability of a social engineer to create a malicious USB or DVD that will entice the employee to use it on his or her work computer, compromising the business

Of course, more areas will be tested, but what I try to do is outline closely the goals the company has for this audit. What I find is that companies often do not know what they want. The auditor's job is to walk them through different avenues into the company and to determine which of those they want tested.

When these goals are clearly defined, you should also include a list of things that are never to be included in an audit.

What Should and Should Not Be Included in an Audit

Many different ways exist for testing the outlined goals to see clearly whether a security hole exists in a company. Using all the principles in this book can help outline a good plan for attack. However, avoid some things when planning an attack. Things like:

» Attacking a target's family or friends

» Planting evidence of crimes or infidelity to discredit a target

» Depending on the laws of the land, impersonating law enforcement can be illegal

» Breaking into a target's home or apartment

» Using evidence of a real affair or embarrassing circumstance to blackmail a target into compliance

Things like these should be avoided at all costs because they do not accomplish the goal and leave the target feeling violated. However, the question does come up about what to do if in an audit evidence appears of some of these things. Each auditor must personally decide how to handle these circumstances, but consider a couple of examples.

In one audit, an auditor found out an employee was using the company's high-speed Internet to download gigabytes worth of porn to external hard drives. Instead of risking the employee's getting fired he went to the employee and told him he knew, but he didn't want him to get fired and just gave him a warning to stop. The employee became embarrassed and upset and figured the auditor was going to still report him. He decided he wanted to preemptively combat this attack and he went to the owners and said the auditor was planting evidence of this offense on his computer.

Of course, the auditor had logs and screenshots of when the compromise occurred and the employee was fired anyway. But also the auditor was reprimanded for not coming forward when he found an offense of which the company had a strict policy.

In another account, the auditor found evidence of a man downloading child pornography to his computer and then distributing it to others on the Internet. The auditor knew from the other images on his computer that he had a wife and children and that reporting this would lead to divorce, probably jail time, and the ruination of his career as well as the family's life.

The law of the land was that child pornography was illegal, as well as morally disgusting and vile. The auditor turned the man in to the company as well as the authorities, which cost that man his career, family, and freedom.

Having a clearly defined "do not" list enhances your audits and keeps you from crossing your own moral and legal guidelines. In one interview I had with Joe

Navarro, one of the world's leaders on nonverbal communication, he made a statement about this point. He said that unless you are a law enforcement agent you have to decide what lines you will and will not cross *before* you enter into an engagement. With that in mind then what things should an auditor include in audits?

» **Phishing Attacks:** Targeted email attacks that allow a company to see whether its employees are susceptible to attacks through email.

» **Pretexting In-Person Attacks:** Very precise and controlled pretexts are chosen and then performed over the phone or in-person to determine whether employees will fall for them.

» **Baiting:** An in-person attack where access is gained to the target's building or other property by some method, and USBs or DVDs are dropped that contain malicious files on them embedded with malicious code.

» **Tailgating (or piggybacking):** An in-person attack where the auditor attempts to approach a group of employees to gain access to the building by just following them in.

» **Physical Security (Red Team):** An attempt to gain physical access to an office and take items of value to the company.

This short list can help a professional auditor set some guidelines to define what should and should not be included. Still, one of the largest problems many companies have is trying to pick out a good auditor, one who can accomplish these tasks at hand.

Choosing the Best Auditor

If you broke a limb and the damage was bad, and a doctor told you that you have a chance for only 50% recovery, but that going to see a good surgeon could increase those odds, wouldn't you search high and low for a good surgeon to fix your problems? And when you found him, what questions would you ask? Wouldn't you want to see his past work? You would want some proof of his ability to grasp the concepts and perform the tasks that would increase your chances of recovery.

You follow a similar process to find the right auditor. Here are some of the basics that you might want to find out as you speak to an auditor:

» **Knowledge:** Has the team released any research, papers, speeches, or other materials that display they are knowledgeable about social engineering? Are they known in the community for being leaders in this field? You do not want to trust your audit and security to a team that is using outdated methods and is not up on the most recent tactics being used.

Determining the amount of knowledge an auditor and team has is hard to do without a little research. Asking auditors about any papers, articles, or information they have written on the topics is not a bad idea. Make sure the team you hire is at the top of its game.

» **Experience:** Clients often do not want to be identified or named. In my case, many clients do not want to be put on a website or marketing material because they feel this will embarrass them or make them vulnerable. But you can determine the experience of the auditor in other ways. Ask him about the methods he has used and how he implemented solutions in the past.

An auditor often does not want to let all the secrets out of the bag in an initial meeting, but ask him for one or two accounts of attacks he launched, which will help you determine his level of skill.

» **Contract:** Having the audit completely outlined, documented, and limitations set can go a long way toward a successful audit. Personally, I do not like to work with a ton of limitations because most malicious social engineers do not have any at all. But at least a small subset of rules written out on what is and is not allowed should be agreed upon.

A social engineer wants permission to record phone calls; video-record the building and interactions; and especially if an audit includes physical security, to have written permission to remove items from the premises. An auditor doesn't want to finish the audit just to be presented with a warrant or a lawsuit.

Also designate an emergency contact person who knows about the audit and can vouch for the auditor and team. If an auditor finds himself in a legal jam he'll want a number to call. No one wants to be performing a late-night dumpster dive to be met by the police and have to sit the night in jail. Having a contact person provides a "get out of jail free" card and can save a lot of hassle in the long run.

» **Rapport:** Apply the principles in this book to find a good auditor. When you speak with him on the phone or in person how does he make you feel? What do you see? Do you get the sense he is very professional and his goal is to really help you?

Does the team portray itself and its business as one you want to be associated with? If you are the project manager who is hiring an auditor, a load of responsibility rests with you. The auditor may not want to meet with a team. The fewer people who know what the SE team looks like, the better for physical security audits. The team, as a result, may only want to meet with one or two people. This means you must ensure the auditor is high quality and can do the work needed.

» **Time:** One of the biggest mistakes companies make when seeking auditors to help them is not giving them enough time to perform the job. They figure that a few phone calls or one site visit can all be accomplished in one day. Although that may be true, what about information gathering, planning, and scoping out the targets? These things take time. Time is important but it is also a double-edged sword—allow enough time for the auditor to do a good job, but not so much time that it becomes a cost problem. Manage, but do not micro-manage.

These are just a few of the areas to consider when choosing the right auditor for your company. In the end you must feel comfortable and good that the social engineering team will have your best interests at heart, will do their best to remain professional, and stay within the guidelines.

Concluding Remarks

> *Knowledge is of no value unless you put it into practice.*
> —ANTON CHEKHOV

The information that I provide in this book is not light-hearted. Much of the information shows serious vulnerabilities in the way people think and act. When I teach security classes with my mentor, Mati, he talks about a payload encoder called "shikata ga nai," which is Japanese for "it cannot be helped" or roughly translated, "there is no hope."

I thought about making that the epigraph, but I thought the phrase "there is no hope" is a little more fatalistic than I like to be normally. Instead, I feel the thought about practice and knowledge fits more of the theme of the book. I have stated time and again that perfecting the skills as well as the ability to detect these skills in use takes a lot more than just knowledge. Being too afraid about the things I have mentioned in this book leads to anger at all the ways people get hacked, which only leads down a path that will cause us to close our minds. Instead I suggest a different approach to the information in this book besides fear: A new mindset that encourages you to learn and think and understand the methods the "bad guys" use so you can be protected from falling prey to them.

Now I am not saying that there is no place for fear. There definitely is room to feel some healthy fear. Protecting your data, your personal information, and your identity, but at the same time understanding the "hacker" mindset combined with the information in this book, might be more beneficial to you.

This section touches on a few things I hope you can take away from this book and use in your life, especially if you are in charge of security for your company, your clients, or reading this for your own personal security..

Social Engineering Isn't Always Negative

I hope that I impressed upon you that social engineering is not always negative. It is not always the hackers or the con men who use social engineering tactics. Doctors, therapists, social workers, parents, children, bosses, employees—everyone uses social engineering tactics to some extent. The art of persuasion is used often in normal everyday social situations.

Learning that social engineering isn't always scary, dark, and evil can go a long way toward uncovering how certain skills are used. After you understand those skills, practice and become skilled or proficient in them; discerning how they are being used against people then becomes much easier.

You can find places to analyze these skills that are not in the dark corners of the world. You can read books on psychology, persuasion, and sales, then observe in the field to see how these skills are used.

The Importance of Gathering and Organizing Information

I cannot really reiterate enough how important quality information gathering truly is. The quality, professionalism, and the very success of every social engineering engagement depends on the level of information gathering you do. The Web is a boundless and endless resource of information. Companies post their financial records, employees' names and titles, contact information, pictures of physical location, security policies, contracts, vendors and suppliers' names, people's personal files, and so much more. On a personal level, employees as well as everyday people post personal pictures, their addresses, their purchases, leases, contracts, favorite foods, teams, music, and so on.

Armed with all this overwhelming amount of information a social engineer can pick and chose what he wants to use and what kind of attack vector to implement. As the engagement continues the information gathered will give the social engineer the ability to use story lines and pretexts that will have the greatest effect on the target. Without information gathering, as reiterated throughout the book, the engagement will most likely lead to failure.

For example, if a professional auditor is given three weeks for a job, he *should* spend half of that time gathering information. However, professional auditors often have a tendency to get excited and approach the target with the old standby pretexts. Do not fall into this habit; spend a lot of time in information gathering.

Almost as important as the information gathering itself is how you store and catalogue the information—perhaps by using one of the methods mentioned in Chapter 2 to store and organize this information. Learning to not just efficiently collect the information but how to store the information can go a long way toward making it efficient to use. Not simply dumping things into a massive document but categorizing things, cataloging them, and labeling them will make the information easy to use, especially if you are on a phone engagement.

Just remember that a social engineer is only as good as the information he obtains. I personally have seen too many gigs go down the drain because of bad information or lack of information. At the same time I have seen people who might not be the smoothest speakers or the most charming succeed in very difficult situations because of the information they gathered.

Information is the crux of social engineering, and if you take anything away from this book, let it be that.

Choose Your Words Carefully

Just like this section's opening epigraph, this topic lends itself to the thought that information has no value unless you put it into practice. You can have all the information gathered and organized and catalogued, but you need to use it efficiently. The first step in this is to organize what words you will use.

I discussed the skills of elicitation and preloading. These are two of the most valuable skills, and I hope you practice using them. Use anchors, keywords, and phrases to load the target with emotions and thoughts to make him follow your lead. Preloading is a very powerful technique that cannot be mastered in a short while, but practice will enable you to use this skill. The great thing about preloading is that you can practice this skill at home, at work, with your kids, your parents, your clients, really anywhere.

Don't think that practicing this means you will always have to get people to do things against their will. Preloading is used to motivate people's minds to be more open to a suggestion or idea. You don't have to use it maliciously. Kids do it all the time. For example, your daughter says, "Daddy, I love you…" and adds a few seconds later, "Can I have that new doll?" This is an example of preloading, putting a "target" into an agreeable emotional state.

Once you master that skill, or at least become proficient in using it, work on the way you use elicitation. Remember that no one loves the feeling of being interrogated. Elicitation should not mimic a police interrogation; it should be a smooth, seamless conversation that is used to gather intelligence on the target or topic you are seeking.

Learning the methods and process used to come up with questions that can be used in normal conversation will not only enhance your skills as a social engineer but also as a communicator. People enjoy when they feel others are interested in their lives and their work. Using this skill for the good can enhance your ability as a social engineer.

I have a good friend that gets people to tell her anything. It is uncanny. Complete strangers will, at the end of a conversation, say things like, "I just don't know why I am telling you all these things…" She is not a social engineer or even in security, but she is a great elicitor.

Mastering preloading and elicitation can enhance your ability to also plan out what you will say. These skills can put your mind in the frame of seeking and gathering information in a more intelligent and less intrusive way.

Have a Good Pretext

Remember that a good pretext is not a lie or a story. Instead you become and live your pretext for a short time. Every fiber of your being—your thoughts, actions, speech, and motivation—should reflect what the pretext would do. If you can accomplish this then your pretext will be believable to the target.

The other thing to remember is that pretexting is used in everyday life, not just in social engineering. Imagine this scenario: You just had an argument with your mate. Now it is time for work. You don't want everyone to know that things at home aren't that good this day, so when you go to work and meet your coworkers who say, "Hey Jim how's it going?" Your reply is, "Awesome. Couldn't be better."

That is the opposite of the truth but what do you do to make that believable? Shoot someone a smile, or project confidence via your posture or body language. Depending on how private you are and how much you don't want to share with your co-workers you might even have a "cover story" to prove how great life is.

This is just one scenario, but people use pretexting all the time. Whenever you are trying to portray a difference from what is reality to people the "cover story" to make it believable is a pretext. Of course, most people aren't really good at it and are easily detected, but noticing these situations in your life and work will give you a good basis of pretexting to analyze.

Analyzing these scenarios can help you identify areas you want to improve in your pretexts and help you master this very useful skill.

Practice Reading Expressions

I think I can talk for weeks about microexpressions. The topic just fascinates me, and it intrigues me to think that people have built-in mechanisms for displaying our deepest darkest feelings, and most of us will have no control over it. How our emotions cause certain muscles to contract and display a certain expression for milliseconds is just an amazing aspect of creation. But learning how to notice them, read them, and use those very same expressions to manipulate others is something that truly astounds me.

Practice how to recreate the microexpressions discussed in Chapter 5. As you do, notice the emotions the microexpressions conjure up in you. Practicing these expressions will also help you read them when others express them.

As you practice, do not focus just on what it takes to read microexpressions in others but on how to control your own microexpressions and prevent someone using their facial-reading reading skills on you. Remember that reading others is a good skill, but having control over your own microexpressions, body language, and vocal tones is far better. This skill can enhance your security practice as well as your personal relationships. After you master many of those skills, you will begin to see how you can utilize one of the main concepts Chapter 5, the human buffer overflow (HBO). The human mind works much like software, just on a higher level. But it can be fuzzed, examined, and overthrown like software. Re-read that section to make sure you fully understand the principles presented.

Manipulation and Influence

Manipulation and influence are two aspects of social interaction that have some dramatic and powerful effects on the people you interact with. For that reason, use the information in Chapter 6 with extreme care. Learning how to persuade and manipulate people can literally make the difference between success or failure in a social engineering endeavor. Every day, people try to manipulate and persuade others to take actions. Some of these actions are very bad and can cost money, personal freedom, and identities.

Use those situations as teaching tools. Analyze the methods that marketers, psychologists, counselors, teachers, and even coworkers use to try to manipulate you. Pick out points that you think you can learn from and put them into your arsenal.

Remember that persuasion is not always negative: It doesn't always have to mean getting someone to do something they don't want. Persuasion can have very positive effects, and many times, positive persuasion is much more difficult. If you can master those skills and use them to help people stay secure, you will be more readily able to identify when someone is using persuasion tactics in a negative sense.

Be Alert to Malicious Tactics

Being aware of what tactics attackers use will surely keep you from falling victim to them. The professional auditors can use these tactics to educate their customers on what to look for in a possible attack. Be alert to pick out instances of how these are being used.

For example, one tactic the "bad guys" use is to strike during times of trouble. When the planes hit the Twin Towers, the earthquakes hit Haiti, and the tsunami hit Asia, the devastation upon the human population and their lives, psyche, and emotions was insurmountable. During times of people's vulnerability and weakness is exactly when the bad guys strike.

Let me illustrate it this way: I once read an article that spoke about how lions hunt in the wild. It said that a lion, when it wants to confuse and disjoint a group of prey to choose a victim, will roar towards the ground—not toward the prey or sky, but the ground. Why? It's because the massive, fear-inspiring roar will reverb off the ground and surround the prey. They become confused by not knowing which direction the lion is coming from. Some will scatter left, some will scatter right, but they will leave their young, old, infirm, and immature herd members open.

The preceding is not too far off from how professional malicious social engineers operate. They "roar" in such a way as to cause or add to the confusion. They use websites that help find dead loved ones after a natural disaster, or claim themselves to have lost family and friends in the carnage. When the emotions of the "targets" are so involved they can't see straight is when an attack occurs.

The inexperienced and immature (technologically speaking) fall victim first by giving out little bits of information until the attacker has enough to build a profile. That profile helps launch further attacks, and those attacks get more vicious and heartless.

Be alert to these instances, and you will keep your clients and yourself protected from falling victim to them. Also, use these situations as a learning lesson, analyze the methods used, and see whether they worked or failed. Doing so will enhance your ability to be more alert to potential threats.

The unfortunate difference in between a lion and a social engineer (besides the obvious) is that a social engineer gives no audible roar. He is not out there yelling, "I want prey, now run!" Instead malicious social engineers' sly, subtle attacks trick thousands into their traps each year.

Use Your Fear

Now if this chapter has built any kind of fear in you all I can say is, "good." You need it. Because healthy fear can save your life, or at least in this case your identity and your business.

Use that fear to motivate change. Don't get angry and upset. Make a decision to change and to educate yourself, your families, and your companies how to observe, notice, and defend against these attacks. Make a decision to not allow your identities and your companies to be hacked, and then do something about it.

This whole book boils down to "security through education." Human hacking is an art form. Social engineering is a mixture and blending of sciences, art, and skill. When blended in the right amount and right mixture the results are "shikata ga nai."

Companies lose millions of dollars per year to breaches, with a large majority of those breaches stemming from social engineering attacks. Yet, more often than not, when we offer clients the chance to add social engineering auditing to their pentesting services they decline.

Why?

Companies tend to fear change. Countless times in my professional practice I have heard intelligent and successful business owners say things like, "We don't need a social engineering audit. Our people won't fall for those tricks." Then during the pentest we will do a few authorized phone calls to get information and when we present the information in the report they are amazed how easy it was to get the information.

At all levels of various companies, security awareness doesn't tend to change much. When speaking to companies after a pentest about a security awareness training program we launched, many told us they do not perform formal intense training for call center or tech support departments. Yet those are the same departments that most often fall for social engineering attacks.

This points to the core of the problem that I am speaking about here. Security through education cannot be a simple catch phrase; it has to become a mission statement. Until companies and the people who make up those companies take security personally and seriously, this problem won't be fixed completely. In the meantime, those who were serious enough to read this book and to have a desire to peer into the dark corners of society can enhance their skills enough to keep their families, selves, and companies a little more secure.

When the "lion roars," be the one who is at the front of the pack leading the exodus out of the way. Be an example of what to do and how to defend against these attacks.

With enough time and enough effort anyone can be social engineered. Those words are true, as scary as they are. That doesn't mean there is no hope; it means your job is to make malicious social engineering so difficult and time consuming that most hackers will give up and go after "low-hanging fruit" or the prey that is left behind. I know; it sounds cold. I would love it if everyone would read this book and make some massive changes—then companies would be truly secure. But that is just not the world we live in.

That statement, then, raises a very serious question. If there truly is no hope, how can companies, people, families, and everyone protect against this massive vulnerability? Until companies begin to realize their vulnerability to social engineering attacks, individuals will have to educate themselves about attack methods and stay vigilant, as well as spread the word to others. Only then do we have hope of staying if not one step ahead of an attack, then not too far behind.

Summary

As I conclude this book, I hope it has opened your eyes to the world of social engineering. I hope that it will continue to help you take note of the potential for malicious attacks. I hope it has helped you build or maintain a healthy fear of the potential for disaster.

I also hope this book helps you to protect your businesses, your families, your children, your investments, and your life. I hope that the information within has showed you that staying completely secure and protected is not impossible.

Mati Aharoni, my mentor, says in one of his classes that the reason the bad guys usually win is because they have dedication, time, and motivation on their side. Don't let life get in the way of security. Conversely, don't let too much fear of the bad guys keep you from enjoying life.

I hope that applying the principles in this book enhances your ability to read and communicate more effectively with people around you. Using them in many aspects of your life, not just security, can prove to be a life-altering exercise. Social engineering is truly an art form. Enjoy.

Index